This book invaluably fills a vacuum in the literature. Across its 40 chapters, it provides the highest level of scholarship and knowledge around the history, content and scope of critical development studies, covering both material and intellectual developments in a reader-friendly fashion for researchers, students and policymakers alike.

Ben Fine, *Professor of Economics at the School of Oriental and African Studies, University of London, UK*

This is a very important book. Without economic reductionism Petras and Veltmeyer expose the astonishing level of greed, exploitation and inequality associated with the world capitalist system. They also provide a sharp and much-needed class analysis of the contradictions of both capitalism and imperialism, and the propensity towards crisis that has assumed global proportions and undermined the foundations of the system as well as generating powerful forces of resistance and class warfare.

John Saxe-Fernandez, *Professor of Latin American Studies, Universidad Nacional Autónoma de México; author of inter alia,* Crisis e imperialismo, La energía en México, Situación y alternativas *and* Economic Imperialism in Mexico: The Operations of the World Bank in Our Country

The particular value of this timely book is that it provides a critical perspective on the destructive impacts of a world capitalist system in crisis. It not only addresses the worldwide dynamics of capitalist development, but also the forces of resistance generated by these dynamics as well as proposals for alternative futures advanced within both the popular sector and academe. It is an analytical tool of vital interest to both academic researchers and students within the broad field of international development studies, political economy and sociology.

Richard L. Harris, *Professor Emeritus of Global Studies at California State University, Monterey Bay. Managing Editor,* Journal of Developing Societies *and Director of the Transpacific Project*

This timely book superbly analyses in class terms US interventionism, the faltering of Latin America's progressive reforms, right-wing comebacks for neo-liberalism in Brazil, Argentina, and elsewhere, and the combined anti-capitalist, anti-imperialist class struggle in Venezuela. Theoretically and politically acute, it is a must acquisition for libraries, journalists, academics, and activists.

James Cockcroft, *Honorary Editor* Latin American Perspectives, *USA*

This book is a lively, engaging and lucid analysis of the diverse practices of the class struggles taking place in multiple sites by indigenous peoples, unemployed workers, landless peasants, local communities and students. It powerfully illuminates the demise of the 'pink tide' as well as the rise of, and turn to, the right; always persuasively stressing the centrality of class struggle. Required reading for those wishing to gain an understanding of the class forces shaping contemporary Latin America.

Cristóbal Kay, *Emeritus Professor of the International Institute of Social Studies, Erasmus University Rotterdam; and Professorial Research Associate of the Department of Development Studies at the School of Oriental and African Studies, University of London, UK*

In this stimulating book James Petras and Henry Veltmeyer analyse recent social transformations in Latin America. They highlight how despite continual elite opposition, the region's poor attempt and succeed in generating progressive social change. The authors argue, moreover, that struggles from below have the capacity to generate further and more profound transformations in the future. This book will be of great value to anyone interested in contemporary Latin America.

Professor Benjamin Selwyn, *University of Sussex, UK*

# THE CLASS STRUGGLE IN LATIN AMERICA

*The Class Struggle in Latin America: Making History Today* analyses the political and economic dynamics of development in Latin America through the lens of class struggle. Focusing in particular on Peru, Paraguay, Chile, Colombia, Argentina, Brazil and Venezuela, the book identifies how the shifts and changing dynamics of the class struggle have impacted on the rise, demise and resurgence of neo-liberal regimes in Latin America.

This innovative book offers a unique perspective on the evolving dynamics of class struggle, engaging both the destructive forces of capitalist development and those seeking to consolidate the system and preserve the status quo, alongside the efforts of popular resistance concerned with the destructive ravages of capitalism on humankind, society and the global environment.

Using theoretical observations based on empirical and historical case studies, this book argues that the class struggle remains intrinsically linked to the march of capitalist development. At a time when post-neo-liberal regimes in Latin America are faltering, this supplementary text provides a guide to the economic and political dynamics of capitalist development in the region, which will be invaluable to students and researchers of international development, anthropology and sociology, as well as those with an interest in Latin American politics and development.

**Henry Veltmeyer** is Professor of development studies at the Universidad Autónoma de Zacatecas (UAZ), Mexico, and Professor Emeritus of international development studies at Saint Mary's University (Halifax, Canada). He is the author or editor of over 40 books on issues of Latin American and global development, and critical development studies.

**James Petras** is Professor Emeritus of sociology at Binghamton University in New York, and Adjunct Professor in international development studies at Saint Mary's University (Halifax, Canada). He is the author of over 60 books and numerous other writings on issues of world and Latin American developments.

# ROUTLEDGE CRITICAL DEVELOPMENT STUDIES

Series Editors

*Henry Veltmeyer* is co-chair of the Critical Development Studies (CDS) network, research professor at Universidad Autónoma de Zacatecas, Mexico, and professor emeritus at Saint Mary's University, Canada.

*Paul Bowles* is professor of economics and international studies at UNBC, Canada.

*Elisa van Wayenberge* is lecturer in economics at SOAS University of London, UK.

The global crisis, coming at the end of three decades of uneven capitalist development and neo-liberal globalization that have devastated the economies and societies of people across the world, especially in the developing societies of the global south, cries out for a more critical, proactive approach to the study of international development. The challenge of creating and disseminating such an approach, to provide the study of international development with a critical edge, is the project of a global network of activist development scholars concerned and engaged in using their research and writings to help effect transformative social change that might lead to a better world.

This series will provide a forum and outlet for the publication of books in the broad interdisciplinary field of critical development studies – to generate new knowledge that can be used to promote transformative change and alternative development.

The editors of the series welcome the submission of original manuscripts that focus on issues of concern to the growing worldwide community of activist scholars in this field.

To submit proposals, please contact the development studies editor, Helena Hurd (Helena.Hurd@tandf.co.uk).

1 **Moving Beyond Capitalism**
   *Edited by Cliff DuRand*

2 **The Class Struggle in Latin America**
   Making History Today
   *James Petras and Henry Veltmeyer*

3 **The Essential Guide to Critical Development Studies**
   *Edited by Henry Veltmeyer and Paul Bowles*

# THE CLASS STRUGGLE IN LATIN AMERICA

Making History Today

James Petras and Henry Veltmeyer

LONDON AND NEW YORK

First published 2018
by Routledge
2 Park Square, Milton Park, Abingdon, Oxon OX14 4RN

and by Routledge
711 Third Avenue, New York, NY 10017

*Routledge is an imprint of the Taylor & Francis Group, an informa business*

© 2018 James Petras and Henry Veltmeyer

The right of James Petras and Henry Veltmeyer to be identified as the authors of this work has been asserted by them in accordance with sections 77 and 78 of the Copyright, Designs and Patents Act 1988.

All rights reserved. No part of this book may be reprinted or reproduced or utilized in any form or by any electronic, mechanical, or other means, now known or hereafter invented, including photocopying and recording, or in any information storage or retrieval system, without permission in writing from the publishers.

*Trademark notice*: Product or corporate names may be trademarks or registered trademarks, and are used only for identification and explanation without intent to infringe.

*British Library Cataloguing in Publication Data*
A catalogue record for this book is available from the British Library

*Library of Congress Cataloging in Publication Data*
Names: Petras, James F., 1937– author. | Veltmeyer, Henry, author.
Title: The class struggle in Latin America : making history today / James Petras and Henry Veltmeyer.
Description: Abingdon, Oxon ; New York, NY : Routledge, 2017. |
Series: Routledge critical development studies
Identifiers: LCCN 2017003333| ISBN 9781138720213 (hbk) |
ISBN 9781138720220 (pbk) | ISBN 9781351763110 (ebk)
Subjects: LCSH: Social classes–Latin America. | Social conflict–Latin America. | Equality–Latin America.
Classification: LCC HN110.5.Z9 S64723 2017 | DDC 306.098–dc23
LC record available at https://lccn.loc.gov/2017003333

ISBN: 978-1-138-72021-3 (hbk)
ISBN: 978-1-138-72022-0 (pbk)
ISBN: 978-1-351-76311-0 (ebk)

Typeset in Bembo
by Wearset Ltd, Boldon, Tyne and Wear

# CONTENTS

| | |
|---|---|
| *List of figures* | *ix* |
| *List of tables* | *x* |
| *Notes on contributors* | *xi* |
| | |
| Introduction | 1 |
| | |
| 1  Class struggle back on the agenda | 12 |
| | |
| 2  Extractivism and resistance: a new era | 26 |
| | |
| 3  Accumulation by dispossession – and the resistance | 40 |
| | |
| 4  The progressive cycle in Latin American politics | 59 |
| | |
| 5  Argentina: the return of the Right<br>*With Mario Hernández* | 79 |
| | |
| 6  Brazil: class struggle in the countryside<br>*João Márcio Mendes Pereira and Paulo Alentejano* | 105 |
| | |
| 7  Democracy without the workers: 25 years of the labour<br>movement and mature neo-liberalism in Chile<br>*Sebastián Osorio and Franck Gaudichaud* | 134 |
| | |
| 8  Mexico: dynamics of a class war | 151 |

**viii** Contents

9 Paraguay: class struggle on the extractive frontier 182
*Arturo Ezquerro-Cañete*

10 Peru: return of the class struggle from below 207
*Jan Lust*

11 Venezuela: in the eye of the storm 227

12 The return of the Right 250

Conclusion 266

*Index* 273

# FIGURES

| | | |
|---|---|---|
| 7.1 | CUT election results by political party, 1988–2012 | 147 |
| 7.2 | Number of legal strikes, 1987–2014 | 147 |
| 7.3 | Number of workers on legal strike, 1990–2009 | 147 |
| 7.4 | Rate of unionization (employed) and population with union affiliation | 148 |
| 7.5 | Evolution of the nominal real minimum wage by presidency, 1990–2014 | 148 |
| 7.6 | Percentage distribution of the labour force by sector, 1990–2014 | 148 |
| 7.7 | Union affiliation by economic activity, 1990–2014 | 149 |
| 9.1 | Percentage of hectares cultivated with soy, by nationality of producers and farm size, 2008 | 191 |

# TABLES

| | | |
|---|---|---|
| 2.1 | Percentage distribution of FDI by sector in Latin America | 28 |
| 6.1 | Settled families and area occupied – Brazil | 117 |
| 6.2 | Landholding structure according to family farming criteria | 120 |
| 6.3 | Agricultural credit per harvest (2012–15) | 121 |
| 6.4 | Murders of rural workers and judgments – Brazil, 1985–2009 | 124 |
| 9.1 | Socio-economic indicators in Latin America, 2014 | 185 |
| 9.2 | Soybean production and cultivation in Paraguay, 1997–2015 | 187 |
| 9.3 | Land conflicts, 1990–2007 | 192 |
| 9.4 | Transgenic crops approved in Paraguay | 200 |
| 10.1 | Remuneration and exploitation surplus: 2000–06 (as a % of GDP) | 211 |
| 10.2 | Remuneration and exploitation surplus: 2007–14 (as a % of GDP) | 211 |

# CONTRIBUTORS

**James Petras** is Professor Emeritus of sociology at Binghamton University and Adjunct Professor in international development studies at Saint Mary's University (Halifax, Nova Scotia). He is the author and co-author of over 60 books and numerous other writings on the dynamics of world and Latin American developments, including *Unmasking Globalization*; *Social Movements and the State*; *Multinationals on Trial*; *What's Left in Latin America*; and *Social Movements in Latin America: Neoliberalism and Popular Resistance*. A list and an actual file of his periodical writings and journal articles are maintained and can be accessed at Rebelion.org.

**Henry Veltmeyer** is Professor of development studies at the Universidad Autónoma de Zacatecas (UAZ) in Mexico and Professor Emeritus in international development studies at Saint Mary's University (Canada). He is author, co-author or editor of over 40 books on issues of Latin American and world development, including *The Cuban Revolution as Socialist Human Development* and *Development in an Era of Neoliberal Globalization*. Books co-authored with James Petras include *Unmasking Globalization*; *System in Crisis*; *Social Movements and the State*; *Empire with Imperialism*; *What's Left in Latin America*; *Social Movements in Latin America: Neoliberalism and Popular Resistance*; and *Social Movements in Latin America: Neoliberalism and Popular Resistance*.

**Paulo Alentejano** has a PhD in development, agriculture and society from the Rural Federal University of Rio de Janeiro. He is currently an adjunct professor at the State University of Rio de Janeiro (UERJ), São Gonçalo campus. He has considerable experience in the field of agricultural geography, with an emphasis on agrarian reform, rural settlements, the struggle for land, pluriactivity and rural education.

**Arturo Ezquerro-Cañete** is a PhD candidate in development studies at Saint Mary's University, Canada, and Universidad Autónoma de Zacatecas, Mexico. He

**xii** Contributors

is a specialist on issues of agrarian change in Paraguay and has several publications on these issues, including a contribution to a special issue of the *Journal of Agrarian Change*.

**Franck Gaudichaud** is professor of history, sociology and political science at the Université Grenoble Alpes in France, with a specialized interest in Chile and Latin American working-class politics and development. He is also a member of the collective Rebelión and a frequent collaborator with Le Monde Diplomatique. Recent publications include *Chili (1970–1973). Mille jours qui ébranlèrent le monde* (2013) and *Venceremos! Analyse et documents sur le pouvoir populaire chilien (1970–1973)* (2013).

**Mario Hernández** is an Argentine economist and the coordinating editor of the journal *La Maza* and radio station La Urbana (Buenos Aires). He is the author, inter alia, of *El movimiento de autogestión obrera en Argentina*.

**Jan Lust** is a recent graduate from the doctoral programme in development studies at the Universidad Autónoma de Zacatecas, Mexico. His book on the revolutionary struggle in Peru in the 1960s has been published in Barcelona as *La Lucha Revolucionaria: Perú, 1958–1967*.

**João Márcio Mendes Pereira** is professor of the Rural Federal University of Rio de Janeiro postgraduate programme in history (Brazil, contemporary history). He is the author of numerous writings on the World Bank and its agrarian reform and poverty reduction programmes.

**Sebastián Osorio** is a researcher with degrees in history and sociology, and is a member of the NGO Centre for Social and Political Labour Research (Cipstra), with a specialist interest in trade unionism, the history of the trade union movement and the world of work in Chile.

# INTRODUCTION

The history of capitalism is a history of class struggle. This is because each advance in the march of capital, every assault made on working people in the quest for private profit – the driving force of capitalist development – brings about a strategic political response in the popular sector, resistance against the destructive forces engendered by this development.

This book is fundamentally concerned with the dynamics of this process – i.e. the development of the forces of production within the institutional framework of what has evolved into a worldwide capitalist system – and the associated class struggle over the past decade and a half. The history of these dynamics can be traced out in diverse spatial and temporal contexts, and particular conjunctures of the capitalist development process across the world. But in this book the main focus is on Latin America – the development and struggle dynamics that have unfolded, and continue to unfold, in this particular region.

As in other parts of the world that are subject to the workings of this system, this history can be traced out with reference to different phases in the development of the forces of production and corresponding changes in the class struggle. Historians with a particular interest in understanding and reconstructing the dynamics of development and resistance usually trace it back to the end of the Second World War. By this time the sun had set on the British Empire, and the diverse countries and peoples that had been colonized and subjected, in some cases to over a century of imperial rule to the ravages of imperialist exploitation (of their labour power and their wealth of natural resources), had begun to rebel and rise up against their masters. In response, the guardians of the capitalist system and the imperial world order turned towards the notion of 'development' and the project of 'international cooperation' with the efforts of the emerging post-colonial states to emancipate themselves from the clutches of imperial rule and embark on a programme of nation-building and economic development.

**2** Introduction

The aim of this project of international cooperation was twofold. One was to ensure that the emerging leaders of this decolonization and development process would not heed the siren call of communism, and to ensure that they would turn to capitalism in meeting the system requirements of national development. The other was to defuse the revolutionary ferment associated with an emerging class struggle for land and social change – a struggle of small landholding peasant farmers and a dispossessed and impoverished rural proletariat (the 'rural poor', in the development discourse) against the forces of capitalist development.

Within the institutional and policy framework of the new world order – a system dominated by capital and ruled by Washington (the US having emerged from the war as the new imperial power with access to enormous financial and productive resources, not to mention military power) – the architects and guardians of this imperial order, together with the agencies and agents of the system, set about to systematically advance the capitalist development process based on the exploitation of the unlimited supplies of surplus labour generated in the process. The main agency here was the nation state, which provided the necessary conditions for mobilizing the forces of capitalist development. The outcome was a system-wide doubling in the pace of capitalist development – the rate of economic growth – to that date, resulting in what liberal historians have dubbed the 'golden age of capitalism' (with rates of economic growth up to 5 per cent per annum sustained for over two decades – 1948–68).

This development was very uneven, with the benefits of growth concentrated in the Euro-US centres of the system and accruing to the capitalist class while the social and economic costs of this development – including the dispossession and proletarianization of the small landholding farmers and their forced outmigration – were borne by the rural proletariat and the rural landless workers, obliging them to abandon agriculture as a source of livelihood, as well as their communities, to sell their labour power for wages on the urban labour market.

The period, from the 1950s to the 1970s, provides the temporal context not only for this process of capitalist accumulation and labour exploitation but also for a multifaceted class struggle. One of the main fronts in this struggle was in the countryside, where the semi-proletarianized peasants resisted the advance of capital and engaged in a protracted struggle for the land and land reform. In this resistance the rural proletariat and semi-proletariat played a prominent role in the revolutionary movements of national liberation. In this struggle they confronted the imperial and neo-colonial state, which mobilized the repressive arm of the state, followed by schemes of rural development, designed to coopt the rural poor, and turn them away from the confrontational politics of class warfare.

Another dimension in the class struggle was the capital–labour relation in the cities. On this front, the resistance took form as the labour movement, which was also systematically weakened and – in the 1980s, in Latin America – destroyed by the combined powers of capital and the state.

Two other dimensions of the class struggle were formed in this process. One took the form of a political struggle for control of the state – to capture the state as

Introduction **3**

an instrument of class power. There are two fronts of this struggle. One involves a process of electoral politics – the parliamentary road to state power; the other involves the mobilization of the forces of resistance – the revolutionary path to state power. A second front in the class struggle was formed in the popular resistance to the advance of capital in the form of an anti-imperialist struggle. The history of US imperialism, and the resulting anti-imperialist struggle in Latin America, has been told too many times to bear repetition. However, the neo-liberal era, which began in the 1980s with the installation of the so-called 'new world order', created an entirely different context for the class struggle, as did the opening years of the new millennium – the central concern of this book.

From the 1950s to the 1970s the class struggle was primarily a matter of land and labour, while in the 1990s, after a decade-long interregnum in which the forces of resistance that had been brought to ground or dispersed were rebuilt, the class struggle took the form of uprisings and widespread resistance against the neo-liberal agenda of structural reform in macroeconomic public policy. In the new millennium the class struggle once again has assumed a different form under conditions of several epoch-defining changes in the global economy (the ascension of China as an economic power, a consequent primary commodities boom) and the demise of neo-liberalism as an economic doctrine and development model. Under these conditions and the expansion of extractive or resource-seeking capital – the class struggle went in several different directions. First, the struggle to some extent was internationalized or globalized as multinational corporations, international financial organizations and imperial states intervened, directly or by proxy with the assistance and connivance of collaborator states, in the class struggle between labour and capital. This was especially evident in Latin America with the ascendancy of extractive capital. As discussed in Chapter 2, giant agro-mineral corporations have played a major role in shaping state economic policies to the detriment of workers, communities and indigenous peoples.

On the frontier of extractive capital, the communities most directly affected by the negative socio-environmental impacts and the destructive operations of extractive capital rose up and took collective action against the mining companies. On the political front, the dynamics of class struggle brought about a process of regime change – a sea tide of progressive post-neo-liberal regimes committed to 'inclusionary state activism' – the use by governments of the fiscal revenues derived from the export of primary commodities to reduce poverty and bring about a more inclusive form of development.

Changes in the economic configurations of Latin America, especially the expansion of the agro-mineral, financial and commercial sectors and the decline of the manufacturing sector, have had a profound impact in shaping the class structure, trade union organization and class conflict. For example, trade union membership has fallen precipitously. In Brazil, trade union affiliates have declined from 32.1 per cent in the early 1990s (prior to the election of Cardoso in 1994) to 21 per cent in the middle of the following decade under the presidency of the Lula, the leader of the Workers' Party. In 2014, according to ILO data, labour union density in Brazil

**4** Introduction

had fallen to 18 per cent and then 16.5 per cent in 2016 (ILO, 2016; Vásquez, 2014). In Argentina between 1986 and 2005 trade union membership declined from 48.7 per cent to 25.4 per cent (although the ILO has it at 32 per cent for 2014). In Mexico, membership held steady at around 14 per cent from 1986 to 2014. Chile is the exception: from a low level of 11.6 per cent in 1986, trade union membership grew to 16 per cent in 2014. Moreover, the general and overall decline in trade union membership was accompanied by the decline in the number and the political weight of industrial workers, especially in labour-intensive light consumer industries that were negatively impacted by imports of cheap textiles, shoes, toys, etc. from Asia as part of the trade-off between exports of agro-minerals and imports of manufactured goods.

The decline in trade unions was accompanied by a decline of political influence in state policies and a turn inward to narrow corporatist, wage and workplace issues. As a result, there are fewer strikes and they are increasingly focused on immediate issues rather than the demand for substantive if not radical social change. Also, the political and social space in the class struggle vacated by the industrial workers were occupied by mass social movements in the countryside, led by indigenous peasants and rural landless workers, and, more recently, by urban struggles led by low-paid service workers and lower-middle-class employees. This is evident in the million-member mass urban struggles in Brazil of May–June 2013.

The change in the economy and in the form and dynamics of the class struggles has also led to a major shift in the locus of the struggle and the demands. Prior to the 1990s, the major strikes, protests and other class actions were organized at the workplace by employed, unionized industrial workers. During the 1990s, the axis of struggle shifted to the streets, countryside and neighbourhoods as the class struggle was spearheaded by rural landless workers, unemployed workers and the downwardly mobile middle class. In the first decade and a half of the 2000s, the locus of class struggle was focused on the communities adjoining sites of agromining corporate exploitation. The struggles took the form of resisting dispossession, protesting the destructive operations of extractive capital on livelihoods and the environment and reclaiming their territorial rights as well as the right to access the commons of water, land and the wealth of natural resources.

As for the urban mass movements that materialized and sprung up in the major cities of Brazil in particular they engaged people in the lower middle class, informal workers and students. The centre of organization and confrontation of these movements were located in the neighbourhoods and local communities. The primary target: the post-neo-liberal state. The capacity and power of these movements to mobilize the forces of resistance dwarfed the power of trade unions by a ratio of 20:1: two million working people joined marches protesting massive corruption, misallocation of budgetary resources, and declining living standards and quality of basic services in health, education and transport.

The new class struggle is basically made up of the younger generation of non-unionized workers, many in the informal sector, low-paid service workers who are highly dependent on public services and who lack the social protection of the state.

The complex and changing anatomy and trajectory of the class struggle from below was matched by the continuities and changes in the class struggle from above. The ruling classes shifted from a position embracing brute force, via military dictatorships and ultra-authoritarian rule in launching the neo-liberal counter-revolution during the early 1970s and mid-1980s, to support for a negotiated transition to electoral politics as a means of consolidating the model and to implement the neo-liberal agenda.

In the face of the anti-neo-liberal popular uprisings in the 1990s, the agro-mineral elite in Brazil and elsewhere embraced the 'progressive' (centre-left) post-neo-liberal regimes so as to secure a privileged place in the new model, accepting increased taxes and royalty payments in exchange for vast state subsidies and large-scale land grants and land-grabbing (the acquisition by foreign investors of large tracts of land).

With the decline of the mega-boom (in 2008, but particularly in 2012), different sectors of the ruling class have adopted different strategies. Some (mostly in the agro-mineral sectors) have begun to press within the centre-left regime for a return to neo-liberalism. Others, including most notably the agribusiness association in Argentina, have organized mass actions to undermine the post-neo-liberal regimes, while foreign financial and investment houses moved their capital to safer harbours or more lucrative sites in other regions.

## Class struggle from above and below

The role of the class struggle has been the most slighted dimension in the academic study of Latin American development. The most influential writers have paid at best passing reference to the class struggle in discussing the capital accumulation process, while the high priests of underdevelopment, dependency and world systems theory have relegated it to the status of a by-product of global processes. A search of the major development journals and yearbooks over the past 30 years fails to turn up a single systematic study of the role of the class struggle in the formation of the state, productive structures and class relations.

In taking the class struggle as the central point of departure we demonstrate that the class struggle in its diverse forms, locations and geoeconomic configurations has been, to quote Karl Marx, the driving force in the process of historical development – as well as the rise and decline of diverse development models used to give direction to this process.

Focusing exclusively on Latin America over a time period of the last quarter of a century, we formulate a framework that identifies two types of class struggle: one that springs from the ruling classes, which we refer to as the class struggle from above, and a second that reflects class warfare as fought by workers, peasants and other subaltern classes in the popular sector. We term this the class struggle from below.

Recognizing the internal dynamics of these variants we highlight the importance of the intensity of class struggle in determining the direction and advances of the major antagonists in the capitalist development process.

Operationalizing our class struggle framework in the form of six case studies in Latin America (Peru, Paraguay, Colombia, Argentina, Brazil and Venezuela), we analyse the changes in the correlation of force in the class struggle, with reference to forces that can be and have been mobilized to the right or the left, depending on the circumstances, changing conditions and relative strengths of these forces. In this analysis we identify how the shifts and changing dynamics of the class struggle have impacted on the rise, demise and resurgence of neo-liberal regimes in Latin America. Likewise, we show how the progressive cycle of post-neo-liberal regimes in Argentina, Venezuela and Brazil and elsewhere in South America (notably in Bolivia and Ecuador) emerged in conditions of economic and political crisis and intensified class struggle from below. Crises conditions always weaken the institutional constraints on collective action, releasing forces that can be mobilized towards either the right or the left. At the turn into the new millennium these conditions favoured the Left, which, in the form of the political class organized to contest national and local democratic elections, took advantage of a political opening created by a combination of changing conditions, including widespread disaffection and rejection of the neo-liberal policy agenda, and the backing of the social movements in the popular sector, to contest the elections and achieve state power.

In the current conjuncture, the correlation of forces in the class struggle cuts both ways towards the right and the left. In Argentina, for example, the conjuncture favours the Right, and in Brazil, despite the crisis of the bourgeois political system, conditions of the economic crisis also favours the Right. But, as Gaudichaud has shown us, in Chile the growing fissures in the dominant exclusionary neo-liberal model and the crisis of the model of *democracia tutelada* has created an opening for the political left and enormous possibilities for a major leap forwards.

In our case studies we found an inverse relationship between high-intensity class struggle from above and redistributive and welfare policies; conversely, we identify high-intensity class struggle from below and positive regime changes favouring a greater share of national income for wage and salaried workers. In more general terms, we found that periods of class conciliation between rulers and popular classes are temporary and a prelude to the re-emergence of intense class struggle. In strategic terms, we found that the wage and salaried classes make short- or middle-term quantitative and even qualitative gains in periods of conciliation but that the ruling classes benefit in the long run, using these periods to regroup and re-launch the class war.

While orthodox classical, neo-Keynesian and Marxist economists rely on economic categories that are abstracted from the class struggle, we show how different rates of private investment, income shares and budgetary expenditures are profoundly influenced by the class struggle. High private investments tend to coincide with successful class struggle from above, which results in lower wages, environmental regulations and corporate taxation. Increased social expenditures, greater public investment and increases in progressive taxation result from intense levels of class struggle. The latter is found in the Venezuelan experience from 2003 to 2013; the former is found in the Paraguayan, Peruvian and Colombian experience over the past two decades.

The class struggle from above is strongly influenced and in some cases initiated and directed by 'outside actors', namely the multinational corporations run and managed by the chief executive officers of the global capitalist and ruling class, and especially the military and special forces that are embedded in the imperial state and its adjuncts such as the international financial institutions of the neo-liberal/ imperial world order. In other words, we can speak and write of a class struggle from 'above and the outside' – taking account of imperial interventions, boycotts, hard or soft coups, and the financing of domestic ruling class parties, non-governmental organizations, the mass media and press that are generally owned and controlled by the scions of the ruling class and by paramilitaries, as we demonstrate in the leading case of Venezuela. Similarly, the US-financed Plan Colombia, especially during the 2001–10 period, was decisive in the advance of class warfare from above, displacing four million peasants and killing thousands of social activists engaged in the class struggle from below.

The advocates and practitioners of class struggle from below have no comparable support on the 'outside'. Venezuela's successful class struggle from below, which defeated a US ruling class coup (2002) and petrol boycott (2002–03) created the social foundations for Venezuela's turn to nationalist-populist policies and the redistribution of oil rents in a socially progressive direction.

Most of our case studies focus on the dynamics of the class struggle in the countryside (Paraguay, Peru, Brazil) because this is the epicentre of the class struggle on the expanding extractive frontier. Especially with the astronomical rise of agromineral demand, prices and profits, the ruling classes launched a class war to dispossess peasants and indigenous communities provoking a class war from below. We note in the text but it bears repeating that the composition of the class forces acting from below varies from country and region: in Paraguay and Peru, indigenous communities are the moving forces, while in Brazil and Colombia the struggle involves a rural semi-proletariat of landless workers and displaced and uprooted peasants.

## The end of the progressive cycle?

At the time of writing (May 2016), Latin America has entered a new period of class struggle presaged by Mauricio Macri's election on 22 November 2015 as president of Argentina. The elections signalled a change in the correlation of forces in the class struggle and a pendulum swing back towards the right, i.e. the end of the progressive cycle in Latin American politics associated with the 'red' and 'pink' tide of centre-left post-neo-liberal regimes that swept the political landscape in the first decade of the new millennium. The resurgence and in some cases the return to power of the Right is signalled most clearly by Macri's election and the end of the Kirchner era. But a similar change in the correlation of forces on the political front of the class struggle is evident in Brazil, where the forces of the new Right have managed to take advantage of the economic crisis triggered by a fall in commodity prices and a corruption scandal to bring down Dilma's PT regime and install one of

**8** Introduction

its own as temporary president.[1] The device of impeachment used to depose the president was a new tactic in the arsenal of weapons used by the new Right in the ongoing class struggle – a 'soft coup' in lieu of the military coups preferred by the US in the golden age of imperial rule.

Similarly, in Bolivia and Venezuela the Right has made major gains on the political front, changing the correlation of force in the class struggle. Crisis conditions in the economy, fomented by imperialist forces and the capitalist class and abetted by the failure of the Maduro regime to navigate the latest storm of economic sabotage and US intervention, have severely weakened the Maduro regime and changed the correlation of forces in favour of the Right. In these conditions the forces of the far Right and US imperialism are not biding their time but lying in wait to seize the opportunity should it or when it arrives in whatever form. In Peru, the return of the hard Right was signalled by the election in April 2016 of neo-liberal hardliner Pedro Pablo Kuczynski to the presidency. Even in Bolivia, where the progressive cycle in Latin American politics had appeared to be securely entrenched, the regime led by Evo Morales, a leader of a movement of indigenous coca-producing peasant farmers, suffered a serious setback during a referendum for re-election in its struggle against the oligarchy and its allies – the right-wing political opposition. These and other forces of development and change provide the context and set the stage for the issues addressed in this book regarding the dynamics of the class struggle in conditions that are unfolding across parts of Latin America.

## Synopsis of the book

The book begins with four chapters that focus on the regional dynamics of the class struggle in the context of what has been described as the 'neo-liberal era'. Chapter 1 establishes a theoretical framework for thinking about the class struggle in the current context. The framework includes the idea that there are different dynamics of class struggle that can be conceptualized as 'from below' and 'from above'. The aim of the book is to examine these dynamics as they are playing out in diverse contexts and on different fronts of the class struggle.

Chapter 2 reconstructs the geoeconomics of and the geopolitics of capital in the current phase of development that we term 'extractive capitalism' and that involves a system in which the extraction of natural resource wealth is prioritized over the exploitation of labour. We examine the political and policy dynamics of this system, as well as the dynamic forces of resistance that come into play on the new frontier of extractive capital.

Chapter 3 analyses the mechanisms by means of which the capitalist class is able to advance and accumulate capital both in agriculture and industry. At issue here are the enclosure of the commons and the dispossession of the direct producers and their forced outmigration and proletarianization. Both the historical and contemporary dynamics of this process are discussed.

Chapter 4 brings into focus and discusses the political dimension of this capitalist accumulation process and the associated class struggle. At issue here are the struggle

Introduction **9**

for control over the state apparatus and the use of this apparatus to advance the economic interests of the contending classes in the struggle. The specific focus of the chapter is on the dynamics of regime change in the current context, i.e. the class struggle associated with the progressive cycle in Latin American politics in the dusk of the neo-liberal era.

This overview of class struggle dynamics is followed by country case studies. Chapter 5 reviews and analyses the dynamics of the class struggle on the front of electoral politics. The focus of the chapter is on the progressive cycle of Latin American politics in the context of Argentina, which provides a paradigmatic case study of the rise and defeat of the centre-left and the re-emergence of the hard neo-liberal Right.

Chapter 6 analyses the social and political struggles that configured the relations of power in the Brazilian countryside between 1964 and 2015, a period that encompasses both the military dictatorship set up with US support (the coup-makers congratulated by President Johnson for having 'restored democracy') and a series of 'democratic' regimes established within the institutional framework of the New Republic. The central focus of the chapter is on the struggle of the landless rural workers' movement – the MST – widely regarded as one of Latin America's most powerful and consequential social movements in the neo-liberal era. The chapter discusses the organizational processes of the principal social actors in the land struggle, the correlation of forces in the class struggle over land and agricultural production, and the role of the Brazilian state in this struggle.

In Chapter 7 the book turns towards Chile in an examination of the class struggle dynamics of the capital–labour relation and the shifting dynamics of the labour movement in the neo-liberal era. One of the key issues addressed by Franck Gaudichaud and Sebastián Osorio, both experts on Chilean politics, is the legacy of the military dictatorship in the relation between the labour movement and the liberal democratic regime established at the end of the dictatorship in 1989.

Chapter 8 reconstructs the shifting dynamics of a class war in Mexico, a society of intense class conflict. Capitalist expansion and the explosion of class struggles in Mexico follow a very distinct trajectory, which we trace out in summary form. As we see it, the balance of power in the class struggle shifted dramatically towards the capitalist class and the elite in the 1980s. We trace out the complex dynamics of this political development, with a central focus on the capital–labour relationship in the class struggle. We conclude that the working class today in its various forms and contingents retains a powerful capacity to engage millions in direct action but that it lacks the national political and social unity to seize state power, and that the correlation of forces between 'capital and labour' remains subject to permanent contestation. The case of Mexico tells us that the ebb and flow of the class struggle in Latin America is still indeterminate.

In Chapter 9, the book turns towards the class struggle on the new and expanding frontier of extractive capital in the case of Paraguay. The central concern of the chapter is with the dynamics of class struggle associated with the expansion of agro-extractivism in the form of capital invested in the production

**10** Introduction

of soya-based biofuels. The expansion of corporate agribusiness has led to heightened class struggle over land in the countryside and the election of a progressive regime that was quickly ousted by the oligarchy. The ousting of Fernando Lugo from the presidency reveals the inordinate level of influence exerted by the land-owning elite on Paraguayan politics, as well as the very feeble nature of the country's democracy. The vehemence of the opposition to a centre-left president, whose policies were more social democratic than revolutionary and who actually sought and achieved very little, serves as a potent reminder that 'it is hardly necessary for the Latin American governments to adopt social-revolutionary measures before the traditional elite ... feel threatened and act violently in protection of their interests' (Gordon & Webber, 2013: 36). All in all, the Paraguayan experience is a powerful reminder of how fragile the prospects for redistributive land reform continue to be in the post-authoritarian and post-neo-liberal period of Latin American politics.

Chapter 10 turns to Peru, with a focus on three fronts of the class struggle. The first has to do with urban labour. On this front, the working class in its current form, predominantly as a semi-proletariat of workers working 'on their account' in the so-called informal sector, is engaged in a struggle for employment and improved income as well as higher wages. The second front of the Peruvian class struggle is formed on the frontier of extractive capital, where entire communities of small producers and farmers struggle to resist and oppose the destructive operations of extractive capital (predominantly in the form of mega-mining, with up to 72 per cent of the national territory ceded to capital for the purpose of exploring and extracting minerals and metals). The third dimension of the class struggle relates to the front of electoral politics. The chapter analyses the dynamics of this political struggle in the context of several recent neo-liberal regimes.

Chapter 11 focuses on the class struggle in Venezuela within the institutional and policy framework of a regime committed to taking the country towards 'the socialism of the twenty-first century' and the most developed case of advanced social welfarism and state-led extractivism in the region. Venezuela is a classic case of class struggle where the forces of anti-capitalist and anti-imperialist resistance have converged.

In Chapter 12 we review some of the major dynamics of struggle associated with the latest progressive cycle in Latin American politics – a cycle associated with a series of post-neo-liberal regimes formed in the vortex of changing conditions in the new millennium. The major question addressed in this chapter is whether this cycle is indeed over and what this would mean for the class struggle ahead.

The conclusion to the book draws together our theoretical observations based on our empirical and historical case studies.

## Note

1 The impeachment of President Rouseff was a clear expression of the pendulum swing back to the right and a broad if not region-wide change in the correlation of force in the class struggle in the current context – the possible end of the progressive cycle.

## References

Gordon, T. & Webber, J. (2013). 'Post-coup Honduras: Latin America's corridor of reaction'. *Historical Materialism*, 21(3), pp. 16–56.

ILO – International Labor Organisation (2016). *World Employment and Social Outlook*. Geneva: ILO.

Vásquez, H. (2014). 'Salario mínimo, salario medio y trabajadores no sindicalizados en Colombia'. CUT Colombia, 11 December. Available at: http://cut.org.co/salario-minimo-salario-medio-y-trabajadores-no-sindicalizados-en-colombia [accessed 7 November 2015].

# 1
# CLASS STRUGGLE BACK ON THE AGENDA

One of the most important and yet surprisingly most neglected factors of social change and historic development, a fundamental determinant of the way in which capitalism has taken form in Latin America, is the 'class struggle'. In one of his most pithy metaphors, Karl Marx referred to class struggle as 'the motor force of history'. The assumption made here by Marx – a fundamental principle of historical materialism – is that with each advance in the capitalist development of the forces of production can be found a corresponding change in the dominant social relations of production as well as in the correlation of force in the class struggle. At each particular conjuncture of the class struggle the forces of change that are unleashed in the capitalist development process can be mobilized towards either the right or the left, depending on the relative strength of the contending classes – the balance of class power at the national or regional level. In this chapter we will analyse the central role of the class struggle in the process of capitalist development that is unfolding in Latin America, on the periphery of what has emerged as a world system.

There are two parts to this chapter. The first section focuses on the different dynamics of the struggle 'from above' and 'from below'. After clarifying the changing forms taken by the class struggle in the current conjuncture, and the different methods used to advance the struggle on different fronts, we briefly turn to the specific outcomes of class struggles in different parts of the region and selected countries. We then briefly discuss several cases of the class struggle in order to highlight the dynamics of a *class struggle from below* formed to effectively counteract the *class offensive from above*. This brief outline of the panorama of the class struggle prefigures the country case studies detailed in Chapters 5–11.

In the second section we turn towards the contemporary dynamics of the class struggle in Latin America, with a focus on the period 2000–15. The dynamics of class struggle are complex and variegated, but our account focuses on the following:

Class struggle back on the agenda **13**

changing class actors and the context of class action, the ebbs and flows of the class struggle, and the shifts in the correlation of class forces. Rather than providing a regional overview of these dynamics, we profile seven countries where the class struggle in its various fronts and forms have exhibited the greatest dynamism, namely Argentina, Brazil, Chile, Mexico, Paraguay, Peru, and Venezuela.

## 1 The two faces of the class struggle

Too often political analysts conceive of class struggle in rather narrow terms as collective actions taken by workers to advance the economic interests of the working class, overlooking other actors in the class struggle and the equally significant (and in the current epoch even more important) collective actions taken and directed by the ruling class, particularly those that engage the state apparatus, which is normally controlled by different factions of this class.

The entire panoply of neo-liberal policies, from the so-called 'austerity measures' and mass firings of public and private employees to the massive transfers of wealth to the financiers and creditors, are designed to enhance the power and accumulated wealth of capital and its primacy over labour. To paraphrase Marx, class struggle from above is a motor force designed to reverse history – to seize and destroy the advances secured by workers from previous class struggles from below.

Class struggle from above and the outside is waged in corporate boardrooms, stock markets, central banks, executive branches of government, parliaments and congresses, as well as in the political arena. Decision makers are drawn from the ruling class or 'in their confidence'. Many, if not most, strategic decisions are taken by non-elected officials and increasingly located in financial institutions such as the International Monetary Fund, the European Central Bank and the European Commission, which represent and act on behalf of financiers and creditors, bondholders and big banks, and other members of the global capitalist class.

Class struggle from above is directed at enhancing the concentration of wealth, increasing regressive taxes on workers and reducing taxes on corporations, selectively enforcing regulations that facilitate financial speculation and lowering social expenditures for pensions, health and education for workers and their families. In addition, class struggle from above is directed at maximizing the collective power of capital via restrictive laws on labour organizations, social movements and public workers' collective bargaining rights. In other words, class struggle penetrates numerous sites besides the 'workplace' and the strictly 'economic sphere'. State budgets over bailouts are sites of class struggle; banks are sites of class struggle between mortgage holders and households, creditors and debtors.

The fact that *class struggle from above* usually precludes public demonstrations is largely because the ruling class controls the decision-making institutions from which its class policies are imposed. Nevertheless, when institutional power bases are fragile or under siege from labour or other elements of the popular classes, ruling classes have engaged in extra-parliamentary and violent public activity such as coups d'état, assassinations and/or appointing a technocratic regime that is

**14** Class struggle back on the agenda

ostensibly beyond the class struggle; or engaged in lockouts, financial intimidation and blackmail, not to mention the mass firing of workers and co-option of collaborators within the political class.

In times of severe crisis, the ruling class nature of political institutions and policies becomes transparent and the class struggle from above intensifies both in scope and depth. Trillions of dollars are transferred from the public treasury to bail out bankers. Hundreds of billions in social cuts are imposed on workers, cutting across all sectors of the economy. During depressions, the class struggle from above takes the form of an *all-out war to save capital* by impoverishing labour, reversing decades of incremental income and benefits gained in *previous* class struggles from below.

## The class struggle from below

Working-class struggles from below range from workplace strikes over wages and social benefits, to general strikes to secure social legislation (or to defend past gains) or to prevent assaults on living standards. In critical moments, struggles from below lead to social upheavals in the face of systemic breakdowns, destructive wars and autocratic rule. The participants in the class struggle from below and the methods used vary greatly, depending on the socio-economic and political context in which class conflict takes place. What is striking in the contemporary period is the uneven development of the class struggle between countries and regions, between workers in the imperial creditor countries and those in debtor neo-colonial countries. The class struggle from below is especially intensifying among some of the more dynamic capitalist countries in which workers have experienced a prolonged period of intense exploitation and the emergence of a new class of ruling billionaires linked to a dominant one-party elite – the cases of China and South Africa.

## The capitalist crisis and the ruling class offensive

In time of capitalist crisis with declining economic wealth, growing threats of bankruptcy and intense demand for state subsidies, there is no basis for sharing wealth – even unequally – between capitalists, bankers, creditors and workers, peasants and farmers, debtors and rentiers. Competition over shrinking resources intensifies conflict over shares of a shrinking pie. The ruling class, facing what it perceives as a life-and-death struggle for survival, strikes back with all the forces – state and private – at its disposal to ensure that its financial needs are met. The public treasury exclusively finances its debts and stimulates its recovery of profits. Ruling class warfare defines who pays for the crisis and who benefits from the recovery of profits.

In turn, the multifaceted capitalist crisis, rooted in in the deregulation of the banking system and the financialization measures put into practice in the 1980s and 1990s with the installation of the new world order of free-market capitalism, is a temporary threat to the capitalist economic system. In response to this threat, and using the crisis as a pretext for taking action, with the aim of reversing the gains made by labour over previous decades of struggle and reactivating the accumulation process, the political representatives of the imperial and local capitalist classes dismantle the social safety net constructed in the process of class struggle from below, undermining in the process the entire legal and ideological underpinnings of 'welfare capitalism'. 'Austerity' is the chosen term to mark the ruling class's seizure of the public treasury on its own behalf – without regard for its social consequences. 'Austerity' is the highest form of class struggle from above because it establishes the arbitrary and unilateral power of capital to decide the present and future allocation of the social product between wages and profits, affecting thereby conditions of employment and unemployment as well as the returns to creditor states and the interest and principal payments of neo-colonial debtor states.

As the crisis deepened among debtor nations, the global ruling class intensified its class war against the workers, employees in both the public and private sectors, and small-business operators and other segments of the 'middle class', which is being squeezed and hollowed out in a process of economic concentration – transferring financial assets to the big players, major investors and creditors in the system of financial capital. First, the creditor imperial states (in Europe the *Troika* – the European Commission, the International Monetary Fund and the European Central Bank) overthrew the constitutional order by seizing state power. Then they proceeded to dictate market-friendly macro- and micro-socio-economic policies. They decreed employment, wage and fiscal policies. They decreed the present and future allocation of state revenues between imperial creditors and local workers. Class warfare went 'global': regional organizations, like the European Union, which embody formally equal members, revealed themselves as imperial organizations for concentrating wealth among the dominant banks in the imperial centres.

## Class struggle from below in times of crisis

Working-class organizations – trade unions, pensioners' associations etc. – are ill prepared to confront the open and aggressive all-out war waged by the ruling class. For decades they were accustomed to the rules of 'collective bargaining' and occasional strikes of short duration to secure incremental improvements. Their parties, labour or social democratic, with dual loyalties to capitalist profits and social welfare, are deeply embedded in the capitalist order. Under pressure of the crisis, they abandoned labour and embraced the formulae of the ruling class, imposing their own versions of 'austerity'. Labour was abandoned; the working classes were on their own – without access to the state and without reliable political allies. The trade unions, narrowly focused on everyday issues and their immediate membership, ignored the mass of unemployed, especially young unemployed, workers. The class struggle from below lacks the leadership, vision, organization and state resources, which the ruling class possesses, to launch a counteroffensive. Class struggle from below at first was entirely defensive – to salvage fragments of labour contracts, to save jobs or to reduce firings. The fundamental problem in the ongoing class struggle is that the trade unions and many workers failed to recognize the changing nature of the class struggle: the 'total war strategy', adopted by the ruling class, went

**16** Class struggle back on the agenda

far beyond pay rises and profit reports and embraced a frontal attack on the living, working, housing, pension, health and educational conditions of labour. The politics of 'social pacts' between labour and capital was totally abandoned by the ruling classes. They demanded the unconditional surrender of all social demands and seized the executive prerogatives of the state to enforce and implement the massive re-concentration of income and political power.

Under these conditions, prevalent throughout Europe and the US, what can be said of the class struggle from below? More than ever, the class struggle has developed unevenly between the new imperial creditor centres and the debtor working-class regions. The most advanced forms of struggle, in terms of scope, demands and intensity, are found in France, Greece, Portugal, Spain, Italy and, to a lesser degree, Ireland. The least advanced forms of working-class struggle are found in the US, Canada, Germany, England, Scandinavia and the Low Countries. Among the BRIC countries, class struggle is intensifying, particularly in China and South Africa but also in India, Russia and Brazil.

The issues raised in each region are significantly different. In China the working class is demanding socio-economic changes and is securing positive improvements in wages, working conditions, housing and health programmes via 'offensive' class struggles. In the face of pending mass firings in heavy industries, the Chinese workers are preparing a counteroffensive. In Brazil, the working class and the rural proletariat of landless workers have adapted or been accommodated to the neo-liberal/agro-mineral self-styled Workers Party regime in exchange for policies that effectively lowered poverty levels and unemployment between 2004 and 2013. In South Africa, despite bloody massacres by the state and yawning social inequalities, struggles over wages and salaries have intensified. This was a defining feature of Lula's legacy.

For most of the rest, the class struggles are defensive and, in many cases, unsuccessful efforts to defend or minimize the loss of employment, labour rights, social insurance and stable employment. The most intensive militant working-class struggles are taking place in countries in which the offensive of capital – the class struggle from above – has been most prolonged, widest in scope and deepest in terms of the cuts in living standards.

The working-class struggle has been weakest in the Anglo-American countries, especially the US, where the tradition of class struggle and general strikes is the weakest. Trade unions in these countries have shrinking memberships (in the US 50 years ago, one-third of all workers were members of a union; today less than 12 per cent are – compared to 18 per cent in Germany, 22 per cent in Greece, 26 per cent in Canada and well over 50 per cent in the Scandinavian countries); trade union leaders are generally closely linked to capitalist parties and there is a very weak or non-existent political identification with class solidarity, even in the face of massive transfers of state revenues to private wealth and earnings from workers to capital. On the other hand, during the 2016 US presidential primaries over 60 per cent of voters under 40 years declared in favour of socialism, a possible harbinger of change. However, this possible change is not at all reflected in data on union membership in the US, which dipped to an all-time historic low in 2014 as a percentage of total workers – 11.5 per cent, according to the Bureau of Labor Statistics (2016).

## Class struggles from above (and the outside) and from below (and within)

The most sustained and successful advances in social welfare and public services over the past decade have occurred in Latin America, where the crisis of capitalism led to militant, broad-based class movements, which overthrew neo-liberal regimes and imposed constraints on both speculative and productive (extractive) capital and – in the case of Argentina – debt payments to investors and rentiers in the imperial centres. Subsequently, nationalist and populist resource-based regimes re-oriented state revenues derived from the export of natural resources and primary commodities to fund poverty reduction and employment generation programmes. The sequence of popular revolts and political intervention, followed by the election in most cases of nationalist-populist regimes, ameliorated the crisis and sustained policies incrementally advancing working-class interests.

In Southern Europe, in contrast, the collapse of capitalism led to a capitalist offensive led by imperial creditors. They imposed the most retrograde neo-colonial regimes, engaged in savage class warfare – while the organized working class fell back on defensive strategies and large-scale social mobilization within the institutional framework of the existing capitalist state. No political offensive, no radical political changes and no social offensive ensued. Movements that do not move forwards move backwards. Each defensive struggle, at most, temporarily delayed a new set of social reversals, setting in motion the inexorable advance of the class struggle from above. The ruling classes have imposed decades of debt payments while pillaging budgets for the foreseeable future. The result will be the lowering of wage structures and social payments. New employment contracts are designed to concentrate greater shares of wealth in the hands of the capitalist class for the foreseeable future. The policies, imposed via the class struggle from above, demonstrate that welfare programmes and social contracts were temporary, tactical concessions – to be definitively discarded once the capitalist class seized exclusive prerogative powers and ruled through executive decrees.

The financial classes of the West have been bailed out and profits have returned to the banks, but the stagnation of the 'real economy' continues. The working classes have, in thought and via militant action, realized that 'collective bargaining' is dead. The state, especially the foreign/imperial creditor-banking state, holds power without any electoral mandate or claim to broad representation. The façade of parliamentary electoral parties remains as an empty shell. Trade unions, in the most militant instances, engage in almost ritualistic mass protests, which are totally ignored by the imperial ruling class bankers and their local political collaborators. The *Troika* dons earplugs and blindfolds while chanting for 'greater austerity' for workers; in the streets, the mantra of the destitute – *basta* – echoes in executive palaces.

**18** Class struggle back on the agenda

## 2 Dynamics of struggle

One looks in vain among the writings of historians and contemporary social scientists for any systematic study of the role of class struggle in the shaping of economic systems, class structures and state power. Yet social classes are ever present in each and every discussion of the policy and political dynamics involved in the distribution of wealth or income by the state or the market, the concentration or deconcentration of property, representation in the state and in determining the beneficiaries of government policy and the lead 'actors' and agencies of social change.

To move beyond class analysis as positioning individuals and groups in an economic structure of social relations, and to see classes as changing and dynamic actors whose action shapes and reshapes the social, political and economic institutions through which they act and react, we have to turn from a purely 'structural' form of analysis in which classes are defined purely in term of their position in society and the 'quotient of well-being' (or problems) associated with this position to a 'political' analysis in which classes act with class-conscious determination to change their situation and to bring down the system if necessary. At issue here is Marx's distinction between a 'class in itself' (class viewed in purely structural terms) and a 'class for itself' in which classes are viewed as class-conscious agencies of social change in particular conjunctures of objective and subjective conditions and the correlation of force in the class struggle. To view class in this way in the Latin American context requires us to extend the class struggle beyond the capital–labour relationship and the land question to encompass 'social communities', indigenous people and unemployed and informal workers – all of them conceptualized and viewed in terms of both their social relationship to the system of economic production as well as their role in the class struggle.

To move beyond class analysis as simply points of reference in static structures and to see classes as dynamic actors whose actions shape and reshape the social, political and economic institutions through which they act and react we have to turn from seeing classes as the 'recipients' of economic goods, state decisions and social action to the class struggle. In the course of our class struggle analysis we will extend the concept of 'class' to encompass diverse forces of resistance to the advance of capital, including the rural and urban semi-proletariat formed under conditions of peripheral capitalism, the indigenous and other communities that are negatively impacted by the operations of extractive capital, and unemployed and informal workers – all conceptualized and viewed in terms of their social relationship to the system of economic production.

### *Conceptualizing the class struggle: key dimensions*

A survey of major professional political, sociological and economic journals over the past half-century fails to turn up a single theoretically informed study of class struggle anywhere. Even the few publications that purport to study 'revolution' marginalize or omit the central role that class struggle in its varied forms plays in the success or failure of popular upheavals. To approach the role of class struggle in a dynamic milieu we will focus exclusively on Latin America over the past two and a half decades – 1990–2014 – a period of significant changes in economic models, political regimes and class structure.

To properly address the centrality of class struggle we need to clarify several points and correct certain misconceptions. In conditions of underdeveloped capitalism the industrial proletariat is not the main protagonist in the class war waged by capital against labour. Class struggle is not merely a matter of the long war and many battles fought by proletarianized and semi-proletarianized peasant farmers throughout the twentieth century, or the struggle of workers for improved wages and working conditions in the form of the labour movement. The most active, organized and combative social classes engaged in the class struggle include in their ranks bankers, manufacturers, plantation owners, commodity traders and other 'owners of the means of production'. In Latin America, some of the more militant participants in the class struggle are 'middle-class' public employees: teachers, health employees and municipal workers.

To clarify this issue regarding the polarities of class we distinguish between class struggle 'from above' and 'from below' (see the discussion above). Class struggle 'from above' includes the owners of the major means of production, distribution and finance. Class struggle 'from below' includes both private and public employees, wage labourers, the unemployed, peasants and Afro-indigenous peoples. In other words, while class struggle might indeed be the 'motor force' of history as understood by Marx, the political and economic direction and societal configurations of the struggle is a matter as to which 'classes-in-struggle' succeed in advancing their class interests and imposing their will, and this matter reflects the correlation of force in particular conjunctures of the class struggle. And we also have to make a further distinction, especially central to the present period: class struggle 'from above' includes two important subgroups: domestic and foreign capitalists. Thus, we need to expand the notion of class struggle from above to include 'the outside' since the 'international capitalist class', as it is termed by some in Latin America, is heavily engaged in the class struggle, deploying all of the forces at its disposal.

Our analysis of the class struggle takes account of a complex dynamic: changing class actors, the intensity and changing context of class action, the ebbs and flows of class struggle and the shifts in the correlation of class forces. We view the state and the political and governmental regimes formed within its institutional framework as both a product of the class struggle and as essential actors in determining the direction of the class struggle.

## Three decades of class struggle

In the first three decades of post-war capitalist development the class struggle predominantly engaged the industrial working class and the rural proletariat of landless rural workers, in what took form as the land struggle and the capital–labour struggle

**20** Class struggle back on the agenda

in the cities. Most of the dynamic class struggles over the subsequent three 'development' decades, however have taken place outside the industrial sector and the factory workplace, and have not engaged to any significant degree the traditional working class or the labour movement. The latter's capacity to mobilize workers had been drastically curtailed by a combination of armed force and repression, structural changes (the destruction of productive forces in industry and agriculture) brought about by the transition towards a new world order of free-market capitalism, and projects of 'international cooperation' designed to extinguish the fires of revolutionary ferment in the countryside (Petras & Veltmeyer, 2001).

In this new context, while tens of thousands of landless rural workers in Brazil occupied large estates, and indigenous communities in Peru, Ecuador and Bolivia fought pitched battles with big mining companies over contamination and dispossession of land and water resources, no comparable industrial actions, strikes or worker occupations of factories took place. The only exception here was the 'recovered factory' movement in Argentina, formed in the throes of a major economic – and political – crisis (2001–03). The protagonists in this struggle were the victims of the economic crisis that ensued from the implementation of one of the most radical programmes of neo-liberal reforms in the 1990s, a movement of unemployed workers who moved from a strategy of street 'pickets' (adopting the tactic employed so successfully in the 1990s by the indigenous movement against the neo-liberal policy agenda) to blockading transportation routes (Petras & Veltmeyer, 2003).

In the period 1990–2005, advances in the class struggle from above alternated with substantial gains for the protagonists in the popular sector – the indigenous communities, peasants and rural landless workers who rose up against the neo-liberal regimes installed within the framework of the Washington Consensus. These movements led the resistance against the neo-liberal policy agenda and by the end of the 1990s had managed to either halt this agenda in its tracks or put its agents on the defensive. By the turn of the new millennium the neo-liberal model in much of South America was to all intents and purposes dead, creating conditions that allowed for the resurgence of the Left in the form of centre-left 'progressive' post-neo-liberal regimes, and the emergence of another 'progressive' cycle in Latin American politics.

On the other hand, the period 1990–2000 saw a major successful advance in the class struggle from above. Across Latin America, foreign and domestic capitalists directly succeeded in transferring over 5,000 state enterprises into private hands and the banks of foreign and domestic capitalists, and these included many highly lucrative enterprises built up over decades and society's most strategic resources, which were transferred either directly through the mechanism of the market, or, more generally via the mechanism of state power. On the dynamics of this class struggle over the assets accumulated by the state see, inter alia, Petras & Veltmeyer (2003).

Throughout this period – the 1990s – in which the structural reforms imposed on governments under the Washington Consensus shifted state power in their favour (basically by removing structural barriers to the entry of capital) – the capitalist class's share of both wealth and national income dramatically increased. And in the same context the share of labour in national income was drastically reduced – by as much as 40 to 50 per cent by some estimates. It was not until well into the new millennium, after five years of rapid economic growth, that workers in Argentina managed to recover the value of the average wage of 1970. The labour market, like the capital and product markets, was deregulated, resulting in some cases – notably Mexico – in a 70 per cent decline in the minimum wage, leading to widespread impoverishment within the working class.

With capital in command of the state and the labour movement virtually destroyed, labour was in retreat; flexible labour policies were adopted, strikes and protests were violently repressed. Structural adjustment policies were imposed via the IMF, the World Bank and the IDB – which facilitated foreign takeovers of national banks, telecommunications and other strategic sectors at bargain basement prices. Ruling class neo-liberal ideology promising free markets, free elections and prosperity held sway over the middle class and enabled neo-liberal elites to win elections in Argentina, Bolivia, Peru, Brazil and Ecuador. Structural adjustment policies in Venezuela were imposed by blood and fire: the Perez regime massacred several thousand protesting unemployed and poor people.

The successful outcomes for local and foreign neo-liberal capitalist classes during the decade of the 1990s led to a belief that this 'model' was the 'end of history', instead of the product of a particular moment in the economic cycle and a specific correlation of class forces.

This ruling class illusion would have profound consequences in the next decade following the crises of 2000, the breakdown and discrediting of the neo-liberal model and the upsurge of the class struggle from below. The overthrow and defeat of the neo-liberal regimes and the relative advance of the 'popular forces' established, in most cases, a new post-neo-liberal configuration of regimes and changes in the correlation of forces.

The imperial powers, especially the US, Canada and the EU, refused to recognize and adapt to this new configuration and adopted policies and strategies to reverse this process and reimpose the 1990s 'neo-liberal model'. As a result of this 'nostalgia for the nineties', they suffered a series of defeats during the first decade of the twenty-first century in Venezuela, Bolivia, Ecuador and Argentina. The ruling classes only succeeded via a military coup in Honduras and a civilian putsch in Paraguay. But by the latter part of the decade the capitalist class went on the offensive and regained ground in some countries.

The ascendancy of the class struggle from above in the 1990s was not universal. In Colombia, the armed class struggle of the FARC advanced from the countryside to the periphery of major cities. In Venezuela a military-civilian uprising in 1992 was followed by mass mobilization from below leading to an electoral victory for the popular classes in 1998 with the election of Hugo Chávez.

The economic breakdown and crises of the neo-liberal model at the end of the 1990s, the gross pillage of the public treasury, the rising rates of impoverishment, social polarization and the massive rise of unemployment and informal 'employment' combined to ignite large-scale social uprisings and mass movements. In a word, the class struggle from below went on the offensive: through popular uprisings (Bolivia, Ecuador and Argentina) and social mobilizations linked to elections (Brazil, Venezuela, Uruguay and Peru), the incumbent neo-liberal electoral regimes were toppled or replaced.

The class protagonists (the leading forces) in these struggles varied according to country. The political and social composition of those engaged in the class struggle from below differed significantly from the centre-left political parties and leaders who benefitted from the struggle. Moreover, the political-economic changes implemented by the post-neo-liberal regimes differed markedly from the programmes and demands that ignited the class struggle from below.

For example, in Bolivia the popular social movements that led to the overthrow of the Sánchez de Losada and Mesa regimes were markedly different in composition and programmatically from the leadership of the Movement to Socialism (MAS) party regime. Workers, the unemployed, informal workers, indigenous people and peasants spearheaded the uprising. But lower- and upper-middle-class social liberals and technocrats designed and implemented economic policy. Mass demands for the nationalization of mines, radical agrarian reform and a class-based 'constituent assembly' were replaced by the MAS leaders by joint ventures with foreign capital, the promotion of agribusiness and a constituent assembly based on 'territorial constituencies'. Similar economic divergences occurred in Argentina and Ecuador between the anti-neo-liberal regimes composed of middle-class leaders and the popular classes. The political elites diluted the policy outcomes of the class struggle from below.

The retreat of the capitalist class, the displacement of the US-backed neo-liberal regimes and their replacement by new pro-capitalist social liberal regimes with political and organizational ties to the popular class organizations led to a relative balance of class forces (labour and capital) in the cities and industries.

## Class struggle from below, 2010–14

The period 2010–14 witnessed a decline in class struggle from below in several senses. The demands were narrowly focused on wages and salaries and not 'structural' changes. The modes of struggle shifted to 'tripartite' negotiations rather than mass action. The popular struggles were fragmented by sectoral interests (public–private, mining industry, peasant indigenous) rather than unified by class interests. Neither labour nor capital was decisively defeated or wholly victorious during the ascendancy of the centre-left regimes during the 2002–14 period. Class struggles, extensive and intensive, persisted, but only for limited moments in a few countries and circumscribed circumstances.

In Bolivia, the capitalist class and the US imperial state made an effort to destabilize the MAS regime by mobilizing agribusiness bourgeoisie and the agro-export elite in Santa Cruz. However, they were defeated in a process of mass mobilizations ('the social movements') and the actions of the armed forces loyal to the regime. Subsequently, the MAS regime negotiated an economic pact with the national and foreign capitalist class to promote 'production, investment and growth' on the one hand, and a social pact with labour union leaders to increase wages, especially the minimum wage and other incremental changes. For all intents and purposes, class struggle from above ended because the regime incorporated the capitalist class's economic programme as its own. The class struggle from below was confined to the economistic demands of public-sector workers and social ecological struggle by a sector of the indigenous peasant communities.

Venezuela is the exception to the social pacts signed by the centre-left regimes in the progressive cycle. Class struggle from above and below remained at the highest intensity. The capitalist class and its US imperial backers launched major assaults on state power. These included a military coup in April 2002, a lockout from December 2002 to February 2003, a referendum to revoke the Presidency of Hugo Chávez in 2004, sustained disinvestment in production and a campaign of unlimited economic sabotage throughout a decade and a half, with a violent terrorist campaign between February and May 2014.

In retrospect the 'class struggle from below' based on an alliance between mass movements and the Chávez–Maduro governments, defeated and rolled back the capitalist class's assault on power and went on the offensive. From 2003 onwards, the government, backed by the popular classes, nationalized enterprises and redistributed oil rents from the overseas banks and capitalists to massive social expenditures. Thousands of community councils were organized to buttress the class struggle from below.

In Venezuela, the intense class struggle reflected the deep social class polarization and political-social divisions. As a result, the kind of regime–multinational capitalist pact, which the MAS imposed in Bolivia, was not possible. Venezuela's practice of class politics contrasted sharply with the double discourse of both Morales and Correa – left rhetoric for the masses and lucrative pacts with the capitalist class.

## Conclusion

Over the last three decades the class struggle has played a decisive role in the rise, consolidation and then the demise of neo-liberalism as an economic doctrine and development model. The 1980s was a low point in the class struggle from below, except for Peru, which experienced a high tide of armed struggle, mass mobilization and workers' strikes. The revolutionary movement of national liberation had been brought to ground or defeated; a conservative counter-revolution brought into play a new policy regime that halted and then reversed many of the gains made by organized labour and the impoverished peasantry of small landholding farmers; a neo-liberal policy regime brought about a decade 'lost to development'. As a result, an enormous mass of landless and semi-proletarianized rural workers were forced to abandon the countryside and migrate to the cities and urban centres, where they were forced to fend for themselves in the interstices of the capitalist labour market and modernizing urban economy.

**24** Class struggle back on the agenda

The 1990s saw an advance of the class struggle from above and a massive influx of capital in the form of multinational corporations and foreign investors. This influx of capital was facilitated by the neo-liberal policies of privatizing state enterprises, deregulating the market and eliminating barriers to the free movements of goods and capital. However, the 1990s generally saw a resurgence of popular resistance against these policies, and the formation of social movements that challenged these policies and confronted the state power of the neo-liberal Right. By the turn into the new century these movements had managed to pave the way for an advance of the class struggle from below. This new correlation of force in the class struggle led to the overthrow of neo-liberal regimes and the inclusionary state activism of post-neo-liberal regimes committed to a more inclusive form of national development, large-scale public investment in social programmes, the renationalization of some enterprises, the organization of new class and community-based ethno-ecology movements, an increase in wages and salaries, and a significant reduction in the rate of extreme poverty.

However, lacking independent political leadership the class struggle from below relied on centre-left electoral politicians who leaned in their direction when class pressure was stronger but turned to the capitalist class when the correlation of force shifted. The class struggle from below advanced furthest in Venezuela in terms of social change. But in no country did it lead to the overthrow of the capitalist economy and state.

The class struggle brought to the fore new and old protagonists on both sides of the class divide. Unlike earlier periods, the industrial working class played a subsidiary role, even in the more advanced industrial economies like Argentina and Brazil. The major protagonists of class struggle from below were a constellation of forces operating in different locations.

Despite the shifting configurations of power between capital and labour, neither has suffered a 'historic' victory or defeat over the past quarter-century, as happened in previous decades. For example, the revolution in Cuba in 1959 was a decisive victory for the class struggle from below that changed the social system, state and economy for a historical epoch. The military coups in Chile (1973), Brazil (1964) and Argentina (1976) smashed working-class institutions and organizations and imposed the neo-liberal economic model for over 30 years.

The result of these 'historic defeats' had a profound impact in shaping the class struggle, even today. For example, the powerful role of workers' organizations in occupying factories and self-managed enterprises, and convoking general strikes has diminished. However, that has not meant 'the end of the class struggle'. New dynamic forces of resistance have emerged in the popular sector and other classes have stepped forwards and are leading the struggle. For example, in Brazil million-person demonstrations have marched and blocked streets, demanding that the 'centre-left' Workers Party (PT) regime attend to basic social services, public transportation, low cost housing and other essential needs. The urban mass struggles demand nothing less than a fundamental shift in budget priorities and allocations away from corporate subsidies and sports extravagances to public needs.

In Chile, mass struggles have been led by secondary and university students demanding quality free public education provided by progressive taxes on the corporate elite; slum dwellers demand an end to the worst social inequalities in the region.

In Argentina, entire communities adjoining agro-mineral mega-corporations have engaged in class warfare resisting toxic chemical farming and mining by Monsanto, Barrick Gold and other extractive enterprises. Urban trade unions have engaged in class resistance to the centre-left regimes' policies imposing the costs of anti-inflationary policies on labour.

In Colombia, Peru, Ecuador and Bolivia, mass resistance is based on rural communities, predominantly peasants, farm workers and indigenous people, and challenge the state-agro-mineral alliances, which are dispossessing them of land, water and clean air. They are promoting state aid for local productive activity. The traditional 'labour organizations' that were formerly at the forefront of the class struggle have become, at best, the rearguard of these mass struggles.

The most significant engagement of labour in the class struggle occurred in Argentina between 2002 and 2006, when hundreds of thousands of unemployed workers organized *piqueteros* (roving pickets), blocked major road arteries, seized work sites and posed, temporarily, an alternative basis for political power.

The new protagonists of class struggle from below represent the principal source of resistance to the current capitalist class offensive from above. In the current conjuncture they are in search of allies in the cities, new political instruments, national organizational structures and a strategy for power.

What is now clear is that the alignment of the social movement activists with reluctant centre-left regime allies has exhausted its progressive possibilities. The centre-left has embraced the agro-mining developmentalist model based on the dispossession and semi-proletarianization of peasants, indigenous communities and small producers. From being reluctant allies of labour, the 'progressive' regimes on the centre-left have become accomplices of the new capitalist class offensive from above. However, this political shift has not stopped the class struggle from below or lessened the weight of the conditions that motivated the exploited, dispossessed and oppressed classes to organize and struggle for substantive social change.

## References

Bureau of Labor Statistics. (2016). *News release*. 28 January. USDL-16–0158. Washington, DC: US Department of Labor.

Petras, J. & Veltmeyer, H. (2001). *Globalization unmasked: Imperialism in the 21st century*. London: ZED/Halifax: Fernwood.

Petras, J. & Veltmeyer, H. (2003). *Cardoso's Brazil: A land for sale*. Boulder, CO: Rowman & Littlefield.

# 2

# EXTRACTIVISM AND RESISTANCE

## A new era

Capitalism as we know it, and as Marx theorized it, originated with the exploitation of the (theoretically) unlimited supply of surplus labour provided by the countryside, and it is based on the capital–labour relationship, a relationship of economic exploitation and class conflict. However, land and the resources bound up with it (forest, water, minerals and metals, etc.) have played a crucial role in the capitalist development process. For several centuries prior to the advance of industrial capitalism in the nineteenth century, capitalism was based on the extraction and pillage – and commodification – of natural resources. True, extraction also required and was based on the exploitation of labour, so in this sense labour exploitation is at the bottom of capitalism as a system of commodity production. That is, as Marx theorized, labour is the source of value, which can be calculated by counting the hours of labour used to produce a commodity and bring it to market. However, under the dominion of extractive capital (capital invested in the acquisition of land and the extraction of natural resources), the capital accumulated in the process – the value of the product brought to market (the natural resources extracted from below or above the ground) – is not entirely or even predominantly based on the extraction of surplus value from the direct producer or worker. A large part of the accumulated capital, and the value of the primary commodities on the world market, is derived from natural capital (the wealth of land and natural resources), which takes the form of ground rent rather than surplus value and is extracted by means of taxes and royalties charged by the owner of the land. In addition, given the high organic composition of capital – the ratio of physical capital or technology to living labour – in the natural resource extraction sector, labour under conditions of extractive capitalism plays a relatively reduced role in the production of value compared to labour in an industrial capitalist regime and environment. The implications of this for both the dynamics of capitalist development and the dynamics of the resistance generated by this development have an enormous significance. This chapter seeks to unravel this significance.

## Extractive capitalism as a new phase in the development process

In the post-World War II period, the capitalist development of the forces of production – what we term 'capitalist development' but what in mainstream development discourse is presented as 'economic development' or 'economic growth' – can be divided into two phases: three decades of state-led development based on the exploitation of the 'unlimited supply of surplus labour' released from the countryside (the agricultural sector) via various forces of change (capitalism, industrialization, modernization); and three subsequent decades of free-market capitalism and neo-liberal 'structural reforms' mandated under the Washington Consensus (Petras & Veltmeyer, 2001; Williamson, 1990).

The neo-liberal 'structural reform' agenda of the Washington Consensus not only caused a massive destruction of productive forces in both agriculture and industry. It also facilitated a massive inflow of capital in the form of foreign direct investment directed towards non-traditional manufacturing, financial and high-tech information-rich services, and natural resource extraction.

The 1990s saw a sixfold increase in the inflows of FDI in the first four years of the decade and then another sharp increase from 1996 to 2001; in fewer than 10 years the foreign capital accumulated by MNCs in the region had tripled (ECLAC, 2012: 71) while profits soared. Saxe-Fernández, a well-known Mexico-based political economist, determined that over the course of the decade the inflow of FDI had netted enormous profits, reflected in the net outflow of US$100 billion over the entire decade (Saxe-Fernández & Núñez, 2001).

Another major inflow of capital in the form of foreign direct investment occurred in the first decade of the new millennium in the context of a major expansion in the worldwide demand for natural resources and a consequent primary commodities boom – primarily in South America (Ocampo, 2007). This boom in the export of primary commodities in the energy sector of fossil and biofuels (oil and gas), as well as minerals, metals and agro-food products, primarily affected South America, which led a worldwide trend towards the (re)primarization of exports from the periphery of the system and the expansion of extractive capitalism (ECLAC, 2012).

The main destinations for FDI in Latin America over the past two decades have been services (particularly banking and finance) and the natural resources sector, namely, the exploration, extraction, and exploitation of fossil and biofuel sources of energy, precious metals and industrial minerals, and agro-food products. In the previous era of state-led development, FDI had predominantly served as a means of financing the capitalist development of industry and a process of 'productive transformation' (technological conversion and modernization). This was reflected in the geoeconomics of global capital and the dynamics of capital flows at the time. However, in response to two generations of neo-liberal reforms, conditions for capital had dramatically improved, opening up and expanding in Latin America a market for goods manufactured in the north (the US, Canada and Europe), and providing greater opportunities for 'resource-seeking' (extractive) capital – consolidating the role of Latin America as a source and supplier of natural resources and exporter of primary

## 28 Extractivism and resistance: a new era

commodities, a role that is reflected in the flows of productive investment in the region towards the extractive industries (see Table 2.1).

At the turn of the new millennium the service sector accounted for almost half of FDI inflows, but data presented by ECLAC (2012: 50) point towards a steady and increasing flow of capital towards the natural resources sector in South America, especially mining, where Canadian capital took a predominant position, accounting for up to 70 per cent of FDI in this sector (Arellano, 2010). Over the course of the first decade of the new millennium, the share of 'resource-seeking' capital in total FDI increased from 10 to 30 per cent. In 2006 the inflow of 'resource-seeking' investment capital grew by 49 per cent to reach US$59 billion, which exceeded the total FDI inflows of any year since economic liberalization began in the 1990s (UNCTAD, 2007: 53).

Despite the global financial and economic crisis at the time, FDI flows towards Latin America and the Caribbean reached a record high in 2008 (US$128.3 billion), an extraordinary development considering that FDI flows worldwide at the time had shrunk by at least 15 per cent. This countercyclical trend signalled the continuation of the primary commodities boom and the steady expansion of resource-seeking capital in the region.

The rapid expansion in the flow of FDI towards Latin America in the 1990s reflected the increased opportunities for capital accumulation provided by the neoliberal policy regimes in the region, but in the new millennium conditions for capitalist development had radically changed. In this new context, which included a major realignment of economic power and relations of trade in the world market, and the growth in both the demand for and the prices of primary commodities, the shift of FDI towards Latin America signified a major change in the geoeconomics and geopolitics of global capital. Flows of FDI into Latin America from 2000 to 2007 for the first time exceeded those that went to North America, surpassed only by Europe and Asia. And the global financial crisis brought about an even more radical change in the geoeconomics of global capital in regard to both its regional distribution (increased flows to Latin America) and sectoral distribution (concentration in the extractive sector). In 2005, the 'developing' and 'emerging' economies attracted only 12 per cent of global flows of productive capital but by 2010, against a background of a sharp decline in these flows, these economies were the destination point for over 50 per cent of global FDI flows (CEPAL, 2012). In the same year, FDI flows into Latin America increased by 34.6 per cent, well above the growth rate in Asia, which was only 6.7 per cent (UNCTAD, 2012: 52–4).

**TABLE 2.1** Percentage distribution of FDI by sector in Latin America

|  | 2000 | 2001 | 2002 | 2003 | 2004 | 2005 | 2006 | 2007 | 2008 |
|---|---|---|---|---|---|---|---|---|---|
| Resources | 10 | 12 | 12 | 11 | 12 | 13 | 12 | 15 | 30 |
| Manufacturing | 25 | 26 | 38 | 35 | 38 | 37 | 36 | 35 | 22 |
| Services | 60 | 61 | 51 | 48 | 46 | 48 | 51 | 49 | 47 |

*Source:* adapted from Arellano (2010, Table 2), based on ECLAC data.

The flow of productive capital into Latin America has been fuelled by two factors: high prices for primary commodities, which attracted 'natural resource-seeking investment', and the economic growth of the South American subregion, which encouraged market-seeking investment. This flow of FDI was concentrated in four South American countries – Argentina, Brazil, Chile and Colombia – which accounted for 89 per cent of the subregion's total inflows. The extractive industry in these countries, particularly mining and to a lesser degree farmland, absorbed most of these inflows. For example, in 2009, Latin America received 26 per cent of global investment in mineral exploration (Sena-Fobomade, 2011). Together with the expansion of oil and gas projects, mineral extraction constitutes the single most important source of export revenues for most countries in the region.

## The new geopolitics of capital in Latin America

As just determined, a wave of resource-seeking FDI was a major feature of the political economy of global capitalist development at the turn into the first decade of the new millennium. Another was the demise of neo-liberalism as an economic doctrine and strategy. In South America powerful social movements successfully challenged this model. Over the past decade, a number of governments in this sub-region have ridden a wave of anti-neo-liberal sentiment generated by these movements. Latin America in this context experienced a sea tide of regime change – a tilt towards the left and what has been described as 'progressive extractivism' (Gudynas, 2010).

The political victories of these democratically elected 'progressive' regimes opened a new chapter in the class struggle and the anti-imperialist movement. The wide embrace of resource-seeking extractive capital has generated deep paradoxes for those progressive regimes in the region committed to addressing the inequality predicament and conditions of environmental degradation that are fast reaching crisis proportions as a result of the operations of extractive capital.

Some political leaders and social movements in this context speak of revolution in the context of moving towards 'the socialism of the twenty-first century' – Venezuela's 'Bolivarian' Revolution, Bolivia's 'democratic and cultural revolution' and Ecuador's 'Citizens' revolution' – and, together with several governments that have embraced the new developmentalism (the search for a more inclusive form of development), these regimes have indeed taken some steps in the direction of poverty reduction and social inclusion, using the additional fiscal revenues derived from resource rents to this purpose. Yet, like their more conservative neighbours – regimes such as Mexico and Colombia, committed to both neo-liberalism and an alliance with 'imperialism' – the left-leaning progressive regimes in the region find themselves entangled in a maze of renewed dependence on natural resource extraction (the 'new extractivism') and primary commodity exports ('reprimarization'). Further, as argued by Gudynas, this new 'progressive' extractivism is much like the old 'classical' extractivism in its destruction of both the environment and livelihoods and in its erosion of the territorial rights and sovereignty of indigenous

**30** Extractivism and resistance: a new era

communities most directly affected by the operations of extractive capital, which generate relations of intense social conflict.

Despite the use by 'progressive' centre-left governments of resource rents as a mechanism of social inclusion and direct cash transfers to the poor, they were not able to pursue revolutionary measures in their efforts to bring about a more inclusive and sustainable form of development, or a deepening of political and economic democratization, allowing the people to 'live well' (*vivir bien*), while at the same time continuing to toe the line of extractive capital and its global assault on nature and livelihoods. The problem here is twofold. One is a continuing reliance of these left-leaning post-neo-liberal regimes (indeed, all but Venezuela) on neo-liberalism ('structural reforms') at the level of macroeconomic public policy. The other problem relates to the so-called 'new extractivism' based on 'inclusionary state activism' as well as the continued reliance on FDI – and thus the need to strike a deal with global capital in regard to sharing the resource rents derived from the extraction process. This relation of global capital to the local state is asymmetrical: the former is dominant. This is reflected in the tendency of the governments and policy regimes formed by the new Latin American Left, even those like Ecuador and Peru that have articulated a populist rhetoric, to take the side of the multinational mining companies in their relation of conflict with the communities that are directly affected by the extractive operations of these companies (see the various country case studies in Veltmeyer & Petras, 2014).

Another indicator of the relation of dependency between global extractive capital and the Latin American state is the inability of the latter to regulate the former and the extraordinary profits that are made by the companies that operate in the extractive sector. It is estimated that given very low or, as in the case of Mexico until recently, non-existent royalty rates and the typically lax and low tax regime on the exportation of minerals and minerals – a major factor in the export regime of a number of countries in the region (particularly Chile, Bolivia, Colombia and Peru) – over 70 per cent of the value of these minerals and metals on the global market is appropriated by different groups of capitalists in the global production chain. For example, the *Financial Times* reported on 18 April 2013 that from just 2002 to 2006, during the height of the primary commodities boom, the biggest commodity traders harvested US$250 billion in profits on their 'investments'. At the same time, given the capital intensity of production in the extractive sector it is estimated that workers generally received less than 10 per cent of the value of the social product on the world market. Typically, the benefits of economic growth brought about by the export of Latin America's wealth of natural resources are externalized, while the exceedingly high social and environmental costs are internalized, borne by the communities most directly affected by the operations of extractive capital.

The continued reliance on the neo-liberal model of structural reform within the framework of a post-Washington Consensus, together with the turn towards and a continued reliance on extractive capital ('resource-seeking' FDI), constitutes serious economic, social and political problems for Latin American states seeking to break away from the dictates of global capital and the clutches of imperial power. However, the turn of the 'progressive' neo-liberal regimes towards regulation of the operations of extractive capital, as well as the growing popular resistance and opposition to their destructive and negative socio-environmental impacts of these operations, also raises major problems for global capital. Even so, the capitalists and companies that operate in the extractive sector are able to count on the support, resources and powers of the imperialist state to counter these pressures.

Regarding the issue of regulation, the states and international organizations that constitute imperialism have been able to mobilize their considerable resources and exercise their extensive powers to create a system of corporate self-regulation based on the doctrine of corporate social responsibility (CSR) (Gordon, 2010; Mining-Watch Canada, 2009). With this doctrine, the Latin American governments that have turned to a strategy of natural resource development have been pressured to allow the companies that operate in the extractive sector to regulate themselves.

The resource wars and social conflicts that have surrounded the operations of extractive capital (particularly in the mining sector) over the past two decades have resulted in the imperial state coming to the rescue of extractive capital time and time again. In this regard, the Canadian state, under the previous hard-line conservative regime led by Stephen Harper, was particularly aggressive in its unconditional and relentless support of the Canadian mining companies that dominate foreign investment in the industry – accounting as they do for upwards of 70 per cent of the capital invested in this subsector in Latin America. The support of the Canadian government for these companies is expressed via diplomatic pressures exerted on Latin American governments, a major sell-job in favour of CSR, and substantial financial support and assistance in overcoming the widespread resistance to the extractive operations of Canadian mining companies. Ottawa has placed virtually the entire international development programme of Canada at the disposal of these companies (Engler, 2012; Gordon, 2010; Gordon & Webber, 2008).

## The contradictions of extractive capitalism

In a book on 'the study of natural resource extraction in resource-rich countries', Paul Collier, the former director of development research at the World Bank, and Tony Venables, director of the Oxford Centre for the Analysis of Resource Rich Economies, concluded that 'often plunder, rather than prosperity, has become the norm in the industry' (Collier & Venables, 2011). In line with the post-neo-liberal agenda of improving social outcomes through better natural resource management and inclusionary state activism (using export revenues derived from the export of natural resources), Collier and Venables set out to improve the management of natural resources in developing countries by 'highlight[ing] the key principles that need to be followed to avoid distortion and dependence'. They do this by focusing on the decision-making process in the management of natural resources but ignoring the capitalist system dynamics that generate the distortion and dependence in the first place.

**32** Extractivism and resistance: a new era

A more sophisticated variant of this approach ('inclusive economic growth' or 'sustainable resource development') is to focus on the economic growth potential of an extractive strategy, rather than resource pillage and labour exploitation, environmental degradation and class conflict. Viewed from this angle, governing regimes in Latin America and elsewhere in the global south have responded to the growing demand for primary commodities by shifting their economic growth strategies towards the extraction of natural resources, in response to the high prices for primary commodities. The result has been a reversion to an international trade structure based on the export of these commodities, which, Latin American structuralists have warned, has been very disadvantageous to countries on the periphery of the world system. This economic growth strategy in Latin America was abandoned when the world market collapsed during the Great Depression in favour of an alternative economic growth strategy based on an industrial policy focused on import substitution (ISI). This strategy was designed to overcome what development economists have theorized as a 'resource curse': more often than not a policy based on extracting a country's abundant natural resources such as industrial minerals and fossil fuels (oil and gas) and exporting them in primary commodity form has resulted in underdevelopment and impoverishment (Acosta, 2009; Norman, 2009: 183–207; Sachs & Warner, 2001: 827–38).

Economists have given different explanations for this 'resource curse'. Explanations range from the negative impact of natural resource development on the exchange rate in other sectors (the so-called Dutch disease), the volatility of commodity prices on the world market with a propensity towards a boom–bust cycle, and an overreliance on foreign direct investment that leads even progressive governments to take the side of the mining companies in their conflicts with the local communities, to the formation of an enclave economy with few backwards or forwards linkages ('multiplier effects' in terms of income and jobs) to other sectors of the economy, and a social structure characterized by polarization, a high level of social inequality in the share of wealth and the distribution of income, and social conflict.

The conflict between the purported aim of extractivism (sustainable and inclusive economic development) and its likely medium-term outcome (volatility, crisis, social inequalities, poverty and social conflict) is a major contradiction. Other contradictions include the conflict between the goal of 'living well' in social solidarity and harmony with nature or mother earth – the stated goal of the development plans elaborated by the progressive policy regimes formed in Bolivia and Ecuador – and the outcome of the actual policies pursued by these regimes: degradation of the environment and dislocation of local communities (see Chapter 3 on this).

In addition, extractivism as a form of capitalism, and as a particular phase in the capitalist development process, also suffers from the conflict between labour and capital that lies at the base of the capitalism system and what the French economist Thomas Piketty (2014) views as the 'central contradiction' of capitalism: a tendency towards social inequality and uneven development, which is reflected in the propensity of capitalism towards crisis and class conflict. How this contradiction plays out today in Latin America in the current context can be traced out not only at the level of the class struggle but in terms of the policy dynamics of extractive capitalism.

These dynamics reflect the relatively high organic composition of capital (productive investment in machinery and technology vs. living labour) in extractive capitalism compared to industrial capitalism. As a result, living labour (wages) is a relatively small or reduced factor of economic production in extractivist economies such as Bolivia, Ecuador and Peru, and entails a much lower production cost relative to technology; consequently, labour in these countries receives a much lower share of the social product – more like 10 per cent (compared to 40–60 per cent in most cases of industrial capitalism). Given the relation of dependency – dependence on foreign direct investment – between the (neo)extractivist economies of South America and the multinational companies in the extractive sector, and the need of the former to strike a deal with the latter, these extractivist regimes – even the most 'progressive' in terms of a commitment towards inclusionary state activism and inclusive development – in actual fact receive but a fraction of the value of the commodities on the world market. For example, in neo-liberal regimes such as Mexico the effective tax rate in the mining sector in 2012 was less than 2 per cent,[1] and royalty payments were done away with in the early 1990s (as a means of attracting foreign investment). As a result, the state receives little in exchange for allowing the pillage of its natural resource wealth. In 'progressive' or 'neoextractivist' regimes such as Bolivia and Ecuador, the state's share of the exported natural resource wealth is greater than in countries such as Mexico and Colombia, which have a neo-liberal policy regime, but even so this share is normally not above 10 per cent.

This means that the lion's share of the value of the social product in the extractive sector is appropriated by the global capitalist class along the global value extraction/exploitation chain. For example, it is estimated that foreign investors and the multinational corporations in the sector receive as much as a 60 per cent rate of return on their investments. Needless to say, the relative share of the popular classes of these resource-rich exporting countries in these 'benefits' of 'economic growth' are negligible. At the same time, the popular sector and the communities on the front line of the class struggle have to bear the brunt of the exceedingly high social and environmental costs of this development process – costs that force them to resist, pushing or pulling them into a relation of conflict with extractive capital and the state.

Over the past decade there have been numerous scientific studies and many reports on this relation of conflict and associated struggles (see, for example, CEDIB, 2010).

## Class struggle on the frontier of extractive capital

There are two ways of understanding the dynamics of resistance in current conditions of the new extractivism. One is in terms of the response to the negative socio-economic and environmental impacts of extractivism and the agency of social

**34** Extractivism and resistance: a new era

and environmental movements formed from the social base of indigenous and farming communities contiguous to the mines and extractive operations (Svampa, 2012; see Leff, 1996, Toledo, 2000, and Tetreault, 2014, with regard to the dynamics of this resistance in Mexico, and Bebbington, 2011, in regard to Peru and elsewhere in the Andes). Through the political ecology lens used by these authors, the resistance movement today is, as Tetreault (2014) phrases it,

> on the cutting edge of a search for an alternative modernity ... impl[ying] greater participation in decision-making, local control over local natural resources ... and a rationale that draws attention to and emphasizes the importance of the matrix of environmental, social and cultural factors.

Exponents of this political ecology approach emphasize the negative impacts of extractive capital and mega-mining projects such as opencast mining – one of the world's most polluting, devastating and dangerous industrial activities – on the environment and the habitat of indigenous and farming communities, particularly as they relate to access to clean or potable water. Examples of these impacts and associated struggles abound.

Another way of understanding these resistance movements and explaining their dynamics is in terms of their connection to the class struggle. Lust (2014), in the case of Peru, and Sankey (2014), in the case of Colombia, take this approach to conclude that the forces engaged in the struggle, and the social base of the social movements formed in this resistance, constitute in effect a new proletariat composed of waged workers and miners, communities of peasant farmers and semi-proletarianized rural landless workers. These sectors of the working class broadly understood serve as a reserve army of surplus labour to the requirements of extractive capital. Most significantly, indigenous communities concerned with retaining access to their share of the global commons, securing their livelihoods and protecting their territorial rights and ways of living are deeply engaged in the new forms of class struggle. As Sankey (2014) has shown in the case of Colombia, the social and political struggles that surround resource extraction, and the associated upsurge in the forces of resistance, have 'been accompanied by the entrance of new actors onto the scene'. While waged workers continued to play an important role in the class struggle and the broader resistance movement – accounting for close to half of the collective acts of protest since 2005 – at least 25 per cent of collective actions involved the communities negatively affected by the operations of extractive capital, and these communities were the major driving force of a growing resistance movement, as they clearly are in Mexico. Looking more closely at the forces engaged in the class struggle, it is possible to identify the contours of a new class structure.

First, we have those social groupings and classes that share what Svampa (2012) has termed 'the commodity consensus' (*consenso de los commodities*). This includes elements of the middle class, including those that take the form of an associational-type social organization or non-governmental organization, which for the most part have been formed within the urban middle classes. Notwithstanding the environmental concerns of many of its members and its organizations – the middle class can best be defined in terms of the relationship of individuals to consumption rather than to production – this social class to some degree is complicit in the operations of extractive capital, hiding this complicity with a mild or muted opposition and resistance to the environmental implications of unregulated resource extraction and to the social justice considerations regarding issues of class and excessive social inequality in the distribution of wealth. These forces are left-leaning but occupy the 'centre' of the ideological and political spectrum, and are readily accommodated to both capitalism and extractivism via a reformist programme that combines extractivism with the new developmentalism.

Another major actor in the resistance to extractive capitalism are community-based movements, i.e. the indigenous and other communities located close to and negatively impacted by the operations of extractive capital and associated mega-projects. These communities have led the resistance to the incursions of extractive capital. These communities have not only resisted the incursions of extractive capital and its destructive operations – what Zibechi (2012) has termed 'subterranean forces of resistance' – but they have formed a broad socio-environmental resistance movement of small landholding farmers concerned with protecting their territorial rights to water and the land, securing their freedom from labour exploitation and the degradation of their habitat, and maintaining their relationship to nature.

The resistance also includes certain sectors of organized labour. But it is predominantly made up of proletarianized and semi-proletarianized rural landless or near-landless workers, or small landholding family farmers and peasants whose concerns relate to accessing land and the commons, resisting corporate land-grabbing and the impact of government-supported corporate agribusiness practices on their livelihoods, as well as the policies derived from the neo-liberal model and the capitalist system.

On this broad social base, the forces of resistance predominantly take the form of social movements opposed to extractive capitalism as such, but extractive capitalism as well as the neo-liberal model used to make public policy and govern them.

For many in this social and political sector – the resistance – 'socialism' is not understood as an economic system as much as a matter of principle (equality and social justice) that can be actualized in public policy. It can even be accommodated to capitalism in the form of local development in the local spaces of the power structure formed within and on the basis of the broader capitalist system. In this context, some elements of the resistance movement are simply looking for a bigger piece of the pie, on both the local level (greater monetary compensation and investment in community development) and the national level (higher taxes and royalties from the mining companies for social redistribution) (Tetreault, 2014). Other elements are radical, articulating an emphatic 'no' to projects that imply the (de facto) privatization or destruction of land, natural resources, territories or culturally significant landscapes. Furthermore, the fact that these movements are anti-capitalist does not necessarily imply that they seek to conserve anachronistic social and

**36** Extractivism and resistance: a new era

production relations; nor does it mean that they intend to overthrow the dominant capitalist system. It simply means that theirs is a project to share the wealth more equitably.

There are additionally two forces of resistance, one located in the urban middle class and taking form as an environmental movement operating within 'civil society', the other located in the indigenous communities of proletarianized peasant farmers – the resistance to corporate capital and extractive capital, and to government policy in the service of capital and the empire. The latter is once again taking the form of organized labour. An example of this is the recent formation in Bolivia of an anti-capitalist coalition of diverse social forces, including groups of organized public-sector workers and miners, that have come together to engage the class struggle against extractive capital, agribusiness and the agrarian elite.

## Conclusions

Several conclusions can be drawn from this general overview of the class struggle in Latin America today. One is that the struggle under current conditions assumes multiple forms, including a struggle over land, ownership of natural resources and improved access to the global commons, as well as the model used to organize agricultural production. Such a model is based on large-scale capitalist production, with inputs of imported capital and advanced modern technology, and oriented towards the world market; the other is based on small-scale production and geared to the domestic market. The corporate model is geared to a development strategy based on large-scale foreign investment in land, natural resource extraction and the formation of joint venture partnerships between the private sector (multinational corporations that provide both capital and technology) and the state in a new association with capital. In opposition to this corporate model, the resistance movement, which includes Vía Campesina (a global movement of small-scale peasant and family farmers) and a coalition of indigenous communities negatively impacted by extractivism in its diverse forms, is oriented towards small-scale local production and alternative non-capitalist forms of development and trade (Abya Yala, 2009).

Another conclusion is that a large part of the resistance movement is anti-neoliberal and anti-imperialist but not necessarily anti-capitalist. The resistance movements discussed in this book as anti-capitalist and anti-imperialist (as well as anti-neo-liberal) are part of a network ('articulation') of social movements that over the past decade has converged around Hugo Chávez's proposed model of an alternative (non-neo-liberal) system of international trade – ALBA. From 16 to 20 May 2013, over 200 social movement delegates from 22 countries met to debate a continent-wide plan of action constructed around the principles of this alliance, which included the need 'to do battle against the transnational corporations and the processes of privatization' and 'to defend the rights of mother earth and to live well' (in harmony with nature and social solidarity) as well as 'international solidarity' (*Minga Informativa de Movimientos Sociales*). At this 'founding assembly' of a continental social movement network (Social Movements for ALBA), the anti-systemic nature of the network was articulated in the declaration of the need to mobilize and unify the diverse sectors of the popular movement – indigenous communities, peasant farmers' organizations, the organized working class, rural landless workers, the proletarianized rural poor, the semi-proletariat of informal sector street workers, the middle classes (intellectuals and professionals, university students and the youth, and small-business operators) and a civil society of non-governmental organizations – around a programme of opposition to capitalism, imperialism and patriarchy (the *voracidad capitalista, imperialista y patriarcal*) in a struggle for 'authentic emancipation with socialism on its horizon'.

But, as Tetreault (2014) notes in his analysis of the resistance to extractivism in Mexico, and as emphasized by Lust (2014) and Sankey (2014) in their studies on extractive capitalism and the resistance in Peru and Colombia, neither the founding of this continental network of social movements nor the formation of a resistance movement in each country where extractive capital has made major inroads means the end of capitalism. For one thing, while the resistance movement is generally opposed to the dominant extractivist development model and its destructive effects on the environment and livelihoods, very few are as yet prepared to abandon the operating capitalist system.

## Note

1 In 2012, Mexico's Auditor General submitted a report that documented the fact that up to 23 per cent of the national territory had been conceded to mining companies for the purpose of exploration and mining, and that the effective tax rate on the export of minerals and metals was as low as 1.2 per cent (López Bárcenas, 2012: 31).

## References

Abya Yala – Movimientos Indígenas, Campesinos y Sociales (2009). 'Diálogo de alternativas y alianzas'. *Minga Informativa de Movimientos Sociales.* La Paz. 26 February. Available at: http://movimientos.org/es/enlacei/show_text.php3%3Fkey%3D13864 [accessed 12 August 2010].

Acosta, A. (2009). *La maldición de la abundancia.* Quito: Ediciones Abya Yala.

Arellano, M. (2010). 'Canadian foreign direct investment in Latin America'. *Background Paper.* Ottawa: North-South Institute, May.

Bebbington, A. (ed.) (2011). *Minería, movimientos sociales y respuestas campesinas. Una ecología política de transformaciones territoriales.* Lima: Instituto de Estudios Peruanos/Centro Peruano de Estudios Sociales.

CEDIB. (2010). 'Crónica de conflictos mineros en América Latina en diciembre 2009-enero 2010'. *PetroPress,* 18, pp. 34–5. Available at: http://cedib.org/bp/PP18/pp. 182.pdf [accessed 10 November 2010].

CEPAL. (2012). *Anuario estadístico de América Latina y el Caribe.* Santiago: CEPAL.

Collier, P. & Venables, A. J. (2011). *Plundered Nations? Successes and Failures in Natural Resource Extraction.* London: Palgrave Macmillan.

ECLAC. (2012). *Foreign Direct Investment in Latin America and the Caribbean 2012.* Santiago: ECLAC.

Engler, Y. (2012). *The ugly Canadian: Stephen Harper's foreign policy.* Halifax: Fernwood.

## 38 Extractivism and resistance: a new era

Gordon, T. (2010). *Imperialist Canada*. Winnipeg: Arbeiter Ring.

Gordon, T. & Webber, J. (2008). 'Imperialism and Resistance: Canadian mining companies in Latin America'. *Third World Quarterly*, 29(1), pp. 63–87.

Gudynas, E. (2010). Desarrollo, extractivismo y post-extractivismo. Available at: www.redge.org.pe/sites/default/files/DesarrolloExtractivismoPostExtractivismo-EGudynas.pdf [accessed 9 January 2011].

Leff, E. (1996). 'Ambiente y democracia: los nuevos actores del ambientalismo en el medio rural mexicano', in H. de Grammont and H. Tejera Gaona (eds) *La sociedad rural mexicana frente al nuevo milenio, Vol. IV, Los nuevos actores sociales y procesos políticos en el campo*. Mexico: Plaza y Valdés Editores, pp. 35–64.

López Bárcenas, F. (2012). 'Detener el saqueo minero en México'. *La Jornada*, 28 February. Available at: www.jornada.unam.mx/2012/02/28/opinion/023a1pol [accessed 9 March 2012].

Lust, J. (2014). 'Peru: mining capital and social resistance', in H. Veltmeyer and J. Petras (eds) *The new extractivism: A post-neoliberal development model or imperialism of the twenty-first century?* London: Zed.

Mining Watch Canada. (2009). *Land and conflict – resource extraction, human rights, and corporate social responsibility: Canadian companies in Colombia*. Available at: www.miningwatch.ca/publications/land-and-conflict-resource-extraction-human-rights-and-corporate-social-responsibility [accessed 12 February 2010].

Norman, C. S. (2009). 'Rule of law and the resource curse'. *Environmental and Resource Economics*, 43(2), pp. 183–207.

Ocampo, J. A. (2007). 'Markets, social cohesion and democracy', in J. A. Ocampo, K. S. Jomo & S. Khan (eds.) *Policy matters: Economic and social policies to sustain equitable development*, London: Zed, pp. 1–31.

Petras, J. & Veltmeyer, H. (2001). *Globalization unmasked: Imperialism in the 21st century*. London/Halifax: ZED/Fernwood.

Piketty, T. (2014). *Capital in the 21st century*. Cambridge: Cambridge University Press.

Sachs, J. D. & Warner, A. M. (2001). 'The curse of natural resources'. *European Economic Review*, 45, pp. 827–38. Available at: www.earth.columbia.edu/sitefiles/file/about/director/pubs/EuroEconReview2001.pdf [accessed 13 March 2016].

Sankey, K. (2014). 'Colombia: The mining boom: A catalyst of development or resistance?' in H. Veltmeyer and J. Petras (eds) *The new extractivism: A postneoliberal development model or imperialism of the twenty-first century?* London: Zed.

Saxe-Fernández, J. & Núñez, O. (2001). 'Globalización e imperialismo: La transferencia de excedentes de América Latina', in J. Saxe-Fernández et al. *Globalización, imperialismo y clase social*. Buenos Aires and México: Editorial Lumen, pp. 87–186.

Sena-Fobomade. (2011). Se intensifica el extractivismo minero en América Latina. Foro Boliviano sobre Medio Ambiente y Desarrollo, 3 February 2005. Available at: http://fobomade.org.bo/art-1109 [accessed 17 December 2014].

Svampa, M. (2012). 'Consenso de los commodities y megaminería', in *América Latina en movimiento. Extractivismo: Contradicciones y conflictividad*. Quito: Agencia Latinoamericana de Información (ALAI), pp. 5–8.

Tetreault, D. (2014). 'Mexico: The political ecology of mining', in H. Veltmeyer and J. Petras (eds) *The new extractivism*. London: Zed, pp. 172ff.

Toledo, V. (2000). 'El otro zapatismo: luchas indígenas de inspiración ecológica en México', in V. Toledo, *La paz en Chiapas: ecología, luchas indígenas y modernidad alternative*. Mexico City: Ediciones Quinto Sol.

UNCTAD. (2007). *World Investment Report 2007. Transnational corporations, extractive industries and development*. New York, NY, and Geneva: United Nations.

UNCTAD. (2012). *World Investment Report 2012. Towards a new generation of investment policies*. New York, NY, and Geneva: United Nations.

Veltmeyer, H. & Petras, J. (2014). *Neoextractivism: A new model for Latin America?* London: Zed.

Williamson, J. (ed.) (1990). *Latin American adjustment. How much has happened?* Washington, DC: Institute for International Economics.

Zibechi, R. (2012). *Territories in resistance*. Oakland, CA/Edinburgh: AK Press.

# 3

# ACCUMULATION BY DISPOSSESSION – AND THE RESISTANCE

This chapter analyses the class dynamics of capitalist development and the resistance on the new frontier of extractive capital that has opened up with the primary commodities boom at the turn into the new millennium (see the discussion in Chapter 2). In this analysis we make reference to and use the concept of 'accumulation by dispossession' popularized by David Harvey in recent years.[1] In the temporal and spatial context of these dynamics, different parts of the rural population have been mobilized in protest against the advance of capital. They have undertaken a variety of collective actions against the destructive operations and negative impacts of large-scale foreign investment in the acquisition of land and the extraction of natural resources for export. The forces of resistance engendered in this process have targeted the policies of governments that have facilitated the foreign investment in land and the operations of extractive capital. The class struggle and conflicts associated with this resistance have taken various forms but generally pit the multinational corporations in the extractive sector and the governments that have licensed their operations against the rural communities that are most directly impacted by these operations. At issue in these conflicts and struggles are various conditions and forces that compel some or many members of these communities to abandon their communities and to separate them from the land and their means of production – what David Harvey (2003) conceptualizes as 'accumulation by dispossession'.

In some cases (Bolivia, for example), accumulation by dispossession has taken the form of a government policy to privatize access to productive resources (in this case, natural gas and water), turning over to foreign investors and the agents of global extractive capital the right to market these resources, and denying members of the communities affected open access to what for millennia had been the commons, in effect, a new form of the enclosures that helped bring about capitalism in nineteenth-century England. In other cases, multinational corporations in the extractive sector have been granted a concession on a long-term (30-year) lease to explore for and exploit natural resources – oil and gas, or minerals and metals – that might be found in these concessions, which in some cases include anywhere from 23 per cent of the nation's territory (in the case of Mexico) up to 70 per cent (case of Peru). And more recently a number of countries in the region, like their counterparts in Africa and Asia, have been subjected to the large-scale inflow of foreign investment in the acquisition of land – 'land-grabbing', in the discourse of critical agrarian studies (Borras et al., 2012). To purchase the tracts of land for the purpose of what might be described as 'agro-extractivism' (the extraction of agro-food or biofuel production for export) or to gain privileged access to the region's subsoil mineral resources, multinational corporations in the extractive sector have taken maximum advantage of their 'economic opportunities' provided by these purchases, signing lucrative agreements with state officials that allow them to appropriate up to 60 per cent of the value of the exported and traded commodities. In many cases, the land and ancestral territorial rights of the population and indigenous communities who live on and work the land involved in these concessions and who have customary use of water and elements of the commons, were or have been violated. In most cases, the rural population affected by the operations of extractive capital have been dispossessed and forced to abandon their communities and way of life.

## Agrarian change as a lever of capital accumulation

In the context of seventeenth-century England, which Marx used as a benchmark to construct his theory of capitalist development, the separation of the direct producers from their means of production – 'primitive accumulation' in Marx's formulation – marked the origins of capitalism. However, a number of Marxist scholars, including Rosa Luxemburg and more recently David Harvey, have argued that the dynamics of what Marx conceived as the 'primitive' or 'original' accumulation is not only found at the outset of the capitalist development process but throughout the history of capitalism – as a permanent condition or, as Harvey (2003: 144) argues, in times of crisis such as at that which precipitated the neo-liberal era.

In Marx's day, the basic mechanism of 'primitive accumulation' was the enclosure of the commons, denying direct producers access to vital resources for subsistence and forcing them to abandon their way of life and their communities, in the process creating a proletariat (i.e. a class dispossessed of their means of production, in possession only of their capacity to work, their labour power, which they are compelled to exchange for a living wage). However, as Harvey argues, this dynamic and situation is by no means limited to the beginnings of capitalism. For one thing, in its propensity towards crisis capitalism creates forces of change similar to those that materialized in other periods in the capitalist development of the productive forces, resulting in a similar process of proletarianization and productive-social transformation. An example of this is the capitalist development process that unfolded in the 1970s in the midst of a systemic crisis. This crisis led to the transition from one form of capitalism (state-led development) to another (free-market capitalism).

**42** Accumulation by dispossession

The advance of capital in these conditions – including the submission of the state to the dictates of capital and a 'structural adjustment' of macroeconomic policy to the new world order – resulted in the massive destruction of productive forces in both agriculture and industry, and a massive inflow of capital in the form of foreign direct investment.[2] It also led to an acceleration of a long-term process of productive and social transformation in which large masses of proletarianized peasant farmers (rural landless workers, or the 'rural poor' in the jargon of World Bank economists) were forced to emigrate, to abandon both their source of livelihood (agriculture) and their rural communities (Delgado Wise & Veltmeyer, 2016).

A key issue in the debates that have surrounded and still surround this process was what Marxists and other scholars in the field of critical agrarian studies conceived as the 'agrarian question' is whether the peasantry can survive the transition to capitalism in agriculture and industry. But David Harvey, with his contributions regarding capitalism in the 'neo-liberal era' on the periphery of what is now a global system, has opened up a new line of debate regarding the contemporary dynamics of capitalist development in the process of productive and social transformation. At issue in this debate are the forces of change generated in this process and the precise mechanisms of 'accumulation by dispossession'.

Here we engage Harvey's concept of accumulation by dispossession. The argument is that the advance of extractive capital on the Latin American periphery of the system can be viewed as a contemporary form of what Marx had described as 'primitive accumulation'. Further, this implies a new form of 'enclosures' – enclosing the global commons – and a new dynamic of resistance and class struggle. The argument can be summarized as follows.

First, the territorial advance of capital and capitalism requires the separation of direct producers from the land and their means of production. Second, the mechanism for doing this is through the enclosure of the commons – land, water and other resources necessary for the subsistence of the direct producers. Third, in the current context of a system of neo-liberal policies – privatization, market deregulation and the liberalization of goods and capital flows – conditions are created that allow for and facilitate the accumulation and the advance of capital. Fourth, the same conditions generate a new proletariat disposed towards systemic transformation. Finally, the new proletariat consists of diverse social classes, including a mass of semi-proletarianized peasants and landless rural workers, that are adversely affected by the destructive operations of extractive capital and the policies of the neo-liberal regimes formed in this context. The forces of resistance mobilized in this struggle derive from the social relations of capitalist production and are directed against the advance of capital as well as the social and environmental depredations of extractive capital, and the policy measures of the regimes formed in these conditions.

This argument is as follows. First, we outline and briefly describe the dynamics of a transition from the Washington Consensus on the virtues of free-market capitalism towards a new consensus regarding the need to 'bring the state back into the development process in order to secure a more inclusive form of development' (Infante & Sunkel, 2009). We then go on to describe what might be understood as the new geoeconomics of capital in the region. Third, we outline the contours of a new model under construction, a model characterized by what has been described as 'inclusionary state activism'. The model is constructed on two pillars, with reference to the post-Washington Consensus regarding the need for a more inclusive form of national development – *new developmentalism*, as understood by economists at ECLAC (see Leiva, 2008, and Bresser-Pereira, 2006, 2007) – and *extractivism*, which, when combined with the inclusionary state activism prescribed by the theorists of the new developmentalism, has been described as 'progressive' or 'neo-extractivism' (Gudynas, 2009). The argument is made with reference to the experiences of Bolivia and Ecuador, paradigmatic cases of a post-neo-liberal model of social change and post-development oriented towards a system conductive of social solidarity and harmony with nature. Fourth, we discuss the different forms taken by the assault of capital on the commons and the diverse mechanisms of accumulation by dispossession involved. The chapter ends with a brief review of the dynamics of struggle and resistance against capitalism in its extractive and neoextractive form.

## From the Washington Consensus to neo-developmentalism

No economic model has had as much influence on public policy regarding development in Latin America over the past three decades as the Washington Consensus model of free-market capitalism and 'structural reform'. The consensus took the form of an argument regarding the virtues of free-market capitalism and the need to liberate the 'forces of economic freedom' (the market, private enterprise, foreign investment) from the regulatory constraints of the welfare-development state. On the one hand, proponents of the Washington Consensus lauded a neo-liberal policy regime for the benefits that it would bring. On the other hand there was the harsh reality that, of the benefits that did materialize, most accrued to capital. Public policies of structural reform facilitated corporate entry and expansion, while both the rural and urban proletariat were excluded and further marginalized, and those elements of the peasantry that retained some access to the land were forced to abandon their livelihoods and communities. Under these conditions, which prevailed in the 1980s and 1990s, the widespread destruction of the forces of production caused by neo-liberal politics led to a new round of capital accumulation in the region – the influx of a large volume of profit- and resource-seeking foreign direct investment and with it an upsurge of the resistance against neo-liberal policies and the new capitalist world order (Petras & Veltmeyer, 2013).

The Washington Consensus was put into practice in the early to mid-1980s as a set of 'structural reforms' in macroeconomic policy imposed on governments via the mechanism of debt repayment and as a condition for 'aid' (debt payment negotiation). It was given official form and was codified by the economist John Williamson (1990). The irony is that this codification of the basic principles of 'structural reform' was made precisely at the point when the architects of these reforms, including the World Bank, came to the conclusion that they were dysfunctional and that they had 'gone too far' in the direction of free-market

**44** Accumulation by dispossession

capitalism and that what was needed was a more inclusive form of development based on the agency of the state.

The neo-liberal model was constructed with reference to three fundamental principles/policy prescriptions: macroeconomic equilibrium and discipline, liberalization of trade and the flow of capital (foreign direct investment), and market deregulation. The combination of these three policy prescriptions was expected to reactivate the capital accumulation process and stimulate economic growth. But the results were disastrous – a decade lost for development, an increase of poverty and inequality without economic growth – resulting in the formation of powerful forces of resistance in the form of social movements with their social base in the indigenous communities and peasant organizations (Petras and Veltmeyer, 2009). Another result was a new consensus regarding the need to bring the state back into the development process (Infante & Sunkel, 2009; Ocampo, 2005).

Whither the Washington Consensus? On the one hand, the guardians of the new world order, and the architects of neo-liberal reform, came to the conclusion that the Washington Consensus was too simplistic and paid insufficient attention to issues of equity, poverty, the environment and cultural diversity. On the other hand, the prescribed labour reforms – deregulation of the labour market and the flexibilization of labour – worked to the advantage of capital, opening up economic opportunities for multinational corporations via the provision of an abundant supply of cheap and docile labour for the *maquila*, a new sector of manufacturing firms based on assembly operations. However, liberalization of trade and foreign private investment, and the deregulation of the labour market, did not lead to economic growth or create more jobs and improved working conditions. On the contrary. The failure of the neo-liberal model to deliver on its promise of economic growth, and the host of problems associated with the destruction of forces of production in both agriculture and industry, led policy analysts to the conclusion that what was needed was to achieve 'a better balance between state and market' (Ocampo, 2005), which would lead to a more inclusive form of capitalist development.

The new paradigm and policy agenda based on this post-Washington Consensus was defined by the following measures implemented by many if not most Latin American governments in the 1990s. First, governments needed to stay the course of 'structural reform' to ensure an effective process of productive transformation and modernization. Second, to ensure that the poor would receive some of the benefits of economic growth there was the need for a 'new social policy' focused on poverty reduction. Third, inclusive development required a more democratic form of governance and local development based on a policy of administrative decentralization and social participation, i.e. the incorporation of civil society into the development process (Fine & Jomo, 2006).

In the 1990s, practically all governments in the region conformed to this new consensus and implemented some version of the new social policy of poverty reduction based on a neostructural model of inclusive development – the 'new developmentalism' as understood and formulated by Bresser-Pereira (2006, 2007).

## The new geoeconomics of capital: the pattern of foreign direct investment inflows

To trace the flow of productive capital or foreign direct investment over the past two decades is a good way of understanding the new geoeconomics of capital in the region today as well as the associated development dynamics.

A good starting point in tracing the dynamics of productive capital in the region is the transition from the era of the developmental state into the new world order of neo-liberal globalization in the 1980s. The neo-liberal policy regime of structural reform – privatization, liberalization, decentralization and deregulation – facilitated a massive and historically unprecedented inflow of capital in the form of FDI.[3] According to UNCTAD the inflow of private capital in the form of FDI increased from around US$8.7 billion in 1990 to US$61 billion in 1998 (1998: 256, 267–8, 362; 2002).

It has been estimated that up to 40 per cent of this capital was invested in the purchase of the shares of privatized state enterprises in the strategic sectors of the economy such as the telecommunications industry and the industry. Compared by sector, up to 50 per cent of this capital was invested in services, including banking, while the manufacturing sector absorbed 25 per cent and the extractive sector only 10 per cent (Arellano, 2010). However, certain forces of change in the world economy, including the ascent of China and the emergence of a 'commodity boom', radically changed the geoeconomics of capital in the region. First, in the first decade of the new millennium the volume of FDI flows to Latin America exploded. Second, by the end of the decade the share of the services sector in FDI flows had been reduced from 60 to 47 per cent, while the share of the extractive sector in these annual flows grew from 10 to 30 per cent (Arellano, 2010).

In 2011, FDI in the region experienced a growth rate of 34.6 per cent, well above that of Asia, which grew by only 6.7 per cent (UNCTAD, 2012). A critical datum: the inflow of resource-seeking capital in South America, the main recipient and destination point for extractive capital in this period, reached and was valued at US$150 billion in 2011, 15 times greater in volume than in the early 1990s (Zibechi, 2012). In absolute numbers, the inflow of FDI in the region for the first time exceeded the flows to the US and was only surpassed by FDI flows to Europe and Asia.

The expansion of extractive capital in Latin America in the new millennium is reflected in the composition of exports, i.e. in a process of '(re)primarization – a growing trend to export the social product in the form of' commodities (natural resources and raw materials, unprocessed with little to no value added) (ECLAC, 2010: 17). This is evidenced by data provided by ECLAC that show a decrease in the degree of primarization in the 1990s but then a process of reprimarization in the first decade of the new millennium. The data also indicate a more pronounced primarization trend in countries such as Brazil and Colombia that are the major recipients of FDI flows in the region. Brazil, for example, received 32.8 per cent of regional flows of FDI in 2000 but in 2008, a year of global financial crisis (and the

**46** Accumulation by dispossession

largest inflow of FDI flows over the decade), Brazil received 45 per cent of total regional inflows of FDI (CEPAL, 2012: 50).

The flow of productive capital towards Latin America over the past decade has been driven by two factors: commodity prices, which remained high during most of this period, and the strong economic growth of the South American subregion, which encouraged market-seeking investment. This flow of FDI is concentrated in four countries of South America – Argentina, Brazil, Chile and Colombia – which represent 89 per cent of total FDI inflows in the subregion. The extractive sector in these countries, especially mining, has absorbed most of these flows. For example, in 2009 Latin America received 26 per cent of global investment in mining exploration (Sena-Fobomade, 2011). And, with the expansion of oil and gas projects, mineral extraction is the most important source of export earnings for most countries in the region.

The explosion of foreign direct investment in the extractive sector responded to a growing demand on the world market for commodities (natural resources such as metals and minerals, energy in the form of fossil fuels and biofuels, and agricultural products).[4] The commodity boom not only was the driving force of a rising tide of extractive capital but encouraged the election of progressive centre-left governments that were oriented towards a combination of extractivism and the new developmentalism.

## A new economic model: new developmentalism and extractivism

Capitalist development in the 1990s caused not only a large inflow of foreign investment but the formation of powerful social movements that engaged in collective action against the neo-liberal policies of governments that subjected the people to the dictates of capital (Petras & Veltmeyer, 2009). By the end of the decade the uprisings and actions of these forces of resistance had managed to halt the advance of capital and the neo-liberal policies of governments in the service of capital, provoking the formation of a political movement concerned with 'going beyond neo-liberalism' in the search for 'another world'.

Another result of the dynamics of resistance in the popular sector was a left turn in electoral politics and the rise of political regimes seeking ways of exploiting (capitalizing on) the forces of change generated by the social movements. Analysts and observers of this trend spoke and wrote of a sea change – a 'red' wave of regime change (reference here to regimes such as Venezuela, Bolivia and Ecuador, with a resource nationalist and radical populist or socialist orientation) and a 'pink' of post-neo-liberal regimes with a more pragmatic approach to social change and capitalist development (Grugel & Riggirozzi, 2012; Levitsky & Roberts, 2011; Macdonald & Ruckert, 2009; Petras & Veltmeyer, 2009).[5]

Notwithstanding the distinction between policy regimes with a radical populist complexion (presented as the 'socialism of the twenty-first century') and those with a more pragmatic orientation, the 'progressive' post-neo-liberal regimes that emerged in the space generated by the activism of the social movements share several features. They include deployment of a new economic model constructed on the basis of two pillars: (i) new developmentalism (including what has been described as 'inclusionary state activism') and (ii) a new more progressive form of extractivism in which the state regulates the operations of extractive capital and uses fiscal revenues/resource rents (derived from the extraction and exports of natural gas, oil, metals and minerals) to finance social programmes of poverty reduction (Dávalos & Albuja, 2014).

In this conjuncture, two countries – Bolivia and Ecuador – driven by the political and intellectual activism of the indigenous communities and organizations have sought to go beyond both neo-liberalism and the new developmentalism in constructing not an alternative form of development but an alternative model – a post-development form of social change expressed in the notion of '*vivir bien*': to live well in social solidarity and harmony with nature (Acosta, 2009; Huanacuni, 2010; Prada, 2013). The idea of this *vivir bien* model of social change and entrenching it in a new constitution that recognizes not only the identity and territorial rights of the indigenous peoples in the country but also the rights of nature have led to a great debate on the construction of another possible world: another development or post-development? (Gudynas, 2014).

This debate has several axes. One has to do with the viability of a model and policy regime based on the notion of living well in social solidarity and harmony with mother earth. Another has to do with the policies actually implemented in recent years and the model underlying these policies. Alberto Acosta, an economist who helped draft the Ecuadorian government's development model and national development plan (*Para Vivir Bien*) but today is one of the government's fiercest critics, has argued that the extractivist strategy pursued by the government, and the policies that it has implemented based on this strategy, is in irreconcilable contradiction with the concept of *vivir bien* (living well).

As Dávalos and Albuja (2014) argue in their discussion of the contradictory features of the government's actual policies regarding economic development, Correa has emerged as one of the strongest and ardent supporters of both 'new developmentalism' (inclusionary state activism) and 'extractivism' (the use of resource rents to achieve poverty reduction). Correa's position on this is that the extraction and export of natural resources of the country in a partnership with foreign investors signifies an 'economic opportunity' that the country and government cannot afford to not take advantage of. This is despite the forces of resistance that this policy has generated in the indigenous movement and the communities most directly affected by the destructive operations of extractive capital. A manifest form of this resistance is the fight led by CONAIE, an organization of indigenous peoples that has led the opposition to the neo-liberal policy agenda of Ecuadorian governments since 1989, against the government's extractivist policies in recent years. More recently, CONAIE has called for an 'indigenous and popular uprising' and a 'national strike' against the government on 11 August 2015 (CONAIE, 2015).

As for the indigenous movement and the opposition to extractivism in Bolivia, the government's recent announcement of its intention to resume its project to

**48** Accumulation by dispossession

build a road through the TIPNIS national park, and to continue with the policy of allowing oil exploration in the protected areas of this park, has sparked a revival of indigenous protests against the policy of allowing the invasion of capital in indigenous territories (*Hoy Bolivia*, 2015; IBCE, 2015).[6]

As Dávalos and Albuja have argued in the case of Ecuador, Correa's policies exemplify all the contradictions and pitfalls of the new extractivism and submission to foreign capital. This includes the enclosure of the commons; the commodification of land, natural resources and water; and the violation of the territorial rights of indigenous peoples and communities, and their marginalization or integration into the circuits and global dynamics of capital accumulation. It also includes the expansion of the extractive frontier – the exploration and exploitation of the country's oil reserves – in the country's pristine glacial waters and tropical forests as well as the open sea and significantly in nature reserves such as Yasuni-ITT and in the indigenous territories (the 'political ecology of territorial transformation'). The resistance and the struggle against the depredations of extractive capital also encompasses bituminous shale industrialization; opencast mining; corporate agro-extractivism, including the use of pesticides, seeds/genetically modified organisms and plantation monoculture; the privatization of public services (including water, carbon markets and the picturesque landscapes of the tourism industry); and the use of biotechnology and geotechnics in the conversion of farmland for the production of biofuels.

In 2007 President Rafael Correa launched the Yasuni-ITT project by means of which the government proposed permanent suspension of oil extraction in the Yasuni Ishpingo-Tambococha-Tiputini National Park (ITT) in exchange for payments of US$3.6 billion by the international community. The project was received with enthusiasm by environmentalists, post-developmentalists, and the indigenous movement and supporters. The Yasuni-ITT park has around 846 million barrels, or 20 per cent of the country's proven oil reserves. The aim of the initiative was the conservation of biodiversity, protection of indigenous peoples living in voluntary isolation, and prevention of the release of $CO_2$ emissions. The Yasuni-ITT Trust Fund was officially launched on 3 August 2010, but by 2012 only US$200 million had been committed, prompting a 180-degree turn in the Yasuni-ITT project. 'The world has failed us', Correa announced, and spoke of the rich countries as hypocrites because they emit the most greenhouse gases while expecting poor nations like Ecuador to sacrifice their economic progress to preserve the environment (*Guardian*, 2013).

As with the TIPNIS controversy in Bolivia,[7] Correa's abandonment of the Yasuni-ITT project shed light on the contradictions of government policy, particularly in regard to the insurmountable contradiction between the government's post-development *Plan Nacional Para el Buen Vivir* (living well) and the government's economic development policies based on capitalism and extractivism (Acosta, 2009).

The plan to extract oil from the Yasuni-ITT reignited a debate on the appropriate development strategy for Ecuador (Chimienti & Matthes, 2013). Many economists and environmentalists, as well as advocates for indigenous territorial rights, have pointed towards a serious defect in the logic of government policy, namely, that the aim is to generate economic growth and reduce poverty through extractivism implies a fatal contradiction with the *Plan Nacional Para el Buen Vivir.*[8]

Since his election in 2007, Correa has embarked on a process of aggressive negotiations with mining companies in order to get for Ecuador a greater share of the value of the product, and thus increase the government's fiscal revenues in service of a strategy aimed at a more equitable distribution of the country's social product. And it appears that Correa's strategy bore fruit. According to the UNDP's 2014 *Human Development Report* from 2003 to 2013, Ecuador's poverty rate was reduced by 50 per cent over the course of Correa's administration. Needless to say, this success in meeting the UN's Millennium Development Goal regarding poverty reduction was attributed by the government to the government's policy of expanding expenditures on social welfare programmes.[9] But at what cost was this achieved? This is one of the core issues of the debate.

Correa's economic development strategy demonstrates the extraordinary importance of the extractive sector in contemporary Ecuador. With the abandonment of banana production for export, oil revenues have come to account for almost one-third of the national budget, although Dávalos and Albuja (2014) argue that resource rents from the extraction of oil contributed next to nothing to the revenues used by the government to reduce poverty. Moreover, under Correa Ecuador has experienced not only the negative socio-environmental impacts of expanded oil production but also an expansion of the palm oil sector and large-scale mining projects that are notoriously destructive of both the environment and livelihoods. Moreover, in the context of the government's efforts to justify its extractivist policies by reference to the overriding need to combat both underdevelopment and poverty, Correa's concern for the environment and the rights of mother earth has been reduced to vague rhetoric. In this context, Acosta points out, Correa has been unable or unwilling to recognize the ecosystem – and political – limits to the dependence on natural resource extraction. In fact, Correa continues to invoke the importance of exploiting the country's wealth of natural sources:

> Our way of life is unsustainable if we do not use our oil and minerals in the next 10 or 15 years while developing alternative energy sources. Those who say that we should not exploit our resources put at risk programs designed to place Ecuador in the forefront of Latin American nations. They would have us return to the status of being a poor nation without a future.
>
> *(Correa, 2013)*[10]

## A new enclosure of the commons?[11]

David Harvey has argued that the policy of privatization (turning public assets over to the private sector) has served as the principal mechanism to enclose the commons (land, water and other natural resources needed for subsistence or sustainable livelihoods) and sacrifice biodiversity on the altar of extractive capital. Enclosure in this

## 50 Accumulation by dispossession

and other forms has served as a lever for capital to jump-start or activate a process of accumulation – an 'accumulation by dispossession' as Harvey has it – in the neo-liberal era of capitalist development.

The dawn of this era can be traced back to the early 1980s in the context of a conservative counter-revolution, construction of a new world order of free-market capitalism in conditions of a systemic crisis, and a consensus on the need to free the 'forces of freedom' (private property, capital and the market) from the regulatory constraints of the welfare-development state. The 'new economic model' constructed in this context included privatization of the means of production, a policy of liberalizing international trade and the flow of foreign investment, and deregulation of the market. The stated aim of these policies was to reactivate the process of capital accumulation and stimulate economic growth by creating favourable conditions for investors and the expansion and operations of capital. Privatization, in particular, according to Harvey (2003: 149), played a crucial role in this process by serving as a mechanism of accumulation by enclosing the commons.

This argument of Harvey's was used by Spronk and Webber (2007) in their analysis of the revolutionary struggle associated with the water and gas wars in Bolivia between 2000 and 2005. Spronk and Webber used Harvey's concepts of 'accumulation by dispossession' and 'enclosure of the commons' in analysing the dynamics of resistance (against neo-liberal policies of the government) and a struggle that brought together indigenous and peasant communities as well as workers and the urban poor. As they see it, these dynamics exemplified the connections made by Harvey between the neo-liberal policy agenda of the state, capital in the form of FDI and the multinational corporation, and organized resistance in the form of social movements formed to challenge the enclosure of the commons and the privatization (and commodification) of vital and productive resources (gas and water in the case analysed by Spronk and Webber). A key aim, and mobilizing force, of the resistance was to 'reclaim the commons'.

We conclude from this and our own research into the contemporary dynamics of the class struggle that privatization as a mechanism of accumulation by dispossession is an undeniable importance in the analysis of both the dynamics of capital expansion in the region and the dynamics of resistance and the struggles that they generate. To illustrate this point, we can point to the case of Mexico in the electricity sector, where in June 2015 the project to strip commoners of their land and property so as to gain access to oil and gas reserves was extended to the power plants in the electricity sector (*La Jornada*, 14 June 2014).

Another dimension of the same problem, which anticipated by decades the neo-liberal policy of privatizing the commons, is manifest in the policy of constructing dams and other infrastructure mega-development projects (García Rivas, 2014). In the cases studied by García Rivas relating to the construction of three hydroelectric dams in the Mexican state of Nayarit, the collusion of the political class with foreign capital and investors for mutual benefit was well documented and analysed as an example of the state as a facilitator of a process of enclosing the commons and a mechanism of accumulation by dispossession.

Privatization has long been used by 'international financial institutions' such as the World Bank and the IMF as a mechanism of accumulation by dispossession. However, it is by no means the only one. Our own research has led us to identify other mechanisms as discussed below.

In addition to the extraction of oil and gas, mining for industrial minerals and precious metals (gold and silver) has proven to be a useful lever of capital accumulation in recent years. At issue here are the gold and silver mines worked by Canadian mining companies that dominate foreign investment in this sector, as well as the opencast mines (*minas a cielo abierto*) created to extract coal, iron ore, copper and other minerals and metals. These opencast mines, which use much less labour per unit of capital invested than the underground mines of earlier years, are notorious for their enormously destructive and devastating impact on both the environment – raping the land and polluting the water needed by nearby communities and those downstream both for their livelihoods and their very existence – and the conflicts and resistance movements that they have generated within the communities affected by the destructive operations of extractive capital. Giarracca and Teubal (2014) have documented and analysed in detail the way in which these open mines in the case of Argentina have served both as a lever of capital accumulation and as a means by which the local population and entire communities have been violently dispossessed, forced to abandon their communities and way of life.

Another mechanism of accumulation by dispossession that has proven to be particularly useful for foreign investors in the agriculture sector (the agro-extractivism) is land-grabbing, termed 'large-scale foreign investments in the acquisition of land' in official development discourse (Borras et al., 2012). According to Borras and his colleagues in the critical agrarian studies (ICAS) network, since 2007 this process of land-grabbing implicates a vast expanse of land, estimated at 220 million hectares worldwide, with significant consequences for the livelihoods of affected populations and communities.

In Latin America this land-grabbing process has been driven by the world market demand for energy and the search for alternatives to fossil fuels. In response to this demand in the Southern Cone of Latin America (Argentina, Brazil, Bolivia and Paraguay), there has emerged a rapidly growing economy based on the conversion in the use of land from the production of grains and food for local consumption and exports into the production of biofuels for export. Not only has this economy of large-scale agribusiness and agro-extractivism come to threaten the local economy of family farmers and peasants but it has accelerated a process of forced outmigration.

The scale of this phenomenon – land-grabbing, natural resource extraction, environmental degradation and violent expulsion of local inhabitants from the land and their communities – is enormous. In the case of Argentina, an important destination for extractive capital in the form of opencast mining and the production of soy-based biofuels, it is estimated that nearly 30 million hectares of the best land and fertile soil, water basins and natural reserves, including strategic reserves of minerals in 23 provinces, are now foreign-owned, and 13 million hectares are

## 52 Accumulation by dispossession

currently for sale (http://laangosturadigital.com.ar). On reviewing the data for other countries in the region it is clear that, even with the emergence of resource nationalist regulatory regimes such as Bolivia, Latin America has in recent years ceded much of its territory for exploration and the exploitation of its natural wealth, and an increasing part of its extractive industries has fallen under the sway of transnational companies based in the imperial centres (Veltmeyer & Petras, 2014).

Land- (and water-) grabbing has served capital in the form of multinational agribusinesses and 'commodity traders' not only as a means of facilitating access to marketable agro-food resources but also to energy in the form of biofuels based on soy and sugar cane, which is in great demand and has more value on the world market. Recent years have seen the expansion of different lines of research in this area. They include research into the dynamics of biofuel production based on a process of land-grabbing, environmental degradation and dispossession in which the big landowners and the agents of foreign capital have managed to further enclose the commons and commodify natural resources needed by local inhabitants and the communities affected by the operations of extractive capital for their social existence.

Norma Giarracca and Miguel Teubal (2014) among others have researched extensively the political economy of soya production (*soyazicación de la agricultura*) and the enclosure of the commons in the form of land-grabbing. As described and explained by Borras and his colleagues, the land at issue or in dispute is in many cases considered 'empty' and 'ownerless' – the property or territorial rights based on customary or traditional use ignored or disrespected.

Land-grabbing and the eviction of the villagers who have customary usage of the land but do not have legal title, and who are therefore vulnerable to being evicted either by legal means (when the invaders turn to the state) or violent confrontations, have begun to assume the form of a class struggle. That is, they are generating not only protests and disputes over territory but broader movements organized to mobilize the forces of resistance against the operations of extractive capital and the neo-liberal policies that facilitate these operations (Giarracca & Teubal, 2010, 2014).

Until the recent collapse in the price of oil the dominant movement of extractive capital had been in the direction of fossil fuels. And, as discussed above, another major destination point for extractive capital has been mining – the production of metals and minerals for industry or middle-class consumption. The conditions to facilitate the accumulation of this capital included a neo-liberal policy of structural reforms – privatization, liberalization, deregulation – as well as financialization. According to studies undertaken by Evans, Goodman and Lansbury (2002), the global mining industry experienced a system-wide process of privatization, deregulation and financialization in the 1980s and 1990s under conditions promoted by the World Bank and other agents of global capital and the imperial state. Warhust and Bridge (1997: 1–12) note that 'more than 90 countries ... reformed their laws mining investment and mining codes in the past two decades', i.e. the 1980s and 1990s. These reforms included the abolition of royalties to encourage FDI inflows. Mexico and Peru, for example, in the 1990s fully complied with this dictate of the

World Bank. With no royalty regime in the mining sector, and, according to the auditor general of Mexico, an extremely lax regulatory system and an effective tax rate that is below 2 per cent, Mexico's policy regime for the extraction and exportation of minerals and metals functions not only as a lever of capital accumulation but as a system designed for looting the country of a precious resource – a haemorrhaging or deep bleeding, in the colourful language of Galeano – with an absolutely minimal compensation for the heavy environmental and social costs that the extraction of these minerals and metals represent (López Bárcenas, 2012).[12] Moreover, instead of integrating these reforms into a national development plan they are designed as a sectoral approach designed to favour corporate interests (Canel, Idemudia & North, 2010: 5–25).

In some cases we should recognize that the strategy of the mining companies is not to separate the direct producers from their means of production, forcing them to abandon their communities and their way of life or their ancestral territory. Strictly speaking this cannot be argued in that mining companies in the extractive sector are evidently willing to negotiate a mutually beneficial agreement with residents and the communities affected by their operations. However, the problem for these companies is that many if not most of those affected are not willing to negotiate with them. Understandably, given what is at stake for them – their very survival as well as their ancestral and territorial rights – they invariably choose or have chosen the path of resistance, thus entering into a relationship of conflict with companies and capital (Bebbington, 2011; Bebbington & Bury, 2013; Veltmeyer & Petras, 2014).

## Resistance on the expanding frontier of extractive capital

Harvey argues that accumulation by dispossession has led to multifaceted forms of struggle that have some new features. One is that these struggles do not come under the banner of labour or a trade union, or the leadership of the working class, but rather of 'civil society' broadly understood as all manner of associative forms of organizations that inhabit the wide expanse between families and the state. This excludes class-based organizations such as the social movements formed within the same expanse. Given the wide range of interests and groups involved in these struggles, it is postulated that they involve 'a political dynamic less focused on social action' (Harvey, 2003: 168). It is possible to argue that they also lead to more social but less political forms of collective action, a 'non-power approach towards social change', as argued by Holloway (2002). Some political analysts have gone further in stating that, given that these movements are rooted in civil society rather than a class structure based on social relations of production, they therefore do not engage a class struggle but rather a multifaceted struggle with a broader and more heterogeneous base.

This conception of the social movements that emerged in the context of resistance against the neo-liberal policies of governments in the 1990s has its origins in a postmodernist theory of social change that can be traced back to the 1980s but that

**54** Accumulation by dispossession

has lost its relevance in contemporary times in that it does not and cannot explain the dynamics of the anti-extractivist movements that have emerged in recent years (Petras & Veltmeyer, 2013; Veltmeyer & Petras, 2015). Although it resorts to some ideas advanced in this failed theory of 'new social movements', a more relevant line of research has been elaborated by Raul Zibechi in terms of the notion of 'subterranean struggles' (Zibechi, 2013). Zibechi, together with the authors presented in a recent book by Bebbington and Bury (2013), argues that these struggles are an integral part of the new extractive economy in Latin America. But the reference here is not to the movements that have emerged on the new frontier of extractive capital, but rather the everyday struggles and cries of 'the excluded', those seeking to adapt their livelihoods to the conditions generated by mining and other extractive operations in the spaces available to them. These analysts argue that these struggles, which are an integral part of the new extractive economy in Latin America, have a basic flaw. These struggles are documented and described in considerable detail but without adequately theorizing their dynamics and their structural and political roots in the functioning of capitalism as a system. That is, they see these localized struggles and movements as anti-extractive – and, indeed, anti-neo-liberal (in terms of government policy and the agribusiness corporate model) – but not as anti-capitalist or anti-imperialist (Veltmeyer & Petras, 2014).

## Conclusion

Today we are in a new phase in the capitalist development of the forces of production, with a corresponding transformation in the social relations of production and the dynamics of class struggle. In terms of the type of capital involved in the process, we can conceive of this stage as extractive capitalism. This does not mean that it has replaced the classical form of capitalism theorized by Marx, with its base in the capital–labour relationship. This relationship undoubtedly remains the basis of the capitalist mode of production. Reference to a new phase of capitalism implies a combination of different forms of capital, including industrial capital which dominates the global production system and financial capital which dominates the structure of power relations within this system. As extractive capitalism is now advancing on the periphery of the system, not within the policy framework of the neo-liberal model, which has been rejected and is in decline, but within the framework of the post-neo-liberal state which has created conditions that if not ideal are functional for the expansion of capital in its neoextractive form and current conjuncture.

The advance of capital on the extractive frontier is facilitated by four main mechanisms, each working to accumulate capital by dispossessing the direct producers from their means of production, forcing them to abandon their livelihoods and their rural communities. One is the neo-liberal policy of privatization, which is to turn over the means of production in the strategic sectors of the economy to the so-called 'private sector', i.e. the CEOs of the multinational corporations that dominate the global economy, or the 'international capitalist class' – or, as Bernd Hamm (2014) has it, the global ruling class. The second is the mechanism of land-grabbing, which allows capital and foreign investors – and governments such as China in search of food security or energy – direct access to agro-food products, agrofuels and other sources of energy and natural resources. The third mechanism, which operates in the mining sector (mining and metals) and the extraction of carbohydrates (oil and natural gas), takes the form of concessions of large tracts of land and territorial space extended to foreign investors and mining companies on long-term contracts to allow them to explore for and exploit the valuable resources of the subsoil. The fourth major mechanism of accumulation by dispossession is also found in the extractive subsector of mining. It works by means of destroying the ecosystem on which the economy of small-scale producers and peasant farming depends.

The institutions and policies that permit the functioning of these diverse forms of accumulation lead to an enclosure of the commons that breeds new forces of resistance, creating conditions of political conflict on the frontier of extractive capital. In these conditions the advance of extractive capital generates new forces of resistance. In the current juncture of the capitalist development process this struggle assumes a very particular form, resulting in the formation of a new proletariat and an anti-extractive socio-political movement – a socio-environmental movement of 'those affected' by the operations of extractive capital. These movements have demonstrated considerable dynamism in the struggle against capitalism in the current conjuncture of its historical trajectory.

## Notes

1 As Gudynas (2015) points out, notwithstanding the repeated invocation of David Harvey's concept of 'accumulation by dispossession' in literally hundreds of studies on Latin America and by Latin American scholars themselves, the idea advanced by this concept is nothing new. On the contrary, it has been formulated in different ways by many Latin American scholars over the years. Although I am in total agreement with Gudynas's criticism of the concept as often applied to capitalism in the current Latin American context, I nevertheless believe that, although not new or any advance on Marx's original formulation, the concept has some analytical utility and relevance for understanding the contemporary dynamics of capitalist development.

2 In the 1990s, Latin America was the recipient of a massive wave of private capital in the form of FDI, increasing from about US$8.7 billion in 1990 to US$61 billion in 1998 (UNCTAD, 1998: 256, 267–8, 362; 2002). This invasion was facilitated by the neo-liberal 'structural reforms' in macroeconomic policy' (privatization, liberalization, deregulation …) mandated by the Washington Consensus in the new world order established in the early 1980s.

3 This capital was both unproductive – namely, in the purchase of the assets of privatized state enterprises, reflected in a process of 'acquisition and mergers' that is estimated to have consumed up to 40 per cent of the capital invested in the 1990s – and productive in the transfer of new modern technologies.

4 The region remains the world's leading source of metals: iron (24 per cent), copper (21 per cent), gold (18 per cent), nickel (17 per cent), zinc (21 per cent), bauxite (27 per cent) and silver (Campodónico, 2008; UNCTAD, 2007: 87). Oil made up 83.4 per cent of total exports of Venezuela from 2000 to 2004, copper accounts for 45 per cent of Chilean exports, nickel 33 per cent of Cuba's exports, and gold, copper and zinc 33 per cent of Peru's. Along with agricultural production, extraction of oil, gas and metals

## 56 Accumulation by dispossession

remains essential for the region's exports. From 2008 to 2009, exports of primary products accounted for 38.8 per cent of total exports from Latin America (ECLAC, 2010).

5  For an analysis of these post-neo-liberal regimes see, among many others, Barrett, Chávez and Rodríguez Garavito (2008), Gaudichaud (2012) and Veltmeyer and Petras (2014).

6  The indigenous movement in both Bolivia and Ecuador continues to urge Presidents Morales and Correa to be faithful to the principles of their national development plan (designed for living well) and to make way for a post-extractivist strategy.

7  On Evo Morales's controversial project to build a road through a national park that contains one of the largest reserves of natural biodiversity in the world, against the resistance of the indigenous communities who inhabit the reserve, see Prada (2012) and Achtenberg (2012).

8  The *Plan Nacional Para el Buen Vivir 2009–2013* emphasizes the importance of redeployment and reduction of inequality, in addition to environmental protection.

9  Dávalos and Albuja (2014) dispute this claim with substantive empirical evidence.

10  This comment is from President Rafael Correa's weekly broadcast to the nation in April and was translated by *Ecuador Digest*. www.cuencahighlife.com/post/2013/04/11/ECUADOR-DIGEST3cbr3eCorrea

11  For an elaboration of the 'commons' paradigm see Bollier (2014).

12  According to the Auditor General (López Bárcenas, 2012: 31), Mexico receives only 1.2 per cent of the value of the metals extracted in the country to sell on the world market.

## References

Achtenberg, E. (2012). 'Bolivia: TIPNIS communities plan national march and resistance to government'. *Rebel Currents*, 23 March.

Acosta, A. (2009). 'El Buen Vivir, una utopía por (re)construer'. *Revista Casa de las Américas*, 257, La Habana, October–December.

Arellano, J. (2010). 'Canadian Foreign Direct Investment in Latin America'. *Background Paper*, North-South Institute, May.

Barrett, P. S., Chávez, D. & Rodríguez Garavito, C. A. (eds) (2008). *The New Latin American Left: Utopia reborn.* London: Pluto.

Bebbington, A. (ed.) (2011). *Minería, movimientos sociales y respuestas campesinas. Una ecología política de transformaciones territoriales,* Lima: Instituto de Estudios Peruanos/Centro Peruano de Estudios Sociales, pp. 53–76.

Bebbington, A. & Bury, J. (eds) (2013). 'Subterranean struggles: New dynamics of mining, oil and gas in Latin America. Austin, TX: University of Texas Press.

Bollier, D. (2014). 'The commons as a template for transformation'. *Great Transformation Initiative*, April. Available at: www.greattransition.org/publication/the-commons-as-a-template-for-transformation.

Borras, S. M., Kay, C., Gómez, S. & Wilkinson, J. (2012). 'Land grabbing and global capitalist accumulation: Key features in Latin America'. *Canadian Journal of Development Studies*, 33(4), pp. 402–16.

Bresser-Pereira, L. C. (2006). 'El nuevo desarrollismo y la ortodoxia convencional'. *Economía unam*, 4(10), pp. 7–29.

Bresser-Pereira, L. C. (2007). 'Estado y mercado en el nuevo desarrollismo'. *Nueva Sociedad*, 210, July–August.

Campodónico, H. (2008). *Renta petrolera y minera en países seleccionados de América Latina.* Santiago: CEPAL.

Canel, E., Idemudia, U. & North, L. (2010). 'Rethinking extractive industry: Regulation, dispossession, and emerging claims'. *Canadian Journal of Development Studies*, 30(1–2), pp. 5–25.

CEPAL. (2012). *Anuario estadístico de América Latina y el Caribe*. Santiago: CEPAL.

Chimienti, A. & Matthes, S. (2013). 'Ecuador: Extractivism for the twenty-first century?' *NACLA Report on the Americas*, 46(4), Winter.

CONAIE. (2015). Porque nuestra lucha histórica es junto a las comunas, pueblos y nacionalidades {IEM}Vamos todos al levantamiento indígena y popular! Quito: CONAIE. Available at: www.pueblosencamino.org/index.php/asi-si/resistencias-y-luchas-sociales 02/1425-ecuador-conaie-vamos-todos-al-levantamiento-indigena-y-popular.

Dávalos, P. & Albuja, V. (2014). 'Ecuador: Extractivist dynamics, politics and discourse', in H. Veltmeyer and J. Petras (eds) *The new extractivism: A post-neoliberal development model?* London: Zed, pp. 144–71.

Delgado Wise, R. & Veltmeyer, H. (2016). *Agrarian change, migration and development*. Halifax: Fernwood.

ECLAC – UN Economic Commission for Latin America and the Caribbean. (2010). *Time for equality: Closing gaps, opening trails*. Santiago: ECLAC.

Evans, G., Goodman, J. & Lansbury, N. (2002). *Moving mountains: Communities confront mining and globalization*. London: Zed.

Fine, B. & Jomo, K. S. (eds) (2006). *The new development economics: After the Washington Consensus*. London: Zed.

García Rivas, M. A. (2014). 'El proyecto hidroeléctrico en Nayarit como una manifestación de la acumulación por desposesión'. Seminario de investigación III, Estudios del Desarrollo, Universidad Autónoma de Zacatecas, 23 May.

Gaudichaud, F. (2012). *El volcán latinoamericano. Izquierdas, movimientos sociales y neoliberalismo en América Latina*. Otramérica. Available at: http://blogs.otramerica.com/editorial.

Giarracca, N. & Teubal, M. (2010). 'Disputa por los territorios y recursos naturales: el modelo extractivista'. *ALASRU*, 5, América Latina, realineamientos políticos e projetos em disputa. Brazil, December.

Giarracca, N. & Teubal, M. (2014). 'Argentina: Extractivist dynamics of soy production and open-pit mining', in H. Veltmeyer & J. Petras (eds) *The new extractivism: A post-neoliberal development model?* London: Zed, pp. 47–79.

Grugel, J. & Riggirozzi, P. (2012). 'Post neoliberalism: Rebuilding and reclaiming the state in Latin America'. *Development and Change*, 43(1), pp. 1–21.

*Guardian* (2013, 15 August). 'Yasuni: Ecuador abandons plan to stave off Amazon drilling'.

Gudynas, E. (2009). 'Diez tesis urgentes sobre el nuevo extractivismo. Contextos y demandas bajo el progresismo sudamericano actual', in *Extractivismo, Política y Sociedad*. Quito: CAAP.

Gudynas, E. (2014). 'El postdesarrollo como crítica y el Buen Vivir como alternativa', in G. C. Delgado Ramos (ed.) *Buena Vida, Buen Vivir: imaginarios alternativos para el bien común de la humanidad*. Mexico City: UNAM-CEIICH, pp. 61–95.

Gudynas, E. (2015). 'La necesidad de romper con un colonialismo simpatico'. *Rebelión*, 30 September.

Hamm, B. (2014). 'Power and the global ruling class. Who rules the world?' *Global Research Newsletter*, 4 June.

Harvey, D. (2003). *The new imperialism*. Oxford: Oxford University Press.

Holloway, J. (2002). *Change the world without taking power: The meaning of revolution today*. London: Pluto.

*Hoy Bolivia*. (2015, 6 August). '5 leyes autorizan actividad petrolera en un parquet'.

Huanacuni Mamani, F. (2010). *Buen Vivir/Vivir Bien: Filosofía, políticas, estrategias y experiencias regionales andinas*. Lima: Coordinadora Andina de Organizaciones Indígenas – CAOI.

IBCE. (2015). 'Indígenas del tipnis vuelven a reactivar movilizaciones', 10 August. Available at: http://ibce.org.bo/principales-noticias-bolivia/noticias-nacionales-deta.

## 58 Accumulation by dispossession

Infante B. R. & Sunkel, O. (2009). 'Chile: hacia un Desarrollo inclusivo'. *Revista CEPAL*, 10(97), pp. 135–54.

*La Jornada*. (2014, 14 June). 'Buscan legalizar despojo de tierras también en el sector de electricidad'.

Leiva, F. I. (2008). *Latin American structuralism: The contradictions of postneoliberal development*. Minneapolis, MN: University of Minnesota Press.

Levitsky, S. & Roberts, K. (eds) (2011). *The resurgence of the Latin American Left*. Baltimore, MD: Johns Hopkins University Press.

López Bárcenas, F. (2012). 'Detener el saqueo minero en México'. *La Jornada*, 28 February. Available at: www.jornada.unam.mx/2012/02/28/opinion/023a1pol [accessed 3 March 2012].

Macdonald, L. & Ruckert, A. (2009). *Post-neoliberalism in the Americas*. Basingstoke: Palgrave Macmillan.

Ocampo, J. A. (2005). 'Mas allá del Consenso de Washington: Una agenda de Desarrollo para América Latina'. *Series Estudios y Perspectivas*, 26. Naciones Unidas-CEPAL México.

Petras, J. & Veltmeyer, H. (2009). *What's Left in Latin America*. Farnham: Ashgate.

Petras, J. & Veltmeyer, H. (2013). *Social movements in Latin America? Neoliberalism and popular resistance*. New York, NY: Palgrave Macmillan.

Prada Alcoreza, R. (2012). 'Misería de la geopolítica: Crítica a la geopolítica extractivista' *America Latina en Movimiento*, 18 October. Available at: www.alainet.org/es/active/58901 [accessed 22 October 2012].

Prada Alcoreza, R. (2013). 'Buen Vivir as a model for state and economy', in M. Lang & D. Mokrani (eds) *Beyond development: Alternative visions from Latin America*. Amsterdam: Transnational Institute, pp. 145–58.

Sena-Fobomade (2011). 'Se intensifica el extractivismo minero en América Latina'. *Foro Boliviano sobre Medio Ambiente y Desarrollo*, 2 March. Available at: http://fobomade.org.bo/art-1109 [accessed 14 April 2015].

Spronk, S. & Webber, J. R. (2007). 'Struggles against accumulation by dispossession in Bolivia: The political economy of natural resource contention'. *Latin American Perspectives*, 34(2), March, pp. 31–47.

UNCTAD – United Nations Conference on Trade and Development. (1998, 2002, 2007, 2012). *World Investment Report*. New York, NY, and Geneva: UNCTAD.

UNDP – United Nations Development Programme. (2014). *Human Development Report. The Real Wealth of Nations: Pathways to Human Development*. New York: UNDP.

Veltmeyer, H. & Petras, J. (2014). *Neoextractivism: A new model for Latin America?* London: Zed.

Veltmeyer, H. & Petras, J. (2015). *The new extractivism: A post-neoliberal development model?* London: Zed.

Warhust, A. & Bridge, G. (1997). 'Economic Liberalization, innovation and technology transfer: Opportunities for cleaner production in the minerals industry'. *Natural Resources Forum*, (21)1, pp. 1–12.

Williamson, John (ed.) (1990). *Latin American adjustment. How much has happened?* Washington, DC: Institute for International Economics.

Zibechi, R. (2012). 'La nueva geopolítica del capital'. *ALAI – América Latina en Movimiento*, 19 April. *Le Monde Diplomatique*, Colombia.

Zibechi, R. (2013). 'El modelo extractivo rechazado en las calles', *Rebelión*, 12 October 2013. Available at: www.rebelion.org/noticia.php?id=175380 [accessed 9 February 2014].

# 4

# THE PROGRESSIVE CYCLE IN LATIN AMERICAN POLITICS

At the turn of the new millennium, several forces of change – including the rise of China as a world economic power, a subsequent primary commodities boom and the demise of neo-liberalism as an economic doctrine and model – created an entirely new context for the capitalist development process in Latin America. Features of this new context included the rapid expansion of 'resource-seeking' or extractive capital and a red and pink sea tide of regime change, leading to the formation of left-leaning ('progressive') regimes oriented towards both the new developmentalism (post-neo-liberal inclusionary state activism) and extractivism (natural resource extraction and primary commodities exports as a strategy of national development). Not that the outcome of these trends and associated developments, such as a pronounced primary commodities boom, were uniform. In fact, it is possible to trace out three different patterns of subsequent political developments.

One was the formation (or continuity) of regimes aligned with the US and that continued to follow the neo-liberal line in their economic policies. These included Chile, which was nominally socialist but whose policies were no different from traditional neo-liberal regimes except for less dogmatism and more pragmatism; Peru, where the government was taken over by a populist who nevertheless stuck with the neo-liberal policies of his predecessors; Colombia, the US's staunchest ally and fully committed to a neo-liberal policy regime; and Mexico, another staunch US ally and advocate of free-market capitalism. In 2016, these countries signed the Trans-Pacific Partnership (TPP) agreement, a massive trade and investment pact promoted by the US but written in secret by the ideologues of some of the US's largest corporations. With the text of the trade pact reviewed by over 600 corporate lobbyists, the Alliance for Democracy (2016) justly describes it as 'NAFTA on Steroids'.

A second pattern was related to the formation in South America of a bloc of post-neo-liberal progressive regimes oriented towards the new developmentalism

**60** The progressive cycle

(inclusionary state activism) as well as extractivism, i.e. the use of resource rents, collected or extracted from the multinational companies given concessions to exploit and export the country's natural resources, to finance their social programmes designed to bring about a more 'inclusive' form of development (i.e. poverty reduction). This included the two largest countries on the continent, Argentina and Brazil, which together accounted for over 70 per cent of the regional economy and exports and which in the early 1990s joined Uruguay and Paraguay to form a subregional trading bloc (Mercosur) in opposition to various subsequent efforts of the US to create a continental free trade zone. The governments in both countries pursued this neo-developmentalist and extractivist policy regime until it was brought to an abrupt end in Argentina by the election on 22 November 2015 of Mauricio Macri, who represented the forces of right-wing opposition and reaction – and the rejection of the post-neo-liberal development model. Behind this event and associated political developments, which can also be traced out in Brazil, Venezuela and Bolivia, was a pendulum swing in the correlation of forces engaged in the class struggle, a 'development' that responded to and reflected the evident end of the commodities boom (around 2012) and with it the end of the capacity of these regimes to sustain their progressive policies. Indeed, in the wake of recent regional developments along this line analysts have begun to write about and debate the 'end of the progressive cycle' in Latin American politics (Gaudichaud, 2016; Katz, 2016).

A third pattern of policy experiments and political developments associated with the demise of neo-liberalism and the 10-year primary commodities boom (2003–12) concerned Venezuela, Bolivia and Ecuador – more 'radical' post-neo-liberal regimes that were oriented in theory (political rhetoric and development discourse) if not in actual fact towards a post-development model in which, in the cases of Bolivia and Ecuador, people would 'live well' (*vivir bien*) in social solidarity and harmony with nature; or, in the case of Venezuela, engaged in a process of revolutionary transformation (the Bolivarian Revolution) oriented towards the 'socialism of the twenty-first century'. At the level of trade, these regimes joined Cuba and several smaller countries in the Caribbean to form the *Alianza Bolivariana para los Pueblos de Nuestra América* (ALBA), a post-neo-liberal intergovernmental alternative trade regime. In the case of Venezuela, the revolutionary process can be traced back to the regime formed by Hugo Chávez in 1998. Like the other post-neo-liberal regimes in the region, the Venezuelan government's development strategy was financed by and hinged on an extractivist approach, but unlike the other post-neo-liberal regimes it was not dependent on foreign direct investment or on the state to strike a deal with global extractive capital. However, as in the case of these two regimes the collapse of the commodities boom and the dramatic fall in the price of oil, the one commodity on which the entire policy regime was dependent, together with the machinations of US imperialism funding of the sabotage of and right-wing opposition to the proto-socialist regime, have pushed the country towards the brink of a severe economic crisis. Whether the combined effect of this crisis, US intervention, right-wing opposition and economic sabotage are enough to overthrow the regime or lead to its collapse is anyone's guess, but there is no doubt that the revolutionary process in the country – like the progressive cycle in Latin American politics – are today in serious jeopardy.

The election of Macri in Argentina, together with the recent elite-directed coup in Brazil and the referendum in Bolivia – as well as the institution of the Trans-Pacific Free Trade regime – are indications of a new conjuncture in the capitalist development process and another pendulum swing in the correlation of class forces, and with it the likely end of the progressive cycle and the return of the Right. At issue in this pendulum swing is what has turned out to be a reactionary rather than progressive developmentalist model, which served initially to de-radicalize and demobilize the popular movements and ultimately to cultivate the return of the Right. With Macri, the country has entered a new political phase in which the goal is no other than to implant a new model of capital accumulation.

## Three decades of class struggle: the left–right pendulum

As noted in the introduction to this volume, the process of capitalist development set in motion by the architects of the Bretton Woods system and the advocates of 'development assistance' – international cooperation with the development agenda of the 'economically backwards' countries seeking to escape the yoke of colonialism and imperialist exploitation – advanced in two stages: a phase of state-led development (1948–80) and the subsequent 'neo-liberal era', in which the forces of national development were advanced within the institutional and policy framework of the Washington Consensus as to the virtues of free-market capitalism. As for the neo-liberal era, the process of development and social change – the development of the forces of production and the corresponding changes in the social relations of production and the resulting dynamics of class struggle – can be traced out decade by decade. The 1980s in Latin America saw the institution of a new economic model, which was used as a template for adjusting the macroeconomic policies of governments in the region to the requirements of the new world order. Because of the manifest dismal failure of this 'structural adjustment programme' and the Washington Consensus to bring about any advance in the economic development process, the architects of the development idea at the end of the decade revised the neo-liberal policy agenda by adding to the basic menu of structural reforms a 'new social policy' oriented towards 'inclusive development' (i.e. poverty reduction).

The 1990s saw a dramatic growth in the influx of capital in the form of foreign direct investment, a deepening and extension of the 'structural reform' agenda (to include Argentina, Brazil and Peru, which had not participated in the first cycle of neo-liberal 'structural reforms') and the growth in the countryside of powerful anti-neo-liberal social movements. By the end of the decade, most countries in the region had adopted the 'new social policy' (poverty reduction, inclusive development) agenda of the post-Washington Consensus and the associated neo-developmentalist strategy devised by economists at ECLAC and the policy framework for 'comprehensive development' devised by economists at the World

**62** The progressive cycle

Bank. However, this agenda did not sway the leadership of the anti-neo-liberal social movements that dominated the political landscape in many countries. By the end of the decade, notwithstanding the massive influx of capital and the widespread adoption of a social reformist and assistentialist policy agenda, the ideologues and advocates of the neo-liberal policy agenda were very much on the defensive in countries such as Ecuador with a powerful anti-neo-liberal resistance. In Peru the political cycle played out in much of South America from Venezuela to Argentina and Brazil seemed to have been about 10 years behind.

At the turn of the new millennium and the third decade of the neo-liberal era, widespread discontent and the rejection of neo-liberalism across the region gave way to a tidal wave of new regimes on the centre-left with a progressive agenda regarding the search for a more inclusive form of development. Even hard-line neoliberals and the proponents of the erstwhile Washington (and now Davos) Consensus had come to the view that the reduction of extreme poverty was an essential part of what was now described as an 'inclusive economic growth' policy agenda and strategy based on the agency of the free market. This agenda was – and is – advanced by conservative private foundations and neo-liberal policy forums across the world, which are heavily financed by the super-rich and the global ruling class and their corporations. However, under conditions in Latin America at the turn of the new millennium it was the post-Washington Consensus on the need for inclusionary state activism and greater income and wealth distribution that prevailed. The resulting progressive cycle in Latin American politics implicated the governments of Argentina and Brazil in what has been described as a 'pink' tide of regime change, and the governments of Venezuela, Bolivia and Ecuador in a 'red' tide.

In this chapter we will briefly review the dynamics of class struggle associated with this progressive cycle.

## Brazil: corporatism, class struggle and klepto-leftism

Two types of class struggle have dominated Brazilian social relations in recent decades. For over two decades of military dictatorships (1964–84) the dominant classes waged war on the workers, employees and peasants, imposing tripartite agreements between state, capitalists and appointed 'union' leaders. The absence of authentic class-based unions and the economic crises of the early 1980s set in motion the emergence of the 'new unionism'. The CUT (Central Única dos Trabalhadores), based on heavy industry, and the MST, the rural landless workers' movement, in the rural areas, emerged as leading forces in the class struggle. The deteriorating political control of the military led to opposition from two directions: (i) the agro-mineral and export bourgeoisie, which sought to impose a civilian-electoral regime to pursue a neo-liberal economic development strategy, and (ii) the new class-based unionism which sought to democratize and expand the public ownership of the means of production.

The class-based CUT allied with the liberal bourgeoisie and defeated the corporatist, military-backed candidates of the Right. In other words, the combined class

The progressive cycle **63**

struggle from below and from above secured electoral democracy and the ascendancy of the neo-liberal bourgeoisie. Under the neo-liberal regimes at the time, three changes that further conditioned the class struggle from below took place:

1 CUT secured legality and collective bargaining rights and became institutionalized.
2 CUT and the MST backed the newly formed Workers Party (PT), a party that was dominated by leftist middle-class professionals intent on taking power through electoral processes.
3 CUT increasingly depended on financing by the Ministry of Labour, while the PT increasingly looked towards private contractors to finance their election campaigns.

From the mid-nineties to the election of Lula da Silva in 2002, the CUT and the MST alternated direct action (strikes and land occupations) with electoral politics – backing the candidates of the PT, which increasingly sought to moderate class disputes. Class struggle from below intensified during the impeachment of neo-liberal President Collar. However, once ousted the CUT moderated the workings of the class struggle from below.

With the hyperinflation of the 1990s, the CUT and the MST engaged in defensive class struggles, opening the way for the election of hard-line neo-liberal Fernando Henrique Cardoso. Under his presidency a severe 'adjustment' that prejudiced workers was implemented to end inflation. Strategic sectors of the agro-mineral sector were privatized. Lucrative public oil and mining enterprises were privatized and banks were denationalized; agribusiness took centre stage.

The class struggle from 'below' intensified, while Cardoso supported the class struggle from above for capital. The MST-led land occupations intensified, as did violent repression; and workers strikes and popular discontent multiplied. The PT responded by harnessing the class struggle to its electoral strategy. The PT also deepened its ties with private contractors and replaced its social democratic programme with a clientelistic version of neo-liberalism.

The rising tide of class struggle from below led to the presidential victory of the PT, whose economic programme was based on IMF agreements and ties to the dominant classes. Under the PT, the class struggle from below weakened and dissipated. The MST and the CUT subordinated their struggles to the PT, which promoted negotiated solutions with the capitalist class. The dynamics of this moderate form of class struggle excluded structural changes and revolved on incremental changes of wages and consumption and increases in poverty spending.

The electoral success of the PT depended on ever-greater financing by private contractors based on awarding billion-real public contracts for multimillion-dollar bribes. The lower- and working-class vote was secured by a well-funded antipoverty programme and the vote-getting campaigns of the CUT and the MST. The high price of export commodities based on the booming Asian market provided a vast increase in state revenues to finance capital loans and social welfare.

**64** The progressive cycle

The 'moderate class struggle' led by the PT ended with the bust of the mega-commodity boom. After the second election of Dilma Rousseff in 2014, the exposure of massive corruption involving the PT further exacerbated the crisis and mass support for the PT. As the economy stagnated, the PT adapted to the crises by embracing the structural adjustments of the ruling class. As the PT leaders shifted to the class struggle from above they ignited protest from below among the middle class, workers and employees – and even within the PT itself. Mass demonstrations protested over the decline of public services.

By 2016 the 'middle' or 'moderate' class struggle in Brazil bifurcated into a mass class struggle from above and a much weaker struggle 'from below'. As the right-wing judicial system selectively exposed deep corruption in the PT regimes and the economy spiralled into the worst recession in 50 years, the right wing mobilized three million street demonstrators seeking to overthrow the Rousseff regime, whose popularity plunged to single digits. The counter response of sections of the Left drew less then a million. The class struggle from above was advancing and the Left was in retreat, as demonstrated by subsequent events (the success of the forces on the Right to finally depose President Rousseff).

## Argentina: high-intensity class struggle

Argentina has been the centre of high-intensity class struggle from above and below over the last half-century. A ruling class-backed military dictatorship from 1966 to 1973 harshly repressed trade unions and their political parties (mostly Left Peronist). In response, industrial workers led major uprisings in all of the major cities (Cordoba and Rosario included), ultimately forcing the military-capitalist rulers to retreat and convoke elections.

The period between 1973 and 1976 was a tumultuous period of rising class and guerrilla struggle, high inflation, the emergence of death squads and successful general strikes. A situation of 'dual power' between factory-based committees and a highly militarized state, ostensibly led by Isabel Perón and death squad leader José López Rega, were ended by a bloody US-backed military coup in 1976.

From 1976 to 1983, over 30,000 Argentines were murdered and made to 'disappear' by the military-capitalist regime. The vast majority were working-class activists in factories and neighbourhood organizations. The military-capitalist class victory led to the imposition of neo-liberal policies and the illegalization of all workers' organizations and strikes. The high-intensity class struggle from above ended the class struggle from below.

The loss of authentic factory and community-based workers' leaders was a historic defeat with an impact that persisted for decades. The subsequent military defeat of the Argentine armed forces by the British in the battle of the Malvinas led to a negotiated transition in which the neo-liberal economic structures and military elite remained intact. The electoral parties emerged and competed for office but offered little support to the legalized trade unions.

Between 1984 and 2001 Radical and Peronist presidents pillaged the treasury, privatized and denationalized the economy, while the re-emerging right-wing Peronist trade unions engaged in ritual general strikes to defuse discontent from below and collaborated with the state. The economic crash of 2000–01 led to an explosion of class struggle, as thousands of factories closed and over one-quarter of the labour force was unemployed (*los desocupados*, the social base of the class struggle led by the *piqueteros*).

In this conjuncture and situation members of the middle class lost their savings as banks failed. A major popular demonstration in front of the Presidential Palace (*Casa Rosada*) was repressed, resulting in three dozen killings. In response, over two million Argentines engaged in general strikes and uprisings, seized the Congress and besieged the banks. Millions of unemployed and impoverished workers and middle-class assemblies, representing nearly 50 per cent of the population, took to the streets. But fragmentation and sectarian disputes prevented a serious alternative government from emerging even in the midst of intense class struggle from below.

Intense class struggle from below toppled three presidents in less than two years (2001–02), but the mass protest remained without leaders or a hegemonic party. In 2003 a left-of-centre Peronist, Nestor Kirchner, was elected and, under pressure from the mass movements, imposed a moratorium on debt and financed an economic recovery based on rising commodity prices and rechanneling debt payments. Unemployment and poverty levels declined sharply, as did the class struggle from below.

In the decade from 2003 to 2013, a low-intensity class struggle led by the middle class emerged as the dominant feature of the political landscape. Militant leaders of the unemployed workers and the trade unions were co-opted. The Kirchner regime ended military impunity. It tried and jailed hundreds of military officials for human rights crimes, gaining the support of all the human rights groups.

This middle class led struggle stimulated labour reforms and the recovery of capitalism, ending the capitalist crisis and de-radicalizing the workers. The Kirchner regimes (Nestor and Cristina Fernández) channelled the revenues from the mega-commodity boom to increases in wages, salaries and pensions. It also subsidized and attracted foreign and domestic agro-business and mining capitalists.

By the end of the decade the capitalist class felt relatively secure and the threats from below were diluted. High growth led to increases in class struggle from above. Agro-business organized boycotts to lessen taxes; Buenos Aires business and professional groups regrouped and organized mass protests. Leftist parties and trade unions, co-opted or fragmented, engaged in economistic struggles. Some sectarian leftist groups, like the Workers Party, even joined the right-wing demonstrations.

By 2012 the commodity boom came to an end. The hard Right dominated the political horizon. The Kirchner–Fernández regime leaned to the right, embracing extractive capitalism as the economic paradigm.

From 2013 to 2015 the centre-right and Right dominated electoral politics. The trade unions were once again under the leadership of right-wing Peronists (Moyano,

**66** The progressive cycle

Barrionuevo etc.). Popular movements were in opposition but without any significant political representation.

After a decade and a half, the cycle of the class struggle had gone round. From intense class struggle from below, to middle-class mediated class struggle, to the resurgence of the class struggle from above.

## Bolivia: from popular uprisings to Andean capitalism and communalist socialism

For the better part of half a century Bolivia had the reputation of possessing the most combative working class in Latin America. Led by the Bolivian Labour Confederation (COB) and the mineworkers, dynamite in hand they led the revolution of 1952, which overthrew the oligarchy, nationalized the mines and, with the support of the peasantry, carried out a far-reaching agrarian reform. However, in the aftermath of the revolution, the workers and trade unions disputed power with an alliance of middle-class politicians, the National Revolutionary Movements (MNR) and peasants.

The uprising and revolution were aborted. Over the following decade, pitched battles between leftist miners and a re-assembled military–peasant alliance led to a US-backed coup in 1962. The US backed Rene Barrientos as 'president'. Between 1964 and 1968 the dictatorship imposed draconian measures on the mining communities and liberalized the economy, in the form of IMF structural reforms. In reaction, a nationalist-military revolt led by General Ovando succeeded to power and proposed to nationalize Gulf oil.

In 1970 a major working-class revolt installed J. J. Torres to power. Even more importantly, the uprising installed a worker–peasant legislative assembly. With a majority of worker legislators and a substantial minority of peasants, the 'Popular Assembly' proceeded to pass radical legislation, nationalizing major banks, resources and factories. A sharp polarization resulted. While civil society moved to the radical left, the state apparatus and the military moved towards the right. The workers' parties possessed radical programmes; the Right monopolized arms.

In 1971 the Torres regime was overthrown, the workers' assembly dissolved, the trade union made illegal and many militants were killed, jailed and exiled.

From 1972–2000, military rulers, right-wing and centre-left regimes alternated in power and reversed the changes instituted by the 1952 revolution. Radical or revolutionary movements and trade unions demonstrated a great capacity for class struggle and the ability to overthrow regimes, but were incapable of taking power and ruling.

Between 2000 and 2005, major popular rebellions took place, including the 'water war' in Cochabamba in 2000; a mass worker–peasant uprising in La Paz in 2003, which ousted neo-liberal incumbent President Sánchez de Lozado; and a second uprising in 2005, which drove incumbent President Carlos Mesa from power and led to new elections and the victory of radical coca peasant leader Evo Morales to the presidency.

Morales and his MAS (Movement to Socialism) party has ruled since 2006, ending the period of intense class struggle and popular uprisings. In this period the government implemented a series of piecemeal socio-economic reforms and cultural changes while incorporating and co-opting the indigenous movement and the trade union leadership. The net effect was to demobilize the popular movement. The key to the stability, continuity and re-election of Morales was his ability to separate socio-economic and culture reforms from radical structural changes. In the process, Morales secured the electoral support of the mass of peasants and workers, isolated the more radical sectors and ensured that the class struggle would revolve around short-term wage and salary issues that would not endanger the stability of the government.

The key to the periodic recurrence of revolutionary class struggle in Bolivia has been the fusion of a multiplicity of demands. High-intensity class struggle resulted from the multiple points of socio-ethnic, national and cultural oppression and class exploitation. Immediate economic demands were linked to class struggles for long-term, large-scale systemic changes.

The major protagonists of the social upheavals demanded an end to deep and pervasive ethno-racial discrimination and indignities. They rejected foreign capitalist pillage of natural resources and wealth that provided no positive returns for the mining and rural communities. They fought for indigenous self-rule and a role in governance if not the government. They resented the denial of symbolic indigenous presence in public or private spaces. Wages that were low relative to profits and hazardous employment with no compensatory payments radicalized the miners. In this context, where workers and Indians were denied governmental access and representation, they relied on direct action – popular upheavals and demands for social revolution were the route to secure social justice.

The coming to power of Evo Morales opened the door to a new kind of mass politics, based essentially on his ability to fragment demands. He implemented cultural and economic reforms and neutralized demands for a social revolution. President Morales convoked a new constituent assembly that included a strong representation of Indian delegates. Bolivia was renamed a 'plurinational' state. Formal recognition and approval of the 'autonomy' of Indian nations was approved. He frequently met and consulted with Indian leaders. Symbolic representation de-radicalized the indigenous movements.

The government took a majority share in a number of joint ventures with gas and oil corporations and increased the royalties and tax rates on profits of mining companies. Morales rejected outright nationalization under workers' control. Morales denounced imperialist intervention in Bolivia and elsewhere, and expelled US Ambassador Goldberg for plotting a coup with the extreme right-wing opposition in Santa Cruz. He expelled the Drug Enforcement Agency and the US military mission for meddling in internal affairs. He increased social spending and salaries and wages incrementally each year by between 5 and 10 per cent.

These reforms were compatible with long-term contracts with dozens of major foreign multinational mining companies that continued to reap and remit

**68** The progressive cycle

double-digit profits. Although the government claimed to 'nationalize' foreign-owned mining companies, in most cases it meant simply higher tax rates, comparable to the rates in the major capitalist countries. The revolutionary demands to socialize the 'commanding heights of the economy' faded and revolutionary mass energies were diverted into collective bargaining agreements.

While the Morales regime spoke of respecting *pachamama* – mother earth – he pursued the most blatant exploitation of land reserves of any president – opening eight of 17 to foreign and domestic extractive capitalist exploitation, arguing that development would provide the revenues to reduce poverty – ignoring the villagers uprooted in the process of losing access to water and land

While the government celebrated indigenous culture, all of its major decisions were made by *mestizo* and 'European'-descended technocrats. MAS bureaucrats overruled local assemblies in the selection and election of candidates. While government legislation proposed 'land reform', the 'hundred families' in Santa Cruz still controlled vast plantations, dominating the agro-export economy. They continued receiving the vast majority of government credits and subsidies. Poverty, especially extreme poverty, was reduced but still affected the majority of the population in the indigenous communities. Public lands, offered for Indian settlement were located far from markets and with few support resources. As a result, few families were resettled.

While Evo articulated an anti-imperialist discourse to the people, he constantly travelled abroad to Europe seeking and signing off on lucrative private investment deals. Corruption crept into the MAS party and pervaded its officials in Cochabamba, El Alto and La Paz. The net effect of Evo's domestic reform and cultural inclusive agenda was to neutralize and marginalize radical critiques of his macroeconomic adaptation to foreign capital.

His affirmation of indigenous ('*Indio*') culture neutralized the opposition of indigenous peasants and farmworkers to the Euro-Bolivian plantation owners who prospered under his 'extractive export strategy'.

The class struggle focused on narrow economic issues directed by trade union leaders (COB), who consulted and negotiated agreements in accordance with Evo's economic guidelines. In short, under President Morales, the class struggle from below diminished, popular rebellions disappeared and collective bargaining took centre stage. The Morales decade witnessed the lowest intensity of class struggle in a century. The contrast between the 1995–2005 decade and the 2006–15 period is striking. While the earlier period under Euro-Bolivian rulers witnessed several general strikes and popular uprisings, during the later decade there was none. Even the hostile, racist landed and mining oligarchy of Santa Cruz eventually came to political agreements and ran on joint electoral platforms with the MAS, recognizing the benefits of fiscal conservatism, social stability, capitalist prosperity and class peace.

Under Morales's conservative fiscal regime, Bolivian foreign reserves increased from under US$4 billion to over US$15 billion – an achievement that pleased the World Bank but still left the vast majority of peasants below the poverty line. In large part, the success of Evo in defusing the class struggle and channelling 'radicalism' into safe channels was due to the incremental changes that were underwritten by a decade-long rise in commodity prices.

With the primary commodities boom the prices of iron ore, oil, tin, gold, lithium and soya soared, allowing the regime to increase state expenditures and wages without affecting the wealth and profits of the agro-mineral elite. But, as the mega-boom ended in 2013–15 (exports fell by 50 per cent in 2015) and nepotism and corruption in official circles flourished, the MAS lost provincial and municipal elections in major cities. The MAS regime, plagued by corruption scandals, attempted to foist unpopular candidates on the mass base and lost. The main opposition to the regime was from the centre-right elements of the middle class. The dormant and thoroughly co-opted COB and peasant movements continued to back Morales but faced an increasingly rebellious rank and file. The electoral decline was most evident in the defeat of a government-sponsored referendum in February 2016, asking the electorate to vote in favour of Evo's re-election, potentially extending his presidency until 2025. Most of the big cities voted against the MAS initiative, rebelling against corruption and abuses by government officials. As for the progressive policy regime of poverty reduction pursued by the Morales-Linera regime – a progressive regime undercut by the insistence of the government to assuage foreign investors by accumulating one of the biggest reserves of foreign currency in the region, and even lending money from this reserve fund to the World Bank and foreign investors at ridiculously low interest rates rather than investing it productively – the end of the commodities boom has effectively curtailed this regime (Almeyra, 2016).

## Ecuador: the dynamics of middle-class radicalism in a citizen's revolution

The last decade of the twentieth century began and ended with an uprising of the indigenous communities that formed the most powerful social movement in opposition to the neo-liberal agenda of the governments at the time. These movements played a major role in the subsequent demise of neo-liberalism as an economic doctrine and development model. But, notwithstanding this important political development, Ecuador has had a long history of palace coups of little socio-economic consequence, at least up until the first half-decade of the twenty-first century. The prelude to the popular upheavals of the recent period was a 'decade of infamy'. Right-wing oligarchical parties alternated in power, pillaging billions from the national treasury. Overseas bankers granted high-risk loans that were transferred to overseas accounts. Major oil companies, namely Texaco, exploited and contaminated large tracts of land, and water, with impunity. Client regimes granted the US a major military base in Manta, from which it violated Ecuadorean air and maritime sovereignty. Ecuador surrendered its currency and dollarized the economy, eliminating its capacity to elaborate sovereign monetary policy.

**70** The progressive cycle

The ethno-class struggle in Ecuador is deeply contradictory. CONAIE (the Confederation of Indigenous Nationalities of Ecuador), founded in 1986, led major uprisings in the 1990s and was the driving force in toppling oligarch Jamil Mahuad in 2000. Yet it allied with right-wing Colonel Lucio Gutiérrez and formed a three-person junta which eventually gave in to US pressures and allowed the vice president and oligarch, Gustavo Noboa, to assume the presidency.

In the run-up to the presidential elections of 2002, CONAIE and the trade union led by the oil and electrical workers' unions intensified the class struggle and mobilized the working class and Indian communities. However, in the 2002 presidential elections CONAIE's political arm, Pachakutik, and most of the militant trade unions backed Lucio Gutiérrez. Once elected, Gutiérrez embraced the agenda of the Washington Consensus, privatized strategic sectors of the economy and backed US policy against Venezuela and other progressive governments in the region. Gutiérrez arrested and dismissed militant oil worker leaders and promoted agro-mineral exploitation of indigenous territory.

Despite CONAIE's eventual disaffection, Pachakutik remained in the government up until Gutiérrez was ousted in 2005 by a movement largely made up of a disaffected middle-class 'citizens movement'. Subsequently, during the 2005 elections, the trade unions and CONAIE backed Rafael Correa. Less than two years later they denounced him for supporting petroleum company exploitation of regions adjoining Indian nations.

CONAIE and the trade unions intensified their opposition in 2008 precisely when Correa declared the national debt illegitimate and defaulted on Ecuador's US$3 billion debt and reduced bond payments by 60 per cent. CONAIE and Pachakutik were marginalized because of their opportunist alliances with Gutiérrez. Their attacks on Correa, as he proceeded to increase social expenditure and infrastructure investment in the interior, further diminished their strength. In the elections for a constituent assembly, Pachakutik received barely 2 per cent of the vote.

While the trade unions and CONAIE continued to mobilize in support of ethno-class demands, Correa increased support among indigenous communities via infrastructure programmes financed by the mega-commodity boom, large-scale loans from China and the reduction of debt payments.

Faced with declining support from the popular classes, CONAIE and sections of the trade unions supported a US-backed police coup attempt on 30 September 2010. Pachakutik leader Clever Jimenez called the right-wing coup a 'just action', while tens of thousands of people demonstrated their support for Correa and his Country Alliance Party (Alianza PAIS).

Correa's 'Citizen Revolution' (*Revolucion Ciudadana*) is essentially based on the deepening of a capitalist developmental model rooted in mining, oil and hydroelectric power. Over the past decade of Correa rule the government has embraced big oil and has sought World Bank loans to finance the agro-mineral growth model while harshly repressing the indigenous movement (CONAIE) and dissident urban social movements. As discussed in Chapters 2 and 3, this repression is rooted in the government's embrace of an extractivist model of capitalist development and its dependence on foreign direct investment, an embrace – and dependency – that has led the government to take the side of multinational corporations in the extractive sector in their conflict with the communities on the extractive frontier.

During the commodity boom from 2006 to 2012 Correa expanded health, education and welfare provisions, while limiting the power of the coastal elite in Guayaquil. With the end of the boom and a subsequent decline in prices, Correa attempted to weaken left-wing and trade union opposition by passing restrictive labour legislation and extending petrol exploration into the highlands where the indigenous communities are concentrated.

In November 2013, trade unions, especially those in the public sector, formed a 'United Workers Front' to protest against Correa's legislation designed to curtail the organization of independent public sector unions.

In the 2014 municipal elections, the right-wing oligarchical parties defeated Correa in the major cities, including Guayaquil, Quito and Cuenca. Once again, CONAIE and the trade unions focused their attack on Correa and ignored the fact that the beneficiaries of his decline was the hard neo-liberal Right.

In June 2015, the hard Right, led by the mayor of Guayaquil, Jaime Nebot, and millionaire banker Guillermo Lasso, led a series of massive protests over a progressive inheritance tax. They sought to oust Correa via a coup. Pachakutik supporters participated in the protests. CONAIE attacked Correa and called for an uprising rather than backing his progressive inheritance tax.

In other words, the anti-extractive indigenous-labour coalition, the United Workers Front and CONAIE, favoured the ousting of Correa and rejected many of his policies but in reality facilitated the ascent to power of the traditional oligarchical Right.

The class struggle in Latin America as elsewhere over the years has unfolded in cycles that reflect changes in the correlation of forces in different conjunctures of the capitalist development process, forces that can be mobilized either towards the right or the left depending on the relative strength of these forces.

We can identify four major cycles in this struggle over the past six decades of capitalist development – three decades under the agency of the state (state-led development) followed by three decades under the sway of the neo-liberal model of free-market capitalism. In the first two decades of this development process the class struggle took the form of a struggle by organized labour for higher wages and to improve working conditions, and a struggle by proletarianized peasants for land reform and to reclaim their right to pursue a livelihood based on agriculture. Over the course of these decades both the labour movement and the land struggle were somewhat successful in bringing about a decided if only relative improvement in the social condition of their members. However, by the end of the 1970s both movements had been either defeated or brought to ground, their capacity to organize and their forces of resistance disarticulated. Under these conditions, with the political left in disarray and the political right on the offensive and in full control of the state apparatus, the movement for

**72** The progressive cycle

revolutionary change gave way to a neoconservative counter-revolution that halted and to some extent reversed the gains made by the peasantry and the working class over the previous decades.

With this swing in the pendulum of force in the class struggle, the 1980s on the Latin American periphery of the world capitalist system saw the steady advance of capital in both agriculture and industry, a resulting destruction of the forces of production in both sectors reflected in what has been analysed as 'a decade lost to development' (no economic growth, a deterioration in the social condition of people in the popular sector) – and a slow but steady reorganization of the resistance in the countryside. To facilitate the advance of capital, a programme of structural reform in macroeconomic policy was imposed on governments in the region, and a new world order was established in regard to international relations of trade and the flow of capital. In the 1990s, capital in the form of multinational corporations and foreign direct investment moved into the region big-time, expanding sixfold by volume from 1990 to 1997 – having purchased at bargain basement prices many of the assets of the lucrative state enterprises and banks placed on the auction block. Under these conditions – and within the framework of the Washington Consensus on the virtues of free-market capitalism – the 1990s have been described as the 'golden age of US imperialism', with reference to its having facilitated an invasion of capital that by one account resulted in a net outflow of US$100 million over the course of the decade (Saxe-Fernández & Núñez, 2001).

The new millennium, however, would see another major swing in the pendulum of forces in the class struggle – a sea tide change in the politics of this struggle. Conditions of this change included (i) an effective organized resistance against the neo-liberal policy agenda mounted by new socio-political movements rooted in the peasantry and the rural landless workers, and in some contexts the indigenous communities; (ii) conditions of an economic and political crisis that came to a head in Argentina in 2001; (iii) a resulting disenchantment and widespread rejection across the region of neo-liberalism as an economic model; and, at a different level, (iv) a number of changes in the world economy, including the ascension of China as an economic power and the demand for natural resources to fuel the rapid growth of the Chinese economy.

Under these conditions, the new millennium opened up with the formation of a series of left-leaning regimes that responded to the challenge that the peasant and indigenous social movements provided to the existing neo-liberal regimes and the political forces ranged in their support. Taking advantage of the political opening provided by the social movements, and in response to the growing demand in some circles for a more inclusive form of development, centre-left post-neo-liberal regimes with a progressive policy agenda were established in Venezuela (1998), in Argentina and Brazil (2003), and then in Bolivia (2006) and Ecuador (2007).

Milestones in the dynamics of sea tide regime change – and resulting utopias and dystopias – include: (i) a popular rebellion in Venezuela in 1998 that brought Hugo Chávez to power and with him the Bolivarian Revolution: (ii) an uprising, in 1990 and then again in 2000, of the indigenous nationalities and communities of Ecuador organized in the form of CONAIE; it placed the neo-liberal policy agenda on the defensive not only in Ecuador but throughout the region, creating conditions that would bring to power Rafael Correa and his 'progressive' left-leaning post-neo-liberal policy regime and 'citizens' revolution; (iii) in Bolivia, a period of revolutionary ferment (2000–05) marked by the gas and water wars, the rise of Evo Morales to power, the creation of the Movement for Socialism (MAS) as an instrument for the sovereignty of the people, and the formation in 2006 of a new multi-ethnic and plurinational political regime backed by the social movements and oriented towards 'socialism' and a post-development model of 'living well' in social solidarity and harmony with nature; (iv) in Argentina, the transmutation of an economic crisis – with its low point in 2001 – into a political crisis, giving rise to a historic movement of unemployed workers (*los piqueteros*) and in 2003 a 'progressive' political regime headed by the Kirchners; (v) the emergence of 'local initiatives of organization for taking and exercising popular power', 'virulent street protests of rejection of decisions made by the national and transnational power' and widespread resistance albeit in 'subterranean' forms and localized arenas (Gaudichaud, 2016; Zibechi, 2012); (vi) a turnaround in the fortunes and the capacity of the US imperial state to dictate or influence policy – marked by the emergence of anti-imperial regimes in Argentina, Brazil, Bolivia and Ecuador as well as Venezuela; and (vii) the rejection, in 2005, of the proposed Free Trade Area of the Americas (ALCA).

Even though the US lost access to some military bases in Ecuador and Bolivia it has regrouped and refigured its military alliances in the region – expanding its bases in Peru and Paraguay as well as in Honduras – and succeeded in the project of rejigging a free trade regime in the form of the Trans-Pacific Free Trade Alliance, the capacity of the US to exercise its imperial power – both the hard power of military force and the soft power of development assistance and cooptation – has drastically diminished in the region. In this context of diminished imperial power the US continues its policy of supporting various attempted coups (in Honduras and Venezuela) and right-wing economic destabilization efforts (Venezuela), and strategic support of US-based capital in its Latin American operations, it has had to rely more and more on trickle-down economics in the form of assistentialist neo-developmentalism – tacit support for the new economic model of inclusionary state activism.

## The transition from intense to limited class struggle, 2000–14

The intensity and scope of the class struggle varied in the post-neo-liberal countries. During the onset of the progressive cycle of centre-left regimes and the start of the commodity boom the class struggle was intense and linked to major social advances. Subsequently, between around 2006 and 2010, capitalists were ensured protection from expropriation, granted subsides, export incentives and tax relief. Labour received jobs, wage and pension increases and access to cheap credit to finance consumer purchases.

**74** The progressive cycle

At the start of the second decade, with the end of the commodity boom, a slow-down in the dynamics of economic growth in the global economy, persistent economic crises and the massive growth of consumer debt, and the end of large-scale foreign capital flows, the class struggle from above regained strength. The capitalist class pressed for greater support and incentives; labour strikes multiplied especially in the face of rising prices and lagging wages.

In the most recent period of regime change (2013–15), the class struggle from above has re-emerged as an influential determinant of regime policy. In Argentina, the Kirchner II (Cristina Fernández) regime signed off on lucrative agreements with major agro-mineral companies, effectively devalued the peso to favour agro-business exporters and turned towards greater support for foreign debt holders. The right turn of the regime, its embrace of the leading capitalist sectors, has provoked a general strike by one of the trade union confederations (headed by Moyano) and 'road blockages' by dissident leftist union activists. The Kirchner regime has come full circle – from accommodating the demands of the unemployed workers for public investment and wage increases in 2003–06 to promoting tripartite social pacts between labour and capital in 2007–11 to a right turn as the end of the commodity boom reduced the windfall of additional fiscal revenues and the capitalist class went back on the offensive.

In Bolivia, the MAS regime came to power by means of mass mobilizations from below, and adopted (at least rhetorically) a plurinational and nationalist agenda. But by the beginning of Evo Morales's second term in office (2008) it pursued and implemented an open door policy regarding foreign agro-mining extractive capital. Incremental wage and pension improvements and extensive cooptation of peasant and trade union leaders created a quasi-corporate state structure embellished by ethno-populist rhetoric. The class struggle from below was harnessed by the MAS to beat back different coup attempts by the Santa Cruz elite in 2008–09. Subsequently the MAS moved to reconcile the elite via a political-economic pact based on the mutual accommodation of the regime and capital.

From the end of 2010 to 2014, the MAS regime embraced a 'developmentalist strategy' based on an alliance with extractive capital, orthodox fiscal policy and the accumulation of foreign reserves managed by foreign bankers.

Paradoxically, the class struggle from below has over the past decade led to regimes that are responding favourably to the demands of the foreign and domestic capitalist class. The Argentine and Bolivian experiences of the class struggle follow a trajectory whereby class struggle from below gains leverage over 'centre-left' regimes for several years but then gives way to class accommodation and demobilization. This is followed by the revival of class struggle from above and the conversion of the 'centre-left' regimes into patrons and promoters of capitalist interests via 'developmentalist policies'.

Even in Venezuela, where the Chavista government under Maduro has attempted to stay the course of the socialist-oriented Bolivarian Revolution under enormous pressures from within and without, the government has turned towards a 'production pact' with capital under pressure from a violent capitalist class offensive launched in February 2014. The Venezuelan masses in the form of a 'class struggle from below' have responded to a powerful capitalist offensive, but are largely dependent on the Maduro government, which has attempted to divide the opposition, repress the violent sectors and offer concessions to productive capitalists and oppositional forces.

## The end of the progressive cycle?

The class ethnic alliances in Bolivia and Ecuador have had divergent outcomes. In the former they brought to power the centre-left government headed by Evo Morales. In the latter they led to opportunist alliances, political defeats and ideological chaos. The class struggle from below has led to a variety of political outcomes, some more progressive than others. But, despite the claims of some popularly elected presidents like Evo Morales, none resulted in a worker–peasant–indigenous regime.

The class struggle over the past two decades has demonstrated a cyclical pattern, rising in opposition to right-wing neo-liberal regimes (De la Rua in Argentina, Cardoso in Brazil, Sánchez de Lozado in Bolivia, Mahuad in Ecuador), but then ebbing with the coming to power of a new cycle of centre-left regimes. The exception here is Ecuador, where the main protagonists of the class struggle backed the rightist regime of Lucio Gutiérrez before falling into disarray.

The key to the success of the centre-left regimes was the decade-long boom in commodity prices, which allowed them to dampen the class struggle by piecemeal assistentialist and welfare reforms, as well as an increase in wages and salaries. However, the incremental reforms weakened the revolutionary impulses from below. The decompression of the class struggle and the channelling of the struggle into institutional channels led to the co-option of sectors of the popular leadership, and the separation of economic demands from struggles for popular political power.

From a historical perspective, the class struggle succeeded in securing significant reductions in unemployment and poverty, increases in social spending and the securing of legal recognition. At the same time, the leaders of the class-based movements more or less abided by the extractive capitalist model and its devastating impact on the environment, economy and communities of indigenous peoples.

Minority sectors of the popular movements in Brazil struggled against the Workers' Party regime's devastation of the Amazon rainforest and the displacement of indigenous communities. In Bolivia, President Evo Morales spoke at international forums in defence of mother earth (*pachamama*) and in Bolivia opened the TIPNIS national reserve to oil and mining exploitation, committing matricide! Likewise, in Argentina President Cristina Fernández faced limited trade union opposition when she signed a major agreement with Monsanto, to further deepen genetic altered grain production and a major oil agreement with Chevron–Exxon to exploit oil and gas exploitation by fracking in the *Vaca Muerto* (Dead Cow) complex. In Ecuador, the CONAIE–Gutierrez agreement and subsequent support of Correa led to a deepening of ecological degradation and diminished opposition to Correa's extractive capitalism.

**76** The progressive cycle

The biggest blow to the extractive capitalist model did not come from the class struggle but from the world market. The decline of commodity prices led to the large-scale reduction of the flow of overseas extractive capital. However, the decline of commodity prices weakened the centre-left and led to a resurgence of the class struggle from above. In Argentina, Bolivia, Ecuador and Brazil, the upper classes have organized large-scale street protests and were victorious in municipal and state elections. In contrast the class struggle organizations remain wedded to defensive economic struggles over wages and welfare cuts by their former centre-left allies.

In this situation we can observe the rise of the class struggle from above under conditions that included the demise of several centre-left regimes, the economic crises of a commodity-based extractive capitalist development model, and the cooptation and or demobilization of the class struggle organizations.

In Brazil, Argentina, Ecuador and Bolivia, the right wing-led class struggle from above aims for political power: to oust the centre-left, and the reimposition of neo-liberal free trade policies. They seek to reverse social spending and progressive taxation, dismantle regional integration and reinstate repressive legislation. The election in Argentina is the clearest signal of this turn in the pendulum and change in the correlation of force in the class struggle. Over the next five-year period 2015–20, we can expect the return of the hard neo-liberal right, the break-up of tripartite (labour, capital, government) cooperation and the return of bipartite capital–state rule.

Cut loose from easy negotiations involving steady incremental gains, the popular movements are likely to combine the struggle for short-term gains with demands for long-term structural changes. Revolutionary class consciousness is likely to re-emerge in most cases.

The return of the Right will result in regressive socio-economic measures across the board and intensify the class struggle as a result. For example, almost immediately on assuming power the new Macri government embarked on a rapid-fire series of conservative economic reforms, threatening public-sector employment and social programmes. By March 2016, with Macri barely three months in office, 200,000 state workers had been fired and 54,000 workers were laid off just in the construction industry. These and other such policy measures can be expected not only to spark a working-class revolt but to bring together disparate sectors of the urban and rural working population. The stage may be set to put in motion the dynamics of another revolutionary class struggle.

The demise of the neo-liberal era, signalled by the rise to power of Hugo Chávez in Venezuela and the emergence of post-neo-liberal regimes in a number of countries in South America over the course of the first decade of the new millennium, has evidently come to an end according to some pundits. The clearest expression of this 'reflux in the post-neo-liberal decade' – to use Gaudichaud's expression – was the rise to power of the hard-right Mauricio Macri in the November 2015 elections, which not only brought to power a regime ideologically committed to a return of the neo-liberal policy agenda and friendly relations with the US, but, according to many Latin American pundits, reflected a clear change in the correlation of force in the regional class struggle.

The progressive cycle **77**

Chapter 5 elaborates on the significance of this electoral contest and the triumph of Macri for Argentina and the broader class struggle, but its meaning is clear enough: seemingly the end of the progressive cycle in Latin American governments. The return of the Right is also evident in Brazil, where President Dilma Rousseff appointed a neo-liberal 'Chicago Boy' economist, Joaquin Levy, as finance minister and has launched an IMF-style regressive structural adjustment policy designed to reduce social expenditures and attract financial speculators. His failure led to his early retirement from office. The Right is also gaining momentum in Ecuador, as a result of the government's deceitful double discourse regarding 'living well' and extractivism. In Peru, the daughter of Fujimori, the author of one of the most drastic neo-liberal programmes, representing diverse interests on Peru's neo-liberal middle class and the far Right, led the polls for the next presidential election. As it turned out, another right-wing hardliner (Pedro Pablo Kuczynski) won the elections. Even in Venezuela, where President Maduro has attempted to assiduously stay the course of a socialist-oriented Bolivarian revolution under pressures from both within and without, under pressure from a violent capitalist class offensive launched in February 2014 the government has had to turn towards a 'production pact' with capital. Washington has channelled millions of dollars to parties on the far Right and violent extra-parliamentary and paramilitary groups as a means of destabilizing the centre-left Maduro government. This aided the right-wing Democratic Unity Movement (MUD) in its victory in the legislative elections in December 2015 by a better than a two to one margin over the Chavista Venezuelan United Socialist Party (PSUV).

In support of this diagnosis and prognosis, progressive social legislation in the region has come to a virtual halt, even before the recent political advances of the US-backed right-wing parties with their neo-liberal economic agenda. However, paralysis and even retreat – and several electoral defeats of the centre-left regimes – do not mean a return to the neo-liberal 1990s, the heyday of US imperialism in the region, a period of privatizations, pillage and plunder which plunged millions into poverty, unemployment and marginality. Whatever the recent voting results and the situation on the front of electoral politics, the collective memory of hardship resulting from 'free-market' neo-liberal policies is seared in the memory of the vast majority of the working population. Evidence of this was the immediate and subsequent responses of the social and political left both in Argentina and elsewhere to Macri's ascension to political power. In less then three months after taking office and after firing nearly 200,000 public employees, Macri faces a general strike convoked by all the trade union confederations.

In this context any attempt by the newly elected officials to 'unmake and reverse' the social advances of the past decade will undoubtedly meet with militant resistance if not open class warfare as well as a range of institutional and political constraints. Also, a careful analysis of the policies proposed by the neo-liberal right suggests that their implementation and impact will demonstrate their likely failure and the rapid demise of any new right-wing offensive, aborting the reflux of the neo-liberal cycle.

## Conclusion

The victory of the hard-right, neo-liberal Mauricio Macri in Argentina and the right-wing coup of the presidency in Brazil do not necessarily augur a new right-wing cycle in Latin American politics. For one thing, Macri's economic team quickly confront mass opposition – and they lack any political support outside the upper-class neighbourhoods. Their policies will polarize the country and undermine the stability that investors require. Brutal devaluations and the end of capital controls is a recipe for inciting general strikes. Conflict, stagnation and hyperinflation will put an end to the enthusiasm of local and foreign investors. Moreover, Macri cannot embrace Washington because Argentina's natural trading partner is China. Macri's regime is the beginning and the end of a reversion to the neo-liberal disaster, similar to what took place at the end of the 1990s.

As for the PT, its fall from grace is more a product of judicial prosecution than the action of trade unions and social movements and that opens political space for new working-class struggles, free from the constraints of corrupt leaders and bureaucrats. The Right's return to power in Brazil is tainted with the same corruption: its capitalist partners are in jail or facing prosecution. In other words, the fall of the PT is only part of the decline and decay of all the capitalist parties.

Over time, the crisis of the 'new Right' may stimulate the formation of a new authentic Left that is free from corruption and links to big business. Under these conditions an authentic working-class party may emerge that pursues socio-economic policies that will put and end to the exploitation of labour and the pillaging of the country's natural resources and the public treasury. In other words, a Left that in word and deed sustains the environment and respects nature and the rights of Afro-Brazilians, indigenous people and women.

## References

Alliance for Democracy. (2016). *Stop the Trans-Pacific Partnership*. Available at: www.thealliancefordemocracy.org/tpp.html [accessed 18 July 2016].

Almeyra, G. (2016). 'Bolivia: un tiro en la pie'. *La Jornada*, 28 February.

Gaudichaud, F. (2016). 'Fin de ciclo? Los movimientos populares, la crisis de los "progresismos" gubernamentales y las alternativas. Dossier: América Latina: crisis de los "gobiernos progresistas" y alternativas actuales'. *Revista Herramienta*, 58. Available at: www.herramienta.com.ar/node/2540 [accessed 3 August 2016].

Katz, C. (2016). 'Is South America's 'progressive cycle' at an end?' *The Bullet*, 1229, 13 March. Available at: www.socialistproject.ca/bullet/1229.php [accessed 24 June 2016].

Saxe-Fernández, J. & Núñez, O. (2001). 'Globalización e imperialismo: La transferencia de excedentes de América Latina', in J. Saxe-Fernández et al. *Globalización, imperialismo y clase social*. Buenos Aires and México: Editorial Lúmen.

Zibechi, R. (2012). *Territories in resistance*. Oakland, CA/Edinburgh: AK Press.

# 5

# ARGENTINA

## The return of the Right

*With Mario Hernández[1]*

The new millennium in Latin America witnessed what has been generally described as a progressive cycle of policy measures implemented by a scattering of centre-left post-neo-liberal regimes that rode a wave of social discontent and rejection of the neo-liberal model that had been in place since the early 1980s in much of the region. This pink and red wave of progressive policies reflected a fundamental change in the correlation of class forces that prevailed in the 1980s. The political left in the form of the labour movement and the land struggle had been thoroughly defeated, and the right-wing opposition in many countries rallied to take advantage of the opening for a neo-liberal policy regime as per the Washington Consensus provided by a neoconservative counter-revolution and the intervention of the World Bank and the IMF. In the 1990s, the rise and collective actions taken by powerful anti-neo-liberal social movements in the countryside changed the correlation of force in the class struggle. Neo-liberal regimes were put on the defensive, creating conditions that the political left saw as an opportunity for achieving state power, which they did in a number of countries in South America. First in Venezuela, then in Argentina and Brazil, and then in Bolivia and Ecuador, the regimes that rode the wave of discontent with neo-liberalism created by the social movements implemented a progressive policy agenda. But as we noted in Chapter 4 this progressive cycle appears to have come to and end with another pendulum swing in the correlation of forces engaged in the class struggle.

We will examine the changing dynamics of this struggle in the context of Argentina. First, we review developments associated with the 'progressive' regime of the Kirchners established in conditions of economic crisis that spelled the end of the neo-liberal policy agenda. We then review some salient features of the presidential elections that spelled the end of the Kirchner regime. We then proceed by outlining the programme and expectations of the newly elected hard-right, neo-liberal Mauricio Macri and then proceed to analyse the implementation and impact of his

## 80 Argentina: the return of the Right

measures on the class structure and the class struggle during Macri's first six months in power (Aznárez, 2016). The third part of the chapter reviews the dynamics of a new emerging class struggle from below.

## The Kirchner regime: taking stock of a decade of 'progressive' policies[2]

The events of 19 and 20 December 2001, the culmination of a long cycle of class struggle since the uprisings in the 1990s (Cutral-Co, Tartagal, Mosconi) should be understood as an insurrection in the strict sense, i.e. as a challenge of the masses to the authority of the bourgeois state. It was the first time in Argentina's history in which a mass mobilization got rid of a democratically established government. The uprising also ended the convertibility of the peso (at parity with the dollar), although privatization, flexible labour and the export orientation of big capital, among many others, would remain structural features of Argentine capitalism. Nor does it mean that workers were better off in terms of their immediate interests. For one thing, their wages would lose on average about a third of their purchasing power as a result of the 2002 devaluation. But none of this belies the fact that the insurrection ended the assault against labour launched by the big bourgeoisie and the neo-liberal Menem regime in the 1990s

In some countries like Bolivia and Venezuela it is easy to find a line of continuity between those in the early years of the new millennium who staged the popular rebellion against the neo-liberal policy agenda and then took over the government. In Argentina, however, the leadership group within the political class that rose to the challenge provided by the anti-neo-liberal social movements not only did not participate in the popular rebellion but was part of the government and neo-liberal regime, though it fell apart. We could say that a part of the political and ruling class managed to adjust to the new scenario created by the popular movement.

The first concern of the Kirchner government, formed in the midst of an economic and political crisis, was to re-establish political order. This task had two dimensions. First, it meant the reconstitution of consensus in the exercise of political power as the basis for stabilizing the political and economic dominion of capital. As it turns out, this meant equating the economic and political interests of the capitalist class as a whole with the interests of society in response to a crisis that affected all classes. But it also meant the need to build consensus around the figure of the new president (Nestor Kirchner, or NK), who was saddled with a weakness deriving from the crisis of the post-2001 political system. After the crisis broke out, the two great historical parties, the UCR and the PJ, confronted the presidential elections of 2003 in a fragmented state – and a crisis of political representation. The UCR response to this crisis crystallized in the formation of several new political forces. As for the PJ, which represented what was left of the once-powerful Peronist party, it presented three internal candidates for the position of president, including the neo-liberal former president Carlos Menem, who had the backing of the party Congress. Under these conditions, NK gained the presidency with 22 per cent of the popular vote, plunging the country into a crisis of representation.

Argentina: the return of the Right **81**

Kirchnerism did not represent the anti-neo-liberal resistance but rather the forces of order. That is, he became president in order to complete the task of restoring order that his predecessor, Eduardo Duhalde, had begun with significant success. The first step was the forced devaluation of the peso, which ended the convertibility of the peso in early 2002.

By way of its inflationary effect, the devaluation imposed in real terms a deep cut in wages, which, combined with cuts in utilities rates and energy prices and interest rates, resulted in a significant recovery in the profitability of productive capital. This was due to the strengthening of the competitiveness of export-oriented capital and the protection of capital that is less competitive and oriented towards the domestic market.

This devaluation, combined with the improved terms of trade in the world market, led to a sustained expansion of exports and a record trade surplus. And this export expansion, combined with an increase in the pace of economic recovery, generated a fiscal surplus and the accumulation of foreign exchange reserves.

Renegotiation and containment in real terms of tariffs for public utilities and energy prices and fuel in return for concessions regarding remaining contractual and regulatory matters, and the liberal use of subsidies to promote both investment and consumption, were the measures taken in response to the crisis of the system of privatized and franchised businesses. Broadly speaking, the restoration of order that prompted these measures had been completed by the end of 2005, i.e. during the government of Nestor Kirchner. From 2007 or 2008 onwards, however, these measures reached their limits and were replaced by others that would be much less successful implemented by the governments of Cristina Fernández de Kirchner.

## Convertibility and wages

It is possible to distinguish two stages in the convertibility of the national currency: the first from 1991 to 1994 and the second from 1995 onwards. Between 1995 and 2001, real wages fell below the 1991 level, which had fallen to below 60 per cent of purchasing power achieved in 1970. Under these conditions the relative impoverishment of many urban workers and the rural proletariat gave way to absolute impoverishment, and the growing concentration of capital led to the proletarianization and impoverishment of a larger stratum of the middle class – what statisticians in Argentina have termed the 'new poor' (Petras & Veltmeyer, 2002a, 2002b).

In this context, the ability of the state to exercise its hegemonic political control function vis-à-vis an anti-hegemonic movement of unemployed workers had been weakened, confronting the regime with the beginnings of a process of social mobilization, particularly of the urban middle class. The formation of the Front for Victory (FPV), a broad centre-left electoral alliance forged by Nestor Kirchner in 2003 can be linked to this process of mobilization of the middle-class.

An analysis of the evolution of the class struggle in 2001 shows that the state's mechanisms of coercion in regard to sectors of the middle strata, insurgent unemployed workers (who also began to take over factories abandoned or closed down

## 82 Argentina: the return of the Right

by their owners) and the urban poor failed miserably, forcing the government to make a number of concessions. For these sectors, hyperinflation was no longer the threat that it once was. Even so, the working class was trapped between fragmentation and the threat of unemployment or precarization.

### The new expansionary phase beginning in late 2002

As of 2002, improved terms of trade and the sharp reduction in real terms of public spending led to a surplus on both the current and fiscal account – the so-called 'twin surpluses'. At the same time, by defaulting on the external debt owed to the IMF and other creditors the government had at its disposal a huge pool of fiscal resources, which it used to finance a programme of social reforms and productive investment, giving rise to a process of economic growth, buoyed by the primary commodities boom on the world market, that was sustained until 2012, when the boom went bust.

The increased availability of fiscal resources, combined with the end of convertibility and the subordination of the Central Bank and the Ministry of Economy to the executive, gave the government a greater capacity to respond to diverse social demands and to arbitrate between fractions of capital. This was one aspect of the mode of accumulation promoted by the government. A second aspect of this mode of capital accumulation was the question of financial dependency. To the extent that the combination of devaluation and high commodity prices maintained a high trade surplus, to which was added in the short term a reduction in interest payments on the foreign debt, the balance of the current account surplus. In the first instance this led to a reduced dependence on capital inflows and money at a lower rate of external debt, a condition reflected in the evolution of the capital account. It was expected that in the medium term higher interest payments and a reduced trade surplus, even without a fall in international commodity prices, would turn into a current account deficit. At that point, the rhythm and continuity of accumulation would again depend on the inflow of private capital (foreign direct investment) and access to capital markets. That is, the accumulation model in place still presented an element of latent financial fragility.

While the government's policy, by means of what has been described as 'inclusionary state activism', changed in a 'progressive' direction vis-à-vis the distribution of wealth and income, the central features of the accumulation mode had not changed. Hence the reference by the leftist economist Katz (2008) to a 'repeated decade'. The reference here was to the 'reproduction of structural imbalances in Argentine dependent capitalism at all levels'. This was evident in a regressive tax policy, conditions of debt payment resulting in under-capitalization, expansion of soy primarization and mineral and petroleum extractivism with all of its pitfalls, perpetuation of a concentrated and very unbalanced industrial structure, and a financial system that blocks investment. In other words, a progressive social policy belied the hidden fact that the fundamental pillars of social inequality that had prevailed in Argentina for decades still remained in place. Nor had there been a pattern

Argentina: the return of the Right **83**

of expanded productive investment – to turn the economy away from external financial dependence and an extractivist strategy that has resulted in increased dependence on external financing, destruction of the environment and rural livelihoods, and growing political conflicts in the countryside. For the case of Paraguay, see Chapter 9.

After 12 years of the Kirchner regime there were no significant innovations or improvement in the structure of production, and this is notwithstanding a pattern of significant growth in public investment made possible by a sustained external trade surplus and a bonanza of additional fiscal resources derived from the default on the accumulated debt from the 1990s and increased exports of the country's agri-mineral resources. Public investment between 2002 and 2014 saw a fourfold increase in its share of the GDP – from 0.9 per cent in 2002 to 3.7 per cent in 2014. However, the payback or recovery in the rate of productive investment was quite slow. For one thing, the rate of private capital formation or productive investment throughout this period was low – only 16 per cent from 2004 to 2008, and around 13.5 per cent thereafter. As for public productive investment, this increased fourfold from 2002 to 2014, its contribution to GDP increasing from 0.9 per cent in 2002 to 3.7 per cent in 2014. The rate of gross domestic fixed investment (IBIF) grew from 8 per cent in 2002 to 21 per cent in 2014, but even so the contribution of public productive investment under the Kirchner regime was limited. Its contribution to the GDP reached 20 per cent in 2006 – which was quite low in comparison with, say, Chile. It continued to grow in the following years, reaching a ceiling of 21.7 per cent in 2008 before beginning to fall the next year as a result of the global financial crisis. In 2011 it would finally exceed the 2008 level, reaching 22.7 per cent of GDP. But since then the level of productive investment has substantially fallen, reflecting the end of the commodities boom on which the government had come to depend for its financial resources.

Also, evident in the period 2002–14 was a huge increase in the rate of profit on the investment made by the large domestic and foreign companies that reaped profits far in excess of their investment. An important part of these profit gains, however, were based on the acquisition of foreign exchange rather than productive investment, and took the form of capital flight rather than productive reinvestment. The recovery in the rate of profit was also the result in part of a fall in real terms of tariffs for gas, electricity etc. and lower interest rates. These facts, to which should be added the result of the renegotiation of the foreign debt, account for a change in the correlation of forces between different fractions of capital. This change favoured productive capital, especially in the export-oriented sector, to the detriment of financial capital and sectors whose insertion into the economy was based on the acquisition of the shares of privatized state enterprises. This change in the balance of forces is correlated with an increase in the relative autonomy of the state.

The trend since 2003 towards the further growth of MIO (manufactures of industrial origin) relative to MOA (manufactures of agricultural origin) and primary exports is a feature of continuity, and not a break with the restructuring process initiated in the 1990s. Wherein, then, is the specificity of this period? First, the

**84** Argentina: the return of the Right

devaluation acted as an umbrella that allowed for a certain degree of import substitution industrialization. However, unlike in the classical period of the 1930s to mid-1970s, the import substitution was articulated with the predominantly export orientation of the big industrial bourgeoisie of highly standardized products and relatively low added value. The hypothesis that is most consistent with the available data is that the accumulation process in this period has been predominantly capital-intensive, and that economic growth since 2003 has been based on the foundation of the capital restructuring process in the 1990s. This was made possible in a context of high exchange rates and historically low labour costs. The predominantly capital-extensive character capital investment explains the strong employment growth, i.e. the high employment/product elasticity relative to the 1990s – at least until 2007 – and the consequent fall in unemployment. In turn, the fall in unemployment in a context of historically low labour costs was a condition of rising real wages – from 2002 to 2007, when the growth in the labour force/employment as well as the gradual but steady increase in real wages came to an abrupt end. At this point the period of relatively successful negotiations over wages between the government and organized labour also came to an end, with the demand for higher wages exceeding the tacit limits set by the government. The impact of this change in the labour–state relationship on the class struggle is discussed below.

### The growth of employment and the collective bargaining power of workers

The volume of production increased threefold from 1991–98 to 2003–11. The counterpart to these data was the strong rise in employment and the fall in unemployment, an essential aspect of the reconstruction of political consensus. The employment rate increased from 38.8 per cent in the third quarter of 2003 to 43.4 per cent in the third quarter of 2011, while the unemployment rate decreased from 16.1 per cent in the second quarter of 2003 to 7.3 per cent in the second quarter of 2011.

This fall in unemployment was the foundation of the recovery in the power of the working class to demand change, evident in the pattern of real wage growth, especially since 2005, especially for private-sector workers and employees. The combination of reduced productivity gains, a fall in hours worked per worker, and the recovery of real wages, led to a fall in the rate of exploitation in the industrial sector and likely also in other productive activities.

Overall, these findings suggest that the fall in unemployment and the strengthening of the bargaining position of workers have allowed workers to improve their situation – an increase in real wages, a lower rate of exploitation, greater participation in the social product, even a decline in inequality according to some measures – but did not reverse the results of the strong offensive launched against the working class in the 1980s (via hyperinflation) and the first half of the 1990s. However, this improvement implies that the process of capital accumulation was based on a more favourable correlation of force for the working class than in the 1990s. But this correlation of force, in turn, only made its way through state action, and this is where the analysis of the specific political dimension of economic policy and its relationship to the dynamics of capital accumulation becomes important.

The implementation of the government's Heads of Household Plan during Eduardo Duhalde's administration, and the return to more targeted social policies during the early years of the Kirchner presidency, sought to contain the social and political impact of rising inequality and poverty resulting from the crisis. Welfare, employment growth and the recovery of middle-class consumption supported a reactivation of the accumulation process and articulating it with the reconstruction of political legitimacy. However, the pressure on government and capital to permit wages to rise only began to be felt in 2005, along with a sharp increase in labour and trade union conflicts.

Beyond cyclical and conjunctural trends, the labour conflict between 2003 and 2010 maintained essential features, notwithstanding the increased capacity of the government to both contain and channel the forces mobilized in the struggle. The movements of unemployed workers (*los piqueteros*) were the protagonists of the 2001 cycle of mobilizations, and the number of collective actions taken by these movements in its struggle against the state grew until 2003. A first quantitative approximation shows that the number of collective actions after rising in 2004 fell in 2005 and especially in 2006, after which the level of class conflict never reached the levels attained in the first two years. Below we provide some more detail on this dynamic of class struggle. Also, the radicality of class actions declines sharply. Radical actions (*cortas de ruta*, occupations, takeovers etc.) represent over 80 per cent of the actions taken by workers in 2004 and 2005, less than 40 per cent of actions in 2006 and only 30 per cent thereafter (Petras & Veltmeyer, 2002a). These data demonstrate the government's success in normalizing the conflict of the movement of unemployed workers.

## The significance of Lavagna's departure

Overall, economic policy under the Kirchners was articulated with an accumulation process driven by the export of primary commodities and products with low added value and based on relatively low labour costs. Tensions between economic policy and the capital accumulation process began to appear in 2005 and, from this perspective the departure of Economy Minister Roberto Lavagna was a significant event. The dispute between the Ministry of Economy and the Minister of Planning and Labour that led to the resignation of Lavagna had as its axis fiscal and wage policy. Lavagna's position was in the direction of moderating the expansion of public spending and containing wage increases. This last point was particularly important in the context of a return to joint negotiations since 2004 and increased labour conflict to levels not seen since the late 1980s.

The departure of Lavagna is symptomatic of the point where the logic of reconstruction of political consensus on the path of gradual satisfaction of popular demands came into conflict with an accumulation strategy driven by exports and

**86** Argentina: the return of the Right

limited industrialization supported by lower wage costs. But even this scenario of timid gradual concessions to the working class cannot be separated from the need to rebuild the legitimacy of political power after years of a downward trend and major conflicts between 2004 and 2005 staged by different fractions of the employed working class – telephone and railway workers, etc.

The end, in 2007, of this period of harmonization between the capital accumulation process and concessions made to the working class showed that the logic of accumulation based on low wage costs has its limits regarding the class hegemony based on this logic. First, wage increases higher than productivity gains and fluctuations in the exchange rate negatively affected the competitiveness of capital. Second, monetary policy became more expansionary by currency intervention owing to increases in the exchange rate in conditions of a trade surplus and the so-called 'Dutch disease', and monetary policy validation of the increased costs of labour.

One policy response of the government to this post-devaluation scenario was to subsidize transportation, energy and other utility costs as a way of tamping down social unrest and growing political conflict while maintaining the institutional and policy framework of privatization. But, to the extent that the increase in the cost of privatized utilities and services came into conflict with the construction and maintenance of political consensus, the pressure of rising costs could no longer be contained with further subsidies, leading to an acceleration in the rate of inflation and a fiscal crisis. As of 2008, and particularly since 2010, this has become a serious problem, one element in the recurrence of fiscal deficits.

The gap between economic policy and capital accumulation developed fully after 2007. In this regard, the 2008 conflict with the agrarian bourgeoisie and the changing international context signalled a new twist in that relationship. What expresses this gap? A change in the correlation of forces favourable to workers on the basis of which the governing regime after the crisis had to reconstruct its relation of political power over contending forces in society and the political arena. This constitutive dimension of the state – the reconstitution and reproduction of its political power – overdetermines economic policy and makes it difficult, if not impossible, for the state to maintain a balance between its 'ideal typical' functions regarding economic policy and the requirements of capitalist accumulation.

It is noteworthy that the government tried to reduce subsidies and limit wage increases with little success, having to retreat from a massive and potentially explosive rejection, until the years 2013 and 2014, years in which the government was forced to make a gradual wage adjustment and to reduce several subsidies in the midst of a recession and increasing difficulties in the external sector.

The main change in recent years is that, despite the deceleration of the economic growth process, which was sustained – from 2003 to 2012 – by the export of agri-mineral commodities, unemployment fell drastically, reducing the pressure of labour on the government. This is an important qualitative change in Argentine capitalism that directly affects the situation of the working class, although we must bear in mind that the struggles of the period do not go beyond immediate economic issues.

While the neo-liberal policies imposed by the Menem administration in the 1990s were based on the political defeat of the working class and the hyperinflation of the late 1980s, the events of 2001 were not a defeat; it was lived as a popular triumph, and what followed was the realization of the popular force to oust the government. The governments of Nestor Kirchner and Cristina Fernández managed to channel and counteract that force, with the power of the vote on the one hand and on the other the threat of forcing the removal of opposition politicians from office via popular mobilisation (*amenaza destituyente*). In the end the voices raised from within the ramparts of participatory democracy and popular assemblies in 2001 were almost entirely silenced or trapped within the institutional framework of representative, formal bourgeois democracy. This was one of the main tasks carried out by the Kirchners.

This was possible because they advanced policies that responded to the situation of crisis lived by all sectors of the population, in both the working and middle classes. The political left did not have any policies that went beyond Kirchernism, allowing the Kirchners almost a free hand in the project to channel and institution-alize the forces of popular resistance. First, we can observe a significant increase in consumption in the post-crisis period. This fact, associated with the phases of recovery and growth, impacted especially on the middle class with access to credit and the acquisition of durable goods. Second, the policies of the regime signifi-cantly decreased levels of unemployment and underemployment. Simultaneously, they increased the real wages of all workers, although for workers in the private sector there was a recovery of pre-devaluation levels. In the case of unregistered private- and public-sector workers, a strong delay compared with the fourth quarter of 2001 persists. Since 2003 the government has been able to use its powers of coercion, including the threat of hyperinflation and high unemployment, and con-cessions to the working class to forge a broad consensus and hold the subordinate classes in line. The consensus has been maintained mainly because of the govern-ment's ability to grant concessions and bring about gradual improvements in the social condition of the subaltern classes

## *The re-composition of state power*

The first Kirchner government was able to rebuild the power of the state through the construction of a broad consensus between 2003–07. Cristina's government managed to reconstruct this consensus after the so-called 'agrarian conflict' (*conflicto de campo*) that broke out in 2008. In both cases, consensus was achieved by the means of a gradual satisfaction of the middle class's demand for a restoration of democracy and the popular resistance and working-class opposition to the govern-ment's neo-liberal policy agenda that led the country into a period of economic and political crisis. But the *conflicto del campo* divided the political waters, hence the attempt to put in place a neo-developmentalist strategy, which required the state to capture a greater share of resource rents (revenues derived from the export of soy-beans), the reintroduction of a state monopoly of foreign trade, and the end of

## 88  Argentina: the return of the Right

subsidizing a bourgeoisie more concerned with currency speculating and exporting its capital than making productive investments.

The issue of agriculture in Argentina's economy and the transformations generated by 'agribusiness' in recent decades came to the fore with the confrontation between Kirchner and the agrarian elite that formed the Liaison Bureau in the first year of Cristina Fernández de Kirchner's mandate. The government then faced defeat because it could not impose Resolution 125 or further increase its share of agricultural resource rents. In the political arena, the result was more uneven. Although the missteps taken by the government and the problems generated by the impact of the global crisis of 2008–09 increased the wind under the sails of opposition groups inside and outside Peronism in the 2009 elections, the government maintained a hard core of support that, aided by the mystique generated by this conflict, allowed it to recover from this mini-crisis in 2010. At the bottom of this fight within the government and the political class was that Kirchner needed cash to allow her to both represent the general interest of society and reconcile the conflicting interests of different factions of the bourgeoisie. And for this she needed to appropriate a greater share of the resource rents derived from the operations of agro-extractive capital and the export of soy and other commodities. At issue here was the potential additional income derived from the technological advance related to the production of transgenic soybeans, which allowed for a quantum leap in labour productivity, which in turn reduced by half the hours demanded by farming while the planted area doubled. The government was intent on capturing a significant part of the revenues derived from these productivity gains and primary commodities boom. The agro-export elite (*el campo* in the conflict), on the other hand, also wanted to capture a larger share of this income, which multiplied like manna from heaven thanks to the high prices of agricultural commodities on the world market. What we have here basically is a dispute between different capitalist interests, in which the workers and popular sectors were mere bystanders, their aspirations and interests ignored.

A key development in this conjuncture of conflicting interests was the reversal over the last decade of a long multi-decade trend for the terms of trade between the products exported from the periphery and from the centre of the world system to deteriorate. Since 2002, the prices of commodities and raw materials in particular have tended to increase significantly, leading to an improvement in the terms of trade with a positive impact on Argentina's balance of trade. This phenomenon is linked to the impact on the global market of the growth of the Chinese economy and to a lesser extent that of India.

If in other historical moments the asymmetric competition faced by big and small capitalists in agriculture led to conflicting interests, the conversion of many small and medium producers into rentiers led many of these rentiers to go along with the big landlords and the agro-export elite in their capacity as owners, and to form a common front against the government in its attempt to increase their share of agricultural rents.

The defeat of Kirchner in the 2008 agrarian conflict was less a question of the homogeneity and social strength of the bloc that opposed it than a disproportion between the alleged 'epic battle' fought by the government against the oligarchy as outlined in the government's discourse and the actual scope of the dispute. The dispute over the government's 'retention' of agricultural rents, its nationalization of AFJP (the pension and retirement fund) and the confrontation with some sectors of the financial bourgeoisie over the use of central bank reserves undoubtedly responds to the need for fiscal resources in order for the government to maintain its subsidies to companies and, to a lesser extent, to pay the foreign debt. But it is significant that that was the government's policy response rather than fiscal adjustment. Kirchner's strategy here was to try to contain the tensions and political conflict through a combination of currency devaluation accompanied by higher interest rates and the use of its firepower based on functional finance and the acceleration of public spending. The aim was to postpone the pressure on the exchange rate and avoid a new sharp devaluation before the national elections in late October, which, as it turned out, she lost, and also to counteract the general decline in the profitability of capital by increasing the fiscal deficit.

## Bourgeois nationalism fails again: from boom to stagnation

As of 2008, Kirchnerism lacked the resources and economic achievements that characterized the 2003–07 stage of economic recovery. The rate of economic growth had begun to slow down, inflation began to depress wages and the ability of the labour market to integrate a growing workforce was seriously reduced. To some extent, this situation was due to the global crisis of capitalism as well as the geoeconomics of capital in the region. In any case, it posed a major challenge to the reformist neo-development model used by the centre-left governments that had assumed state power at the turn of the new millennium by riding a wave of anti-neo-liberal sentiment generated by the social movements. The inclusionary state activism and progressive policy stance of the post-neo-liberal regimes (increased social spending, etc.) – including the Kirchner regime – formed in the new conjuncture of the capitalist development process in Latin America was only possible because of a highly favourable international economic situation.

In the emergence of these processes there was the confluence of diverse forces and changing conditions. One of these was the virtual collapse of the traditional political parties that had been the guarantee of capitalist stability for decades in Latin America. Then there were high growth rates based on the commodities boom, low inflation and budgets that were balanced or even in surplus. Under these conditions, according to economists at the United Nations Economic Commission for Latin America and the Caribbean (ECLAC, 2015), almost 50 million people in the region were lifted out of poverty over the course of the last decade. Poverty had decreased, from 43.9 to 28.1 per cent of the population, between 2002 and 2012, although the structure of social inequality, and the social polarization between the rich and poor, remained the same, and Latin America continued to be the most unequal region on the planet.

**90** Argentina: the return of the Right

In conditions of the global capitalist crisis, the political economy of national development in Latin American economy changed dramatically. In the new context the various 'nationalist' development and policy experiments in the region, including the one furthered by the Kirchners, failed in an attempt to structure an independent economy and state – to escape the clutches of global capital (dependence on foreign direct investment and capital markets) and initiate a process of autonomous industrialization, destroying the supremacy of finance capital. Rather than creating a national bourgeoisie, what was created instead was a 'boli-bourgeoisie' (in Venezuela) or the 'crony capitalism' of the Kirchners that bled financially to the state. In the nationalizations that took place, the companies received compensations from the state that exceeded what the market would have paid (Sidor, YPF). In any case, the state, or more precisely the Kirchner regime, controlled or managed collectively the nationalized property but did not touch the banks.

Global crises provide opportunities for developing countries but to take advantage of these opportunities requires a policy independent of both the national bourgeoisie should one exist and global capital in the form of multinational corporations and foreign direct investment. The additional fiscal resources provided by the extraction of its natural resource wealth and the export of these resources in primary commodity form allowed some governments such as Venezuela and Bolivia to finance major health and education campaigns and poverty reduction programmes, but it did not permit them or lead them to lay the economic foundations of national autonomy and support a long-term plan for an alternative, more viable form of national development. The cycle of progressive policies in the region financed by natural resource rents is over. Programmes of limited tax reforms, royalties and increased taxes on oil and gas, and other natural resources extracted from the multinational companies in the extractive sector offered a temporary advantage in the context of the primary commodities boom. But now that the boom has gone bust, as these booms always do, and the era of high international prices for the commodities, especially oil, is over – at least for now – the inclusionary state activism that has characterized the progressive cycle is also over, creating conditions for the return of the Right to power.

This less favourable context created by the current conjuncture in the capitalist development process exposed the limits of the neo-developmentalist project that the Kirchners had pursued. Faced with the evident limits of this political project and the Kirchner regime, dominant factions in the political class increased their opposition to the regime in the hope of forcing changes in the correlation of forces and promote changes in government policies that would allow them to avoid the growing fiscal deficit and the dollar shortage.

In what could be called the first phase of instability, Kirchner sought to shore up the weakening economy (the decline in the rate of economic growth) through increased public spending based on an easing of monetary policy and the appropriation of funds from non-tax sources. This did indeed result in some economic recovery in the period 2009 to 2011. It was combined with an expansion of pension coverage, the implementation of the Universal Child Allowance (AUH) and policies to allow for increased borrowing (and the assumption of household debt) to offset wage stagnation. These policies were reflected in an election result of 54 per cent for the re-election of Cristina Fernández de Kirchner in 2011.

## The demise of the Kirchner regime

The political imperative for the Kirchner regime to extend its stay in power forced it to face the systemic need for fiscal and external adjustment, a condition of which was devaluation of the currency. This transition to this policy regime began in late 2011 with the 'fine-tuning' of a heterodox adjustment marked by political control over the exchange market, a policy that was deepened in late 2013 with the appointment of Axel Kiciloff as minister of economy.

The devaluation of the peso in early 2014, a gradual return to the international financial capital market with payment to the Paris Club, compensation of Repsol for the partial expropriation of YPF, a financial agreement with China, allowing for the growth of consumption based on the expansion of personal debt (via the Procrear, Procreauto, Argenta card and Ahora 12 plans) and raising the wage ceilings were the key policy tools used in this new stage.

The transition towards this new policy regime took place in an increasingly negative global and regional environment. Brazil, Argentina's largest trading partner, is stagnating and embroiled in a possibly terminal economic and political crisis. The economic growth of China, Argentina's second-largest trading partner, has begun to slow down, and the US has raised interest rates. The government in this context turned towards a policy of increasing international reserves to pay for the growing external debt and imports, and fiscal adjustment policies of personal debt to maintain the social peace, but this policy collided with a stagnant economy and an investment strike from big capital, which decided to accentuate its demands for a structural adjustment and to await the elections of 2016.

Organizations in the popular sectors do not have an alternative policy programme and continue to bet on the 'lesser evil'. The auspicious electoral convergence of the Left's anti-capitalist forces in the form of the Workers' Left Front (FIT) is not enough to form a mass option in the electoral field. With its limitations this convergence is part of a medium-term bet to build political unity in a diversity of political practices and traditions within a broad strategy of popular power.

Groups like Pueblo en Marcha, a party built from within the popular movements by the Frente Popular Darío Santillán, Socialist Democracy and the Movement for Latin American Unity and Social Change (MULCS) or the Popular Movement Dignity, which participated in the Worker's Left Front (FIT) in the April 2015 elections, set up a debate on the possibility of advancing towards a new coalescence of political forces on the left. This left pole should be based on the agreement to form an anti-capitalist political front, independence from the government in power and the rejection of all projects of class conciliation. The construction of this front should be comprehensive, with one foot in the mobilization of popular power and the other in the electoral struggle for state power.

In April 2016, the editor of *Le Monde Diplomatique* wrote that

> The Kirchners, regardless of the outcome of the October elections, remain a political culture ... the major political orientations of the last decade – state intervention, social policies, Latin Americanism, human rights – constitute a core of values shared by most of society.

Further, Eduardo Jozami (2015) in *El futuro del kirchnerismo* (*The Future of Kirchnerism*) argued that

> we should not be fear an opposition victory nor of the current governor of the province of Buenos Aires (Scioli), since the reforms of the last decade would be so deep and have achieved so much social consensus to be considered irreversible.

Nevertheless, for the Left the legacy of Kirchnerism regarding consciousness and organization is disappointing.

There are two ways of promoting social inclusion: snatching businesses away from the bourgeoisie or distributing super-profits, which appear to be the same but are not. Those who merely distribute super-profits are left exposed inexorably to neo-liberal adjustment policies, because they have to maintain the profits of the bourgeoisie, which controls businesses a whole. Brazil's Lula and Dilma are good examples of this.

The collapse of the Kirchnerist political project goes hand in hand with never having been able to go beyond the horizon of building a slightly less bad capitalism. Furthermore, over the decade Kirchnerism paved the way for the emergence of a political and social movement with a strong conservative bent structured around traditional sectors of the upper middle and upper class: landowners, the infamous *corpo* (economic groups tied to the opposition), institutional groups (sectors of the judiciary), etc. These sectors were able to dominate the streets on several occasions in 2008, with the conflict in the countryside in 2012, with *cacelorazos* against the dollar and stocks in 2015 and in the Nisman case. This political-social conservative movement at different times managed to capitalize on the weakening of the government's ties to its social base. This is how the Right won the legislative elections in 2009 in the province of Buenos Aires (De Narváez) and returned to it again in 2013 (Massa).

The Right, through the mediation of the conservative political-social movement, managed to occupy the political vacuum left by the crisis of Kirchnerism. Its legacy is Macrismo but in a radically different context. Without an organic crisis and considerable legitimacy in some circles, or legitimacy at the beginning, Macrismo promises to deepen the adjustment to correct various imbalances in the capitalist project and recover the macroeconomic conditions for an expanded process of capital accumulation. This will mean or necessitate an accelerated devaluation of the local currency, an exacerbation of the external debt and above all a reduction in fiscal spending on subsidies and social programmes, reduced consumption and various austerity measures that will bring about a downward 'adjustment' of wages and the cost of labour, in other words adjusting the working classes to the requirements and dictates of capital. However, it would appear that the popular resistance to this agenda has already started and the class struggle has joined in.

## President Macri and the neo-liberal rollback

In the upper-income neighbourhoods of Buenos Aires there was singing and dancing in the streets on the night of 15 November 2015 as the presidential election results rolled in and Mauricio Macri was pronounced the victor. Wall Street, the City of London and their financial mouthpieces, the *Wall Street Journal* and the *Financial Times*, announced the coming of a new era, and the end of 'anti-investor, populism and nationalism [and] wasteful social spending', referring to the increases in pensions, family allowances and wages approved by the previous, centre-left, government.

To put this enthusiastic response in perspective Macri does not merely represent the plutocracy; he is one of its richest members. He not only boasts of a 'carnal relationship' with Washington, in his acceptance speech he pleased Obama by announcing he would work to expel Venezuela from Mercosur, Latin America's foremost regional economic integration organization.

Announcing a cabinet made up of a uniform collection of neo-liberal economists, former supporters of the military dictatorship and even a rabid right-wing rabbi, he then spelled out his policy agenda, which was cleverly hidden during his electoral campaign, in which his raucous rhetoric for 'change' spoke to everybody and nobody.

He promised to end capital controls, export taxes and retentions on agro-business exports; devalue the peso and pay the Wall Street speculator Paul Singer over $1.2 billion in debt that he bought for $49 million dollars; privatize and denationalize the state-owned airline, oil company and pension funds; sign off on EU- and US-centred free trade agreements, thus undermining Latin America integration projects like Mercosur; terminate a joint memo of understanding with Iran so as to investigate a terror bombing as requested by Israel; and expel Venezuela from Mercosur.

The millionaire playboy president called for harsh austerity for the working class and bountiful handouts for the economic elite.

The day after the elections local and overseas speculators boosted Argentine stocks 40 per cent, anticipating a free-market bonanza. George Soros and hedge fund mogul Daniel Loeb 'piled into Argentine assets'. Investment fund managers incited Macri to act swiftly in implementing what they dubbed 'sweeping reforms' before mass popular resistance was organized to stymie his policies.

However, Macri's Wall Street and Washington patrons are well aware that their client's boisterous big business bombast faces serious political obstacles because his policies will provoke severe economic hardships. For one thing – apart from the massive resistance his policies will provoke among the working class and in

**94** Argentina: the return of the Right

the popular sector – Macri does not have a majority in Congress to approve his radical proposals. Congress is controlled by a coalition of right-wing and centre-left Peronist parties that will have to be co-opted, bought or coerced.

Congress would balk at supporting Macri's entire neo-liberal agenda, and he would have to violate the constitution by resorting to 'executive decrees' to bypass Congress, which will be contested in the courts, streets and legislature. It is doubtful that he will be able to face down all his critics and implement his radical neo-liberal agenda. Also, the head of the Central Bank, Alejandro Vanoli, appointed by the previous, centre-left Fernández government, is not likely to be amenable to Macri's tight money policy, radical devaluation and fiscal austerity. Macri would have to – and undoubtedly will – invent flimsy pretexts to purge the incumbent public officials and appoint free-market ideologues.

Macri ignored the institutional damage that his authoritarian approach would have and the likelihood of an increase in the public's sense of a lawless regime willing to trample constitutional rules to impose his free-market dogma. But Macri's ending of the tax retention on agro-exports had a boomerang effect as it decreased government revenues, exacerbating the fiscal deficit and necessitating deeper reductions in social expenditures. The contrast between higher earnings for the agribusiness elite and lower living standards for labour was an invitation to greater class hostility and strife.

Even more decisive Macri's 'export strategy' was badly undermined by the low prices of Argentine commodity exports. Ending capital and price controls on his first day in office provoked a major devaluation, which now exceeds 60 per cent. This resulted in severe increases in the prices of consumer goods and increased profits for the export elites, while provoking mass unrest across the occupational spectrum.

Macri met with the 7 per cent of speculator holdouts who demanded full payment on Argentine's debt to them – the so-called 'vulture funds' led by Paul Singer of Elliott Capital Management. Macri's capitulation to the speculators and agreement to pay US$1.2 billion on an original US$49 million purchase of Argentine debt to Wall Street speculators provoked a firestorm of opposition from the vast majority of Argentine workers and employees who will shoulder the added burden. Moreover, the 93 per cent of debt holders who had agreed to the previous financial haircut of 70 per cent have demanded full payment according to the law, multiplying tenfold the demand on the treasury.

The devaluation and decline of domestic purchasing power did not attract a tidal wave of foreign investment to lift the economy and provide the jobs and general prosperity that Macri promised. Foreign capital inflows did not create new enterprises; they concentrated on buying existing privatized public enterprises. Incoming capital did not expand the forces of production; it only shifted the direction of the flow of profits from public coffers to private pockets, from the domestic economy to overseas investors.

The general foreign and domestic political climate is vastly different today from how it was in the 1990s, when the previous failed neo-liberal experiment was launched. In the late 1980s, Argentina suffered from acute inflation, stagnation and declining incomes, conditions that (together with Brazil and Peru under Fujimori) facilitated one of the most dramatic and drastic turns towards neo-liberalism in the region. Working-class organizations and the labour movement at the time were still recovering from a murderous decade of military rule. Moreover, in the 1990s the US was at the pinnacle of its power in Latin America (manifested in its capacity to dictate macroeconomic policy and bring most governments in line with its interests and foreign policy). China was only at the beginning of its dynamic growth cycle. The USSR had disintegrated and Russia was transformed into a vassal state. Latin America was ruled by a motley collection of neo-liberal clones under the thumb of the IMF.

But today Macri faces an entirely different scenario – the working class, trade unions and militant popular movements are organized and intact, having experienced a decade of substantial gains under a centre-left government. By the fourth month of his regime he was confronting a wave of strikes from Buenos Aires through Patagonia to Tierra del Fuego. The IMF experience is a poisonous memory. Hundreds of military officials responsible for crimes against humanity have been arrested, tried and prosecuted. The threat of a military coup, ever present in the 1980s and 1990s, is virtually non-existent. Macri's belligerency to Chinese fishing boats – the navy sank one of them – has created a major diplomatic incident, threatening the key market for Argentine agro-exports (soya). His declared passion to serve Washington could cause Macri to prejudice strategic commercial relations with China and bankrupt the agro-export elites. In this new situation, Macri's move to leave Mercosur and embrace the US-engineered Trans-Pacific Trade Partnership prejudices Argentina's strategic trade links with Brazil, Venezuela, Uruguay and Paraguay. Today Macri finds an inhospitable climate in Latin America for his embrace of the US. His proposal to expel Venezuela from Mercosur has already been rejected by its members.

Macri is finding it impossible to replicate the neo-liberal policies of the 1990s for all the above and one additional reason. The earlier experiment with free-market capitalism led to the most severe economic depression in Argentine history: double-digit negative growth, unemployment rates exceeding 50 per cent in working-class districts (and 25 per cent nationally), and rates of poverty and indigency that exceeded sub-Saharan Africa.

By the end of the first half-year of his regime, his neo-liberal policies are leading Argentina into another major crisis. To pay the extortionate demands of the vulture funds, Macri proposes to float a US$15 billion bond at upwards of 8 per cent, which would lead to the same debt cycle that led to the crash in 2000–01. The debt will not finance economic activity, which can provide revenues to pay back the loans; instead it will result in new and bigger borrowings. Already the regime talks of a further US$10 billion bond flotation, which even Wall Street cautions is 'too risky'.

Macri mistakenly believed that he could rush through a dose of 'harsh medicine' – and thus avoid the inevitable mass protest – and attract thereby a massive inflow of capital that would rapidly 'grow' the economy. He was gravely mistaken. After

## 96 Argentina: the return of the Right

the initial giveaways and uptake of the stock market, the Soros and Loeb speculators took their profits and left. Weakened domestic consumption and the depressed global commodity market did not attract long-term, large-scale productive capital.

First, a US Appeals Court ruled against the immediate lifting of sanctions based on the pact with the vulture funds. Second, earlier debt holders – the 93 per cent – are demanding full payment of the 65 per cent reduction. If successful, these claims will bankrupt the Macri regime. Third, the regime's 300 per cent increase in household expenses for gas and light, added to a major increase in taxes and 40 per cent devaluation and 30 per cent inflation in rents, food and clothing, has already pushed one million workers under the poverty line, according to a study by the National Council of Statistics, Science and Technology. Fourth, a wave of bankruptcies has rippled through the retail commerce sector and threatened to spread throughout the economy, doubling the unemployment rate. And, fifth, a massive strike wave has gained momentum, rippling out from the public sector to the private sector, culminating in a call by the three major labour confederations for a general strike. But the real question is not – as the financial pundits claimed when he was elected – whether Macri would 'seize the moment and his opportunity', but how soon his regime will crash amid the ruins of a depressed economy, raging inflation and general strikes.

The general foreign and domestic political climate is vastly different today than it was in the 1990s when the previous failed neo-liberal experiment was launched. In the late 1980s, Argentina suffered from acute inflation, stagnation and declining income, conditions that (together with Brazil and Peru under Fujimori) facilitated one of the most dramatic and drastic turns towards neo-liberalism in the region. Working-class organizations and the labour movement at the time were still recovering from a murderous decade of military rule. Moreover, in the 1990s the US was at the pinnacle of its power in Latin America (manifest in its capacity to dictate macroeconomic policy and bring most governments in line with its interests and foreign policy). China was only at the beginning of its dynamic growth cycle. The USSR had disintegrated and the resulting Russia was transformed into a vassal state. Latin America was ruled by a motley collection of neo-liberal clones under the thumb of the IMF.

However, today Macri faces an entirely different scenario – an organized working class, the trade unions and militant popular movements intact, having experienced a decade of substantial gains under a centre-left government. The IMF experience is but a poisonous memory. Hundreds of military officials responsible for crimes against humanity have been arrested, tried and prosecuted. The threat of a military coup, ever present in the 1980s and 1990s is non-existent. China has become the key market for Argentine agro-exports (soya). Despite his declared passion to serve Washington Macri is obligated to accommodate to China. In this new situation any move to leave Mercosur and embrace of the US-engineered Trans-Pacific Trade Partnership will prejudice Argentina's strategic trade links with Brazil, Venezuela, Uruguay and Paraguay. Today Macri will find a hostile climate in Latin America for his proposed embrace of the US. His proposal to expel Venezuela from Mercosur has already been rejected by its members.

In short, Macri will find it impossible to replicate the neo-liberal policies of the 1990s for all the above and one additional reason. The earlier experiment with free-market capitalism led to the most severe economic depression in Argentine history: double-digit negative growth, unemployment rates exceeding 50 per cent in working-class districts (and 25 per cent nationally), and rates of poverty and indigency that exceeded sub-Saharan Africa.

If Macri believes that he can rush through a dose of 'harsh medicine' – and thus avoid the inevitable mass protest – and attract thereby a massive inflow of capital that will rapidly 'grow' the economy, he is gravely mistaken. After the initial give-aways and uptake of the stock market, the Soros and Loeb speculators will take their profits and run. Weakening domestic consumption and a depressed global commodity market do not attract long-term, large-scale capital. The real question is not – as the financial pundits claim – whether Macri will 'seize the moment and his opportunity' but how soon after he tries to impose his free-market model his regime will crash amid the ruins of a depressed economy, raging inflation and general strikes.

## After six months of Macri working-class resistance is growing

Argentina has a long history of working-class struggles led by the Confederación General de Trabajadores (CGT) and the Association of State Workers (ATE). However, in the context of the war launched by capital and the state against the working class in the 1980s, and the sad history of subsequent tripartite deals with the state and capital, together with the corruption of the union leadership, many of whom enriched themselves at the expense of the social base, the CGT and the ATE have totally lost their legitimacy in leading the struggle of organized labour. But it turns out that the rise of Mauricio Macri to state power has helped to revive somewhat both the agency and the tattered reputation of Argentina's two major federations of organized workers.

On 10 March 2016, in response to the assault of the right-wing Macri regime on the working class in the form of various decrees to the effect of laying off thousands of state workers – 200,000 in just the first 100 days of Macri's regime – the Association of State Workers (ATE) held a plenary meeting of the country's 24 secretaries general, at which it was unanimously decided to continue the struggle on lines elaborated at the end of the year, which led to milestone mobilizations on 29 December and 29 February. Another outcome of the meeting was the declaration of a national day of struggle, with a series of strikes and mobilizations throughout the entire country a week later (16 March).

While the Association of State Workers (ATE-CTA) announced plans for a general strike, the agribusiness minister, Ricardo Buryaile, agreed to receive the workers of the Family Agriculture Secretariat, who had been camping for days in protest against their dismissal (part of a government plan to trim the public sector by laying off state workers). On this, Hugo 'Puppy' Godoy, secretary general of ATE, declared:

The situation is serious. In addition to the 16 dismissed workers in Jujuy, three of whom are ATE delegates, the authorities have given notice that on March 31 up to 13,000 contracts will be voided. This means closure. In other words, we have a triple problem: workers being laid off, destruction of a central government agency created to address the problems of poor farmers in our country, and pursuing the union that it represents, flagrantly violating the law. We will not allow this, so we are now in a state of permanent mobilization. The Agribusiness Minister will see us on Monday at 11:00, and depending on what happens at that meeting the assembly will decide what steps to follow.

Ana Laura Lastra, delegate of the Internal Board of ATE-INDEC (Buenos Aires province), confirms this situation:

The strike of February 24 was a huge sign that workers are willing to fight. It was the strongest demonstration of state workers from all over the country in years. The fear has begun to dissipate and we are overcoming the intimidation of the Macrista regime and the betrayal of UPCN policy. But between 24F and the new strike called for Wednesday the ATE leadership '*le dio aire al*' government, which launched a new wave of layoffs.

Luana Simioni, delegate of ATE-IOMA Board (Buenos Aires) also confirmed the current political climate:

In all ministries of the province of Buenos Aires there was massive resistance to layoffs and the holding of popular assemblies ('*procesos asamblearios*') not seen for a long time. For many the layoffs are at the limit of their tolerance. And there was a very good response from the permanent workers at the plant, especially where ATE were in command, in backing their comrades with insecure contracts ('*los precarios*'). The example of the Ministry of Social Development is one of the most emblematic struggles, having after 11 days of fighting managed to ensure the restatement of the laid-off workers. There can be found a very strong organization that is now denouncing the layoff of state workers at the Ministry and advancing the struggle for higher wages. And there were similar responses in many other agencies.

Both delegates participated in the open plenary, attended by more than 150 activists and state delegates to prepare the strike the following Wednesday (16 March). Also, ATE Capital convened for the following Monday a plenary of delegates open to all activists and laid-off workers to organize the strike, roadblocks and pickets to ensure that it would be as massive as the 24F strike. This general assembly of workers convened by the Internal Board of ATE voted to continue the struggle and to open up the plenary to all delegates. However, the ATE leadership, mired in internal debate, called for strikes without continuity and without any serious plan. For this reason we should demand a national plan of unified struggle, arising from the bases, and insist on periodically holding assemblies and plenaries of the rank and file open to all activists, whether members or not, and especially those laid off. Neither the degenerate leaders of the past or Kirchnerists can divide us again to serve their selfish interests. We must impose the broadest unity for struggle, reorganizing the union from the bottom up. This is the demand of the classist Left opposition.

On 16 March there was a national day of action with strikes and demonstrations of health workers registered with the Federation of Unionized Health Professionals (FESPROSA), an organization representing more than 30,000 physicians, health professionals and health workers from across the country. The National Secretariat of FESPROSA had convoked the action with the following demands: salary and wage incomes equal to the professional family basket, with the floor set at an increase of 40 per cent; free bargaining; the convening of national health bipartite negotiations; the end of job insecurity and indiscriminate dismissals; pensions (retiree income) valued at 82 per cent of wages and salaries; tax repeal of the tax on wages and salaries; full freedom of association; no to the criminalization of social protest and repeal of the anti-terrorist law.

With the presence of 73 delegates of 21 grass-roots associations, the Extra-ordinary Congress of Historical CONADU voted in favour of a national plan of struggle with 48-hour strikes, demanding the immediate opening of joint negoti-ations for a 45 per cent wage increase. The Congress was held on 10 March in the city of Buenos Aires. The national plan of struggle would take place in two stages. The first was a 48-hour strike on 16–17 March; the second strike occurred on 29–30 March, with the installation of a tent in front of the Ministry of National Education.

The state workers of Tierra del Fuego were on strike for 13 days and engaged in various marches and demonstrations to protest the increase in the retirement age, the loss of retirement income at 82 per cent of current wage rates, and wage cuts.

The general assembly decided unanimously to ratify the strike action. Then, by a large majority, it determined that a partial roadblock would be organized on the Monday in different parts of the city of Ushuaia and then mobilize from the courts to the High Court. It was also determined that at 8 o'clock in the evening an informative and decisive general assembly would be held by torchlight. At the same time, a massive general assembly in Rio Grande called for a concentration of force in San Martin and Belgrano to march on to Channel 13 and the hospital.

On Wednesday, 9 March, 15,000 teachers in Santiago del Estero took to the streets to demand action on their claim for improved wages and to protest state repression suffered the week before. Teachers' wages in Santiago are among the lowest in the country: the base salary is only US$2,900. The mobilization aroused enormous popular sympathy, and support for the teachers' fight against poverty and the impunity of the provincial government is growing. Romina Plá, general sec-retary of Suteba-La Matanza, who was speaker at the closing ceremony of the public demonstration stressed that

**100** Argentina: the return of the Right

the struggle of the teachers in Santiago de Esteras is a beacon for all teachers across the country to protest the miserable bipartite agreement between the national government and the union bureaucracy. We demand that all unions call for a national strike of all teachers and an educational national march in solidarity with the teachers of Santiago.

## Bonapartism and bipartism: the state of state-labour relations

Despite the government's efforts, most wage agreements that were reached during its 100 days in office ignored the official guideline of 25 per cent for the year. In the best case the validity of the bipartite agreement is biannual, leaving open the possibility of negotiating a higher percentage in the second half of the year if government inflation forecasts are not met. So far, only the bipartite agreement with the state of commerce employees approached the benchmark set by the Casa Rosada: a wage increase of 20 per cent until the end of August was agreed to, plus payment of a fixed sum of US$2,000 in two instalments.

The mechanics' union SMATA, a pioneer in implementing short agreements, had ratified this methodology a week beforehand and agreed with automotive manufacturers an increase of 11 per cent for the April–June period, which, added to the increase agreed to in the first quarter, meant an improvement of 19 per cent in the wage over the first six months of the year. In the coming days, the six-month restructuring agreements would be replicated for employees of dealerships and workshops.

The non-teaching staff at universities and private schools reached an agreement for a 31 per cent salary increase for the whole year. It would be implemented in two stages: 25 per cent in March and another 6 per cent payable in August or September. This agreement includes 15,000 private university workers.

The Board of the Confederation of Transport Workers (CATT) demanded an urgent meeting with President Macri, to demand the repeal of income tax on wages while warning that they would resort to more 'forceful' measures (*medidas de fuerza*) in April if their demands were not met. They also questioned the lay-offs.

On this point, the government had a setback in the Bicameral Commission for Legislative Procedures because it failed to obtain a judgement in favour of its necessity and urgency decree (DNU), by which Macri had sought to raise the minimum level of non-taxable minimum profits. The centre-left alliance put together by Cristina Fernández, the Front for Victory, had a majority in the committee.

## The lay-offs in figures

By a number of accounts the Macri regime is not only shrinking the state but also the country: 54,000 lay-offs already in construction, the possibility of 10,000 more in the metallurgical sector and promise of 10,000 lay-offs in the public sector.

As for the lay-offs in the construction sector, the president of Argentina's Chamber of Construction (CAC), Juan Chediack, admitted that the industry is 'going through a very difficult transition, which we had anticipated' and said that the number of lay-offs was equivalent to '50 per cent of the job posts that have been lost in the country' in the previous three months (*The Dawn News*, 9 March 2016). However, the businessman justified these lay-offs with the argument that '[f]ixing Argentina's economy can't be done from one day to the other'. When asked about the causes of this situation, he replied that 'two factors came together: the fiscal deficit of 2015, which caused non-payment to workers and, on the other hand, high inflation, which stopped private developments'. Argentina, he continued, 'comes from a decade with more than 20 per cent inflation, [which makes it] very difficult ... to make public works'. This is 'because the economic equation in the [labour] contracts is distorted'. In addition, he noted that 'in 2015 the amount of money allocated by the government to subsidies exceeded the amount destined to public work', further distorting the economic equation. 'This economic alchemy', he added, 'can never end well, because the financing must come from somewhere. If you do not want [costs to rise and] fees to climb because you don't want to generate inflation, then you need to generate spurious money to subsidize'. Either way 'there will be a deficit', which can only be resolved by reducing public spending and, he might have added, reducing the size of government and the state's direct engagement in the national economy. In other words, lay off public-sector workers, in sync with the decisions of many private-sector employers to restructure and reduce labour costs by laying off workers. The alternative mechanism of restructuring (reduce labour costs) by cutting back or slowing down the rise of wages is more complicated and fraught with labour conflict.

Regardless of the purported cause, or the motivation behind the policy of the government and the decisions made by many CEOs to lay off workers – and in both cases the undoubted motivation is the quest for private profit and personal enrichment – the massive laying off of workers is the order of the day for the Macri regime. Macri and his ideological henchmen and right-wing backers have evidently calculated that they can weather the storm of labour conflicts to come. The class struggle is thus fully engaged, with the capitalist class in effective command of the instruments of state power, which can and will be turned against the working class as needs be. However, in order to gauge the correlation of forces in this class struggle we need to have a clear idea or understanding of the concrete situation in which the working class finds itself. This is particularly so in regard to the issues of wages, lay-offs and other government 'restructuring reforms' that by a number of accounts have not only massively increased the ranks of the poor but are resulting in a massive mobilization of the working class. In the following we provide some examples and detail to illustrate what, at the time of writing, was already a general pattern after barely 100 days of the Macri regime.

In March 2016 the workers of Menoyo mobilized to demand the reinstatement of 21 laid-off workers. They also denounced the compulsory conciliation issued by the Buenos Aires cartera laboral for a factory in Munro (Buenos Aires province) and said that they had been prodded by a thug who responded to orders from the owners of the company. Similarly, in March one of the most important companies

**102** Argentina: the return of the Right

in the country, Techint, continued the wave of lay-offs. Paolo Rocca, the leader of the business group involved, let nearly 1,000 workers go. It was also learned that Siderar, the country's largest steelmaker and part of the Techint Group, reached an agreement with eight contractors to fire around 1,000 workers. In Ramallo, lay-offs would reach 700, while in Campana nearly 300 workers at the metallurgical firms Loginter and Camau, both contractors for the Techint group, were laid off. Meanwhile, Rocca took advantage of the lack of the government's regulatory control to raise the prices of Siderar products, creating difficulties for the local companies that depend on Techint for raw materials. As a result, the companies supplied by Techint were also forced to lay off workers. Ruca Panel, a company dedicated to the production of modular buildings, had to let 90 workers go while the construction company Eleprint laid off 400 workers.

The Atucha nuclear power plant, located the city of Lima, confirmed the lay-offs of 600 workers, while company Ar-Zinc iterated its decision to not revive its plant dedicated to the manufacture of zinc ingots and sulphuric acid. The company informed the labour authority of 243 agreements for voluntary withdrawals (88 per cent of the staff) and that it 'would execute the closure of the plant according to environmental legislation in force'. Nevertheless, various municipalities in the region, the province and several unions joined forces to insist on the plant being reopened, and it was likely that the CGT-San Lorenzo would call for a new 48-hour general strike in the industrial belt.

Workers laid off by the firm Ricedal Alimentos in Chabás (Santa Fe) were camped out at the plant on the edge of Route 33 in protest and to demand reinstatement and reopening of the firm.

The lay-offs that the government implemented in the public sector triggered a parallel trend in the private sector. From 1 December to mid-March, 68,563 lay-offs were recorded across the country, of which 37,627 were in the public sector and 30,936 in the private sector. This is a detail that emerges from a survey produced by the Observatorio del Derecho Social de la CTA Autónoma, headed by Paul Micheli.

In the private sector, meanwhile, suspensions expanded, hitting the petroleum, automobile, textile, auto parts and steel industries especially hard. The general secretary of the UOM, Antonio Caló, reported that about 3,000 workers in the sector had been dismissed and another 4,000 were suspended. He warned that the number could rise 'if there are changes in importing foreign items affecting domestic production' and said that the governing council approved the call for a march in defence of jobs. But, as noted at the outset, the sector most affected by lay-offs was construction. The national leadership of the Uocra denounced the loss of between 25,000 and 30,000 jobs over the past three months – 50 per cent of all lay-offs in the country. This situation particularly affected the housing sector, as the vast majority of companies were SMEs and could not survive if not paid what they are owed.

Returning to the more general figures, the report of the CTA differs from that reported by Economic Trends, which required 107,000 lay-offs so far in 2016, showing a sharp contrast to lay-offs recorded in the same period last year, when 1,432 people were left without work. Specifically, the number of lay-offs increased more than 70 times. The total figure is broken down into 41,920 redundancies in January and 65,799 people who lost their job between January and February, with a preponderance in the private sector. In this context, the head of the CTA, Hugo Yasky, warned that the country was in a 'peak of unemployment', with between 85,000 and 90,000 workers having lost their source of employment in the public or private sector. He also announced his intention to present draft legislation to Congress that would prohibit dismissals without cause for one year.

On 23 May 2016, in the aftermath of mobilizations in which several hundreds of thousands of workers took part, the CGT announced that it would not respond to Macro's vetoing of the anti-firing law with force or a general strike, announcing instead that it would push for the demand of 2.7 billion pesos promised by the government for short-term jobs via an expanded public works programme – the same tactic that led to the demobilization of the unemployed workers (*los piqueteros*) movement in 2003. In effect, by rejecting calls for a general strike the CGT effectively offered the Macri regime a virtual truce until August, when the various sectors of the organized labour would presumably be brought together. As for the government, it stated that the promised jobs funding would be made available mid-year.

## Conclusion

As an epilogue to this selected summary of lay-offs in both the public and private sectors over 100 days of Macri class rule, the Observatory of the Social Debt (Observatorio de la Deuda Social) of the Catholic University (UCA) reported on 3 April that from the assumption of the presidency by Macri on 10 December over 1.4 million had been added to the ranks of the poor, estimated at 34.5 per cent (up 5 per cent), and 350,000 of these were in a state of indigence (Calloni, 2016). And, the authors of the report add, these figures will undoubtedly climb with the announced new increases in the cost of gas (up 300 per cent), water and gasoline (up 375 per cent), electricity (up 300–500 per cent) and transportation (up 100 per cent) – and with the new wave of lay-offs. In this regard, in just one day (1 April) the government dismissed 2,300 public-sector workers. Additionally, the Association of State Workers (ATE) warned that, according to the government's schedule, another 25,000 more lay-offs were expected. Added to these lay-offs was the expected impact of the government's 'reform' measures on the country's small and medium-sized businesses (*pymes*, in Spanish), which, in the short run, included the loss of 200,000 jobs (Calloni, 2016).

The conclusion that we draw from these statistics and from our analysis of the working class's immediate response to the Macri government's policy regime is that the government has sown the seeds for a possibly dramatic advance in the class struggle from below – a mobilization that will undoubtedly change the correlation of class forces in the class struggle. One of the major problems in this struggle is the CGT, the country's largest federation of organized labour, formed in 1930 but over the past 80 years acting more as a brake to the mobilization of the working class against one regime after another. Given the historic and current accomodationist and reformist stance of the CGT leadership and a history of tripartism and betrayal, the advance of the working class in its struggle against both capital and the state in the current conjuncture will require a new leadership. Without this leadership and without a more active engagement of the political left it is possible, if not likely, that the conditions and opportunity for revolutionary change that the Macri regime, despite its intentions to the contrary, is creating will be lost.

## Notes

1 Mario Hernández is an Argentine political economist, the editor of the political journal *La Maza* and a political commentator and analyst. He is also a frequent collaborator of the authors. Most of the information and interpretation of events given in this chapter were also published and can be found in the weekly news reports given by *Resumen Latinoamericano y del Tercer Mundo*, *Diariodeurgencia/The Dawn News*, Buenos Aires. www.resumenlatinoamericano.org.
2 Unless otherwise cited and referenced, all of the data given in the following discussion were provided by co-author Mario Hernández, who has also published some of these data in multiple reports and issues of *Resumen Latinoamericano*, *Diariodeurgencia*, Buenos Aires.

## References

Aznárez, C. (2016, 8 September). 'Mauricio Macri: A balance of his first 10 months'. *Resumen Latinoamericano*/The Dawn News.
Calloni, S. (2016). 'Con Macri de presidente, un millón 400 mil nuevos pobres'. *La Jornada*, 3 April, p. 17. Available at: www.jornada.unam.mx/2016/04/03/mundo/017n1mun [accessed 18 April 2016].
ECLAC – Economic Commission of Latin America and The Caribbean. (2015). *Social panorama of Latin America*. Santiago de Chile: ECLAC.
Jozami, E. (2015). *El futuro del kirchnerismo*. Buenos Aires: Penguin Random House.
Katz, C. (2008). *Las disyuntivas de la izquierda (The dilemmas of the left in Latin America)*. Buenos Aires: Luxemburg Editions.
Petras, J. and Veltmeyer, H. (2002a). *Argentina: Entre desintegración y la revolución*. Buenos Aires: Editorial la Maza.
Petras, J. and Veltmeyer, H. (2002b). Argentina: 18 months of popular struggle – A balance. *Mind and Human Interaction*, 13(3), pp. 169–81.
Resumen Latinoamericano y del Tercer Mundo. (2016). *Diariodeurgencia/The Dawn News*, Buenos Aires. Available at: www.resumenlatinoamericano.org/category/diarios-de-urgencia/ [accessed 16 September 2016].

# 6

# BRAZIL

## Class struggle in the countryside

*João Márcio Mendes Pereira and Paulo Alentejano*

This chapter analyses the class struggle over land and land reform over the course of what has been described as the neo-liberal era, which in Brazil can be dated from the political regimes established by Fernando Collor de Mello and Itamar Franco in the 1990s. We then focus on the dynamics of class and political struggle that took place during the regime of Fernando Henrique Cardoso and the Workers Party (PT) regime under the successive administrations of Lula da Silva and Dilma Rousseff. In this context we discuss the salient features of the socio-economic reality of the Brazilian countryside, which include agrarian reform settlements, the concentration of land ownership and the structure of production, the internationalization of agriculture, food insecurity, violence and environmental degradation, the dynamics of land occupations, and the agro-strategies of capital at the beginning of the twenty-first century. The chapter concludes with a brief discussion on the recent and current dynamics of class struggle in the Brazilian countryside.

## The neo-liberal pivot of agrarian reform and the class struggle in Brazil's countryside

As elsewhere in Latin America, the turn towards neo-liberalism in Brazil occurred in the context of an external debt crisis and the consequent collapse of the economic model that in the case of Brazil was put into place by the military regime that took power in 1964. While the collapse of the economic model that hitherto had been hailed as the progenitor of an 'economic miracle' (rapid economic growth sustained by both exports and domestic consumption), in the countryside and cities popular pressure increased not just for the return of the democratic regime, but for effective social democratization. The limits of the transition from a military dictatorship to a return towards democracy and the rule of law became visible with the 'pact from above' that defeated the campaign for direct elections for president in 1984 (Fernandes, 1985).

Despite, or perhaps because of, these limits the coalition government formed in the redemocratization process ended up engaging a range of heterogeneous and even contradictory political forces. In a context of growing violence in the countryside and an increase in conflicts and peasant mobilizations, in 1985 the federal government created the Ministry of Reform and Agrarian Development (Ministério da Reforma e do Desenvolvimento Agrário – MIRAD). In May, during the IV Congress of CONTAG, the president of the republic proposed the National Agrarian Reform Plan (PNRA). At the same time that CONTAG's support for the government was sealed, the announcement made it appear that the time for agrarian reform had arrived (D'Incao, 1990; Graziano da Silva, 1985; Gomes da Silva, 1987).

What reform was proposed? Expropriation as the principal instrument for obtaining lands, rather than an exceptional resource; payment for the indemnification of expropriated lands was to be based on the value of the property declared by the landholders for taxation purposes; the centrality of the settlement programme for landless families, relegating other actions (such as colonization, the granting of land deeds, and taxation) to complementary measures; the establishment of a settlement target of seven million of the estimated 10.5 million landless peasants or those with insufficient land within a period of 15 years; the establishment of 'priority areas' for agrarian reform, in which there was a concentration of settlements, which broke with the pattern of occasional intervention in foci of conflict; and the participation of organizations which represented rural workers in all phases of the process.

With the PNRA it was proposed to emphasize the use of expropriation through payment of compensation in TDAs and under the value declared by landowners for the purposes of revenue collection – which reduced the value of the indemnifications by about 60 per cent (Gomes da Silva, 1987: 65). This had been the central point of political conflicts on the eve of the 1964 coup and two decades returned to the fore. However, the times were different. The focus of the proposal was the expropriation of 'unproductive' *latifúndios* maintained for the purpose of speculation. It was anticipated that the capacity of the semi-feudal agrarian elite and the 'backwards' landholders to resist this policy and political development would have been weakened as a result of the modernization of agriculture. However, it was in the south-east, particularly in São Paulo state – the richest and most industrialized in the country – where there emerged the most intransigent reaction to the proposal (Veiga, 1990). As one of those involved at the time stated, 'precisely because we directed our fire against speculation we hit the system at its heart' (Palmeira, 1994: 56).

Having lost control of the instruments of state power, the forces of right-wing reaction and resistance in the countryside turned to the mass media, all in the hands of the most reactionary elements of the ruling class. Deploying these instruments of ideological power against the proposed agrarian reform the large landholding agrarian elite initiated their anti-reformist campaign with the intention of terrorizing the population with the idea of an imminent 'social convulsion' in the countryside and 'chaos', branding the government as 'communist' and accusing it as intending to 'confiscate private property' (Veiga, 1990: 82; Gomes da Silva, 1987: 74).

In this context there emerged the right-wing Democratic Ruralist Union (União Democrática Ruralista – UDR), which brought together ranchers from the south-east and centre-west. The UDR rapidly made a name for itself on the national stage by calling on landholders to defend and arm themselves against land occupations. With its intransigent defence of the right to property, it managed to organize land-holders from all over the country – both modern and backwards, large, mid-sized and small. With the aim of representing the forces of freedom in the countryside, the UDR presented itself as the principal spokesperson for the 'rural producers' in the country (Dreifuss, 1989; Bruno, 1997).

The category 'rural producer' emerged in the political discourse during this period as an instrument of combat and political identity, substituting for the negative image of *latifundiário* a positive one associated with the generic image of production. In this context, any reference to the private monopoly of land was avoided. Camouflaging the glaring inequalities that existed among different categories of landholders, the category of 'rural producer' was used to generate a false image of agricultural producers united in a common struggle against the PNRA.

So intense were the pressures on the legislators that between May and October 1985, when the final version of the PNRA was approved, the original proposal had been significantly modified after 12 different versions. Various legal norms were instituted, which restricted still further the expropriation process. In 1989 MIRAD was ended. PNRA's settlement target for 1985–89 was 1,400,000 families on 43,090,000 hectares. However, it turned out that only 10.5 per cent of the total land was recovered for the landless and only 6.4 per cent of the families settled (Leite & Ávila, 2007: 83).

## *The constitutional battleground*

Following the failure of the PNRA, the peasant organizations moved their energies and dispute to the National Constituent Assembly (1987–88), where the theme of 'agrarian reform' condensed the most bitter class conflict in the entire legislative process. Various organizations were involved in the National Campaign for Agrarian Reform, which proposed a popular amendment for which more than 1,200,000 signatures were collected. The core of the proposal consisted of the idea of the 'social function' of property, non-compliance with which would result in sanctions varying from summary loss of the property to compensation of the value declared for fiscal purposes. Also proposed was the establishment of a maximum limit of property which an individual or company could own, to be calculated in accord-ance with regional parameters.

Employer groups were also mobilizing. In the end, all of them converged on the unconditional defence of the 'right to property' and 'free enterprise' to block any possibility of reform, with the support of representatives of urban industrial business and international capital. As in the 1960s, there was no support for agrarian reform from the 'progressive' and 'modern' sectors of the Brazilian bourgeoisie.

**108** Brazil: class struggle in the countryside

Although the 1988 constitution, owing to popular pressure, had expanded the sphere of citizenship rights in Brazil, the same could not be said for the democratization of access to land. For the first time, the expression 'agrarian reform' appeared in a constitutional text where it was stated that property had to fulfil its 'social function', understood as rational use adapted to natural resources and the preservation of the environment, compliance with labour legislation, and production methods that favoured the welfare of workers and owners. However, the definition of the criteria for compliance vis-à-vis the social function of land remained ambiguous (with the exception of references to labour legislation). All references to the *latifúndio* were deleted from the text, a maximum limit for land ownership was not established and 'settled' workers were not defined as a priority for agricultural policy, as demanded by the peasant organizations. Moreover, the decision about landownership for purposes of expropriation remained with the judiciary, allowing for legal delays and thereby delaying the creation of settlements.

As for the issue of expropriations, prior just compensation, in the form of TDAs that were redeemable up to 20 years, was established after the second year, with the guaranteed preservation of the real value of land. In this way, the policy of compensating landholders based on market values was strengthened, rewarding rather than punishing landholders who did not comply with the policy of expropriating land that did not have a social function.

The constitution prevented the expropriation of small and medium-sized rural properties as well as productive properties. 'Productive property' was supposed to be regulated by means of complementary legislation, which would be enacted five years later. Meanwhile the legal vacuum made land expropriation unfeasible. Following the approval of the Agrarian Law in February 1993, modest constitutional mechanisms for regulating agrarian reform were established but only for economic reasons, ruling out expropriation for social and environmental reasons.

This legislation established mechanisms that attributed to the judicial decision-making authority for operationalizing any land policy, creating conditions for the growing judicialization of the agrarian question. This highlighted the fact that the predominant juridical socialization among the operators of law in Brazil was – and still is – based on a vision of the right to property as something inviolable and absolute (Fachin, 1993), which fed an unfavourable attitude towards the landless among the majority of judges.

The correlation of forces institutionalized in the 1988 constitution and in the subsequent legislation undermined the possibility of implementing large-scale agrarian reform in Brazil. The legal framework allowed at most a limited land settlement policy susceptible to cyclical fluctuations.

### *The class struggle and the 1989 presidential election*

After the constitutional battle, the following chapter of the agrarian class struggle in Brazil was the 1989 presidential election. During the electoral campaign, the dispute ended up polarized between Collor de Mello and Lula da Silva. Popular movements returned to the streets, at the same time that strikes exploded all over the country, demanding profound social reforms. Meanwhile, business sectors and the military used slogans such as anti-communism, the modernization of the country and the struggle against corruption. The electoral result represented the defeat of a popular democratic project fed by a decade of social struggles in the countryside and cities. At the same time, the Cold War ended and the Washington Consensus emerged as a policy framework for the new world order.

## The Collor and Itamar regimes (1990–94)

The Collor government (1990–92) introduced neo-liberalism to Brazil. Among other measures, it implemented an economic policy that severely worsened living and employment conditions in the countryside and cities. The treatment given to popular struggles was summarized in repression and criminalization. Furthermore, this government did not make any new expropriations for the purposes of agrarian reform and the existing settlements were abandoned to their own fate (Medeiros, 2002; Ferreira et al., 2009).

During the Itamar administration (1992–94) there was an inflection in the government's way of dealing with social movements in the countryside. For the first time, a Brazilian president met with representatives of the MST, recognizing the organization as a legitimate interlocutor for the forces of resistance. People with credibility and who were connected to the social movements were appointed to the board of the National Institute of Colonization and Agrarian Reform (Instituto Nacional de Colonização e Reforma Agrária – INCRA, created in 1970) at the beginning of 1993. Moreover, after the approval of the Agrarian Law in May the same year, the modest constitutional measures related to agrarian law were regulated, allowing expropriations to be carried out. The question of expropriation regained space in the government agenda, both because of the pressure of social movements and owing to its association with the fight against hunger. However, in the context of the implementation of the Real Plan (the monetary stabilization programme), various political pressures inside and outside the government undermined the execution of this timid programme of 'agrarian reform'. Only 23,000 families were settled in 152 projects (Stédile & Fernandes, 1999; Medeiros, 2002; Ferreira et al., 2009).

## The Cardoso government and the agrarian question (1995–2002)

In the context of the transnationalization of the Brazilian economy, the government took the large inflow of capital in the form of FDI and access to the international capital market as marking the end of the era of state-led development and Brazil's entry into the new world order of neo-liberal globalization (Petras & Veltmeyer, 2003). As a result, the previous decade's policy of maintaining a positive balance on the trade account was abandoned (Delgado, 2010: 92). On the other hand, the enormous international liquidity, maintenance of high domestic interest

**110** Brazil: class struggle in the countryside

rates, and the currency overvaluation, practised until 1998 – the three pillars of the Real Plan's 'success' – combined with unilateral commercial liberalization and the dismantling of the agricultural regulation model, had a drastic impact on Brazil's agricultural sector. The volume of agricultural imports shot up, reaching levels that were unprecedented (Delgado, 2009: 20). On the other hand, the accelerated decline of agricultural prices was not counterbalanced by price support policies, with a resultant negative impact on agricultural income, pushing numerous firms and establishments into bankruptcy.

Agrarian reform only appeared in a diluted and muted form in the 1994 presidential election, which was contested by Lula, the leader of the Workers' Party (PT) with which the MST was aligned, but won by Fernando Cardoso, formerly a Marxist sociologist who made a major contribution to what development theorists described as 'dependency theory'. But the confluence in Cardoso's first government between 1995 and 1997 helped to radically alter the agrarian scenario. The first was the national and international repercussion of police violence in actions against peasants in Corumbiara (August 1995) and more especially in Eldorado dos Carajás (April 1996). Both episodes resulted in dozens of dead peasants and fed a series of protests in Brazil and abroad against violence in the countryside and in favour of agrarian reform.

The second factor was the increase in land occupations practically all over the country. The MST was the principal organizational force in this process, but in some states unions linked to CONTAG also entered the fray. A struggle of particular importance was related to a series of land occupations in Pontal do Paranapanema – a region in São Paulo state characterized by *grilagem* (illegal claims of land) of public land. Various MST leaders were arrested and social tensions increased with the violence of the police and armed groups at the service of the *latifundiários*.

Another decisive factor was the holding of the successful National March for Agrarian Reform, Employment, and Justice. Organized by the MST, the march lasted for three months, departing from various parts of the country and reaching the capital on 17 April 1997, a year after the massacre in Eldorado dos Carajás. The march managed to gain the sympathy of part of urban public opinion. Along with the 'landless' were the 'homeless' and 'jobless', among others, bringing around 100,000 people to the streets of Brasília in the first mass demonstration against neoliberal policies.

These events not only gave land occupations and the demand of agrarian reform greater visibility, but they also propelled the MST to prominence in diverse national and international political scenarios. At this point, this movement could no longer be treated as a simple 'police case', nor could its demands be ignored. The federal government's response came shortly after the massacre in Eldorado dos Carajás, with the creation of the Extraordinary Ministry of Land Policy (Ministério Extraordinário de Política Fundiária – MEPF). MEPF started a set of initiatives aimed at reducing tension in the countryside and weakening the political rise of the MST.

In the first place, in 1997, a series of measures were enacted to make the expropriation process faster, to reduce the compensations paid to landholders and to accelerate the settlement of families (MEPF, 1998). Not all were applied and some did not have a relevant effect, but this showed that the government was concerned with accelerating its capacity to respond to social pressure.

Second, the de-federalization of agrarian reform commenced, transferring to states and municipalities the competence to conduct processes to obtain lands and settlements, thereby converting them into the objects of locally negotiated bargaining (MEPF, 1997). This policy was against the position taken by the peasant organizations. Moreover, combined with other measures, it allowed for the incorporation of trade union organizations and excluded the MST from participation in some public policies, dividing the peasant organizations and stimulating them to compete among themselves.

These initiatives took place in a context of widespread repression in the countryside in which the federal police were used to monitor the landless, evictions were carried out in a truculent and illegal manner and leaders were imprisoned. The extreme agrarian right joined the struggle, mobilizing private instruments of violence reinforced by the state judiciary and police.

At the same time, the major vehicles of communication began to disseminate a negative image of social movements, in particular the MST. In general, the landless and the MST were associated with rioting, violence, corruption and a lack of vocation for agriculture.

Finally, the government initiated a programme of 'market-assisted land reform' (MALR), propagated by the World Bank. This programme was designed as an alternative to the strategy and tactics adopted by the MST to that point – to 'occupy' and 'settle' on the land and initiate negotiations with the government rather than the landowners. The 'market-assisted' land reform programme entailed lending money to poor peasants for them to buy the land via direct negotiations with the landholders. In this transaction, landholders would be compensated at the market price while the purchasers assumed the costs of land acquisition. Along with a loan, the purchasers received a subsidy for investment in infrastructure and production. This market land reform mechanism stimulated a process of bargaining, since the lower the price of the land the more funds that were left over for investment (van Zyl & Binswanger, 1996). In other words, MALR was an operation for buying and selling land between private agents financed by the state, with the addition of a subsidy. Politically, this model was one of the World Bank's strategies for alleviating rural poverty within the framework and complementary to its structural adjustment programme of macroeconomic policy reform.

According to the Bank (IBRD), Brazil offered ideal conditions for MALR because an economic policy which impacted negatively on the social fabric of rural society was under way, and there existed an enormous demand for land as well as a tendency for the price of rural property to fall in some regions. As for the government, the MALR provided a non-confrontational and palatable solution to the agrarian question. It was this convergence of interests that allowed the World Bank to convert Brazil into a laboratory for experimenting with its new market-assisted land reform programme (Pereira, 2007).

The first project under this programme was initiated in August 1996 in the state of Ceará. Out of this experience was born the Land Bank (Cédula da Terra – PCT) pilot project, which was extended to another four states in the form of a new loan approved by the Bank in April 1997. PCT would finance the purchase of land for 15,000 families in four years, but the expectation was to later finance a million families in six years (IBRD, 1997). The north-east region was chosen as a target, since the poor rural population of the country was concentrated there. The project financed the purchase of any rural property, including those that could be expropriated, and was criticized by the MST and CONTAG as an expression of neoliberalism and incapable of democratizing the agrarian structure.

In the meantime, the government majority in Congress approved the creation in February 1998 of the Land Bank, a public fund capable of raising funds from various sources, including international, to finance the purchase of land by poor peasants and the landless (MEPF, 1999a). In other words, without any assessment of the ongoing experiences and against the position of *all* peasant movements, the Congress approved the creation of an instrument to implement MALR at the national level. Based on the idea of 'negotiated' access 'without conflicts', the federal government made use of intense propaganda to divulge the supposed advantages of the new model, while at the same time criminalizing the MST's strategy of land occupations.

Cardoso's second mandate began in 1999 with the crisis of the Real Plan and the adoption of a fiscal adjustment programme agreed to by the IMF. In this context, the external adjustment policy was once again 'adjusted'. Returning to the strategy adopted in 1994, a balanced trade policy was implemented to meet the current account deficit. As had occurred in the 1982 crisis, the primary export sectors were called upon on to generate this balance. At this moment, just one word echoed in the mainstream media: agribusiness. A generic term created and spread by employer organizations, agribusiness was elevated to the position of 'saviour' of the Brazilian economy. However, from a critical development studies perspective, agribusiness denoted 'an association of large agro-industrial capital with big landholders [in a] strategic alliance with financial capital in the pursuit of profit and income derived from the land under the sponsorship of the state' (Delgado, 2010: 93).

The strategy adopted by the government consisted of a combination of four initiatives: (i) priority investment in territorial infrastructure, means of transport and routes to transport production abroad; (ii) the reorganization of the public system of agricultural research to harmonize them with the large agro-industrial enterprises; (iii) low regulation of the land market, in order to allow private control of the land resources necessary for the expansion of agriculture; and (iv) currency devaluation that would raise the profitability of the export sector (Delgado, 2010: 94).

Alongside this strategy the government concentrated on: (i) decentralizing the agrarian reform programme to states and municipalities; (ii) outsourcing and privatizing technical services and activities linked to settlements (such as technical assistance); (iii) giving settlers ownership of their land in three years, in order to make them pay for the expropriated rural property; (iv) transferring to settlers responsibility for various attributions over which INCRA had previously had jurisdiction (such as topography, demarcation of lots etc.); (v) maintaining the agrarian reform programme as a policy to alleviate rural poverty, without any intention of structural change; (vi) repressing land occupation and economically strangling the MST, forbidding the liberation of public resources for activities it carried out; and (vii) implementing MALR on a large scale through the mechanism of the Land Bank (MEPF, 1999a, 1999b; Alentejano, 2000).

Owing to the repression of land struggles and the implementation of MALR, peasant movements sought greater political unity in the National Forum for Agrarian Reform and Justice in the Countryside. In October 1998, the Forum submitted an investigation request to the IBRD Inspection Panel, with a series of criticisms and accusations against PCT. In May 1999, the Panel found all of the Forum's arguments to be unfounded and did not recommend to the board of the World Bank that the requested investigation be carried out. The Brazilian government used this as proof of the project's efficiency. Three months later, based on documents that contained numerous irregularities and evidence of the corruption of the administration of PCT, the Forum asked for a new investigation from the Panel, once again receiving a negative answer.

However, a number of assessments showed the incapacity of MALR to stimulate economic development and social justice in the Brazilian countryside and elsewhere where the programme was implemented (Borras, 2003; Sauer, 2009; Pereira, 2007, 2012). Despite technical advances and measures which improved programmes of this type – increased participation and transparency mechanisms through trade union mediation – these measures were not sufficient to overcome the structural limits of the MALR model, such as the dependency of the offer of land on landholders and the incapability of democratizing the landholding structure and achieving this social scale, owing to prior payment in money at market prices.

In 2001–02 the Cardoso administration carried out two important actions. The first was the registration of requests for access to land in post offices all over the country. With intense propaganda in the means of communication, the campaign promised 'agrarian reform without conflicts'. The number of people registered reached 839,715. However, none was settled. The second action consisted in halting for two years INCRA inspections of occupations, which undermined the expropriation process.

While the 'rural landless workers' gained notoriety during the 1990s as a political force, arguably agricultural producers in the category of 'family farmers' had a greater impact. Factors decisive in its emergence included: (i) the increase in the social differentiation of agricultural labour; (ii) the decline of the political weight of rural wage earners; (iii) disputes within the peasant trade union movement, particularly between CONTAG and DNTR-CUT; (iv) evaluation of the effects of the modernization of agriculture and neo-liberalism and the growing conviction of the need for an alternative model of rural development that is more 'democratic' and 'inclusive'; and (v) discussions within the trade union movement about the role of

**114** Brazil: class struggle in the countryside

family farming in development, taking the European experience as a principal reference point (Favareto, 2006; Medeiros, 2001, 2010).

The mobilization led by CONTAG and DNTR-CUT and the progressive convergence between them resulted in CONTAG affiliating with the CUT in 1995, leading to the extinction of DNTR. It also resulted in the creation of a National Program for Strengthening Family Farming (Programa Nacional de Fortalecimento da Agricultura Familiar – PRONAF) in 1996, consecrating 'family farmers' as a political category. The spread of this category reconfigured the terms of the debate about public policies related to production, commercialization, credit, agro-industrialization and cooperativism, as well as agrarian reform itself, which lost its central position for the trade union movement. Nevertheless, the divergences between the CUT and CONTAG trade unionism continued in a permanent dispute over which one was the spokesperson for 'family farmers' as a group, which resulted in the emergence of another organization, the Federation of Workers in Family Farming (Federação dos Trabalhadores na Agricultura Familiar – Fetraf) (Medeiros, 2010; Picolotto, 2011).

On the other hand, the predominance of this group in the field of identity politics was reflected in an analysis of the rural world that led to an abandonment of the concept of the peasantry in the 1990s. The MST and Via Campesina were concerned with redeeming this concept as a question of political identity in the 2000s, sometimes in a complementary form and sometimes competing with the concept of family farming depending on the specific antagonist, became a matter of debate and dispute regarding the best way of understanding the world of rural labour (Via Campesina, 2002; MST, 2013a).

## The Lula da Silva (2003–10) and Dilma Rousseff (2011–16) PT regime

The victory of Lula in the 2002 elections was a landmark in Brazilian history. After three defeats the PT candidate finally reached the presidency, supported by a broad political coalition that included both popular and conservative forces. 'Hope has defeated fear', stated Lula, whose election signalled a change of direction after a decade of neo-liberalism. However, campaign commitments including the promise that there would be no 'breaching of contracts', the composition of ministers, the profile of the government's support in Congress and the first measures adopted – such as the reform of social insurance that was socially regressive in terms of rights – and, above all, the regime's economic policies would soon show that there would be no rupture in the structure of power.

Even so, the beginning of the government was marked by an enormous expectation on the part of the rural poor and peasant movements regarding the realization of an effective agrarian reform programme. The number of occupations and of families in campsites organized by the MST shot up, returning the agrarian question back to the centre of the political agenda. Individuals supported by the organization were appointed to the board of INCRA, heightening the expectation of action on the agrarian question.

Employer reaction was immediate in the form of violence against peasants and movement activists, which soon returned to the levels of the 1980s (IPEA 2011: 238). The judiciary was also called into action in the states by issuing arrest warrants and eviction notices that reached record levels. A media campaign conducted in the country's principal means of communication criminalized social movements, in particular the MST, and accused the federal government of omission or connivance.

Meanwhile, at the request of the government a team of researchers prepared a new proposal for a National Plan of Agrarian Reform (II PNRA). Based on a systematic study the proposal showed the existence of land available for agrarian reform in all states of the federation. Furthermore, it pointed to the existence of a potential demand estimated at six million families that were landless or from *minifundiárias*, an emergency demand of around 180,000 families in encampments, and an explicit demand of around one million families, consisting of the public registered at the post office in 2001 and in encampments. The proposal also established a target of one million settled families between 2004–07 and returned to the idea of 'reformed areas', with the aim of overcoming the occasional nature of settlement policy and promoting synergy among public policies. The cost and the means of financing this were also detailed, reinforcing its feasibility.

The proposal was delivered to the government in October 2003 and counted on the total support of peasant movements. However, the federal government rejected the document, and in its place announced the II PNRA, with much lower targets. A few days previously the president of INCRA and his team had been dismissed, in the name of governability.

Among other targets, II PNRA stipulated the settlement of 400,000 families by 2006; the regularization of the landholdings of 500,000 families; the expansion of land credit to 130,000 families through the recently created National Program of Land Credit (Programa Nacional de Crédito Fundiário – PNCF), financed by IBRD; the provision of technical assistance, training, credit, and commercialization policies, for all those settled in agrarian reform areas; the promotion of gender equality in settlements; and giving those living in the remnants of *quilombos* title to their land (quilombos are areas where fugitive or freed slaves lived before the end of slavery in 1888; the breach opened by the 1988 constitution stimulated a movement which involved more than 2,000 black rural communities, which now demand their recognition as remnants). Also forecast was the updating of agricultural productivity indices.

Even with the modest targets, lower than those refused by the government, II PNRA performed less well than hoped. At least this is what can be understood from the positions taken by the principal interested parties involved. In a letter sent to President Lula in October 2005, the MST criticized the ongoing agrarian policy, denouncing the non-compliance with settlement targets, the abandonment of thousands of encamped families, and the non-updating of productivity indices. At the same time, they criticized the political and financial support given to agribusiness.

**116** Brazil: class struggle in the countryside

In March 2006, six organizations assessed the agrarian policy of the Lula administration (MST, 2006b). Of the 39 measures assessed, 10 were considered positive and 29 negative. The majority of measures assessed as positive were considered secondary and partial, while the negative ones were structural.

The performance of the agrarian policy of the Lula administration demonstrated in practice what the official documents indicated: the weakening of agrarian reform as a structural policy and its conversion into a measure of reducing rural poverty and social pressure. An examination of the documentation produced by the government and the PT until 2006 showed that the actual conception of agrarian reform had been weakened from a conceptual and programmatic point of view until it became a residual and peripheral action of social compensation, this to the extent that: (i) the establishment of annual settlement targets stopped; (ii) the concept of reformed areas lost importance; (iii) expropriation was no longer considered the principal instrument for obtaining land; (iv) land credit gained importance as an innovative instrument; and (v) the mention of the updating of productivity indices as an indispensable measure for expanding the land available for agrarian reform disappeared (Carvalho Filho, 2007). The promise of a 'widespread agrarian reform, massive and with quality, as a fundamental part of a new project of national development', as stated by Lula's manifesto during the 2006 re-election campaign, was nothing other than mere electoral rhetoric. In the following years, this weakening would mark the agenda of Lula's second mandate, becoming consolidated during the administration of Dilma Rousseff (IPEA, 2013: 336–47; MST 2013b, 2014).

On the other hand, the federal government adopted important public polices for supporting production and commercialization which benefitted family farmers and those settled by agrarian reform, such as the Food Purchase Program (Programa de Aquisição de Alimentos – PAA), the National Policy of Technical Assistance and Rural Expansion (Política Nacional de Assistência Técnica e Extensão Rural – PNATER) and the law which set aside 30 per cent of the funds of the National Policy of School Meals (Política Nacional de Alimentação Escolar – PNAE) for the purchase of products from family farming and from settlements. These policies had a limited scope and suffered from the lack of resources to become massive, but they represented much more than previous governments had done (IPEA, 2011, 2012).

The weakening of agrarian reform in the federal political agenda was one of the results of the power of agribusiness in the Brazilian economy and politics. Its expansion during the 2000s was propelled by the increase in international prices of agricultural commodities, and most especially by the demand of China, Brazil's most important commercial partner. Moreover, agribusiness benefitted from the economic policy, the recurrent renegotiations of the debt of the large borrowers and the channelling of public resources to assist business conglomeration and internationalization strategies. State action, through various instruments and agencies, prioritized the promotion of growing crops for export and the production of animal feed, agrofuels, paper and cellulose, strengthening agribusiness as a power structure (Delgado, 2010).

## Agrarian reform settlements

The existence of agrarian reform settlements in Brazil essentially resulted from three factors: the social mobilization of thousands of landless families, the practice of occupation as the principal form of pressurizing governments, and political actions carried out by social movements in the countryside. However, the real number of settled families is an object of controversy among social movements, researchers and public agencies. Official data indicate the existence of a little more than 1,200,000 settled families in the country, in an area of almost 90 million hectares, as shown in Table 6.1.

The MST and some researchers reject these figures and accuse INCRA of inflating the data to meet their annual settlement targets. In fact, for both the Cardoso and Lula administrations, data were aggregated that should not have been counted as implementation of agrarian reform. For example, families continued to

**TABLE 6.1** Settled families and area occupied – Brazil

| Year | Settled families | Area (hectares) |
| --- | --- | --- |
| Until 1994 | 58,317 | 16,290,069 |
| 1995 | 42,912 | 2,683,062 |
| 1996 | 62,044 | 2,515,865 |
| 1997 | 81,944 | 4,165,754 |
| 1998 | 101,094 | 3,025,000 |
| 1999 | 85,226 | 2,303,118 |
| 2000 | 60,521 | 2,151,574 |
| 2001 | 63,477 | 1,829,428 |
| 2002 | 43,486 | 2,401,925 |
| Total (Cardoso Admin.) | 540,704 | 21,075,726 |
| 2003 | 36,301 | 4,526,138 |
| 2004 | 81,254 | 4,687,393 |
| 2005 | 127,506 | 13,437,558 |
| 2006 | 136,358 | 9,237,949 |
| 2007 | 67,535 | 5,747,068 |
| 2008 | 70,157 | 4,143,246 |
| 2009 | 55,498 | 4,633,822 |
| 2010 | 39,479 | 1,878,008 |
| Total (Lula da Silva Admin.) | 614,088 | 50,194,064 |
| 2011 | 22,021 | 1,902,884 |
| 2012 | 6,132 | 328,745 |
| 2013 | 10,200 | 525,161 |
| 2014 | 2,268* | 205,310* |
| Total (Dilma Admin.) | 40,621* | 2,962,100 |
| GENERAL TOTAL | 1,251,462 | 88,619,077 |

*Source:* INCRA (updated on 31/08/2014).

*Note*
\* Until August 2014.

**118** Brazil: class struggle in the countryside

be settled in projects previously created in lots that were unoccupied, which cannot be configured as the creation of new settlements. More seriously, families who already had possession of land, but not ownership, were also included, settled families who moved from one lot to another were counted as if they were new settled families, and settled families and settlements created by state governments – some in the 1960s – were recognized by INCRA and included in the statistics. Notwithstanding the controversy, the official data show that during the Dilma Rousseff administration (2011–14) little more than 40,000 families were settled, a very low level in comparison with the settlement rate of the previous governments.

INCRA uses various instruments to obtain land for the agrarian reform program. Expropriations were responsible for obtaining the land used in the largest number of settlements created between 1990 and 2010, benefitting some 53 per cent of families. However, in terms of size, the state and federal public areas – obtained through recognition, *arrecadação* (transfer of ownership) and *discriminação* (investigation of ownership) – amount to 64 per cent of the total areas settled. During the FHC administrations, 53 per cent of properties used for agrarian reform were expropriated, while during the Lula administration 30 per cent were. When we consider the area expropriated, FHC administrations were responsible for 42 per cent of the total and Lula administrations for 17 per cent. It can thus be seen that the instrument of expropriation has been increasingly less used, which is directly linked to the non-updating of the productivity indices that are the foundation for expropriations.

In relation to the 'quality' of settlements, a lot of research has been done on the subject, covering various aspects and focusing on a number of areas. Generally speaking, it can be concluded that, despite the poor quality of the land, the precarious productive and social infrastructure, the fragility of the technical assistance and the insufficient financial support for the economic and social development of the settlements, settled families, nevertheless, enjoyed a significant improvement in their living conditions, and in relation to food, health and education. Moreover, settlements have introduced new productive and political dynamics in the municipalities where they were implemented. In some micro-regions where, for diverse reasons, the action of social movements was more concentrated, settlements emerged very close to each other, resulting in a greater political strength and economic expression for this segment (Leite & Ávila, 2007).

However, it should be noted that, over the last two decades, the increase in the number of land occupations and of settlements has undergone a spatial dislocation (Alentejano, 2004). While most occupations have been concentrated in the south-central region of the country, it was in the north where the federal government settled most families. This geographic discrepancy between the mobilization of workers and the settlement policy does not deny the fact that the latter has largely been reactive to land occupations (Fernandes, 2000). However, it indicates the inflection in agrarian policy implemented since the presidency of the FHC, with the aim of responding to social pressure for land and combating rural social movements, especially the MST. While numerous families spent years in encampments in states in the south and south-east of the country, many never managing to be settled, in the Amazon region there proliferate denunciations of 'ghost' settlements, some with fraudulent land granting processes in the name of false owners – known as *laranjas* – who are fronts for loggers (Oliveira, 2010).

## Landholding structure and agricultural production

According to the last agricultural census, the Gini index has remained practically stagnant over the last two decades, changing from 0.857 in 1985 to 0.856 in 1995/96 and 0.854 in 2006. Nevertheless, in some states the index has risen – such as Tocantins (9.1 per cent), Mato Grosso do Sul (4.1 per cent) and São Paulo (6.1 per cent) – owing to the expansion of agribusiness towards the Amazon, propelled by soybean and livestock rearing. In the specific case of São Paulo, this growth was fundamentally due to the expansion of sugar cane production, stimulated by the increase in the consumption of fuel alcohol and the increase in the international price of sugar. This expansion of sugar cane occupied areas of pasture in the states, stimulating the movement of cattle to other regions in the country, especially to the Amazon.

The inequality of landholding structure in Brazil remained untouched, since small establishments (with less than 10 hectares) account for 48 per cent of total establishments, but the area they occupy is only 2.4 per cent of the total; at the opposite end, establishments with more than 1,000 hectares only constitute 0.9 per cent of the total number but occupy 45 per cent of the total area. The contrast is reaffirmed when it is observed that the establishments with less than 100 hectares represent 86 per cent of the total, occupying an area of around 21 per cent, while those greater than 100 hectares total 14 per cent and occupy around 79 per cent of the area. This structure altered little over the last 50 years.

Based on INCRA data, it can be seen that the numbers have changed but landholding concentration remains, since: (i) properties under 10 hectares represent 33.95 per cent of the total but only occupy 1.45 per cent of the area; (ii) the number of properties with less than 100 hectares corresponds to 86.1 per cent of the total, but they possess only 17.5 per cent of the total area; (iii) on the other hand, properties over 1,000 hectares correspond to only 1.5 per cent of total properties but control 52.59 per cent of the total area.

A direct result of the persistent land concentration has been the expulsion of workers from the countryside. Prevented from expanding the lands under their control, or expelled from them, peasants have tended to leave the rural environment fully or partially, which has been accentuated by the modernization of agriculture, which reduces the need for an agricultural labour force.

The average number of workers per establishment has fallen since 1950, with a light oscillation upwards between 1970 and 1975. It should also be noted that establishments with less than 100 hectares are responsible for 84.36 per cent of persons occupied in agricultural establishments, although the total area they occupy represents only 21.2 per cent of the total. On average, establishments with less than

**120** Brazil: class struggle in the countryside

100 hectares used 12.6 times more workers per hectare than the medium-sized establishments (100–1,000 hectares) and 45.6 times more than the large establishments (with more than 1,000 hectares).

What can be observed is that in recent decades the rural population has suffered an absolute reduction (and not only relative, as had been occurring until 1970), falling from 41 million in 1970 to 38.6 million in 1980, 35.8 million in 1991, 31.8 million in 2000 and 29.9 million in 2010 (IPEA, 2010).

The prevalence of business agriculture in the Brazilian agricultural model can also be observed through the comparison of the most recent statistical data about 'family' and 'non-family' agriculture, as shown in Table 6.2.

Family establishments constitute the wide majority (84.4 per cent), although they represent only 24.3 per cent of the area occupied. They are predominantly concerned with the production of foodstuffs for the internal market, being responsible for 87 per cent of the national production of manioc, 70 per cent of beans, 46 per cent of corn, 38 per cent of coffee, 34 per cent of rice and 21 per cent of wheat; in relation to livestock, they produce 58 per cent of milk, 59 per cent of the breeding of pigs, 50 per cent of birds and 30 per cent of cattle (IBGE, 2006).

In relation to the generation of employment, family farming also is important, since 74.4 per cent of rural workers are occupied in family farming establishments, with 8.7 hectares being necessary to generate a job in family farming, while in business agriculture 67.5 hectares are required. In all regions, family farming responds for the majority of those involved in agricultural activities: 52.6 per cent (centre-west), 54.8 per cent (south-east), 76.7 per cent (south) and 83 per cent (north and north-east) (IBGE, 2006).

It is important to highlight that family farming generates 37.9 per cent of the value of agricultural production, although it covers an area 16.8 times smaller than business establishments (18.37 hectares against 309.18 ha). Breaking down the data, it can be concluded that family farming generates R$104 per hectare/year, while business agriculture generates R$44 per hectare/year.

What is most significant, however, is that this performance occurred in a scenario of elevated inequality in the distribution of public credit destined for agricultural activities, which reproduce the inequality existing in the landholding structure. The amount allocated to family farming is always around one-fifth of the value allocated to the business sector. In other words, more than 80 per cent of the

**TABLE 6.2** Landholding structure according to family farming criteria

| Category | No. of establishments | % | Area occupied (hectares) | % |
|---|---|---|---|---|
| Family farming | 4,367,902 | 84.4 | 80,250,453 | 24.3 |
| Non-family farming | 807,587 | 15.6 | 249,690,940 | 75.7 |
| Total | 5,175,489 | 100 | 329,941,393 | 100 |

Source: IBGE – Censo Agropecuário, 2006.

expenditure in the agricultural plans in recent years had been aimed at approximately 15 per cent of producers, while the other 85 per cent of producers have disputed the remaining 20 per cent of funds (IPEA, 2011: 283). To illustrate this, of the public agricultural credit for 2009–10, for example, the funds reserved for PRONAF amounted to R$15 billion, an increase of 15.4 per cent in relation to the previous year. Despite this, the PRONAF funds represented only 16 per cent of the R$92.5 billion in credit announced by MAPA in favour of business agriculture. Moreover, of the 4,367,902 family establishments, only around 1.2 million had access to PRONAF (IPEA, 2010: 264–5).

In the following years these differences were maintained, as shown in Table 6.3.

## A new wave in the internationalization of agriculture

Similar to the concentration of landholding, the internationalization of agriculture is also not a novelty in Brazilian history (Sampaio, 1980) but has been assuming new contours in the last decade, owing to the control exercised over agriculture by large transnational companies and the purchase of land by individuals, companies, states and international financial funds.

Brazil has the largest stock of fresh water and agricultural land of any country in the world; these are resources that are fundamental for mechanized agriculture and extensive livestock raising. Added to this is the dominant tropicality of Brazilian land, which provides a high intensity in photosynthesis processes and conditions favourable to the raising of large animals.

These 'comparative advantages' – understood here not as a 'natural vocation' but as historically valorized attributes – for the expansion of agriculture in Brazil is even more evident when it is taken into account that the total land used or not used for pasture in Brazil is more than double that of the two most important countries in this area after Brazil (the US and Russia). Added to this is the fact that, unlike the US and Russia, which have large areas temporarily covered by snow, in Brazil there are no serious seasonal impediments for the agricultural use of land. It is calculated that the country has no less than 15 per cent of unused agricultural land in the world.

All these associated factors contribute to explaining the ongoing wave of internationalization of Brazilian agriculture, expressed by the control of transnational companies over what is produced and where, for what and for whom. Three aspects

**TABLE 6.3** Agricultural credit per harvest (2012–15)

| Harvest | Family farming | Agri-business |
|---------|----------------|---------------|
| 2012/13 | R$18 billion | R$115 billion |
| 2013/14 | R$21 billion | R$136 billion |
| 2014/15 | R$14 billion | R$156 billion |

Source: MDA and MAPA.

**122** Brazil: class struggle in the countryside

illustrate this corporate power: the determination of technological standards (seeds, machines and agrochemicals), the purchase and transformation of production (large traders and agribusinesses) and the growing wave of land acquisitions by foreigners.

In relation to the final point, this involves a local manifestation of a global process. In effect, the offensive of capitalists (including Brazilians) and states in the rural land of the global south has occurred for various reasons, among which are the search for profit through the production of foodstuffs, pasture, fuels and cellulose, as well as the trade and control of fresh water (Borras et al., 2011). This offensive has been propelled by states and by capitals of various extractions, including large-scale international investment funds, avid for new accumulation fronts in a context of international economic crisis.

It is still not possible to precisely measure the magnitude of this phenomenon in Brazil. According to IPEA (2011: 246), until 2011 foreigners had acquired 46.6 million hectares in countries in the global south, of which only four million were in Brazil. However, this information is not reliable, owing to the fragility – politically constructed and preserved over the decades – of state control and inspection mechanisms. In addition to the lack of consistent data about investors and individuals who own land in the country, there are legal breaches that facilitate the access of foreigners to acquiring property in Brazil. One of the strategies used has been the creation of Brazilian companies in the name of third parties, hiding their owners' identities.

## Increasing food insecurity

The last agricultural census revealed that between 1996 and 2006 there was a small reduction in the total area of agricultural establishments, resulting, above all, from the reduction of the area of natural pasture. On the other hand, there was an increase in the areas used for crops, planted pasture and forestry. However, the expansion in the amount of crops has not resulted in the expansion of food production for the Brazilian population. Comparative analysis of the evolution of the planted area of some of the principal agricultural products, as well as the production of cattle and timber, indicates that the area planted with basic foodstuffs has fallen, while the area used for crops mostly aimed at exports and industrial purposes (production of animal feed, energy and paper and cellulose) has grown.

The area used for the production of the three basic foods in the diet of the Brazilian population (rice, beans and manioc) has fallen by more than four million hectares, decreasing from 11,438,457 to 7,383,731 hectares in 2012. On the other hand, the area used for export or industrial transformation products has almost doubled. Considering only three of these products (sugar cane, soybean and corn), the planted area rose from 27,930,804 to 49,908,175 hectares in the same period. It should also be noted that, between 1990 and 2012, soybean overtook corn in terms of planted area, becoming the largest crop in the country. The three crops

# Brazil: class struggle in the countryside **123**

mentioned above (soybean, sugar cane and corn) are responsible for more than 50 per cent of the agricultural GDP of the country.

Of the crops grown for industrial purposes or export, the greatest growth in proportional terms was sugar cane, used fundamentally for the production of sugar for export and fuel alcohol for the internal market. The planted area more than doubled between 1990 and 2012, concentrated in the south-eastern region – responsible for two-thirds of the sugar cane area in the country – and in the centre-west, while in the north-east there was a reduction in this crop. It is worth noting that this expansion was greatly stimulated by the state. Between 2008 and 2009, for example, it is estimated that the sugar-alcohol sector received more than R\$12 billion from the National Social and Economic Bank (Banco Nacional de Desenvolvimento Econômico e Social – BNDES) (Sauer, 2010).

In the case of soybean, which is grown essentially for export, whether *in natura* or in the form of meal for animal feed, the planted area has more than doubled, with the growth occurring in all regions of the country, especially the centre-west, which has overtaken the south as the region with the greatest planted area.

In the case of corn, although the increase was inferior, there was also a growth in the area planted – principally used for the production of animal feed, both for the internal market and for export. Therefore, Brazil has been increasingly converted into one of the principal centres of grain for animal feed, which already occupies one-third of the cultivated area of the planet (ETC, 2011).

Other revealing data about the trajectory of Brazilian agriculture include the expansion of cattle in Brazil, an activity characterized by its extensive nature and with the number of heads of cattle already having surpassed the number of Brazilians. In this case, the activity expanded in all regions, notably the centre-west (leader) and the north, where the herd has tripled in this period, assuming the vice-leadership and overtaking the south-east region.

Finally, also worth noting is the growth in the production of timber in the country, through the production on an industrial scale of trees for the manufacture of paper, cellulose or charcoal, or timber for the furniture industry, civil construction and other uses.

The comparison between population growth and the growth of agricultural production highlights a scenario of food insecurity. Between 1991 and 2010, the Brazilian population rose from 146,917,459 inhabitants to 190,715,799 inhabitants, a growth of 29.8 per cent. In the same period, the production of three basic food products (rice, beans and manioc) increased by only 14.5 per cent, which means that the availability of these basic foods per inhabitant declined. On the other hand, the production of corn, sugar cane and soybean increased 176.9 per cent, which confirmed the priority of current Brazilian agriculture for export-oriented products or the production of raw materials for industry, to the detriment of the production of foodstuffs for the population.

Finally, it is worth noting that state action has been fundamental in propelling this trajectory and making it feasible. Of the establishments that received funding, 85 per cent had as one of their sources some governmental programme, amounting

**124** Brazil: class struggle in the countryside

to 57.6 per cent of funds. Moreover, the distribution of public funding has been profoundly unequal: in 2006, establishments with 1,000 or more hectares (0.9 per cent of the total) obtained 43.6 per cent of funds, while establishments with less than 100 hectares (88.5 per cent of those who obtained funding) received 30.42 per cent of funds (IBGE, 2006).

Some specific data can illustrate the inequality of power in Brazilian agriculture. For the 2008/09 harvest, for example, agribusiness received R$65 billion for costs and investment, an amount 500 per cent higher than the R$13 billion granted to family farming. Between 2007 and 2009, the national treasury spent R$2.3 billion on the securitization of the agricultural debt, while the Federal Revenue Service estimated at R$8.85 billion the amount of the fiscal waiver related to the exemption of taxes granted to the agricultural sector (Sauer, 2010). This means that the state extracted and channelled resources to the Brazilian people to finance the food insecurity of the population in favour of the profit of a minority.

## Violence, the exploitation of workers and environmental devastation

The dominant agrarian model in Brazil has always been marked by intense violence, the exploitation of labour and environmental devastation. Nevertheless, in recent years, these characteristics have been reinforced by the transformations mentioned above.

Data on countryside violence between 1985 and 2011 indicate that every year on average 61 people were murdered in the struggle for land, 633 families were thrown off their land, 13,351 families were evicted by judicial order in some unit of the federation and 397 people were arrested, while there were 762 conflicts, involving 91,264 families (CPT, 2013). Table 6.4, in turn, provides aggregate data for the 1985–2009 period that show the magnitude of violence against rural workers, as well as the serious impunity which reigns in the country.

On the frontier between violence and the exploitation of labour – since it involves at the same time a violation of human rights and a gigantic source of profit – 3,041 occurrences of slave labour were registered in Brazil between 1985 and 2013. This number rose significantly after 2005, when inspection was intensified. Between 2008 and September 2010, for example, inspection operations of the Ministry of Labour resulted in the release of more than 10,000

**TABLE 6.4** Murders of rural workers and judgments – Brazil, 1985–2009

| Total of cases | Number of victims | Cases judged | Persons who ordered the killing condemned | Persons who ordered the killing absolved | Persons who carried out the killing condemned | Persons who carried out the killing absolved |
|---|---|---|---|---|---|---|
| 1,162 | 1,546 | 88 | 20 | 8 | 69 | 50 |

*Source:* Setor de documentação da CPT (April 2013); IPEA (2011: 238).

workers, with almost 50 per cent being in establishments located in areas of the agricultural frontier in the north and centre-west. The south-east, window of 'modern' agribusiness, registered almost 30 per cent of cases of slave labour in 2009, surpassing all other regions. It is in the sugar-alcohol sector – i.e. in the mono-cultivation of sugar cane, strongly financed by the state – that the greatest number of occurrences in the south-east has been concentrated (IPEA, 2011: 240). Recently, after a two-year debate, the National Congress approved a proposal for a constitutional amendment that allowed for the expropriation of lands where the existence of slave labour is discovered, to be used for the purposes of agrarian reform. However, owing to pressure of the *ruralista* lobby, the definition of slave labour was left to be defined in a complementary law, and there is a fear that this definition will drag out for many more years, and that the regulations will not follow the current parameters (which are in harmony with the definitions of the International Labour Organization – ILO), weakening the fight against slave labour.

Moreover, in recent years Brazil has been transformed into the greatest consumer of agro-toxins in the world, with an average consumption of 5.2 litres per inhabitant per year, having overtaken the US in 2008 and concentrating 84 per cent of sales throughout Latin America (IPEA, 2011: 250). Recent data have shown that between 2000 and 2012 sales of agro-toxins grew 96.7 per cent worldwide, while in Brazil they grew 189.6 per cent (ABRASCO, 2012).

Since the planted area in the country has remained practically the same, what can be seen is the brutal intensification of the consumption of agro-toxins, associated with the growth of export crops, which are the crops that consume them most. According to ABRASCO (2012), in 2010, soybean was responsible for 44.1 per cent of the use of agro-toxins in Brazil, followed by cotton (10.6 per cent), sugar cane (9.6 per cent) and corn (9.3 per cent). On the other hand, the production of foodstuffs, (such as fruit and greens) have also registered alarming indices of contamination, with the use of poison in intensities (not quantities) higher than of soybean cultivation (IPEA, 2011: 251).

The growing poisoning of land, water, fauna, flora and foodstuffs has increased the cases of intoxication from agro-toxins. Between 1999 and 2007, almost 52,000 cases were notified (IPEA, 2011: 252). Even more seriously, between 2000 and 2009, 2,052 were registered in the country (ABRASCO, 2012).

Another dimension of the process of environmental devastation is the deforestation triggered by the expansion of the agricultural frontier. Data from the Laboratory of Image Processing and Geo-processing (Lapig), from the Federal University of Goiás, indicate that the current rate of deforestation of the Cerrado could result in an increase from 39 to 47 per cent of the devastated percentage of that biome by 2050. The research also demonstrates that the destruction of the Cerrado places at risk the availability of hydric resources for the Pantanal and the Amazônia, since biomes are interconnected. There exists a correlation between the expansion of the Brazilian agricultural frontier and the increasing deforestation of the Cerrado and the Amazon region.

**126** Brazil: class struggle in the countryside

## The tactic of land occupations

The analysis of data regarding land occupations in Brazil over the last three decades has revealed that this tactic gained increased relevance in the struggle of rural social movements from the middle of the 1990s onwards, reaching its maximum level at the end of the same decade.

At the end of the 1980s and the beginning of the 1990s this tactic was used almost exclusively by the MST, and was also one of the characteristics that distinguished it from the other rural social movements existing in Brazil, especially the CONTAG trade union movement. However, even the MST could not give this type of action a national amplitude, so until 1995 there were fewer than 100 land occupations per year. The context of the economic crisis linked to the implementation of the Washington Consensus in the Brazilian economy in the first FHC administration, combined with the passing of the Agrarian Law by the Brazilian Congress in 1993 – which regulated, albeit in a limited fashion, the social function of property – created the conditions for a significant growth in land occupations in Brazil. After the occupations reached their peak in 1999, with 593 actions, their number began to fall, which can basically be attributed to the repressive actions unleashed by the FHC administration and by the adoption of MALR.

After the election of Lula, given the hope created by the election of a candidate of a party (PT) historically committed to agrarian reform and the expectations caused by the implementation of the II PNRA, occupations began to rise. However, in the middle of the first Lula administration, they began to fall, faced with the evidence that agrarian reform had been abandoned by the government in favour of the priority given to agribusiness. Since then what has been observed, notwithstanding light oscillations, is a tendency towards the reduction of the number of occupations, in the wake of the increasing strength of agribusiness.

Analysing the average annual land occupations in the FHC, Lula and Dilma administrations, this tendency in the fall of occupations as a tactic in the struggle for land in Brazil is evident. The annual average of land occupations during the 20 years that separate the beginning of the first FHC administration from the end of the first Dilma administration was 314.7. Comparing the averages of each administration, we can note that only in the second Lula administration (271.5) and the Dilma administration (218.25) were annual averages lower than this general average. In the two FHC administrations and the first Lula one the averages were higher, with the highest average being observed in the first Lula administration (427). There can thus be no doubt that, after a long cycle of expansion that ran from the first FHC administration until the end of the first Lula one, occupations declined from the second Lula administration onwards. How can this be explained? The historical anachronism of agrarian reform, as some of the ideologues of agribusiness argue? The co-opting of MST leaders and of other land movements, as argued by some left-wing analysts?

Comparing land occupation data with that of areas in conflict highlights interesting elements for the construction of this response. From 2006 to 2008, the number of areas in conflict decreased together with the reduction of occupations. However, from 2009 onwards the tendencies became disassociated, with conflicts increasing while occupations fell. When the percentage of land occupations in relation to the areas in conflict are considered, the disjunction between them becomes even more evident, since the proportion falls from 40 to 20 per cent.

Two conclusions can be drawn from this. First, there was a retraction in the struggle for land organized by rural social movements, notably on the part of the MST, now more concerned with the administration of public policies created for settlements than the organization of new land occupations. Second, with the agribusiness offensive and other activities related to neo-extractivism – which has advanced in the expropriation of peasant, indigenous and *quilombola* land – there was an inflection in land struggles, which reduced the percentage of occupations in relation to total conflicts. It is also important to consider that the increase in the levels of employment, principally in civil construction and other less qualified activities, connected to a greater availability of credit for family farming and a set of conditional cash transfer programmes (such as the *Bolsa Família* programme), sensitively reduced the appeal of the struggle for land and agrarian reform among poor social groups.

All of this means that rural social movements are more on the defensive than the offensive, in a wider context of the retraction of the struggle for land in the country. However, this does not necessarily signify that these movements have simply been co-opted. We think that the reality is more complex. Medeiros (2013), for example, points to three reasons for the reduction of land occupations: (i) the fall in the rate of expropriations, resulting in encampments which lasted for various years; (ii) the reduction in the public available for occupations owing to new possibilities for employment and social policies until 2013; and (iii) new priorities for rural social movements, ranging from direct actions of confrontation with agribusiness to the struggle for credit and the conditions of production. Our analysis agrees with this approach.

It is important to consider that, during the last two decades, owing to the pressure of rural social movements, various public policies were created aimed at rural workers, especially those who had been settled. Important among these were technical assistance (ATES), credit (PRONAF), commercialization (PAA) and education policies (PRONERA). Some are exclusively for the beneficiaries of agrarian reform, such as PRONERA; others covered the entire family farming sector. All these initiatives are important for the consolidation and development of settlements and their creation represents important victories of the social struggle. However, contradictorily, they involve social movements in some manner in their implementation and administration, absorbing much of their energy that could otherwise be directed towards forms of direct social struggle, such as occupations. The participation of the movements in the administration of public policies has engendered democratic forms of control to a greater or lesser extent, depending on the scale (local, state or national) and a series of political factors, but in all cases they have not managed to alter the structure of political and economic power in the Brazilian countryside.

## Agro-development strategies of capital in the twenty-first century and the intensification of the class struggle in the countryside

Since the beginning of the 2000s, business organizations have sought to expand the volume of land for the expansion of the production of agricultural commodities and to block agrarian reform, using the following measures: (i) redefinition of the legal Amazon, excluding the states of Mato Grosso, Tocantins and Maranhão, thereby allowing the immediate incorporation of 145 million hectares, owing to the reduction of the area used for environmental preservation; (ii) privatization of public land of up to 1,500 hectares without public bidding in the Amazon region; (iii) reduction of the border region where foreigners are forbidden to purchase land from 150 kilometres to 50 kilometres; (iv) repeal of the constitutional clause allowing the remnants of *quilombos* title to their land; (v) elimination of the productivity indices, which supported expropriation for the purposes of agrarian reform; (vi) transfer competence for demarcating indigenous lands from the executive to Congress (PEC No. 215) (Almeida, 2010; IPEA, 2013 and 2012).

In relation to environmental policy, the principal initiative consisted of making the legislation in force more flexible, opposing those who defended public regulation and the socio-environmental function of land and those who defended the absolute right to property and the commercialization of nature. The conflicts concentrated on the approval of the new Forestry Code, which replaced the previous one, from 1965. The *ruralista* caucus defended: (i) the amnesty of rural landholders who had not complied with environmental legislation; (ii) the reduction of areas that had to be preserved in any rural property (the so-called legal reserve); (iii) the expansion of the agricultural frontier through the opening of areas where legally this could not occur; and (iv) provision of credit for those who practised environmental crimes. After an intense dispute, the result was very favourable to the interests of agribusiness (IPEA, 2013: 332–6; Sauer & França, 2012).

At the same time, the expansion of new progressive extractivism in Latin America has to be considered (Gudynas, 2012), since a large part of the improvement in the economic conditions of the region resulted from the exploitation of mineral resources and agro-exports, in a scenario which deepened the divisions in low-income sectors, with some criticizing and others extolling the governments that propelled this model.

The extraction and exporting of primary products was linked with financialization, each complementing the other, since the rise in international prices of commodities made it feasible for Brazil and other Latin American countries to continue remunerating international financial capital and distributing export related earning, both to parts of the internal agri-mineral bourgeoisie and to parts of the low-income sectors, via social policies (Gudynas, 2012).

In this scenario, a connection was established between neo-extractivism, economic growth and poverty reduction, which gave broad legitimacy to the two Lula administrations, and to a lesser extent to the first Dilma administration. However, with the reduction of the price of commodities in recent years and the impacts of the international economic crisis, the possibility of this connection has been exhausted, heightening the political conflict within the support base – which is wide and heterogeneous – of the second Dilma administration, which started in January 2015. In other words, the political pact that sustained the model that connected financial capital (national and international), agri-mineral capital and low-income sectors has exhausted its limits.

New perspectives of class struggle have unfolded given this new scenario, marked by economic recession, the rise in unemployment and the decline in income of the working class. Not by chance did massive new land occupations begin to occur in 2015 and the MST has recently declared a return to prioritizing land occupations.

In the Caruaru letter, resulting from the meeting of the National Coordination of the MST, released at the end of January 2016, there appeared the assessment that 'in the national scenario, the international crisis of capitalism is added to the exhaustion of the neo-development model based on economic growth and on the distribution of income with class reconciliation, initiated in 2003' (MST, 2006a).

Despite the discordance in relation to the more general conception of the nature of the economic model adopted by the Lula and Dilma administrations – since we believe that it was not neo-developmentalism, but rather neo-extractivism, and that there was no redistribution of income, but an improvement of the income of the poorest groups without any penalization of the richest – we agree with the diagnosis of the exhaustion from 2013 onwards of the class reconciliation programme implemented by the governing coalitions led by the PT since 2003. The MST resolution announced in the Caruaru letter marked a posture of a major counteroffensive, by pointing to the intensification of mobilizations and, above all, land occupations:

> Due to the inefficiency and apathy of the government in adopting measures favourable to agrarian reform, we will intensify the popular mobilizations, occupations of unproductive *latifúndios* and ranches, as established in the 1988 Federal Constitution, which do not fulfill their social function.
>
> *(MST, 2006)*

## Conclusion

Despite the gains in productivity in intensive branches of production in the last 50 years, the Brazilian agricultural model has historically supported itself and expanded through the extensive appropriation of new areas. It is a model dependent on the elastic offer of land, which requires the maintenance of a stock of unused and unexploited land without any restriction on its use. The process of modernization of agriculture, instead of attenuating, worsened this structural trait. Resulting from this was the veto of the dominant class on any agrarian reform, the pressure for making environmental laws more flexible and the refusal of any mention of social control over the right to property. Equally there occurred the criminalization of social movements by the media and the state.

**130** Brazil: class struggle in the countryside

The concentration of landholding continued to play a fundamental role in the production and reproduction of injustice and the inequality of power, income, and wealth in the country. Far from the image of 'efficiency' which business interests wished to convey, the 'success' of agribusiness was based on the exploitation of peasants, environmental devastation, the indiscriminate use of agro-toxins, and violence against peasants, indigenous peoples, and *quilombolas*, under the direct and indirect sponsorship of the state. These traits are constitutive of the dominant agrarian model, and not exceptions.

Despite the reinvention and activism of peasant, trade union and other segments of the popular movements, agribusiness has reaffirmed itself as the principal force in the structuring of the social relations in Brazilian agriculture. In this context, half a century later it is evident that the agrarian question in Brazil today is not that of capitalist agriculture, the penetration and corporate makeover by capital of agriculture, but the strategic and political response of the rural proletariat and the forces of resistance in the countryside to the further advance of capital in the form of corporate agribusiness and agro-extractivism. Contrary to the arguments advanced by the right-wing and neo-liberal ideologues of corporate agribusiness and the agrarian elite within the ruling class, agrarian reform is not an anachronistic slogan in Brazil. On the contrary, it continues to be current and assumes new content and meaning in the current context of the class struggle in the countryside, which, as Pedro Stedile, the leader of the MST, points out in an analysis of the current political situation, is entering a new phase.

In the current conjuncture of a system in crisis, a profound and prolonged crisis that has resulted in several years of negative economic growth (including a 3.5 per cent decline in total output in 2015), neither 'big capital' nor the governing political class, nor for that matter the PT regime headed until recently by Rousseff (until she was ousted as part of the impeachment proceedings against her, and her effective impeachment, arguably a coup, on 16 April 2016), has a workable or effective strategic or political response to the crisis. In the face of the crisis, the dominant class continues to advance a destructive agribusiness corporate model, and the interim government headed by Michael Tenner, a right-winger who has been described as a cross between Frank Underwood and Donald Trump, continues to advance a neo-developmentalist model that has clearly exhausted if not exceeded its limits. The response of the current government and interim regime to the crisis of the economic model and the pressures exerted by the political representatives of big capital and the agro-export elite has been to claw back the benefits and put a halt to the progressive social policies and programmes implemented over the years of the commodities boom. In this Brazil follows Argentina down the road of a decisive swing to the right. The response of the popular classes to the announced structural adjustment and austerity measures, which echoed measures implemented by the Macri regime, was perfectly predictable: a wave of popular resistance across the country and a sharpening of the class struggle. The outcome of this struggle remains undecided.

The challenge for the Left in this context of crisis and right-wing response is to mobilize the forces of popular resistance: 'to build class unity and feed the people with the ideals of an advanced, socially just and democratic society' (MST, 2016). What this means for the working class and the movement of landless rural workers is, via its diverse organizational forms and 'mediations' (unions, popular social movements and progressive parties), to collectively build a new political project for the country, a project based on 'the defense and deepening of popular democracy, the distribution of wealth, and national sovereignty'. The unfolding of history will show what forms the class struggle will assume in the Brazilian countryside.

## References

ABRASCO. (2012). *Dossiê ABRASCO – Um alerta sobre os impactos dos agrotóxicos na saúde*. Rio de Janeiro: ABRASCO.

Alentejano, P. (2000). 'O que há de novo no rural brasileiro?' *Terra Livre*, 15, pp. 87–112.

Alentejano, P. R. R. (2004). 'Uma breve análise a partir dos dados sobre ocupações e acampamentos'. *Conflitos no Campo – Brasil – 2003*. CPT-Nacional.

Almeida, A. W. B. (2010). 'Agroestratégias e desterritorialização: direitos territoriais e étnicos na mira dos estrategistas dos agronegócios'. in A. W. B. Almeida et al., *Capitalismo globalizado e recursos territoriais*. Rio de Janeiro: Lamparina, pp. 101–44.

Borras, S. M. (2003). 'Questioning market-led agrarian reform: experiences from Brazil, Colombia and South Africa'. *Journal of Agrarian Change*, 3, July, pp. 367–94.

Borras, S. M., Franco, J. C., Kay, C. & Spoor, M. (2011). *Land grabbing in Latin America and the Caribbean viewed from broader international perspectives*. Santiago: FAO Regional Office.

Bruno, R. (1997). *Senhores da terra, senhores da guerra*. Rio de Janeiro: Forense/Edur.

Carvalho Filho, J. J. (2007). 'O governo Lula e o esvaziamento da reforma agrária'. *Reforma Agrária*, 34(2), pp. 95–102.

CPT – Comissão Pastoral da Terra. (2013). *Conflitos no Campo Brasil*. Goiânia, Goiás: CPT Secretaria Nacional. Available at: http://cptnacional.org.br/index.php/noticias/conflitos-no campo/2042-conflitos-no-campo-brasil-2012 [accessed 18 February 2014].

D'Incao, M. C. (1990). 'O governo de transição: entre o velho e o novo projeto político agrícola de reforma agrária', *Lua Nova*, 20, pp. 89–120.

Delgado, G. (2010). 'A questão agrária e o agronegócio no Brasil', in M. Carter (ed.) *Combatendo a desigualdade social: o MST e a reforma agrária no Brasil*. São Paulo: Ed. UNESP, pp. 81–112.

Delgado, N. G. (2009). *Papel e lugar do rural no desenvolvimento nacional*. Rio de Janeiro: IICA/MDA.

Dreifuss, R. (1989). *O jogo da direita na Nova República*. Petrópolis: Vozes.

ETC Group. (2011). *Quién controlará la economía verde?* 1 November. Available at: www.etcgroup.org/es/content/¿quién-controlará-la-econom%C3%ADa-verde [accessed 3 December 2011].

Fachin, L. E. (1993). 'Depois da Lei Agrária: o que muda no campo brasileiro?' *Democracia na terra*, 10, pp. 15–30.

Favareto, A. (2006). 'Agricultores, trabalhadores: os trinta anos do novo sindicalismo rural no Brasil'. *Revista Brasileira de Ciências Sociais*, 21(62), pp. 27–44.

Fernandes, B. M. (2000). *A formação do MST no Brasil*. Petrópolis: Vozes.

Fernandes, F. (1985). *Nova República?* Rio de Janeiro: Zahar.

Ferreira, B., Alves, F. & Carvalho Filho, J. J. (2009). 'Constituição vinte anos: caminhos e descaminhos da reforma agrária – embates (permanentes), avanços (poucos) e derrotas (muitas)'. *Acompanhamento e Análise de Políticas Sociais* (IPEA), 2(17), pp. 155–223.

Gomes da Silva, J. (1987). *Caindo por terra: crises da reforma agrária na Nova República*. São Paulo: Busca Vida.

**132** Brazil: class struggle in the countryside

Graziano da Silva, J. (1985). *Para entender o Plano Nacional de Reforma Agrária*. São Paulo: Brasiliense.

Gudynas, E. (2012). 'Estado compensador y nuevos extractivismos'. *Nueva Sociedad*, 237, pp. 128–46.

IBGE. (2006). *Censo Agropecuário*. Brasília: IBGE.

IBRD. (1997). *Project appraisal document to Brazil for land reform and poverty alleviation pilot project*. Report no. 16342-BR. Washington, DC: IBRD.

IPEA. (2010). 'Desenvolvimento rural'. *Acompanhamento e Análise de Políticas Sociais*, 18, pp. 189–233.

IPEA. (2011). 'Desenvolvimento rural'. *Acompanhamento e Análise de Políticas Sociais*, 19, pp. 231–86.

IPEA. (2012). 'Desenvolvimento rural'. *Acompanhamento e Análise de Políticas Sociais*, 20, pp. 247–311.

IPEA. (2013). 'Desenvolvimento rural'. *Acompanhamento e Análise de Políticas Sociais*, 21, pp. 323–420.

Leite, S. & Ávila, R. (2007). *Um futuro para o campo*. Rio de Janeiro: Vieira & Lent.

Medeiros, L. S. (2001). 'Sem terra, assentados, agricultores familiares: considerações sobre os conflitos sociais e as formas de organização dos trabalhadores rurais brasileiros', in N. Giarraca (ed.) *Una nueva ruralidad en America Latina?* Buenos Aires: CLACSO, pp. 103–28.

Medeiros, L. S. (2002). *Movimentos sociais, disputas políticas e reforma agrária de mercado no Brasil.* Rio de Janeiro: CPDA/UFRRJ and UNRISD.

Medeiros, L. S. (2010). 'Agricultura familiar no Brasil: aspectos da formação de uma categoria política', in M. Manzanal & G. Neiman (eds) *Las agriculturas familiares del Mercosur: trayectorias, amenazas y desafios*. Buenos Aires: Ciccus, pp. 131–52.

Medeiros, L. S. (2013). *A questão fundiária no Brasil contemporâneo e as dificuldades da luta por reforma agrária*. Seminário Franco-Brasileiro.

MEPF. (1997). *Diretrizes do processo de descentralização da reforma agrária*. Brasília: MEPF.

MEPF. (1998). *Mudanças legais que melhoraram e apressaram as ações da reforma agrária*. Brasília: MEPF.

MEPF. (1999a). *Agricultura familiar, reforma agrária e desenvolvimento local para um novo mundo rural*. Brasília: MEPF.

MEPF. (1999b). *A nova reforma agrária*. Brasília: MEPF.

MST. (2006a). *Balanço das medidas do governo Lula (2002–2006) em relação à agricultura camponesa e reforma agrária no Brasil*. São Paulo: MST.

MST. (2006b). 'BioNatur leva sementes agroecológicas para todo o país'. Available at: www.mst.org.br/mst/pagina.php?cd=727. [accessed 9 August 2008].

MST. (2013a). *Programa agrário do MST – Texto em construção para o VI Congresso Nacional*. São Paulo: MST.

MST. (2013b). *Carta da Direção Nacional do MST à Presidenta Dilma Rousseff*. Arapongas: MST.

MST. (2014). *Carta à Presidenta Dilma Rousseff*. Brasília: MST.

MST. Secretaria Nacional (2016). Estamos entrando en un nuevo periodo de la lucha de classes. *Carta de Caruaru/PE*, 30 January. Available at : www.resumenlatinoamericano. org/2016/02/03/mst-de-brasil-estamos-entrando-en-un-nuevo-periodo-de-la-lucha-de-clases-carta-de-caruaru.

Oliveira, A. U. (2010). 'A questão agrária no Brasil: não reforma e contrarreforma agrária no governo Lula', in João P. A. Magalhães (ed.) *Os anos Lula: contribuições para um balanço crítico 2003–2010*. Rio de Janeiro: Garamond, pp. 287–328.

Palmeira, M. (1994). 'Burocracia, política e reforma agrária', in L. Medeiros et al. (eds) *Assentamentos rurais: uma visão multidisciplinar*. São Paulo: Ed. UNESP, pp. 49–65.

Pereira, J. M. M. (2007). 'The World Bank's "market-assisted land reform" as political issue: evidence from Brazil (1997–2006)'. *European Review of Latin American and Caribbean Studies*, 82, pp. 21–49.

Pereira, J. M. M. (2012). 'Evaluation of the *Cédula da Terra* project (1997–2002)'. *Estudos Avançados*, 26(75), pp. 111–36.

Petras, J. & Veltmeyer, H. (2003). *Cardoso's Brazil: A land for sale*. Boulder, CO: Rowman & Littlefield.

Picolotto, E. (2011). *As mãos que alimentam a nação: agricultura familiar, sindicalismo e política*. PhD thesis, Universidade Federal do Rio de Janeiro.

Sampaio, P. de A. (1980). *Capital estrangeiro e agricultura no Brasil*. Petrópolis: Vozes.

Sauer, S. (2009). 'Market-led agrarian reform in Brazil: the costs of an illusory future'. *Progress in Development Studies*, 9(2), pp. 127–40.

Sauer, S. (2010). 'Dinheiro público para o agronegócio'. *Le Monde Diplomatique Brasil*, 33, April, pp. 8–9.

Sauer, S. & França, F. (2012). 'Código Florestal, função socioambiental da terra e soberania alimentar'. *Caderno CRH*, 25(65), pp. 285–307.

Stédile, J. P. & Fernandes, B. M. (1999). *Brava gente: a trajetória do MST e a luta pela terra no Brasil*. São Paulo: Editora Fundação Perseu Abramo.

van Zyl, J. & Binswanger, H. (1996). 'Market assisted rural land reform: how will it work?' in J. van Zyl, J. Kirsten & H. Binswanger (eds) *Agricultural land reform in South Africa: Policies, markets and mechanisms*. New York, NY: Oxford University Press, pp. 413–22.

Veiga, J. E. (1990). *A reforma agrária que virou suco*. Petrópolis: Vozes.

Via Campesina (2002). *Histórico, natureza, linhas políticas internacionais e projeto para a agricultura brasileira*. São Paulo: Via Campesina – Brasil.

# 7

# DEMOCRACY WITHOUT THE WORKERS

## 25 years of the labour movement and mature neo-liberalism in Chile

*Sebastián Osorio and Franck Gaudichaud*

As in much of Latin America, the early history of Chile was marked by the formation of a workers' movement that burst onto the scene as a political actor at the end of the nineteenth century, when the growth of the saltpetre and urban proletariat placed the demands of the working class on the political agenda with the first general strike in the republic's history (Vitale, 2011). From that point, various forms of worker mobilization were common, which the ruling class and the dominant economic groups have had to confront ever since. The result was a tragic death toll incurred throughout the country incurred by those who sought to control the natural response of workers faced with insufferable living conditions (Garcés, 2003). In this effort, organizations as diverse as mutual benefit societies, resistance groups and grass-roots cooperatives came together, as well as political organizations such as the Partido Democrático (Democratic Party), precursor to the Partido Obrero Socialista (Socialist Workers Party), which would become the first organization to exclusively represent the interests of workers, under the leadership of Luis Emilio Recabarren.

This situation dragged along for many years, becoming increasingly unsustainable, such that from 1921 onwards the political regime carried out a progressive incorporation of limited bands of organized workers by means of a social pact known as a 'State of Commitment', the reach of which extended essentially until 1973. In that period, a constant rise in union struggles and social conquests were recorded, marked by an important politicization that culminated with the Popular Unity government and its 'Chilean Path to Socialism', abruptly interrupted by a coup d'état engineered by the US imperialist state at the hands of General Pinochet (Gaudichaud, 2013).

In order to arrive at an assessment of the union movement during those 25 years of democracy, it is essential to weigh the real impact of the dictatorship on the organization of workers up to the present day. This requires taking into account at least three issues. The first is the systematic military offensive carried out since 11 September 1973 against unions and their leaders, in an attempt to eliminate the 'internal enemy' identified by the armed forces, and which led to the shrinking to a bare minimum of their activities, having been also prohibited from collective bargaining and the right to strike. In the long run, this sudden interruption in the process of creating a political entity enmeshed in the world of labour – which stretched throughout the greater part of the twentieth century – required a long reconstruction that, even with the return to democracy, continued building slowly towards a recovery of the conditions that existed prior to the coup d'état.

The second issue to consider is the set of laws known as the 'Labour Plan', which drove a new institutionalism to control conflicts between capital and labour that was highly favourable to the interests of the business class, with the explicit goal of creating a unionism that worked on behalf of the neo-liberal project: depoliticized, weak and fragmented. Undoubtedly, the continuation of the fundamental pillars of the Labour Code three decades after its creation represents one of the greatest successes of the dictatorship. Collective bargaining was carried out only at the company level; the predictable and excessive bureaucracy which governed strikes, the parallel union, the impediments to negotiating around the organization and orientation of the labour process, and labour flexibility, among other considerations, have put considerable and challenging obstacles into play.

A third and final matter has to do with the economic transformations driven by structural adjustment programmes that outlined what has been called the 'neo-liberal model', and which affected the structure of work, drastically reducing the workforce in those sectors of the economy where the labour movement was strongest, and expanding it where there was no presence or significant union tradition, such as the retail sector and services in general (Ruíz & Boccardo, 2014). As a result, union movements had to create alternative strategies for growth and struggle to incorporate to a greater or lesser degree the new contingents of workers.

The importance of these three factors becomes clear with the return to democracy. In fact, the course taken by the labour movement since 1990 can be described as the fruitless struggle to overcome these challenges within the new political setting that came into being with the 1988 plebiscite. Taking these factors into account, this chapter explores the characteristics of the union movement and its political development, as well as the outcomes of its activities over those 25 years both within and outside the sphere of state institutionality, to come to an understanding of its achievements, its failures and possible future scenarios.

To this end, the chapter is divided into two periods: the first is that which begins with the return to democracy and ends in 2000, a moment marked by the *punto de inflexión* which represented the end of the Asian Crisis for a severely weakened union movement and the replacement of the Workers Trade Union Federation (CUT) leadership, which passed from the hands of the Christian Democratic Party (DC) to an alliance between the Socialist Party (PS) and the Communist Party (PC) that delivered newfound stability; the second period, meanwhile, lies with the 'socio-political' shift of the union movement in the CUT and the reposition of

**136** Chile: democracy without the workers

unions as the leading protagonists with strike actions beginning in 2006, and culminating with the beginning of the second Bachelet government. In terms of a conclusion, the chapter offers an overall assessment that includes the debate on the first two years of the government of the New Majority and the discussion around labour reform.

## The union movement in the face of the new 'neo-liberal democracy'

As with any other social actor following a significant, historic path, taking the union movement as an object of study is a complex task owing to its amorphous and loose characterization. To facilitate the analysis, this is performed at two levels. First, clearly delimited organic benchmarks that group together notable sectors of unionism, such as the CUT and other multi-union bodies, those which often have an explicit political orientation or, at least, which have an orientation that is possible to infer from their actions. Second, that of underground movements that underpin the unions' foundations in terms of labour conflict, and in which the conflicts between capital and labour are most directly expressed. To approach a global understanding, the discussion will attempt to engage both levels.

With due consideration of the leading role played by the union movement in bringing protests into being against the dictatorship, but above all the previous agreements between the reborn CUT and the consensus before the 1989 elections, and which implied significant reforms in the Labour Code, for the union movement the future looked promising with the return of democracy, and their more representative leadership acted in consequence.

Therefore, as soon as Patricio Aylwin took office as president of the republic, a policy of 'social consensus' was put into motion. It consisted of the drafting and signing of agreements between workers, businesses and the state, aimed at establishing a social pact for the harmony and governability of the new democracy. In practice, for the union movement it was supposed to smooth out the degree of conflict and the use of mobilizations, contributing to the preservation of the new policy regime, while on the government's side the business community could expect a reciprocal relationship based on understanding and an acceptance of the demands of the workers.

To put all of this into practice, the 'Tripartite Framework Agreements' (*Acuerdos Marco Tripartitos*) were introduced between 1990 and 1993, which the union organizations embraced with enthusiasm. Under the umbrella of the CUT came the associations of civil servants, the teachers' union and the mining and industrial unions, ensuring the broad participation of workers who represented a potential degree of mobilization. The business associations, meanwhile, were reluctant to sign and introduce those measures, despite the fact that their members would benefit the most (Osorio, 2012). In effect, any analysis of those agreements showed that they included an explicit acceptance of the new economic model and the renouncing of the historical classist policy of the union movement, embracing the principal of cooperation between capital and labour in the bosom of the workplace. Further still, it conceded a series of fiscal benefits for workers that in no way threatened the profits of capital, derived directly from state coffers (Araya, 2011: 43–63).

During these early years, the government simultaneously attempted to fulfil its promises by implementing a series of complementary legal initiatives, which sought to strengthen the ability of unions to negotiate and to make it more difficult to fire workers, although without any intention to return to the old model of labour relations, intending that the changes should lead to innovation within the new framework of production codified in the Framework Agreements (Campero, 2007). These reforms, actually rather moderate in nature, were strongly opposed by the business class and representatives of the opposition in parliament, who held a majority in the Senate despite being an electoral minority (due to the institutionalism enshrined in the 1989 plebiscite) and succeeded in pushing Aylwin towards the politics of consensus, approving essentially 'cosmetic' laws with the support of the right-wing sectors, maintaining a prerogative to fire workers at will and without any concrete measures to strengthen unions. Similarly, the Trade Union Law was approved in 1992, legalizing the CUT but opening the door to the creation of other unions with only a 3 per cent support base from unionized workers in the country, something that threatened to establish parallel unions at the trade union level, precisely that which they had sought to avoid (Araya, 2015). In other words, the logic of the consensuses operated in a fashion that Moulián would years later characterize as 'transformism' (Moulián, 2000).

In view of such negative outcomes, there is a question of why a main trade union body with so much social power – the most important of the popular sectors in quantitative terms – accepted the situation without quickly implementing a more confrontational strategy. Various hypotheses, which centre on the idea of an excess of confidence among the leadership regarding the changes that were carried out at the end of the military regime have been offered, as well as the fact that the government did everything it could within the rules of the game, blaming business sector stubbornness for the failure to deliver on promises, owing to their intransigence on sensitive topics for the workers, which led to the dissolution of negotiations in 1993.

Without putting this aside, what has attracted little attention in explaining this phenomenon is the ability of the political parties in the ruling coalition to represent the positions of the most important unions and associations and translate them into guidelines for action taken by the CUT (see Figure 7.1 in the Annex to this chapter). As the data indicate, since its founding and until the mid-1990s, the union federation was dominated by DC and PS, precisely the political forces that promoted the transition model as it was carried out. Add to this the destruction of a large part of the classist Left by the dictatorship, and indirect electoral mechanisms that lack any form of control by the base and that were denounced in each election for being susceptible to fraud, one can understand the political orientation of Labour Central as adhesion to a well-defined historical project that was not able to fulfil its promises (Osorio, 2015).

The responsibility of the leaders of the CUT for the failure of their programmatic demands is even greater considering the fact that during these first years there was an important union conflict at the grass-roots level through strikes that involved a great number of workers. Interestingly, this fact has given rise to diametrically opposed interpretations. On the one hand, it has been pointed out that these strikes are totally natural at the enterprise level, in line with the institutional framework of the labour movement, and on the other hand, it pointed to the potential for political conflict arising from these actions (Zapata, 1992).

The first is questionable in light of the data presented in Figures 7.2 and 7.3, which point to numerous actions that go well beyond the legal framework of industrial relations. As for the second, although the disposition of workers towards direct action and class struggle may have led to a process of politicization, the important thing is that this was not channelled as a mobilizing force that went beyond corporate demands. Nor did it translate into some kind of alternative union force for disputing the leadership of the CUT beyond positions taken by PC, which in those years had been decimated. On the contrary, many of the large corporate-type mobilizations that took place during the Framework Agreements were led by the Concertación leadership, as in the struggles of public officials, teachers and municipal health workers. In this sense, we can speak of a conscious effort not to escalate the conflict.

Towards the end of Aylwin's presidency, the CUT already took note of the narrow limits of its strategy, although this was only reflected in a more radical discourse and withdrawal from the government. It should be noted that at this point the rise of trade unionism as a political actor began a slow but steady decline, which in practice made it almost impossible to reverse the situation. As shown in Figure 7.4, from 1992 onwards the rates of unionization have declined and stagnated notably, and the absolute number of unions have increased, indicating a runaway dispersion of its forces. At the same time, the impact of economic policy should not be underestimated. Along with raising the minimum wage significantly (see Figure 7.5), it reduced inflation by raising real wages and took advantage of the growth momentum and the reduction of unemployment to assuage some of the most pressing problems of the working class such as poverty and indigence.

The trend towards distancing the main trade union leaders from the government deepened with the less integrative attitude shown by the presidency of Eduardo Frei, whose administration will be responsible for establishing the irreversibility of the model with neo-liberal trade agreements signed with foreign countries. At the same time, the CUT suffered its first breakdown, which, combined with the decline of unionization and its mobilizing incapacity, illustrates the complex scenario that must be faced as diverse authors began to speak of a 'crisis of unionism' (Foxley & Sandoval, 1999). This crisis was in reference to the difficulties imposed by the increasing flexibility and subcontracting of labour, in addition to the changes in the structure of production made during the dictatorship, changes that undermined the sectors where trade unionism maintained its strongest organic enclaves, as shown in Figure 7.6, among others factors.

Chile: democracy without the workers  **139**

If there was already an internal crisis, it would be accentuated by the open power struggles with the CUT's 1996 internal elections, in which DC lost its absolute leadership amid reciprocal allegations of fraud, assuming the PS leader Roberto Alarcón with a political orientation that sought to overcome the bogging down of the trade union movement under the slogan 'Dialogue with mobilization', and that promoted an alliance with civil society organizations such as CONFECH that transcended the labour problem, arriving at proposing a change in the constitution, a prelude to what would later be known as the CUT's 'socio-political' turn.

One of the challenges faced by trade unionism in the late 1990s was the so-called Asian Crisis, which put at the forefront the urgency of ensuring the standards of living that had been achieved by a large part of the working class in spite of growing inequality. To do this, going back to the terms of the Agreements, the government specified a significant increase in the minimum wage for three years. But a second attempt at labour reform had also to be addressed. This involved a project that reflected many of the trade union aspirations but that in practice was impossible to ratify because the Concertación constituted a parliamentary minority in the Congress. After the first rejection of the bill, the contents of the reform were reduced by the agreement between Senator Thayer and the minister of labour, which was not enough to avoid a new defeat in the vote, putting an end to the desire to end the most anti-union aspects of the Labour Code. In any case, there was some doubt whether the government had a genuine interest in approving its reform, or if by taking advantage of its parliamentary minority it opted to stress the right to the upcoming elections, clearly positioning it on the side of the business 'entrepreneurs'.

The frustration of important sectors of workers when they saw that after almost a decade of democracy the promises in the workplace remained unfulfilled was not an obstacle for a continuation of the trade union struggle. In fact, major strikes by teachers, public officials and trade unions from all sectors of the economy continued apace, albeit far from the effervescence of the 'joy' of the transition, and corroborating in each battle the insurmountable difficulties of finding success in collective bargaining without the existence of stronger trade union organizations than those at the enterprise level in dealing with their conflicts. Particular mention should be made of the decisive support given by a sector of the CUT to the coal workers of Lota, in the struggle to avoid the closure of the mine, and also the last significant mobilization that the Labour Central was able to promote in October 1995. This included street blockades and actions taken without requesting permits in various cities throughout the country and that failed to achieve any significant impact.

The challenge of the 1996 election by the DC sectors most committed to the politics of consensus threatened an irreversible break with the project of a unitary unionism beyond ideological divisions, leading to a reformulation of electoral rules to improve the weak internal democracy of Labour Central through open lists and an increase in the number of delegates (from 800 to 30,000), conferring the right to vote to the presidents of all the affiliated unions. In spite of this reorganization, the following elections of 1998 were again marked by scandal, with the aim of

**140** Chile: democracy without the workers

withdrawal from the list by Concertación, which resulted in the victory of the Communist Party through its unknown leader Etiel Moraga, in alliance with the dissident PS group of Arturo Martínez.

As expected, far from solving the CUT's problems, the weakening of DC leadership deepened the victory of PC. However, it should be noted that the change in leadership, which in another context could have marked important changes, occurred at its worst moment in terms of affiliation and legitimacy before the imminent retirement of DC. In addition, the undisputed weight of PS implied a balance that PC could not break if it wanted to protect the credibility of Labour Central so in practice the change from a DC–PS axis to a PC–PS axis did not imply any immediate changes of relevance beyond adoption of more confrontational language. In other words, the emergence of a political tendency aimed at breaking away from the dictatorship's legacy did not yet materialize as a concrete force.

Despite the indicated inertia, it was inevitable that new elections would be held in the following year to dispel the concerns of government parties, and so, without pain or glory, the brief leadership of PC opened the way to the presidency of Arturo Martínez, who had the CUT's political project in his hands, which had shifted from the slogan of the 'Framework Agreements' to that of 'Dialogue with mobilization' without any results. Nevertheless, the election of the first socialist president in the post-dictatorship period, and the departure of the ghost from the break-up of the Central, augured an encouraging panorama.

## The promise of socio-political syndicalism and the rebirth of the workers' strike

The rise of the socialist Ricardo Lagos to the presidency meant, at least initially, a renewal of the relationship between trade unionism and the government. The difference was that after a decade of neo-liberal democracy, and with disenchantment on account of the debts left by the Concertación project, the relationship was now fraught with mistrust and, therefore, it was not an impediment for the CUT to continue advancing in its agenda of alliances with social organizations, and to put on the table its extra-labour demands whenever it could.

But the trade union movement in the early 2000s was not the same as it had been in the 1990s. The balance of the decade was undoubtedly negative in terms of organizing the working class, and beyond the lack of results with regard to the programme of struggle, because unionism had not been able to reactivate according to the expectations generated. In general terms, the unionization rate fell and stagnated below the peak reached in 1992, but over time an ever-smaller number of union members were engaged in the collective bargaining process, a tendency that would extend into at least 2004. This speaks of increasing difficulties for unions in disputing how to distribute the wealth that they generated.

The repercussions of the Asian Crisis in turn limited the margins of manoeuvre for the new government in improving the situation of workers with economic policies that would lead to an increase in the minimum wage, reduce the rate of poverty and indigence, and combat unemployment. The other side of the coin was that, finally, after 10 years, the governing coalition obtained an absolute majority in both chambers of parliament, the reason why in theory the approval of laws or reforms would no longer be conditioned by behind-the-scenes negotiations with the Right. But, as we shall see, the neo-liberal model was already well entrenched, and Lagos did not intend any change in its basic pillars.

In political terms there were at least four trade union movements by the end of the 1990s. The first was represented by the 'moderate' leadership of the CUT, which emphasized the importance of mobilization but above all of dialogue with the government. The second was a 'conservative' policy of sectors of DC that ended up breaking away from Labour Central in 2003 to start the UNT (General Workers Union) the following year, with a corporative and critical discourse regarding the excessive politicization of the CUT. Parallel to these two tendencies, a sector with a more radicalized but still very minority political perspective, which emphasized internal democratization and class independence, was formed with the creation of MOSICAM (Trade Union Movement for Change) and the emergence of the CGT (General Confederation of Workers) following the disaffiliation of the CUT of a sector led by former communist Manuel Ahumada Lillo, from the confederation of the food, hotel and gastronomy industry. But this latter tendency also arose within certain less 'organic' expressions of the class struggle and union organization, sometimes characterized as 'movementist' syndicalism insofar as it sought to extend collective action to non-union social organizations and demand more horizontal and flexible forms of organization.

Finally, among workers, there was a massive presence of a 'depoliticized' and atomized sector that sometimes participated in trade unionism, but with no interest in anything beyond monetary or corporate issues. The latter group was largely 'the son of neo-liberalism' and of the new individualistic subjectivities of the model installed in Chile since 1975, but it is based above all on the immense 'flexi-precarization' of the labour force from the 1980s and 1990s, forging a fragile and fragmented union structure with few prospects (Dasten, 2014: 117–40).

In contrast, the first sector linked to the CUT embodies the traditional trend and historical continuity, but according to several scholars is part of a project that had already seen several degrees of internal decomposition, which explains the emergence of other small Labour Centrals, and at the same time a loss of credibility and representativeness, particularly in the absence of a leadership directly elected by its members or facing what was widely considered a 'bureaucratized' organization.

However, in these years of the Lagos government, the Labour Central began to gradually move towards greater politicization of its goals, despite the fact that some leaders mentioned their fear that this orientation could mean a risk of alienation within the base of the trade union movement. The demands of the CUT in these years were eloquent: from strictly labour demands to important changes in the economic model as a whole. This trend, which was already a few years in the making, had its consecration in the 2003 Congress of the Central, which established as the official position of the CUT a so-called 'socio-political' trade unionism. The reasons for this phenomenon can be found in the maturation of the PS–PC leadership. An

**142** Chile: democracy without the workers

increasing number of union leaders, including those of PC, had come to the realization of the need for certain institutional changes in order to bring about further growth of the union and to strengthen its capacity to wage further struggles.

In the year 2001, President Lagos managed to approve the second labour reform of the post-dictatorship period, but, in the absence of consensus on the part of the leaders of the ruling parties, the end of strike-breaking and other such measures of concern to workers did not materialize as expected. This showed that the problem was not only one of parliamentary majorities but the concern in certain sectors regarding the legacy of the model of industrial relations instituted by the military regime. On the other hand, collective bargaining was much preferred over negotiating agreements, leading as it did to a reduction in the working day and strengthening of the Labour Directorate. All this generated a permanent criticism by the leadership of the CUT, which again saw the opportunity to make major changes.

To protest against this situation, but also to advance the position of Labour Central's new demands and to reject the business offensive that advocated greater labour flexibility (a position that found support from within the ranks of the Lagos administration), in August 2003 the CUT organized the first national strike since the return to democracy. Along with several street blockades that paralysed the capital city, the calculations of the organizers were that around 600,000 workers adhered to the strike nationally; the government meanwhile spoke of total normality.

Despite the show of strength, this mobilization did not achieve anything except to reveal what the multi-union was about and ready to do, and to reaffirm some degree of union independence. Since then, leaders have been involved in the preparation of the CUT's refoundational Congress, which had three long-run consequences. First, it consolidated its 'socio-political' orientation, which involved the generation of social and political alliances to promote structural changes to the Chilean model. Second, the 'conservative' current concretized its threat to break away from the Central and form the National Union of Workers, which in the long run would be immersed in the irrelevance of not having the expected support of the Concertación parties, which strictly were the only ones capable of mobilizing the trade union machinery needed to give a significant boost to the formation of a parallel Central. And the third was the incursion of trade unionism in the 2005 elections in alliance with some parties of the Concertación, which did not manage to achieve any representation.

However, at the grass-roots level in the first five years of this decade, except in the public sector, the labour conflicts that ended in a strike diminished their intensity, probably in the face of the verification of the limits of these trade union instruments that, despite legal changes, continued to favour the business class offensive. There were, as always, important exceptions, such as the efforts of the national coordinator of the Luksic Group (COSILUK), which in 2003 tried to build a union organization based on the financial holdings of the powerful Chilean entrepreneur. But, despite the advances made in this initiative, for various reasons it did not thrive. In spite of this devastating panorama, from 2005 onwards the union struggle re-emerged, albeit in a still limited form, as shown in Figures 7.2 and 7.3. This partial revitalization resulted mainly in the growth of illegal strikes and the growth of a large gap with respect to the number of legal strikes.

This new impulse of trade unionism, or the 'rebirth of the workers' strike', as the sociologists Aravena and Nuñez (2009) have termed it, has been symbolized to a great extent by the great mobilization of the workers subtracted by the CODELCO copper company, which marked the prelude to what would be Bachelet's first government. The founding of the Confederation of Copper Workers (CTC), under the leadership of Communist Party member Cristian Cuevas, the highly combative strike of 2007 of most of its 25,000 subcontractors, combining paralysis, roadblocks, clashes with the police and negotiations with the government, led to important benefits for the miners within a new Framework Agreement. But they also showed the limits to the new president's progressivism in that, rather than solving the problem of subcontracting, the parliament ended up legalizing this widespread practice. At the same time, conflicts in the private sector and strikes against several forest enterprises between March and May 2007 (the Arauco forest of the COPEC holding company), as well as the 'long strike' of thousands of workers for the salmon companies in 2008, shook the country later with considerably fewer favourable results (Álvarez, 2009).

There are several reasons why these mobilizations can be understood as a qualitative change for the Chilean trade union movement, but in broad terms it can be asserted that in particular the paralysis of the CTC came to reposition the strike as the political instrument par excellence for workers. But, for this to happen, the will of a handful of leaders was not enough; what was needed was a mass labour movement from the grass roots, a development that undoubtedly was driven by leaders with a more radical and rupturist orientation. More importantly, in order for the disruptive power of the strike to have an impact on national politics, it had to be deployed in what Womack called 'strategic positions', i.e. those sectors of the economy in which a strike has relevant economic effects that warrant state intervention (Womack, 2007). Thus, what the major trade union referendum could not do with its political turnaround was now carried out by sectors of workers from the corporate struggles, but which pointed to central aspects of labour regulation, such as the subcontract, in the model.

At a different level, these mobilizations marked a turning point in the downward trend in unionization, as shown in Figure 7.4, and also the resumption of greater striking activity, perhaps motivated more by the example of trade union organizations than with their own, had been politically influential. In this sense, it would be necessary to consider the renewed work stoppages organized by state workers at the central and municipal levels and by the mobilization of teachers, among others. Also, in the private sector, attempts were made to replicate similar strategies, with unified mobilizations of precarious workers in the commercial retail sector, although they have been far from reaching the level of their

**144** Chile: democracy without the workers

predecessors in mining, and also have the same level of support from the CUT that was stressed by these types of action that did not adjust to the existing institutionality and that continued to increase. In fact, according to the studies by Armstrong and Águila (2011), in 2009 only 22,000 workers (in an active population of eight million people) participated in legal strikes, while more than 1,500,000 were involved in conflicts considered illegal.

In contrast to the rules imposed by the Labour Code, a second period of labour resistance developed, which spread less drastically during the first democratically elected right-wing government in more than 40 years. Among the most important are the long mobilization (2011–14) of the port transport workers, who had not been able to forge the Port Union of Chile, which has shown the ability to negotiate extensions and pressure to set up agendas (such as the so-called 'Ley Corta Portuaria' in 2014) taking advantage of its privileged position in the economy, by controlling the gateway of most of the country's exports.

While the CUT, the most important trade union referent to this day, tried to reinvent itself by reaching new fringes of workers and installing a programmatic agenda that was elusive until finding a certain harmony in the second Bachelet government, different workers' movements with characteristics other than 'traditional' trade unionism have found their own ways of organizing and action. Their transitory and unstable labour characteristics have given way to forms of unity more adjusted to territorial and communal criteria that transcend the company, which allows them to act collectively around more general interests than the immediate corporations and to negotiate their demands more effectively than have the subcontracted workers. This insurgency from below facilitated the appearance of other union strategies, such as in the case of state workers who are not contracted for a wage but are paid a fee and thus have no labour rights owing to their particular condition. The new unionism of the CUT and several smaller Labour Centrals and unions has resulted in these workers being treated in the same way as other workers. In any case, it is fair to recognize that several of these trade union expressions have grown in contact and dialogue with the CUT, which has moved cautiously and at times with contradictions appropriate to its adaptation to the new context for labour.

Finally, it is essential to emphasize that if the trade union movement has recovered a certain level of activism and organization it is because it is starting from a very low level. The trade union organization today in Chile is an institution with a presence only in large enterprises, in which almost half have a union (48 per cent). In the smaller companies, which constitute the majority of businesses, trade unionism is found in an extreme minority of cases. In fact, according to the Labour Survey of the Ministry of Labour, only 4.5 per cent of small enterprises and 1.6 per cent of micro-enterprises are unionized (ENCLA, 2011). This reality combines with some experiences of trade union revitalization, but that does not allow us to speak of a 'new trade unionism', as the labour movement is rooted in historical experiences and struggles accumulated over the course of the twentieth century (Garretón, 2012).

## Final thoughts

In light of this brief analysis on the trajectory of trade unionism in neo-liberal democracy it is possible to conclude with a general assessment of its struggles and its current situation.

First, 25 years after the transition to democracy, the centrality of macroeconomic equilibrium, the construction of a 'subsidiary' state, the deepening of the asymmetry between capital and labour, the unrestricted support for the export strategy as an 'engine' of macroeconomic growth, the control over natural resources by transnational conglomerates and the hegemony of speculative finance remain the hallmark of the current Chilean economy. In this process the political logic has been subordinated to economic rationality, which had to follow the principles of the market economy – free-market capitalism: this neo-liberal rationality helped shape the country in the mould of a 'mature', albeit peripheral, capitalist society. The Chilean way to neo-liberalism was born in violence and, in the process, the labour movement was largely destroyed and reconfigured to the point of being unable to regain the strength that it had before the coup d'etat. Figure 7.7 illustrates this clearly.

The important thing is that this situation has not been a product of chance, but rather responds to a set of factors of shared responsibility between the trade union movement and the political forces that have managed the institutionality inherited from the military regime. On the one hand, the Tripartite Framework Agreements were the maximum expression of the policy promoted by the Concertación, tying the trade unions to the commitment that the first years of the transition would pass without disruption or disruptive mobilizations. On the other hand, the reforms demanded by the trade union movement did not find room in a democratic context plagued by authoritarian enclaves[1] that blocked the legislative implementation of government programmes, although there is a real doubt as to the political will of Concertación leaders and politicians to effect any change beyond tepid reforms in the direction of poverty reduction. To judge by the facts, these centre-left politicians are uncomfortable with a trade unionism that threatens in any way the value placed on economic stability by the capitalist class. That is, they can be considered to be political representatives or functionaries of this class

From the perspective of labour, the ineffective performance and lack of activism of the most important expression of labour unionism in the country can be explained in part by the partisan axis of union leadership – DC hegemony with PS support – which marks the 'socio-political' commitment of the 'democratic' Concertación regime to a constitutional arrangement engineered by the dictatorial Pinochet regime. This commitment was sealed by the entry of PC into an alliance with the governing regime and the multi-union labour movement, such as it is, under the umbrella of the New Majority. In the hands of its president, Barbara Figueroa, who has embarked once more on the road to collaboration, multiple drafts of a new labour reform bill have been postponed, slowing down and making it difficult to launch a major trade union offensive against capital.

**146** Chile: democracy without the workers

As has been pointed out, the figures show that the result of this trajectory of trade unionism has not been positive; the percentage of the unionized labour force has not managed to grow from a meagre 12 per cent, whereas today less than 10 per cent of workers are covered by collective instruments. Meanwhile, inequality continued to increase until it stagnated in the mid-2000s, making Chile one of the most unequal countries in the world. The situation has also hit the CUT, which by 2014 had only about 22 per cent of Chilean unions (far from its 'unitary' expectation) and maintains a highly questionable internal election system as it lacks such basic aspects as a transparent and verifiable pattern, which has resulted in a move away from important trade union organizations such as CONFUSAM and trade unions in the retail sector.

Meanwhile, the absence of far-reaching reforms to the most harmful aspects of the model identified by the New Majority has led many analysts to speak of a continuation of the 'transformative' project of the Concertación, although now accompanied by timid reformist reforms aimed at solving or reducing the social unrest expressed in the streets since 2011. This thesis finds support in various actions carried out by the government, which, in the long run, show that sectors that are reluctant to take measures that substantially alter the institutional structure of neo-liberalism are a transversal majority, which includes both the Right and the so-called 'Party of Order' (the axis formed by the Socialist Party and the Christian Democratic Party). Thus, to expect full compliance with the programme of Bachelet's second government with the support of its coalition seems to be a chimera.

A legitimate question that arises from this scenario is whether there is another alternative to advance a minimum programme of legal changes that might strengthen the world of trade unions. Although the outcome of the current labour reform project remains to be seen, a tentative response would have to take into account the failed initiatives that have been carried out, some of which have been exposed along these lines. Likewise, considering that the CUT itself does not have the capacity to win its demands from the streets, the key seems to be to manage the little mobilizing power of its main intermediary bodies on the level that the working class knows best: stoppages of activities or strikes, but with clear political objectives. If such a commitment were to be made, it would also be necessary for the CUT, sooner rather than later, to take a generous role in calling for a common struggle for organizations that have withdrawn from it, but above all those that have proved to have a real disruptive power when they paralyse their workplaces, so that the desired changes can be contested no matter how much the business sectors and the politicians who defend them might protest.

Despite the complexity of this challenge, the shaking of the social struggles since 2011 and the significant conflicts in various sectors of the labour market have made it possible to see the rearticulation of union actors who could renew the political agenda of the workers in the medium term and the Chilean left.

# Annex

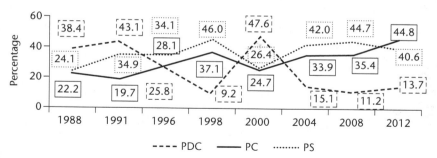

**FIGURE 7.1** CUT election results by political party, 1988–2012.

*Source:* our own elaboration based on Osorio (2015).

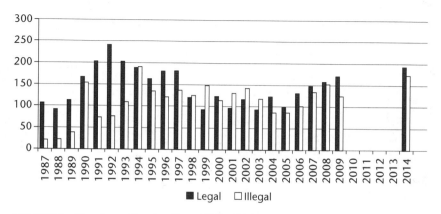

**FIGURE 7.2** Number of legal strikes, 1987–2014.

*Source:* own elaboration with data from Armstrong (2009); Observatorio de Huelgas Laborales (2015).

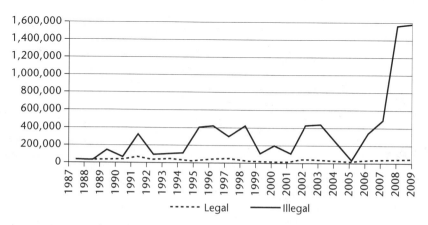

**FIGURE 7.3** Number of workers on legal strike, 1990–2009.

*Source:* own elaboration with data from Armstrong (2009).

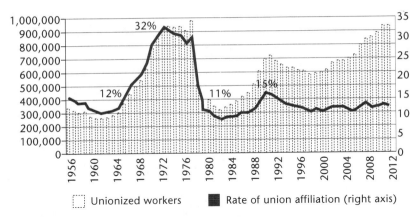

**FIGURE 7.4** Rate of unionization (employed) and population with union affiliation.

Source: own elaboration based on data from DERTO (1977) and Lüders (2010).

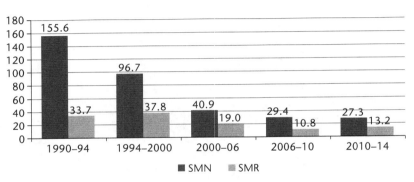

**FIGURE 7.5** Evolution of the nominal real minimum wage by presidency, 1990–2014.

Source: own elaboration with data in Rivas, Gabriel (2014). Available from: www.cipstra.cl/salario-minimo-1.

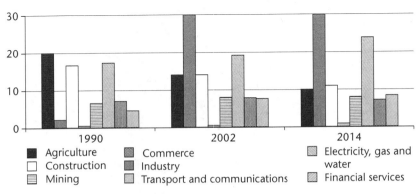

**FIGURE 7.6** Percentage distribution of the labour force by sector, 1990–2014.

Source: own elaboration with data from INE.

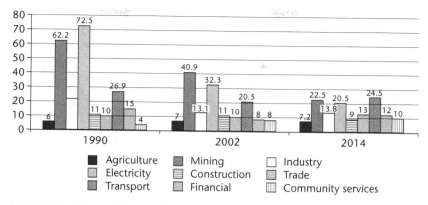

FIGURE 7.7 Union affiliation by economic activity, 1990–2014.

## Note

1 Garretón, Manuel (2012): *Neoliberalismo corregido y progresismo limitado: los gobiernos de la Concertación en Chile 1990–2010.* Editorial ARCIS y CLACSO, Santiago.

## References

Álvarez, R. (2009). 'Desde fuera o dentro de la institucionalidad? La "huelga larga del salmón", y las nuevas estrategias sindicales en Chile (2006–2008)', in A. Aravena & D. Nuñez (eds) *El renacer de la huelga obrera en Chile. El movimiento sindical en la primera década del siglo XXI.* Santiago: ICAL.

Aravena, A. & Nuñez, D. (eds) (2009). *El renacer de la huelga obrera en Chile. El movimiento sindical en la primera década del siglo XXI.* Santiago: ICAL.

Araya, R. (2011). 'El acuerdo marco chileno. Un caso frustrado de pacto social?' *Tiempo Histórico*, 2, pp. 43–63.

Araya, R. (2015). *Organizaciones sindicales en Chile. De la resistencia a la política de los consensos: 1983–1994.* Santiago: Editorial Finis Terrae.

Armstrong, A. & Águila, R. (2011). 'Evolución de las huelgas laborales en Chile, 1979–2009'. *Revista Administración y Economía*, 69. Santiago: Ediciones Universidad Católica de Chile.

Campero, G. (2007). 'La economía política de las relaciones laborales 1990–2006'. *Serie Estudios Socio-Económicos*, 37. Santiago: CIEPLAN.

Dasten, J. (2014). 'Tendencias de un sindicalismo fracturado. Sindicalismo autoritario versus sindicalismo movimientista', in VVAA, *Reconfiguración de las relaciones entre Estado, sindicatos y partidos en América Latina.* Buenos Aires: CLACSO, pp. 117–40.

ENCLA. (2011). *Séptima encuesta laboral*, Dirección del trabajo, Santiago. Available at: www.dt.gob.cl/documentacion/1612/w3-article-101347.html [accessed 12 January 2014].

Foxley, A. & Sandoval, G. (1999). *Conversaciones con Manuel Bustos.* Santiago: Editorial Andrés Bello.

Garcés, M. (2003). *Crisis social y motines populares en 1900.* Santiago: Lom Editorial.

Garretón, M. (2012). *Neoliberalismo corregido y progresismo limitado: los gobiernos de la Concertación en Chile 1990–2010.* Santiago: Editorial ARCIS and CLACSO.

Gaudichaud, F. (2013). *Chile 1970–1973. Mille jours qui firent trembler le monde.* Rennes: PUR.

Moulián, T. (2000). *Chile actual, anatomía de un mito*. Santiago: LOM Ediciones.

Osorio, S. (2012). *El bloque histórico en Chile durante la transición y las transformaciones en la política sindical: El caso de la CUT*. Article 3, Centro de Investigación Político Social del Trabajo.

Osorio, S. (2015). *Trayectoria y cambios en la política del movimiento sindical en Chile, 1990–2010. El caso de la CUT, entre la independencia política y la integración al Bloque Histórico Neoliberal*. Master's thesis, University of Santiago.

Ruíz, C. & Boccardo, G. (2014). *Los chilenos bajo el neoliberalismo. Clases y conflicto social*. Santiago: Ed. El Desconcierto.

Vitale, L. (2011). *Interpretación marxista de la historia de Chile*. Vol. 1. Santiago: Lom ediciones.

Womack, J., Jr. (2007). *Posición estratégica y fuerza obrera. Hacia una nueva historia de los movimientos obreros*. Mexico City: Fondo de Cultura económica.

Zapata, F. (1992). 'Transición democrática y sindicalismo en Chile'. *Foro Internacional*, 2(5), pp. 703–21.

# 8

# MEXICO

## Dynamics of a class war

Mexico is a society of intense class conflict. Indeed, the level of class war in Mexico is probably unparalleled anywhere else in the world. This is partly the result of historical factors and partly because of the country's closeness to and integration with the US and its vulnerability to the forces of world capitalism. The contradictions in Mexican society are evident even to the most casual observer. Apart from the appalling inequalities and the deep pockets of poverty in a society of unsurpassed wealth, and the sheer scale of class exploitation, Mexico is a country of long-established racist oppression, reflecting the consequences of the Spanish conquest of the sixteenth century. Members of the ruling class and its various elites, as well as television personalities, political bosses and anyone who wields any real power and has privileged access to the country's extraordinary wealth, is almost by definition white. The great mass of the population of the working class as well as middle-class business operators and functionaries are of mixed racial descent and can be identified by their dark skins. At the very bottom of society are the indigenous people, mainly peasants, who generally speaking are living at just about subsistence level. The descendants of the Aztecs, Mayas, Zapotecs, etc. are paying the enduring price of their historic defeat.

This chapter will review some of the most important dimensions of the class struggle in various conjunctures of a system in crisis and an economy on the threshold of epoch-defining social change. We began this book with the observation and insight derived from Marx's conception of historical materialism that class struggle is the driving force of social change. Our analysis of the forces of change released in the class struggle substantiates this assertion.

## Six decades of capitalist development and class struggle

The history of capitalism in Mexico can be traced back several centuries to the conquest, the pillage of the country's natural resource wealth, and the imperialist

**152** Mexico: dynamics of a class war

class exploitation of the diverse indigenous nationalities that inhabited the continent. But for a number of reasons we situate our analysis in conditions found at the
end of World War II, when the idea of development as we understand it today, i.e.
as a project of nation-building based on the agency of the state with international
cooperation, was 'invented' (Sachs, 1992). By this time the country had already
experienced many decades of capitalist development and a corresponding process of
productive and social transformation, which saw the conversion of large numbers
of indigenous and indigenous peasant farmers into an industrial proletariat or an
industrial reserve army of surplus rural labour. But with the advance of capital in
both the countryside and the cities the 1950s and 1960s saw the formation of an
insurgent class struggle from below in the form of a powerful labour movement and
a rapid increase in unionization as well as the formation of social movements organized around the demand for land and revolutionary change. These movements
were formed in the revolutionary class struggle tradition established by Emilio
Zapata, the iconic leader of the peasant revolt and the agrarian movement in the
state of Morelos at the beginning of the Mexican Revolution in 1910.[1]

This movement, together with the broader Zapata-led peasant movement that
it inspired, would become one of the two driving forces of the twentieth century's
first major social revolution – a development that led to a massive programme of
land redistribution and agrarian reforms. Paralleling this development in the countryside was the growth of a powerful labour movement that can be traced back to
two labour revolts – the strike, on 1–5 June 1906, of some 2,000 mineworkers
against US-owned Cananea Consolidated Copper Company (CCCC), and another
strike some six months later against a textile firm, Rio Blanco, the operator of a
number of textile production firms in the state of Veracruz. Both labour revolts
were violently repressed by the state but they led to increased class consciousness
within the working class – an awareness not just of the super-exploitation and
oppressive conditions experienced by workers in Mexico's most important industry
at the time, but also of the potential power of an organized working class. The
strike against Cananea, the property of an American colonel, William C. Greene,
was a major catalyst of this growth in class consciousness and precursor to various
struggles leading up to the Mexican Revolution; in the accounts of Mexican labour
historians *la huelga de Cananea* was the 'cradle' of the Revolution.

The embers of an alliance of peasants and workers forged in the heat of the
Mexican Revolution were rekindled in the 1930s in a series of class struggles during
the regime of Lazaro Cárdenas, founder of Partido Revolucionario Mexicano
(PRM), the predecessor of the PRI, which ruled Mexico for 71 years until 2000,
when it surrendered power to the right-wing National Action Party (PAN). The
leading force in this struggle was the workers in the oil production sector, who had
become a major strategic factor of national development. In response to this mobilization of workers and peasants, and to settle the conflict between capital and labour
in both the countryside and the cities, President Cárdenas (1936–40) and his government nationalized the US-owned oilfields and expropriated a large swath of
multimillion landholdings,[2] socializing peasant agricultural production in the form

of the *ejido* system of communal property in land – a development that would be partially reversed with the Agricultural Modernization Act, legislated by the Salinas-led government in 1992.

Over the following three decades the Mexican labour movement saw many ups and downs and different twists and turns, including the formation of a corporatist system of tripartite negotiations linking both labour and capital to the state.[3] This political development, engineered by Cárdenas, can be counted as one of the labour movement's most important strategic defeats, accommodating as it did the leadership of the movement to the PRI and perverting the subsequent course of the class struggle from below, tying the labour movement to the governing PRI regime.

The capitalist class and the forces of US imperialism operating in Mexico responded to the advances of the working class and the peasantry, and the peasant–worker alliance forged in the class struggle, by mustering all the forces available to them by virtue of their control of the state apparatus and the cooperation provided by the US government in the form of development assistance. The result was a countrywide class struggle that engaged both organized labour in the demand for higher wages and better working conditions, the landless or near-landless peasant farmers and indigenous communities in their struggle for land and revolutionary change, and the political Left in a concerted effort to mobilize and unify the diverse forces of resistance and opposition to the advance of capital and its assault on the livelihoods of both workers and peasants. As for the role of the state in this struggle, it involved both the stick (political assassinations of peasant leaders and other forms of violent repression) and the carrot: improving social security and living standards for formal-sector workers in industry, construction and extractive activities; land reform in the countryside; and, for *ejidos* with commercial potential, irrigation, credit, seeds, guaranteed prices.

One of the milestones in this class struggle was the student movement of 1968 when thousands of students across the country protested for greater democracy and joined the forces of resistance mobilized by the land and labour movements to create a near-revolutionary situation in which up to 300 students and citizens were killed by the government's armed forces (Soldatenko, 2005: 111–32).

In the wake of 1968 the forces of reaction, mobilized and led by the state, redoubled the class struggle from above in the form of five tactics. One was to reconcile the conflict between labour and capital in negotiated tripartite settlement of the issues in dispute. Another was to facilitate the labour force participation of rural migrants to the cities by incorporating them in a programme of social welfare measures. This resulted in incremental but steady improvements in the standard of living of the urban population. A third tactic was to extend to offer those peasant farmers and their communities beset by diverse forces of change and capitalist development relief from the pressures created by these forces in the form of a programme of integrated rural development – extending to them the technical and financial assistance needed for them to confront these forces of change. The aim of this tactic was to divide and demobilize the revolutionary social movements by offering the rural poor an alternative to engaging the class struggle. A fourth tactic, used with international cooperation, was to decapitate the social movements by co-opting the leadership or offering community leaders and activists grants to further their studies in the US. The government's tactic of last resort was to deploy the state's repressive apparatus – its reserves of armed force – in a direct confrontation with the revolutionary movements. By the end of the 1970s these movements had been either defeated or, in the case of what would be reborn as the Zapatista Army of National Liberation (EZLN), brought to ground. As for the labour movement, it would also be brought to ground – not via the deployment of the state's repressive apparatus, but rather by the penetration of global capitalism and the working of structural forces released with Mexico's entry into the new world order of neo-liberal structural reform.

## The neo-liberal pivot of the class struggle

The 1980s in Latin America opened with a conservative counter-revolution, a movement to halt the incremental but steady gains made in earlier decades by the working class within the social liberal reform framework of what could be described as a development state.[4] Both the labour movement and the struggle for land in the countryside had been defeated by a combination of state repression and a strategy of integrated rural development designed to turn the rural poor – the masses of dispossessed peasant families forced by the capitalist development of agriculture to abandon their rural livelihoods and communities in the countryside – away from the confrontational politics of the social movements seeking revolutionary change (Delgado Wise & Veltmeyer, 2016).

This defeat, together with the dynamics of an expanding external debt, created conditions that allowed the World Bank and the IMF to impose on the Mexican and other governments in the region a programme of structural adjustments to their macroeconomic policies, initiating what David Harvey among others dubbed the 'neo-liberal era'.[5]

A major aim and a stated goal of the neo-liberal policy reform agenda – namely, the privatization of economic enterprise, the deregulation of the markets, the liberalization of trade and the flow of investment capital, and a decentralization of government administration – was to liberate the so-called 'forces of economic freedom' from the regulatory constraints of the development state. The immediate outcome of these structural reforms, not to mention an extended process of decapitalization associated with the obligatory use of export revenues to service the accumulated external debt, was an advance of capital in both the cities and the countryside, resulting in the destruction of productive forces in both agriculture and industry and a virtual collapse and involution of the labour market, which forced the growing mass of rural migrants to work 'on their own account' on the streets rather than exchange their labour against capital for a living wage. Some economists and sociologists at PREALC and ECLAC have estimated that in the vortex of these 'structural' forces up to 70 per cent of new jobs generated in the 1980s were formed in what was termed the 'informal sector' (Portes, Castells &

Benton, 1989; Klein & Tokman, 2000; Tokman, 1992). It is calculated that today up to 60 per cent of Mexico's working class is found in this sector, which is to say that they do not work for wages but work for themselves on the streets and in the shadows of the labour market, or are led into a life of crime or to seek work in the narco-economy (Rodriguez-Orregia, 2007).[6]

Needless to say, these changes and this 'development' had a dramatic impact on diminishing the organizational capacity and political power of the working class, affecting the ability of workers to negotiate collective contracts with capital and settle with the government. Another result of these changes in the structure and internal composition of the working class was a dramatic decline in unionization and labour union density (the percentage of workers in labour unions). From 1984, at the outset of Mexico's admission into the new world order, to 2000, the year that marked the end of PRI's undisputed control of the government and the state apparatus, unionization declined by 20 to 30 per cent (La Botz, 2005).

Having precipitated what became known as the major external debt crisis of the twentieth century, and having led the World Bank and the IMF to close ranks in coming to the defence of the big banks and creditors within the world capitalist system, Mexico was the first country to be subjected to a programme of neo-liberal reforms described by Lopez Portillo, president of Mexico from 1976 to 1982, as a disease, the disease of 'an obsolete and arrogant hegemonic dogma and blind egotism', 'transmitted by rats' (the 'sorcerers' or 'witchdoctors' of the IMF) with the consequences of 'unemployment and poverty, the ruin of industry and speculative enrichment' (Lopez Portillo, 1982).

The neo-liberal transformation of Mexico can be dated from 1982, when Miguel de la Madrid, who succeeded the hapless Lopez Portillo,[7] adopted an economic agenda that included several structural adjustments to its macroeconomic policy, including the removal of development support for small-scale peasant farmers as well as protective measures designed to support local industry and domestic producers in their battle against the forces of the world market. These and other neo-liberal reforms, imposed on Mexico and other debtor governments in the region as a condition for accessing the capital needed to restructure their external debt, had a dramatic outcome and economic impact in expanding the inflow of capital in the form of FDI and destroying forces of production built up over decades in both agriculture and industry,[8] resulting in an agricultural crisis and a massive increase in rural outmigration of the dispossessed and impoverished peasantry – the 'rural poor' in the World Bank's development discourse – and the formation of a disproportionate semi-proletariat of landless rural workers.[9] Under the impact of forces released by the neo-liberal policy agenda, including an agricultural crisis and a rural exodus of historic proportions, a growing number of impoverished peasant farmers and agricultural workers were forced to migrate to the United States in search of paid work.

The Mexican working class in these conditions was entirely reshaped. The labour market for jobs in both the private sector and the public sector was effectively closed down, forcing new entrants and the swarms of dispossessed peasants

## 156 Mexico: dynamics of a class war

and rural migrants in search of work to fend for themselves on the streets, creating in the process a burgeoning informal sector characterized by a low level of labour remuneration, job and income insecurity and precarization, inadequate housing and the lack of access to basic public services and social security coverage, and crucially the absence of unions and the inability of workers to organize collectively. As thousands of jobs were lost in steel and metal production, and other traditional manufacturing industries, the centre of industrial production shifted towards the north and the US border, the *maquiladoras*, resulting in a major feminization of the labour force as more and more women entered the workforce in response to the growing demand for cheap, flexible, non-unionized labour. Drastic currency devaluations in 1982 and then again in 1994 in the context of the peso crisis effectively cut wages, resulting in a major and continuing loss in the purchasing power of Mexican workers. Under these conditions the income share of labour in the gross domestic product fell or was reduced by 40 to 60 per cent, a statistic that was reflected in a serious deterioration in the social condition of most workers and the impoverishment of many. It is estimated, on the basis of official statistics, that over 50 per cent of Mexicans today still live in poverty, and this after two decades of concerted efforts by the government to reduce the rate of poverty by means of a 'new social policy' adopted under the post-Washington Consensus on the need for a more inclusive – and thus socially and politically sustainable – form of development (Veltmeyer & Tetreault, 2013; World Bank, 2004).[10]

NAFTA, the North American Free Trade Agreement, engineered by the US government, was the centrepiece of the neo-liberal policy agenda, the crowning glory of the US's imperialist strategy. By incorporating low-wage/low-rights Mexico into the continental production system under NAFTA, big business sought both to discourage labour militancy as well as to harmonize labour costs downward in Canada, the US and the older industrialized and unionized regions of Mexico (Roman & Velasco Arregui, 2009).

The eruption of the Zapatista Army of National Liberation (EZLN) on the political stage of the class struggle on 1 January 1994 coincided precisely with the day that NAFTA was designed to take effect. In the words of Marcos, EZLN's spokesperson, it spelled the end of the peasant smallholder economy, the 'death knell' of the rural livelihoods of millions of peasant farmers and their communities.

Although the Mexican government as early as 1983 was forced to give in to the dictates of capital – i.e. to succumb to the demands of the Washington Consensus presented by the World Bank and the IMF – it was the regime of Salinas de Gortari (1988–94) that sealed the fate of the working class and ordinary Mexicans in the popular sector. Salinas began his regime with a political power grab that involved one of the most blatant cases of electoral fraud in Mexico's complicated and sordid political history – the 'theft of Mexico', as it was dubbed by political observers. The PRD, a leftist breakaway group from the governing party, had clearly won the popular vote but was defrauded of its victory, initiating another two decades of neo-liberal regimes. The Salinas regime included not only the signing of NAFTA and a massive privatization programme (placing up to 80 per cent of state enterprises on the auction block), but also a major expansion in the inflow of FDI in response to this privatization policy and in setting up assembly plants, or *maquilas*, across the border.[11] By the end of the decade the *maquilas* accounted for the bulk of Mexico's manufacturing exports – traditional industries, as well as the government's capacity to pursue an independent industrial policy, having been destroyed in the structural adjustment process (Cypher & Delgado Wise, 2010).[12]

This destruction had a profound impact not only on the organizational capacity of the working class but also on the formation and internal structure of this class. For one thing, neither the formal labour market nor the *maquilas* in the north of the country were able to absorb the mass of surplus rural labour released by the capitalist development process. This not only led to the formation of a large informal sector of urban employment, but it forced increasing numbers of the 'rural poor' to migrate further north to the United States. International migration in this context not only provided a safety valve that reduced the pressures on both the government and the private sector to absorb and employ the expanding reservoir of surplus workers, but it also provided an alternative pathway out of rural poverty to the social movements, to some degree diminishing their combustible force. In these conditions, Mexico was soon converted into the world's largest supplier of migrant workers to a rapidly growing world labour market (Delgado, Wise & Veltmeyer, 2016). Undoubtedly, this helped dampen the fire of revolutionary ferment in both the land struggle and the labour movement.

## From Zedillo to Peña Nieto: two decades of neo-liberal reform and class struggle

Salinas was succeeded in the presidency by Ernesto Zedillo, the last of an uninterrupted 70-year line of Mexican presidents from the Institutional Revolutionary Party (PRI). Zedillo assumed state power on the eve of the country's worst ever financial crisis (1994–95), which deepened the destruction of the forces of production in both agriculture and industry caused by Mexico's admission into the new world order of neo-liberal globalization. He both extended and deepened Salina's neo-liberal reform agenda, allowing foreign investors to purchase the assets of all of the major banks save Banorte – and this after a US\$40 billion bailout of US (and some Mexican) private investors in these banks and the stock market. Notwithstanding a financial crisis that destroyed up to 40 per cent of the value of the accumulated capital stock and brought about numerous bankruptcies and the loss of up to a million jobs, most mainstream analysts and many pundits continued to conclude triumphantly that Mexico was on the correct economic and political path.[13]

A flagrant expression of this analysis was *Latin Finance*'s naming of President Ernesto Zedillo as its man of the year for 2000 for having 'set Mexico on the road to strong economic growth, political maturity, and a new more equal relationship with the United States' (Ochoa & Wilson, 2001). On the downside of Zedillo's policies, and well hidden behind the enthusiasm of foreign investors and the

**158** Mexico: dynamics of a class war

government's slogan, 'Well-Being for the Family', living standards and household incomes declined and the number of impoverished Mexicans increased from 50 million in 1994, at the start of the Zedillo regime, to nearly 70 million by 1999 (Mufioz Rios, 2000; Robledo, 2000).[14] On the other side of the ledger, the CEOs of the transnational-dominated *maquiladora* sector were well placed to take advantage of the peso crisis – and the expansion of cheap non-unionized reserve labour created by it – by increasing their investments and operations of the *maquiladoras*. The second half of the 1990s saw a major increase in investment and export production in the *maquila* sector. Employment in the *maquiladoras* doubled between 1994 and 1998, and, along with employment growth, real wages in the *maquiladoras* declined by 21.7 per cent between 1994 and January 1998, making investments more profitable.

Salinas and Zedillo's neo-liberal policy agenda, implemented over the course of two *sexenios* (1988–2000), was extended by subsequent governing regimes to other strategic sectors such as oil production and the generation of electrical power, and labour reform (to give managers more flexibility in the use of labour and make it easier to fire workers).[15] While a number of South American countries in the first decade of the new millennium abandoned or turned away from the neo-liberal policy agenda – largely the result of the political activism of social movements with their social base in the peasantry, particularly in the semi-proletarianized sector of rural landless workers, and the indigenous communities – the Mexican government continued to relentlessly pursue its neo-liberal policy agenda, activating the resistance of thousands of workers in key sectors.

The past two decades of neo-liberal reform are replete with countless cases of local and regional organized resistance, mass demonstrations, work stoppages and class struggle, but generally they have been effectively 'managed' by the state, largely because of the failure of the political Left and the labour movement to unite (La Botz, 2010; Roman & Velasco Arregui, 2009).

The most sustained effort to align the labour movement, as well as the resistance to the neo-liberal policy agenda of all Mexican governments since the early 1980s, with the electoral process of democratic politics – to create a democratic political front for the class struggle – is associated with a political movement led by Andres Manuel Lopez Obrador (AMLO), presidential candidate for the PRD in both 2006, as the head of a citizen's 'Coalition for the Good of All', and 2012, as the leader of another broad 'citizen's movement', subsequently reorganized as MORENA, the National Regeneration Movement. The movement led by AMLO brought and brings together both rural and urban divisions of the labour movement and the organized resistance, particularly workers in the strategic sectors of energy and oil production, and education – since 1996 a leading sector of the labour movement. However, an overview of PRD's byzantine politics over the past three decades at both the national and state levels – the political machinations, the shady electoral deals and shifting alliances, not to mention the not infrequent cases of overt corruption and the failure or lack of any advance on campaign promises or political commitments made by members of the political class on the centre-left – demonstrate all too clearly that the electoral process and liberal democratic politics do not provide an effective means of advancing the economic and political interests of the working class or advance the agenda of substantive change and genuine progress. Even if AMLO or some other centre-left social democratic party had won or were to achieve state power political experience elsewhere in the region – for example Brazil (see Chapter 6) – it would be extremely unlikely that the working class would have found a champion for advancing its interests or a progressive agenda. As Pedro Stédile, leader of the the MST, has argued, in the case of Brazil the system of democratic politics is a poor instrument for advancing the class struggle from below. The only way of advancing this struggle and going forwards with a progressive working-class political agenda is an active mobilization of the diverse forces of resistance formed in the popular sector. Herein lies the challenge for the Left.

## A change of regime, the same struggle (with a few twists)

In 2000 seven decades of PRI rule came to an end with the ascension of Vicente Fox, a landowning businessman and at the time president of Coca Cola's Latin American division, to state power under the banner of the right-wing National Action Party (PAN). However, neither the neo-liberal policy regime of Fox's predecessors – the tactical dimension of the strategy of economic globalization and free-market capitalism pursued by all governments since 1983 – nor the alignment of the government with capital and US imperialism were discontinued. Indeed, under Fox and Calderón the government's ideological and programmatic commitment to neo-liberalism was both extended and deepened, provoking a series of confrontations with organized labour over the government's labour and energy reform agenda and its project for fiscal and educational reform.

This was par for the course. The one additional factor or input of the government into the class struggle had to do with the expansion of the narco-economy, which not only created an enormous illicit revenue stream for the cartels and drug lords, the merchants of cocaine and marijuana and other hard drugs, but also provided an important new form of capital accumulation as well as employment for large numbers of rural unemployed youth. Vicente Fox, as it turned out, was all for legalizing the trafficking of drugs, or at least marijuana, which could be attributed in part to the fact (or allegation) that his presidential campaign was to a large degree financed by fortunes made in drug trafficking and money laundering.[16] In any case, Fox's soft approach to the trafficking of drugs radically changed with the ascension of Felipe Calderón to the presidency. Because the competition among the major drug cartels had begun to escape the tacit and until then effective limits set by the government, and the government had in effect lost its capacity to regulate the trade and to ensure that the competitive struggle among the cartels would not create a generalized state of heightened insecurity, Calderón succumbed to pressures from the US State Department in declaring a war on the narcos (the drug cartels) – Mexico's War on Drugs. The outcome of this war, the main legacy of Calderón's presidency, included at least 100,000 violent deaths and at least 20,000 disappearances,

**160** Mexico: dynamics of a class war

a dramatic expansion of the reach and firepower of the cartels (about a half of the country is now believed to be under their sway), and a generalized culture of fear. Notwithstanding Calderón's declaration – and unsuccessfully waged – war on the drug cartels numerous studies have disclosed clear evidence of an effective alliance between the state and the drug cartels who launder their profits in the major US banks. This could be viewed as an elite alliance from above blocking the class struggle from below. What this, together with the federal military-drug gang murder of 43 *normalistas* in Oaxaca, shows is that mass murder is part of the machinery that allows neo-liberalism to continue despite continued popular opposition.

The current PRI regime, headed by Enrique Peña Nieto, has continued to advance the neo-liberal reform agenda of the previous PAN regime (Fox, Calderón) by privatizing and reforming what remains of the state sector, in particular the utility responsible for the generation of electricity (FyL), Pemex and the education system.[17] The government's planned educational reform has resulted in one of the most intense periods of class struggle in the entire neo-liberal era, pitting the federal government against the activist caucus within the official union, the CNTE, or the National Coordinator of Education Workers, in a protracted struggle that in 2014 saw the murder of 43 teacher trainees, or *normalistas*,[18] and on 19 June 2016 a street demonstration in which federal police killed a dozen teachers and sympathizers protesting the government's neo-liberal brand of educational reform designed to both get rid of teachers and break union power (Hernández Navarro, 2014; Roman & Velasco Arregui, 2014).[19]

Oaxaca has been at the centre of this battleground in the struggle waged by teachers since 2006, when the CNTE's battle against the government's neo-liberal educational reforms galvanized a citizen's movement for democratic transformation that has brought together a broad swath of communities and civil society organizations in support of the teachers' struggle. In 2006, Oaxaca became known worldwide for mounting the first major resistance in Latin America in the twenty-first century. It was a revolt that paralysed this southern state of Mexico for more than six months but resulted in the formation of a popular administration of public services (Esteva, 2016). Ten years later, teachers and communities in eight regions of Oaxaca took to the streets to demand the repeal of the education reform, but, unlike 2006, where the main focus of resistance was concentrated in the city of Oaxaca, in 2016 the resistance, and widespread signs and actions with street blockades in solidarity, spread throughout the state.

On 1 August 2006, in one of the momentous battles in this struggle, a grouping of some 3,000 women marched downtown in Oaxaca City banging metal pots and pans,[20] and gathered in the central town square, where the teachers and other protesters had been encamped for some months, and engaged the state police in an action that culminated in the takeover of the state-wide television and radio company (Gibler, 2006).[21] The most recent act of violence perpetrated by the government in its battle to bring an end to the CNTE's three-year fight against educational reform and break the union took place almost 10 years later.[22] At the time of writing (12 July 2016), the battle between the government and the union is in full swing, with neither side ceding any space in what has turned out to be a major war of position in the relation of conflict between the government and the union. Having managed since 1992 to impose its neo-liberal agenda of structural reform in sector after sector, the government appears intent to break the power of the union, the only force in the labour movement left with the class power to possibly halt the government's agenda. The CNTE for its part has materialized as possibly the labour movement's last redoubt in the class struggle mounted against the government's concerted effort to impose its neo-liberal agenda.

Apart from the current fight led by the CNTE against the government's education reform,[23] the most dramatic example of the class struggle organized from within the labour movement in the current conjuncture pits the powerful electrical workers' union, the SME, against President Calderón's agenda to privatize the public utility responsible for generating electrical power. This struggle unfolded over several years. Unfortunately, despite numerous battles in several years of heroic struggle, in 2009 the once-powerful electrical workers' union had to give up the fight, defeated by the intransigence of a neo-liberal regime committed to destroy it.

Celebrating its ninety-fifth anniversary on 14 December with cultural events and pledges to continue to fight for the jobs of its members, two months after Calderón's liquidation of the state-owned Central Light and Power Company (Luz y Fuerza del Centro), seizure of the facilities and firing of 44,000 workers, and faced with the government's intransigence, the union was forced to change its strategy. With 62 per cent of LyFC workers forced to accept the offered severance pay, union leader Martín Esparza told workers that the SME would continue to engage in powerful peaceful actions. 'We remain firm,' said Esparza. 'We are a peaceful citizens' movement with great power, with clear demands, and with ingenuity. We will continue with our national and our international alliances' (La Botz, 2010). Bold words, but action – that of the government – spoke louder. Despite protestations to the contrary and a promise that it would continue the struggle, the most powerful labour union in the country had been defeated by forces beyond its control.

## The Zapatista factor in Mexican class politics

To understand how the Zapatista Army of National Liberation (EZLN) changed the political landscape in Mexico and the important role that it has played in the class struggle, we need only look at the economic and social conditions suffered by much of the population in Chiapas at the time of the eruption of the Zapatistas on the political stage. In economic terms the statistics are staggering, particularly as relates to the distribution of the state's enormous wealth and the extent and depth of poverty, which in terms of official statistics affected over 70 per cent of the population at the time (vs. 44 per cent nationwide). In a state that accounted for 21 and 47 per cent of the country's oil and natural gas reserves, 35 per cent of coffee production, 55 per cent of its supply of electricity, and the country's second largest

**162** Mexico: dynamics of a class war

production of beef and corn, 47 per cent of the largely rural and indigenous population had no access to potable water; one-third of all households were without electricity; as many as 59 per cent had no basic sanitary facilities such as drainage; and three-quarters of the population consumed less than 1,500 calories a day (vs. the minimum level of 2,155 prescribed by the WHO).[24] Whereas 13 per cent of Mexico's population was defined as illiterate, this figure was 31 per cent in Chiapas. The majority of households had no access to public services, located as they were in an officially defined 'marginal zone' (a *bolsillo de olvido* in Marcos's more evocative description) characterized by an exceedingly high rate of impoverishment, exclusion and deprivation of basic human needs and public services, not to speak of a manifest denial of fundamental human rights and the lack of democracy and social justice.

Ever since Spanish colonial times, but particularly in the 1960s and 1970s, the Lacandon jungle and lowlands, described by Lourdes Arizpe as 'the last social frontier', was subject to a process of massive outmigration involving many thousands of largely indigenous peasants from Los Altos, pushed off their lands by the more powerful agro-export farmers and cattle ranchers. In addition, Tlzeltales from Ocosingo, Choles from the north, Tzotziles from Los Altos, Tojolabales from the Llanos and Zoques from the central valleys of Chiapas were forced to abandon their livelihoods and communities in response to the government's efforts to colonize the Lacandona so as to create a labour force for the construction of a series of hydroelectric and oil exploration mega-projects.[25]

In addition to these and other forces of socio-economic, ecological and demographic change that characterized the Lacandon region in the 1970s and 1980s, which resulted in a particularly volatile and complex multi-ethnic society and the rapid growth of a number of very new and highly marginalized communities, the population in the state was subjected like no others in Mexico to conditions generated by the forces of capitalist development as well as by what in Marcos's poetical language was constructed as the 'bloody jaws' of the 'wild beast' (US imperialism), whose teeth have sunk deeply into the throat of south-east Mexico, drawing out large pools of blood (tribute in the form of 'petroleum, electrical energy, cattle, money, coffee, banana, honey, corn ...') through '[as] many veins – oil and gas ducts, electrical lines, train cars, bank accounts, trucks and vans, clandestine paths, gaps and forest trials ...' (Marcos, 1992). As far as Marcos and the EZLN were concerned, the enemy was US imperialism and the Mexican state, which sustained both it and its globalizing neo-liberal project. This was made clear by Marcos himself as early as 1992, a year and a half before the 1994 uprising, and soon after the Zapatistas' first skirmish with the government's armed forces. And the point was made, not as eloquently but as clearly, both at the moment of the EZLN's unexpected irruption and capture of four cities and subsequently (the spring of 1996) in the convocation of a series of national, tri-continental and intergalactic encounters and forums 'against neo-liberalism and for humanity'.

With the imposition of a neo-liberal policy agenda under Salinas's administration and a resulting deregulation of the market, coffee prices plunged 50 per cent

Mexico: dynamics of a class war **163**

in a single year, with similar developments in the production and marketing of corn and beans – the two staple commodities and consumption goods of the peasant sector of agricultural production. With the government abandoning its rural integrated development programme of protective measures, subsidized credit and technical services and support, the small non-capitalist producers in Chiapas and elsewhere, together with the thousands of small and medium-sized firms and enterprises that made up the petit bourgeois sector of the economy, were suddenly confronted with the naked forces of the world market, and, to use Marcos's evocative language, with 'the bloody jaws of the wild beast'. Under the impact of these forces, agricultural output fell by 35 per cent from 1989 to 1993 on the eve of the inception of NAFTA. Thousands of direct producers were forcibly separated from their means of social production, adding to the dynamics of land struggle reflected in the fact that at least 30 per cent of Mexico's unresolved land petitions at the time came from Chiapas (Hernández Navarro, 1994: 44). Under these and other conditions of 'primitive accumulation' – 'accumulation by dispossession', as David Harvey has it (see our discussion in Chapter 3) – incomes in the depressed rural sector fell even more precipitously than elsewhere in Mexico, from 65 to 70 per cent by some estimates (Harvey 1998).[26] Under these conditions, as Marcos observed at the time, NAFTA would impose a 'death sentence' on the Zapatistas and other small producers in the region and across the country.[27]

This struggle by land-hungry peasants was combined in diverse contexts with a mass line strategy pursued by a number of leftist organizations such as Proletarian Line, Pueblo Unido, the Central Independiente de Obreros Agricolas y Campesinos/ Partido Comunista Mexicana (COAC/PCM) and the Fuerzas de Liberación Nacional (FLN). In the context of this mass line strategy and in the aftermath of the 1968 massacre at Tlatelolco, some urban left-wing intellectuals, mostly UNAM students, moved to the countryside to establish a rural front of the class struggle (Collier & Lowery Quaratiello, 1994).[28] By the late 1980s the rural front of the FLN had established an effective base of operations and training camps in a number of indigenous communities in the area, liaising with a number of organizations such as the Partido Revolucionario Clandestino Union del Pueblo (Procup), formed by the legendary Lucio Cabanas and still maintaining a presence in Guerrero.

By the Zapatistas' own account, their resort to arms was dictated by circumstances and a correlation of forces under particularly adverse conditions.[29] In the conjuncture of 1 January 1994, however, it served as an important catalyst of social and political forces of opposition and an effective means of forcing the government not only to take notice of the demands of indigenous people in Chiapas and across the country but to enter into negotiations designed to address and settle them. At both levels the resort to arms was to some extent successful. On the one hand, the armed rebellion provided a critical stimulus to the formation of a national democratic movement based on forces organized in the wake of the 1985 earthquake and mobilized under conditions of an economic and political crisis that marked the end of the de la Madrid regime in 1988. This movement forced the government to abandon its strategy of armed confrontation with the Zapatistas, to declare a

**164** Mexico: dynamics of a class war

unilateral ceasefire and to enter into negotiations with them in February, within weeks of the onset of the rebellion. On the other hand, the rebellion provided a critical stimulus to a process of direct actions and mobilizations initiated by a number of indigenous groups in 1992 on the basis of organizations formed in the previous decade and at least 20 years of struggle by diverse ethno-campesino organizations formed at local, municipal and regional levels.[30]

The formation in January 1994 of the State Council of Indigenous and Peasant Organizations (CEOIC) was the spark that led to the mobilization of over 800 land petitions by over 100 organizations. In the first six months of 1994, close to 350 farms and ranches were invaded, leading to a process of negotiations over 50,000 hectares of land as well as a backlash of terror and military action by the hired guns of the caciques with the tacit support of the political establishment (Harvey, 1998). Under pressure from the political forces mobilized within the popular sector of civil society, and the direct actions taken by a number of indigenous organizations in support of the Zapatista uprising, the government entered into a process of dialogue and negotiation with the EZLN, treating it reluctantly as a voice of the state's indigenous people and the bearer of their demands for change, albeit with an effort at first to deny its legitimacy then to reduce its significance and scope, limiting it to a local issue and finally seeking to actively undermine its efforts to constitute itself as a national political force with regards to the indigenous question.

What can we conclude from this brief summary of the dynamics of class struggle in Chiapas in the early 1990s – and with the hindsight provided by two subsequent decades of low-intensity class struggle?[31] For one thing, on the local level, the Zapatista uprising was the culmination of more than 20 years of ethno-campesino and class struggle, a manifestation of a long history of indigenous resistance and a shorter history of opposition to neo-liberal capitalism, as well as a model demonstration of the effectiveness and limits of a guerrilla form of armed struggle which had existed in Mexico with few interruptions for at least 30 years. At the national level, however, the story changes. The Zapatistas have been unable to constitute themselves as the nucleus of a broader mass movement.

## Class struggle on Mexico's extractive frontier

Capitalism in Latin America as elsewhere has taken two fundamental forms, driven on the one hand by the exploitation of labour (the appropriation of surplus value), and on the other by the pillage and appropriation of natural resource wealth and the extraction of resource rents from the country's stock of natural capital. From the fifteenth to the nineteenth century the capital invested in the development of the forces of production was for the most part accumulated by means of natural resource extraction rather than the exchange of labour against capital and the exploitation of labour power. Although labour was super-exploited and oppressed in the process, capital was accumulated by dispossessing the direct producers under conditions where '[f]orce, fraud, oppression, [and] looting are openly displayed without any attempt at concealment' (Luxemburg, cited by Harvey, 2003: 137). In the twentieth century, Mexico was the recipient of large pools of industrial capital eager to take advantage of the virtually unlimited supply of surplus labour released in capitalist development of agriculture. In the late 1930s and 1940s, the Mexican government instituted a policy of import substitution industrialization and modernization in order to secure for the country the opportunities for employment and income generation provided by industrial capital. In the subsequent period of capitalist development based on the agency of the welfare-development state (the 1950s–1970s), capital was accumulated predominantly by means of the proletarianization of the peasantry and small landholding agricultural producers, separating them from their means of production and forcing them to migrate to the cities in the search of wage-labour opportunities.

The installation in the 1980s of the new world order of neo-liberal globalization, and a policy of macroeconomic structural reforms under the Washington Consensus, brought about in Mexico (and elsewhere in the region) a change in the geoeconomics – and geopolitics – of capital. Foreign direct investment inflows were increasingly turned away from manufacturing and traditional industries and directed towards the *maquiladoras*, the purchase of the assets of privatized state enterprises, the provision of financial services and advances in information technology – and increasingly towards the mining and extraction of minerals, metals and other natural resources for the purpose of exporting them in primary commodity form. This is to say, labour-seeking capital was slowly but steadily displaced by resource-seeking capital, although nowhere near to the extent as in South America in the context of a primary commodities boom on the world market. Whereas the countries in this subregion that responded to and participated in this boom by (re)orienting production and exports towards primary commodities – Argentina, Bolivia, Chile, Ecuador, Peru, Paraguay, Venezuela etc. – Mexico continued to serve as a major destination and haven of US industrial capital seeking to profit from the low labour costs and the relative freedom from the perils of unionization. This is reflected in the composition of exports, which in the case of Mexico favours *maquiladora* manufacturing and labour in the form of migrant remittances, as opposed to the economies of most South American countries, in which primary commodities constitute anywhere from 60 to 95 per cent of exports.

Notwithstanding the predominance of manufacturing products and labour in Mexican exports, the extractive sector, especially mining, has in recent years been the recipient of massive foreign direct investment seeking to take advantage of the exceedingly generous conditions provided by the state to extractive capital in the mining sector – no royalties and an effective tax rate of less than 2 per cent on the value of the product on the world market.[32] In addition, Article 6 of Mexico's Mining Law[33] states that mining activities 'will be given preference over any other use or exploitation of the land', which gives the federal government the right to expropriate land from small-scale farmers and ranchers as well as sacred sites from indigenous groups, in order to promote private mining operations. Under these conditions a large part of the national territory has been ceded to extractive capital for the purpose of exploration and production. For example, in the first decade of the new millennium the federal government, under the control of the right-wing National Action Party (PAN), delivered over 56 million hectares of mining concessions, equivalent to over a quarter of the country's territory, to privately owned companies (López & Eslava, 2011: 28).

The expansion of extractive capital in Mexico has had a dramatic impact on the dynamics of the class struggle. For one thing, the struggle is no longer centred on the capital–labour relationship or labour conflicts, but on the social environmental conflicts focused on the defence of territory and rural livelihoods. These conflicts and related struggles increasingly pit the multinational companies that operate in the extractive sector and the rural communities most directly and negatively impacted by these operations. The destructive operations of extractive capital in the mining sector have generated a powerful albeit divided resistance movement – a series of local resistance movements – against the incursions of extractive capital and the negative impacts of extractive capital on the environment and their livelihoods. MiningWatch and other NGOs working in alliance with the communities that are negatively impacted by extractivism have followed and continue to support the large and increasing number of communities that are engaged in the struggle – a struggle not so much over land and labour but over territorial rights, access to the commons and, above all, the right of communities to protect their livelihoods, their health and their way of life as well as their habitat.

As noted in Chapters 2 and 3, the class struggle on the new frontier of extractive capitalism has been well documented and studied. In these studies (for example, Tetreault, 2014b), the working class no longer appears as the primary 'actor' in the struggle. In fact, the communities in struggle are deemed by some to be the 'new proletariat'. However, this point needs to be clarified and requires some discussion. Without a doubt the foundation or economic base of the capitalist system is the capital–labour relationship, a relationship of economic exploitation and in some contexts a relation of class oppression. But, whereas the working class thus remains the critical factor and the dominant actor in the class struggle associated with the process of capitalist development – the historic and current incursions of capitalism and the advance of capital both in the region and across the world – other social classes and groups can and do play an important part in the struggle in different contexts and conjunctures.

The point is that the crucial factor in these struggles remains the relationship of individuals and groups to production, even though this relationship has a political as well as a structural dimension. For example, the struggle of unionized miners in Mexico presupposes a capital–labour relationship in the private-sector exploitation of the country's mineral resources, and often mineworkers do not object to the use of highly destructive technologies, such as opencast mining and cyanide leaching, as long as they have paid work. A lousy and dangerous job is better than no job at all. In this way, the interests of unionized miners can collide with those of the radical eco-territorial resistance movements, and their demands might well compete with those of the reform-oriented eco-territorial movements that insist on greater compensation for local populations negatively affected by mining.

Mexico: dynamics of a class war **167**

Another point that needs clarification and some discussion is the role of labour in the class struggles brought about by the expansion of extractive capital – and capitalism. For example, even though labour typically is not as predominant in the structure of extractive capital and the associated dynamics of resistance as it is in the system of industrial capitalism, it still plays an important role in the production process and the class struggle. In some situations, mining operations can bring mineworkers and the communities most directly impacted by these operations into a relation of conflicting interests (the former pressing for work and the continued operations of the mine, regardless of the destructive technologies employed or its negative consequences for the communities; the latter opposed to mining under any conditions). An example of this conflict of interest is in the case the Sierra of Manantlán, between Colima and Jalisco, about 50 km from the coast, where the gigantic opencast iron ore mine Peña Colorada is located, now owned by Ternium and Mittal Steel. The workforce for the mine comes from outside the region and lives mostly in an enclave, a company town called Peña Colorada. On 22 July 2015, approximately 300 Nahua inhabitants of the region blocked the mine's entrance in demand for indemnization for over 30 years of exploiting communal land. Employees from the mine met them with resistance and were soon backed up by state police forces from Colima, who beat protesters and arrested 34 of them.

Another study by Tetreault (2014b) of the resistance to extractivism in the mining sector of Mexico's economy points towards a similar pattern. What these studies show is that, while labour conflicts in the mining sector have a long history, social environmental conflicts revolving around the defence of territory and rural livelihoods are relatively new, with roots in the struggle for land and for indigenous autonomy that stretch back to the conquest. Under the structural and political conditions created by neo-liberal policy regimes, these conflicts have proliferated over the past two decades.[34] At issue in these conflicts and related struggles is the right and power of mining companies, many of them foreign-owned, to plunder the nation's mineral resources without consideration of matters of national and territorial sovereignty or the habitats and livelihoods of indigenous communities or the welfare of Mexican workers and their families.

To illustrate and highlight the role of workers and the continuing relevance of labour to the class struggle on the new frontier of extractive capital we need but take the notorious but not atypical case of the assault on the workers of the city of Cananea, Mexico (population 32,000), 30 miles south of the Arizona–Mexico border, on 6 June 2010. On that day more than 3,000 federal and 500 state police descended on Cananea, where Section 65 of the Union of Miners and Metallurgical Workers (the Mineros) had been on strike for three years. They drove workers out of the mine, pursued them to the union hall and gassed all who took refuge inside, including women and children. Several people were injured in the melee and at least five miners were arrested (Fischel & Nelson, 2010).

The attack on the workers of Cananea was a bitter turn in the prolonged David-and-Goliath struggle between a proud union and a powerful transnational copper mining company, Grupo México, Mexico's largest mining corporation and operator

**168** Mexico: dynamics of a class war

of the largest copper mine in the country, which was solidly backed by the Mexican government from the beginning of the neo-liberal regime.[35] The miners were striking to restore health and safety protections guaranteed by their union contract and to mitigate environmental damage to their region and community. But, more fundamentally, they were fighting for the survival of independent Mexican unions – for the power to organize and to protect workers and their communities from exploitation and corporate abuse.

This was not the first encounter between Mexican miners and the government in this fight. In 1989 the Cananea miners carried out a strike to protest the sale of Compañía Minera Cananea to Grupo México. The strike was part of a series of massive strikes staged by Mexican miners in a vain effort to resist the privatization of state-owned mining companies during the first years of the Salinas administration (1989–1992). The Salinas administration responded with three lines of action: first it declared the company bankrupt; then, in August the same year, it sent in the armed forces to break the strike; and, finally, it imposed a settlement on the company and the union within the tripartite corporatist framework set up to manage industrial (capital–labour) relations. The corporatist relations between the state and unionized labour, forged in the early years of the labour movement but consolidated under the Salinas regime,[36] were maintained by the subsequent regimes of Ernesto Zedillo and Vicente Fox, and continued until they finally collapsed in 2006, during the last few months of Fox's presidential term.

Grupo México became notorious in 2006 for its role in the Pasta de Conchos mining disaster in Coahuila, Mexico, in which 65 members of the Mineros union were killed. In the months leading up to the massive explosion in the mine, workers repeatedly warned of dangerous conditions, including a build-up of explosive methane gas. They were ignored by the company and by regulating agencies charged with overseeing mine safety in Mexico. On 19 February 2006, the mine blew up. Napoleón Gómez Urrutia, general secretary of the Mineros, accused Grupo México of 'industrial homicide' and called for an investigation. Gómez was already well known for his opposition to neo-liberal labour reforms and his focus on international labour solidarity.[37] Under his leadership the Mineros forged alliances with the Steelworkers (United States and Canada) and with Grupo's key union at its Peruvian mines, the Federation of Metal Workers of Peru.

After Gómez Urrutia denounced the state's complicity in the Pasta de Conchos explosion, Calderón's government removed him from his leadership post. Gómez was charged with mishandling union funds and forced to flee to Canada, where he now lives as a guest of the Steelworkers. After an independent audit by a Swiss accounting firm exonerated Gómez and the union, Mexican courts threw out the charges and Gómez was officially reinstated as general secretary. Despite this, the government continued to seek his extradition, although the Canadian government repeatedly refused to comply. The Mineros refused to accept government control of their union and re-elected Gómez Urrutia six times. In the US, the AFL–CIO denounced Gómez's ouster as part of 'the continuing suppression of the independent labour movement ... by the Mexican government'.

The Mineros had been on strike since July 2007, when 1,300 workers walked from their jobs, citing dangerous health and safety conditions and contract violations that threatened the health and safety of the community. The violations were thoroughly documented by the Maquila Health and Safety Support Network (MHSSN), a bi-national group of occupational health experts that toured the mine in fall 2007. Among their findings: piles of silica dust, which can cause silicosis and lung cancer; dismantled dust collectors; and inadequate ventilation systems, respirators and auditory equipment. MHSSN's report documents 'a workplace being deliberately run into the ground' where workers are 'exposed to high levels of toxic dusts and acid mists, operate malfunctioning and poorly maintained equipment, and work in … dangerous surroundings'.

Since then Grupo México and the union have waged a prolonged legal battle, as the company sought repeatedly to have the strike declared invalid. Under Mexican constitutional law, strikes must be honoured unless invalidated by the courts; as long as union workers are striking, companies cannot hire replacement workers or resume production. In January 2008 the courts briefly sided with the company, and police ousted the workers from the mine. Helicopters bombed strikers with tear gas; police beat them with clubs; 20 miners were injured. The next day the court reversed its position and upheld the strike, forcing Grupo México to withdraw from the mine.

In February 2010, two and a half years into the struggle, the Supreme Court again declared the strike invalid and terminated the union's contract. Mexico's Political Coordination Board, a governing body of the National Chamber of Deputies, urged the government to 'avoid the use of public force against the strike movement' and instead consider revoking Grupo México's ownership of the Cananea mine concession 'given their persistent refusal to resolve, by means of dialogue and negotiation, the strike that this mine's workers maintain'. The board called for a 30-day cooling-off period followed by negotiations. Looking broadly at the struggles against Grupo México at all its mining sites in Mexico, it called for a 'legal, comprehensive and fair solution to the Cananea, Sonora, Sombrerete, Zacatecas, and Taxco, Guerrero miners' striking conflicts, within a frame of respect to the rights of unions' autonomy, strike, collective hiring, safety and hygiene and all other labour rights'. Hoping that the Political Coordination Board's recommendations would win out, the workers continued to press their demands.

In a 2008 report the International Metalworkers Federation wrote that '[t]he line between the Mexican government and Grupo México has remained blurry since Calderón took office … and the two have worked in concert to plan and execute the assault on los Mineros'. In fact, Mexico's ruling party, the Partido del Acción Nacional (PAN) at the time had long pursued an openly neo-liberal agenda. One of President Calderón's legislative priorities was to fundamentally restructure the relationships between labour, capital and the state. Since winning the presidency for the first time in 2000, PAN has championed the dismantling of contractual protections for workers. In Mexico, the process is known as 'flexibilization', which allows companies to hire temporary and part-time workers without benefits or job security, and subcontract out jobs previously held by unionized workers (Fischel & Nelson, 2010).

**170** Mexico: dynamics of a class war

Grupo México has played a leading role in implementing flexibilization within the framework of the government's labour reform legislative project. For example, all of the union locals at Grupo's mines have been under assault, and, as in the case of other mining companies over the years, several have been replaced by a *sindicato blanco*, a company union. In the days following the police incursion at Cananea, Grupo México announced that all the strikers were welcome to return to work, as long as they agreed to join the *sindicato blanco*. With the mine secured, Grupo México, Minister of Labour Javier Lozano and Sonora Governor Guillermo Padres quickly unveiled a new partnership: Grupo México would invest $120 million to rebuild and expand the mine while the state would invest almost $440 million in new infrastructure and aid for economic development in Cananea. Par for the course, as reflected in the continuing support for Grupo México provided by the current government headed by Peña Nieta. On 21 December 2013, this government hammered in the final nails in the coffin of what had been for years the country's largest and most important state enterprises.[38]

## Dynamics of the labour movement in the current context

The Mexican labour movement has undergone a profound transformation over the last 20 years, the result of several decades of neo-liberal economic policies and the transformation of the Mexican one-party state into a system comparable to the two-party class dictatorship of the US and Canada. A new independent labour movement emerged which has not only broken with the old state-controlled labour relations system but has also put itself forwards as the leader of the social movements, and, at the moment, appears to be a real and perhaps the only political force that can challenge the combined class power of the state, capital and the ruling class. In 2004, for example, while the economy remained weak, political parties wallowed in corruption and conservatives continued to press their reactionary and pro-capital and pro-business political agenda, Mexico's new independent labour movement stood its ground, fought back and stepped forwards to lead social and political opposition to the government (La Botz, 2005).

Created by two independent labour organizations, in late August and early September 2004 the Union/Peasant/Social/Indigenous and Popular Front (FSCISP) rallied a number of broader forces in a series of collective actions that combined demonstrations and work stoppages in opposition to the neo-liberal agenda of President Vicente Fox and the ultra-conservative National Action Party (PAN). With the EZLN cornered in Chiapas and the centre-left Party of the Democratic Revolution (PRD) in disgrace following the revelation of political payoffs, the FSCISP emerged as a real potential force on the Mexican Left – at least in the judgement of Dan La Botz, an astute long-time observer and analyst of the labour scene in Mexico.

As La Botz constructs it – and Roman and Velasco Arregui (2009), two other seasoned analysts of the Mexican working class, concur – the need for, and the political potential of, an independent labour movement relates to the possibility of bringing together into one movement the diverse groups and organizations aligned with the FSCISP, and to broaden and deepen support for this movement within the labour movement. This development had its beginnings in the spring of 1996, when 21 unions, including 10 from within the government-controlled Congress of Labour (CT), made a series of presentations that they referred to as the Forum: Unions Face the Nation. This forum was designed to promote a debate about the role of unions in Mexico and a variety of issues of importance to labour. The unions that engaged in this debate became known as the Foro group. In November 1997, the Telephone Workers Union, the National Union of Social Security Workers (SNTSS) and six other unions pulled out of the CT and joined independent unions such as the Union of Workers of the National Autonomous University of Mexico (STUNAM) and the Authentic Labour Front (FAT) to create a new labour federation, the National Union of Workers (UNT).

The new UNT put forwards a programme of democratic reform in unions and the workplace. The UNT called upon PRI and later Vicente Fox and the PAN to carry forwards and complete the 'democratic transition' in Mexico, and urged the government to enter into negotiations with the labour and social movements to negotiate 'a new social pact'. The UNT in this context expressed its willingness to work with both employers and the government to increase productivity within the framework of a social pact that gives workers real labour union freedom, i.e. the right to organize unions of their own choosing.

Another independent-minded union, the powerful Mexican Electrical Workers Union (SME), was invited to join the UNT but declined to leave the PRI-dominated CT – a decision that the leaders of the union would come to regret when in 2009 the government, under Calderón's PAN regime, made its final move to privatize the state utility. In any case, in August 1998 SME, while still remaining part of CT, drew together some 40 other unions, peasant organizations and urban poor people's movements into an independent labour coalition (not a formal federation) called the Mexican Union Front (FSM). FSM defined itself as an attempt to create 'an alternative unified, democratic, working class, anti-capitalist unionism', but like UNT it was primarily motivated to fight against the agenda of neo-liberal economic reform, particularly the privatization of the Mexican Light and Power Company, a state-owned firm which employed all of the SME's members.

The fact that UNT put forwards a clearly reformist programme while FSM advanced a nominally anti-capitalist programme does not really explain much about their political behaviour. For one thing, FSM remained in the PRI-dominated CT even after the UNT left it and to this day is still part of it. When the UNT organized the FSCISP, SME and FSM at first declined to join the common front except as observers. However, at present both UNT and FSM are committed or are working to build FSCISP. In truth, La Botz (2005) notes, UNT and FSM both represent independent labour formations, each with its own strengths and weaknesses. But, despite their differences, both have joined together – at least for the moment – in a common fight against the neo-liberal policy agenda (privatization, labour law reform, energy reform) if not capitalism.

**172** Mexico: dynamics of a class war

The appearance of an independent labour movement, and the possible formation of a common front, takes on more significance given the corporatist structure of the labour movement and the inability of the Zapatistas – despite their powerful political imaginary and appeal – to confront the 'capitalist hydra' and the long-standing and current crisis in Mexican politics with a fragmented and largely inconsequential Left and a plethora of unorganized local struggles that are seemingly unable to coalesce into an effective national movement. Over the last decade, the Mexican Left has found expression in various vehicles – the populist left-of-centre PRD, a more radical EZLN and the reformist civil society movement Alianza Civica. However, in none of these movements are the working class and organized labour central to the struggle for social change, and at the moment at least none of these organizations have the ability to lead Mexican society. Whether the Mexican Left can rise to the occasion and join if not lead the labour movement in forming an effective counterhegemonic force to the class power of capital and the Mexican state remains to be seen. It is *the* political question.

## Conclusion

The historic march and advances of capitalism and the resulting dynamics of class struggles in Mexico follow a very distinct trajectory. Large-scale, long-term foreign investment in minerals and land from the late nineteenth to the early twentieth century based on high-intensity exploitation set the stage for the Mexican Revolution. In the lead-up to this major upheaval in Mexico's capitalist development process, the correlation of forces shifted dramatically in favour of peasant armies led by Emilio Zapata and Pancho Villa. But the subsequent counter-revolution, from the 1920s to the mid-thirties, temporarily reversed the process and witnessed the rise of a new post-revolutionary elite allied with the US petroleum multinationals.

The second major social upheaval in Mexico's capitalist development process began in the mid-1930s and lasted to the end of the decade. Large-scale movements of class-conscious oil workers and landless rural peasants expropriated and nationalized the oil fields and large landed estates, establishing indigenous rural cooperatives in the form of *ejidos*.

By the early 1940s the class struggle from below was contained by the corrupt political leadership of the PRI, the self-styled 'revolutionary party'. From then on to the late 1960s, Mexico was ruled by a business elite that deepened its ties to and dependency on the US while retaining some of the social advances of the earlier revolutionary wave.

In the 1980s the balance of power shifted dramatically towards the capitalist class and the elite under conditions of the Washington Consensus and the newly installed neo-liberal order. As a result of forces released in the resulting development process, Mexico's industrial apparatus was dismantled, creating conditions that led to the ascendancy of the class struggle from above and the destruction of Mexico's revolutionary legacy. In these conditions, strategic sectors and the commanding heights of the economy were privatized, and the remaining pillars of the peasant economy of small-scale agricultural producers were severely compromised, releasing forces that allowed for and resulted in the entry of foreign direct investment, an agricultural crisis and a rural exodus of unprecedented proportions. In addition, labour unions were 'incorporated' by the state and Mexico's entire market came under US control through NAFTA.

In the face of this multifaceted capitalist offensive, workers, diverse groups and a significant number of peasants and rural landless workers and the indigenous communities revolted in a wave of regional, sectoral and popular revolt – and defensive struggles.

On the front of electoral politics, some contests, including the battle for the presidency in 1988, were successful but the elite in control of the electoral process denied the victorious outcome in what was notoriously known as the 'theft of Mexico', a development that installed Salinas de Gortari, a cultivated asset of the neo-liberal world order, in the presidency. This provided the guardians of the new world order, via their proxies in the office of the president, both the opportunity and the power to turn Mexico around – to install the new world order and fully implement the neo-liberal policy agenda.

In this context, an uprising of an indigenous peasants' army, in the form of the Zapatista Army of National Liberation, took control of various rural communities in Chiapas but were violently repressed and subsequently 'contained', preventing their spread across the country. Multitudinous marches, protests and barricades by students and professors in Mexico City successfully challenged the president's dictatorial prerogatives in regard to this uprising but they were quelled by mass killings by the army and its death squads. The trade unions, led by electoral workers, teachers and oil and factory workers advanced an agenda of social change but they suffered a massive expulsion and state intervention.

Subsequently, the class struggle in Mexico was advanced in fits and starts, with numerous ups and downs and periodic battles and tactical encounters between the forces commanded by the government and different contingents of the organized working class. Apart from episodic and at times violent confrontations and intense struggles of workers in the labour movement, the epicentre of the class struggle shifted to the countryside – to the resistance of those communities most directly and negatively impacted by the expanding operations of extractive capital, especially in the mining sector.

In this situation, today the working and popular classes in their diverse forms and contingents retain a powerful capacity to engage millions in direct action but they lack the national political and social unity to seize state power. Mexico is the Latin American country with the greatest number of popular struggles but the least capacity to mount an offensive against capital and its political representatives in control of the state apparatus – or capacity to mobilize the diverse forces of resistance and construct a unified revolutionary movement. The class struggle in Mexico in current conditions is very fragmented, even as the working class continues to undertake heroic efforts to engage in regional, factory and provincial social struggles. In this situation the alliance between foreign investors, business billionaires

**174** Mexico: dynamics of a class war

and the state machine is in control of state power, while the workers, peasants and popular movements in some regional and local contexts are able to confront and contest hegemonic power.

The recent history and current dynamics of the class struggle in Mexico illustrate the contradictions and complexities of capitalism and the diverse multiple forms taken by the inevitable forces of resistance. An analysis of these dynamics leads us to conclude that the correlation of forces in the class struggle currently is not favourable for a process of revolutionary change. Even so, in the current context certain sectors of organized labour, particularly the teachers' union, are gathering force. The gross political miscalculation by the governing PRI regime in confronting and dealing with the union appears to have awakened dormant forces of anti-systemic resistance, not only in the south of the country but across the country. Although the capacity of the working class in its diverse forms to confront the combined powers of capital and the state is severely limited, the struggle and collective actions of the teachers' union and diverse sectors of impoverished peasants and indigenous communities point towards a possible change in the current correlation of force in the class struggle. In addition, the class struggle on the expanding frontier of extractive capital is gathering force from below in the form of the Movement of Those Affected (by the destructive operations of extractive capital). The National Indigenous Council (Consejo Nacional Indígena) in this connection needs to be considered, its potential mobilizing power assessed. The correlation of forces between 'capital and labour' in the class struggle is subject to permanent contestation, but both history and the current political situation in Mexico tell us that the ebb and flow of class struggle remain indeterminate.

## Notes

1 A practical revolutionary, and undisputed leader of the Liberation Army of the South, in November 1911 Zapata promulgated the Plan de Ayala that called for the implementation of agrarian rights and the redistribution of lands to the peasants. Zapata's Plan of Ayala also influenced Article 27 of the progressive 1917 Constitution of Mexico that codified an agrarian reform programme.
2 Redistributing to peasants some 45 million acres (180,000 km²) of land owned by large commercial haciendas, Cárdenas fulfilled the land distribution policies written in Article 27 of the constitution. In addition, his government acted on the demand for sweeping change regarding land and labour rights advanced by diverse groups of mobilized workers and peasants who had for so long agitated and fought for their interests. Cárdenas managed to channel the demands of these workers and peasants by bringing them together in an effective alliance under the banner of his party and reformist government.
3 In founding the Partido Revolucionario Mexicano (PRM), the predecessor of PRI, Cárdenas also established the basic corporate structure of sectoral representation, which would govern capital–labour relations in Mexico ever since. His government also established a new welfare programme for the poor and nationalized the railways. But Cárdenas as president is probably best known for the nationalization of the oil industry in 1938 and the creation of Pemex, the government oil monopoly.
4 Throughout what historians have termed 'the golden age of capitalism' but what we might well term the 'age of development' (roughly from the 1950s to the 1970s), the primary agency for social change was the nation state via policies of economic development and

social reform. Organized labour was another key factor, because it could negotiate collective agreements with capital to improve wages and working conditions. However, in the 1960s and 1970s military regimes began to emerge in reaction to the political Left and the slow but steady gains of the popular classes in the development process.

5 In 1983 the government of Mexico announced that it was unable to service the interest on its accumulated external debt, giving rise to what historians have described as the major international (Third World) 'debt crisis' of modern times. Mexico, together with Argentina and Brazil accounted for close to two-thirds of total 'Third World debt'. In response to this crisis, and to prevent the possibility of a concerted policy of countries defaulting on their external debt, the World Bank and the IMF joined forces in a common front to compel indebted countries to open up their economies to the world market and use their export revenues to service the external debt.

6 A sociological study of *los Ninis*, unemployed Mexican youth — the 40 per cent who neither work nor study — found that over 60 per cent saw their prospects for paid work or employment not in the private or public sectors but in the narco-economy.

7 Lopez Portillo has been described as 'the most heartily despised former president in Mexican history', excoriated for his economic policies that included the nationalization of the country's banks and the devaluation of the peso by 40 per cent, and because of his supposedly 'uncontrolled government spending and foreign borrowing' and the suspension of debt payments in August 1982, which helped trigger an international debt crisis and thereby conditions that led to a new neo-liberal era. In any case, the Lopez Portillo regime had a contradictory impact on the neo-liberal agenda advanced under the Washington Consensus. On the one hand, because his *sexenio* coincided with an oil boom, Mexico's entry into the neo-liberal world order was probably delayed. On the other hand, the 'Dutch disease' effect of the oil boom resulted in conditions (a massive growth in the external debt) that provided the agencies of global capital the leverage to impose the structural adjustment programme.

8 Another important dimension of the neo-liberal policy agenda implemented in the 1980s was the dismantling of the government's industrial policy based on import substitution industrialization — a policy prescribed by economists at ECLAC. Forced to abandon this policy, and prevented from implementing an endogenous industrial policy as a cost of admission to the neo-liberal world order — 'globalization' as it came to be known — the government was forced to oversee the privatization and the destruction of the industrial production apparatus built up under the import substitution policy. With the transfer or destruction of this production and employment generation apparatus, which prior to the 1980s had absorbed most of the surplus rural labour generated by the capitalist development of agriculture, in the 1980s this employment generation apparatus, and the labour market that sustained it, was effectively dismantled.

9 Marxists at the time conceptualized the proletariat as an industrial reserve army of surplus labour while modernization theorists such as Arthur Lewis viewed it as a lever of capital accumulation — an unlimited supply of surplus labour that can be used to fuel a process of industrial development. As it turned out, under conditions of peripheral capitalism neither theory proved correct. Given the destruction of forces of production and the prevention of an industrial policy (forced abandonment of ISI) there would be no demand for surplus labour, resulting instead in the formation of an 'informal' sector where rural migrants were forced to fend for themselves on the streets without exchanging their labour power for a living wage.

10 This situation contrasts dramatically with the experience of countries, and the actions taken by governments, in South America that have rejected neo-liberalism as an economic doctrine and turned towards what has been described as 'inclusionary state activism' under the post-Washington Consensus. In these countries — Argentina, Brazil, Chile, Bolivia, Ecuador, Venezuela — extreme poverty has been in some cases virtually eliminated and the overall rate of poverty reduced by 50 per cent on average since 2000, the year in which the UN announced its Millennium Development Goals (including the reduction by 50 per cent of the rate of poverty by 2015).

**176** Mexico: dynamics of a class war

11  Mexican critics have portrayed the profound policy changes introduced by the Salinas regime as *entreguismo* – the handing over of national sovereignty to foreign interests.

12  The major winners under Salinas were business groups with liquid assets that enabled them to monopolize large sectors of the Mexican economy. Salinas's crony-capitalist policies created Mexico's three giant mining companies and the fortunes of the country's three richest individuals today. By 1990, the grossly uneven distribution of wealth in Mexico grew even worse as 2 per cent of the population controlled 78.5 per cent of national income. More than two dozen Mexicans became billionaires under the Salinas administration, mostly through investment in newly privatized industries, while hardships were imposed on peasant farmers, workers and even the middle class. The major losers were workers and small farmers, many of whom joined two million new rural poor as they were driven deeper into poverty by neo-liberal policies (Moguel, 1994: 38–9).

13  The peso crisis of 1994 and 1995 dealt a severe blow to the Mexican economy, underscoring the weak foundations on which it is based. The crisis led to a 70 per cent devaluation of the peso within three months. From approximately three pesos per dollar the exchange rate fell to about 10 pesos per dollar by 1999, greatly compounding the high rates of devaluation between August 1976 and August 1996 (Fernandez Vega, 1996: 45). The cost of imported goods such as basic tools and electronic items such as radios, televisions and light and heavy machinery more than doubled in price in peso terms, affecting both regular consumers and Mexican capitalists. The gross domestic product plummeted by 7.5 per cent in a year and was slow to recover.

14  While socially devastating, the crisis was a boon for foreign capital and internationally competitive national capital. Multinational companies took advantage of the lower wage bill since the December 1994 fall of the peso. Indicative of such growth in foreign investment is that the number of *maquiladoras* increased from 2,085 in 1994 to 2,983 in 1998. In January 1998 17.1 per cent more people were employed in *maquiladoras* than in January 1997 and employment in the *maquiladoras* doubled between 1994 and 1998 (Ochoa & Wilson, 2001: 5).

15  As part and parcel of the neo-liberal agenda, successive governments in Mexico have implemented policies to suppress wages and to deregulate collective labour contracts in order to give employers more prerogatives and greater flexibility. Along the same lines, big Mexican mining capital and right-wing governments have orchestrated concerted political attacks to weaken and divide unionized miners. And this is just the tip of the iceberg, since it only refers to formal-sector employment. There is also an informal sector in the extractive sector (the mining industry) as well the major urban centres, especially in the country's northern coal-mining region where working conditions are similar in many respects to those that existed for the slaves that toiled in the mines of New Spain centuries ago.

16  It has been alleged that the 'Friends of Fox' club that financed his presidential campaign and put him in the presidency included prominent figures and magnates of Ciudad Juarez tied to multiple murders in the border city, as well as various powerful and politically influential families such as Los Zaragoza, Fuentes Tellez Sotelo, Cabada, Karrodi, whose fortunes have their origins in the laundering of drug money (Gallur Santorum, 2010). In addition, the investigative journalist Gallur Santorum (see the 10 postings on the drug cartels in *Contralinea* in 2010) cites sources within the state security apparatus and a number of reports and studies that tie these fortunes made in drug trafficking and money laundering to public functionaries and bureaucrats both in the state and the federal government.

17  The process of energy and educational reform, the latest expressions of the government's neo-liberal policy agenda, is part of the structural reforms programme designed and promoted by the IFIs (World Bank, WB, International Monetary Fund, IMF, and the IDB) as well as – in the case of Mexico – the OECD (re the OECD–Mexico Agreement to Improve the Quality of Education in Schools of Mexico). In total, 11 structural reforms have been approved, including education and energy. Twenty-two more reforms are pending approval.

## Mexico: dynamics of a class war 177

18 On 22 June 2014, the Mexican military killed 22 young people in the town of Tlatlaya in the state of Mexico in what appeared to be executions. On 26 September, the Mayor of Iguala in the state of Guerrero ordered the police to get rid of a group of students from a rural teachers' college. As far as can be determined (see Hernández Navarro's article 'La matanza de Iguala y el Ejército'), the police murdered six and took 43 student teachers into custody. They have not been seen since. There are reports that the police turned the trainee teachers' students over to a local drug cartel, which then murdered the students. To date the whereabouts or remains of these 'normalistas' in the 'killing fields' of Mexican capitalism have not been found, to the continuing anguish of their families.

19 'The government chose force,' said Francisco Bravo, a leader of the National Coordinator of Education Workers (CNTE), the activist caucus within the official union. 'They thought they could end our struggle quickly by arresting our leaders, that we would back down. They were wrong' (Slaughter, 2016).

20 A common tactic in the actions taken by middle-class groups in support of the different working-class struggles.

21 Not a shot was fired in this action. Not a punch was thrown. It took several hours of negotiation before the women were able to fix a live broadcast, during which – still clutching their pots and wooden spoons, dressed in aprons and work clothes – they set out to correct the mistakes in the station's reporting on the violent 14 June attempt by state police to lift the teachers' encampment, and demand on the air that the press 'tell the truth' about the Popular Assembly of the People of Oaxaca and the social movement taking over Oaxaca (Gibler, 2006). On 16 June, two days after the raid of the state television and radio company, some 500,000 people marched downtown to demand the governor's resignation.

22 Teachers have been protesting the government's education reform since 2013 by blocking highways, a common tactic of struggle in Mexico, as well as other countries – for example, the *piqueteros* in Argentina – pioneered by the indigenous movements in Ecuador and Bolivia in the 1990s. Other tactics have included holding ongoing encampments in the main squares of state capitals, and marching through the streets of Mexico City. The CNTE upped the ante on 16 May by calling for a national teachers' strike. Participation was uneven nationally but saw strikes and protests in states where they had not taken place before, such as Coahuila. For a time, teachers in Chiapas blocked four highways. For its part, the government moved quickly to fire 3,360 striking teachers in states other than the four southern states – Oaxaca, Chiapas, Guerrero and Michoacán – where CNTE is strongest. Later, the Department of Education announced it would fire 4,500 teachers in those states, although those firings have not been carried out. On 11 June, 1,000 police using tear gas evicted teachers from their tents in front of the Oaxaca education department. Teachers and supporters resisted with rocks and barricades and moved to the main square in the central city. At the time of writing (29 June), the strike – and the struggle – continues.

23 The stakes in this struggle are very high. For the teachers, educational reform is a model designed to outsource education by replacing their positions with new contract workers without labour rights, and converting education into a privatized financial service. The CNTE estimates that this could mean that 60 per cent of Mexico's 1.2 million teachers would lose their jobs. As for the government, if the national teachers' movement manages to bring down the educational reform, a path would be cleared to bring down all the structural reforms planned for the country's strategic sectors, such as the energy sector. This is the assessment that teachers are making and this is precisely the fear of the federal government.

24 These statistics were provided by official sources at the time of the rebellion and so if anything understated the severity of the conditions they indicated ('A Profile of Chiapas', Embassy of Mexico, Washington, DC, 7 January 1997; *New York Times*, 9 January 1994, Section 4, p. 6). In three of the cities captured by the Zapatistas in January 1994, which form the base of its strength (Ocosingo, Altamirano, Las Margaritas) the situation is even worse. Up to 75 per cent of the population have no electricity and in Las Margaritas 73 per cent lack potable water (Moguel, 1994: 38f).

**178** Mexico: dynamics of a class war

25 On these conditions and the migratory process that brought at least 300,000 into the Lacandona see inter alia Benjamin (1989). Home to 12,000 in 1960, the Lacandona in the early 1990s had over 300,000 people, placing severe pressure on the social and economic systems, not to mention a fragile ecosystem already rendered extremely fragile by illegal logging and oil drilling (La Botz, 1994: 6–8). Tejera Gaona (1997) argues that in the context of this multi-ethnic society and developments the Zapatista rebellion cannot be reduced to the ethnic factor in the same way that so many earlier peasant and indigenous rebellions could be. Although an ethnic factor is clearly present in the struggle, the overriding factor is class, the objective conditions of which had a greater role to play in the rebellion, in unifying diverse ethnic groups, than did a shared ethnic cultural identity, which remains highly fragmented.

26 The purchasing power of wages in 1994, according to Tejera Gaona (1997), was only 44 per cent of what it was in 1981, and this was before the worst wage compression of the past decade, in 1995. In addition, the *jornaleros* of Los Altos continue to experience the most severe conditions of super-exploitation in the country.

27 NAFTA directly affected the producers of coffee and corn, the two main production staples on the *ejidos* in and around La Margarita, Altamirano and Ocosingo. The scope of the problem resulting from the direct exposure to the forces of the world market (that is, the state-subsidized corn producers in Texas) is evident in the huge productivity gap between corn producers in the region and those in the US. Under the conditions of *minifundismo* and extremely low labour productivity in Los Altos, 150 to 300 *jornaleros* are required for 17 in Mexico and one in the US.

28 A striking characteristic of the movement that spawned the Zapatista uprising was the capacity of the FLN rural front, under the command of Marcos, to mix with the population and gain the active support and trust of thousands of indigenous Tzeltales, Tzotziles, Zoques, Choles and Tojozales of Los Altos and La Selva. In this the EZLN achieved in 10 years of ideological and political struggle what no other Marxist oriented political or guerrilla organization had managed to achieve in decades.

29 As Marcos himself explained, the resort to arms was a tactic of last resort adopted in circumstances 'of desperation, when the political scene was totally adverse'.

30 One indicator of the level of organization in the agricultural sector is the number of *ejido* unions, which in the 1980s and early 1990s stagnated in the north but exploded in the south-east: from three to 745 in Oaxaca, four to 45 in Guerrero, and reaching 60 in Veracruz. In Chiapas, the number of *ejido* unions had always been high (Harvey, 1998; Haber, 1996: 171–88).

31 Given the broad mass support of the indigenous population for the Zapatistas in Chiapas, the government has been unable to destroy the movement with standard counter-insurgency measures, forcing the state to embark upon a long-term strategy of low-intensity operations combined with military occupation and encirclement.

32 In his latest report on the government's accounts, the auditor general of Mexico observed that the cost of a mining concession in Mexico is 'symbolic' in that it does not even cover related administrative costs. According to the report, between 2005 and 2010 the federal government collected 6.54 billion pesos from mining companies (equal to approximately US$503 million in 2010, at an exchange rate of 13 pesos to the dollar), which represented barely 1.2 per cent of the value of mining production during the same period (López Bárcenas, 2012: 31).

33 The legal basis for free-market mining in Mexico was established in the 1992 mining law, which, at the behest of the World Bank (as a mechanism for encouraging FDI) abolished the payment of royalties on the extraction of metals and minerals, and opened the door to the full participation of 100 per cent foreign-owned mining companies in all stages of the mining process. Unlike other Latin American countries, which oblige mining companies to pay the state a percentage of their earnings in royalties, in Mexico these companies only have to pay a small fee for the right to explore and extract minerals, starting at five pesos per hectare (38 cents) during the first two years and increasing to 111 pesos per hectare (about US$8.54) after 10 years.

34 By late 2013, 29 high-profile eco-territorial conflicts around mining in Mexico had been detected (Tetreault, 2014a). These movements were led on the local level by people whose livelihoods, health and cultures, and territorial rights, were threatened by large-scale mining projects and who sought to keep natural resources outside of the sphere of the capitalist mode of production. In his review of these conflicts, Tetreault identified 19 of them as 'radical' in that they articulated an emphatic 'no' to mining, at least under a capitalist regime; the rest were focused on obtaining greater material rewards on the local level, mitigating and compensating for the worst environmental consequences and/or obliging mining companies to keep their promises. Twenty-five of them revolve around mining projects carried out by foreign mining firms, 18 of them Canadian.

35 Grupo México began as ASARCO Mexicana, which helped open Mexico to US investment and economic control. ASARCO's mines produced fabulous wealth for its US owners, while ASARCO's railways trekked Mexico's ore across the border to ASARCO's smelters and refineries. At one time, ASARCO had over 95 US mines, smelters and refineries, as well as holdings in Mexico, Chile, Peru, Australia, the Philippines and the Congo (Fischel & Nelson, 2010). In 1998, ASARCO put itself on the market and was purchased by its former Mexican affiliate. In 2005, ASARCO filed for Chapter 11 bankruptcy, citing lack of assets and environmental liabilities as the primary causes. The most prolonged and complex environmental bankruptcy in US history was finally concluded in late 2009, when the company settled its claims and Grupo México regained control, over the strenuous objections of the Steelworkers. Grupo México would subsequently be the first company to take advantage of the opportunity for capital accumulation provided by the new mining law implemented by the Peña Nieto government. It provided authority for the giant corporations in the mining sector to drill for oil and gas in roughly 25 per cent of the national territory under lucrative, essentially untaxed mining concessions – acquired by paying between 18 cents and US$3.88 per acre.

36 Most of Mexico's labour unions are affiliated with the PRI through the Confederation of Mexican Workers (Confederación de Trabajadores Mexicanos – CTM), which is associated with some independent unions and federations in an umbrella organization known as the Congress of Labour (Congreso del Trabajo – CT). In August 1991 the CT confirmed its direct relationship with the government party in a document called the Political Agreement Between the PRI and the Organization of the CT. In relation to the labour sector of the PRI, the CT consists of more than 30 organizations encompassing 85 per cent of the unionized workforce, including the CTM, the largest and most influential organization in the CT, comprising over 11,000 labour unions with more than five million union members and considered the spearhead of Mexico's labour movement. In the early 1990s, Mexico had an estimated 9.5 million unionized workers. The CT mediates between the labour unions and the government. At the same time, it provides the state with a formal mechanism for political manipulation of labour.

37 In 2014 Mexico passed a labour law that made jobs less secure by, among other things, permitting greater outsourcing as well as temporary and part-time work. The law was the culmination of 25 years of struggle waged by political parties, rival unions, employers and workers, in response to a campaign orchestrated since the early 1990s by the World Bank for governments in Latin America to legislate labour reforms for greater economic efficiency (Alexander & La Botz, 2014).

38 On 21 December 2013, Mexico's president, Enrique Peña Nieto, posed for the cameras holding the official decree ending the 75-year history of the national oil company, Pemex. The decree also closed the era in which Mexico's electrical generating and distribution system had been under the control of two public institutions – Central Light and Power (LyFC), from 1960 to 2009, and the Federal Electricity Commission (CFE), from 1937 to 2013. In a literal sense, neither Pemex nor CFE will cease to exist but they will quickly become mere shadows of what they once were: the two largest firms operating in Mexico.

**180** Mexico: dynamics of a class war

## References

Alexander, R. & La Botz, D. (2014). 'Mexico's labour reform: A workers' defeat – for now'. *NACLA*, 18 April.

Benjamin, T. (1989). *A rich land, a poor people*. Alberquerque, NM: University of New Mexico Press.

Collier, G. & Lowery Quaratiello, E. (1994). *Basta! Land and the Zapatista rebellion in Chiapas*. Oakland, CA: Food First.

Cypher, J. & Delgado Wise, R. (2010). *Mexico's economic dilemma: The failure of neoliberal restructuring*. Lanham, MD: Rowman & Littlefield.

Delgado Wise, R. & Veltmeyer, H. (2016). *Agrarian change, migration and development*. Halifax: Fernwood.

Esteva, G. (2016). 'La batalla de Oaxaca'. *La Jornada*, 20 June.

Fernandez Vega, C. (1996). 'Panoptica, estabilidad cambiaria: los factores ajenos'. *La Jornada*, 11 September.

Fischel, A. & Nelson, L. (2010). 'The assault on labour in Cananea, Mexico'. *Dollars & Sense*, September–October. Available at: www.dollarsandsense.org [accessed 3 March 2012].

Gallur Santorum, S. (2010). 'Feminicidios en Juárez: La oligarquia'. *Contralinea*, 31 October. Available at: www.contralinea.com.mx/archivo-revista/index.php/author/gallur [accessed 31 April 2014].

Gibler, J. (2006). 'Scenes from the Oaxaca rebellion'. *ZNet*, 4 August.

Haber, P. (1996). 'Identity and political process: Recent trends in the study of Latin American social movements'. *Latin American Research Review*, 31(1), pp. 171–88.

Harvey, D. (2003). *The new imperialism*. Oxford: Oxford University Press.

Harvey, N. (1998). *The Chiapas Rebellion: The struggle for land and democracy*. London and Durham, NC: Duke University Press.

Hernández Navarro, L. (1994). *Chiapas: la rebelión de los pobres*. Navarra: Gakoa Liburuak.

Hernández Navarro, L. (2014). 'La matanza de Iguala y el ejército'. *La Jornada*, 18 November.

International Metalworkers' Federation (2008). 'An injury to one: The Mexican Miners' struggle for union independence'. *White Paper*, March. Available at: www.workers capital.org/images/uploads/Injury%20to%20One.pdf [accessed 15 June 2016].

Klein, E. & Tokman, V. (2000). 'La estrati cación social bajo tension en la era de la globalización'. *Revista de Cepal*, 72(December), pp. 7–30.

La Botz, D. (1994). *Chiapas and beyond: Mexico's crisis and the fight for democracy*. Boulder, CO: Westview.

La Botz, D. (2005). 'Mexican labour year in review'. *Mexican Labour News and Analysis*, January. Available at: www.ueinternational.org/Mexico_info/mlna.php [accessed 4 April 2008].

La Botz, D. (2010). 'Mexican electrical workers change strategy in face of government intransigence'. *NACLA*, 7 January.

López Bárcenas, F. (2012). 'Detener el saqueo minero en México'. *La Jornada*, 28 February. Available at: www.jornada.unam.mx/2012/02/28/opinion/023a1pol [accessed 1 May 2015].

López Bárcenas, F. & Montserrat Eslava, M. (2011). *El mineral o la vida. La legislación minera en México*. Mexico: Centro de Orientación y Asesoría a Pueblos Indígenas.

López Portillo, J. (1982). 'Mexico Vivirá. Sexto informe de gobierno de José López Portillo el 1 de septiembre de 1982'. *Resumen Ejecutivo*. Available at: www.larouchepub.com/spanish/other_articles/2004/Memoria_JoLoPo/05ONUpararNuevOscur.html [accessed 22 September 2005].

Marcos, Subcomandante (1992). 'Tourist guide to Chiapas'. *Monthly Review*, 46(1), pp. 8–9.

Moguel, J. (1994). 'Reforma constitucional y luchas agrarias en el marco de la transición salinista', in J. Moguel, C. Botey & L. Hernández 'Chiapas y el Pronaso', *La Jornada*, Supplement, 25 January.

Mufioz Rios, P. (2000). 'La canasta básica aumentó 400%'. *La Jornada*, 27 November.

Ochoa, E. & Wilson, T. D. (2001). 'Mexico in the 1990s: Economic crisis, social polarization, and class struggle'. *Latin American Perspectives*, 28(3), pp. 3–10.

Portes, A., Castells, M. & Benton, L. (1989). *The informal economy: Studies in advanced and less developed countries*. Baltimore, MD: Johns Hopkins University Press.

Robledo, E. (2000). 'En México hay 70 millones de pobres: Boltvinik'. *Epoca*, 6 November.

Rodriguez-Orregia, E. (2007). 'The informal sector in Mexico: Characteristics and dynamics'. *Revista Perspectivas Sociales/Social Perspectives*, 9(1), pp. 89–175.

Roman, R. & Velasco Arregui, E. (2009). 'The state against the working class'. *Global Research*, 26 November.

Roman, R. & Velasco Arregui, E. (2014). 'Partners in crime: The continental capitalist offensive and the killing fields of Mexico. Part I: State Terror and the murder of 43 students'. *The Bullet*, 1058, 21 November.

Sachs, W. (ed.) (1992). *The development dictionary: A guide to knowledge and power*. London: Zed.

Slaughter, J. (2016). 'In push for education reforms, Mexican government kills teachers in the street'. *LabourNotes: Putting the Movement back in the Labour Movement*, 28 June. Available at: www.labournotes.org/2016/06/push-education-reforms-mexican-government-kills-teachers-street [accessed 28 June 2016].

Soldatenko, M. (2005). 'Mexico '68: Power to the imagination!' *Latin American Perspectives*, 32(4), July, pp. 111–32.

Tejera Gaona, H. (1997). *Organiacieon étnica, identidad y formación regional en Chiapas*. Mexico: Instituto Nacional de Antropología e Historia.

Tetreault, D. (2014a). 'Mexico: The political ecology of mining', in H. Veltmeyer & J. Petras (eds) *The new extractivism: A model for Latin America?* London: Zed, pp. 172–91.

Tetreault, D. (2014b). 'Free market mining in Mexico'. *Critical Sociology*, 42(4), December.

Tokman, V. (ed.) (1992). *Beyond regulation: The informal economy in Latin America*. Boulder, CO: Lynne Rienner.

Veltmeyer, H. & Tetreault, D. (2013). *Poverty and development in Latin America: Public policies and development pathways*. West Hartford, CT: Kumarian.

World Bank (2004). *Poverty in Mexico: An assessment of conditions, trends and government strategies*. Washington, DC: World Bank. Available at: www.bancomundial.orgmx/pdf/estudiosporsector/povertyinmexico/2.pdf [accessed 13 December 2012].

# 9

# PARAGUAY

## Class struggle on the extractive frontier

*Arturo Ezquerro-Cañete*

On 22 June 2012, the Paraguayan Congress impeached and ousted from office the moderately left-of-centre government of Fernando Lugo and replaced him temporarily with Federic Franco, a figure from a competing faction of Lugo's own Patriotic Alliance for Change (Alianza Patriótica para el Cambio – APC) coalition, bringing to an end the country's halting democratic experiment, ongoing since 1989. Paraguay was suspended from both the Union of South American Nations (Nations Unión de Naciones Suramericanas – UNASUR) and the Southern Common Market (Mercado Común del Sur – Mercosur) for the interruption of democratic rule, and only reinstated after the inauguration of Colorado Party President Horacio Cartes in August 2013.

The above episode is reflective of the intensification of efforts by imperialism and the Latin American Right to turn back the clock on the progressive cycle of the 2000s. In this sense, the Paraguayan case (along with the 2009 military coup in Honduras) signalled, perhaps, the earlier stages of a receding ('pink') tide that has intensified in recent years. For one thing, it inaugurated an emerging regional shift towards 'smart coups', 'whereby Left governments are forced out of office and a new Right-oriented government put in place, with, preferably, relatively little bloodshed and an element of popular and institutional legitimacy' (Cannon, 2016: 119; for the case of Brazil, see Chapter 6).

Although this chapter focuses on the 'rise and fall' of Fernando Lugo and the multifaceted advances of conservative forces thereafter, it starts from the premise that the role of the class struggle cannot be viewed in historical isolation. Indeed, as Marx outlines in his conception of historical materialism, at each stage of capitalist development can be found a corresponding and distinct form of class struggle based on the forces of resistance to this advance. The chapter therefore begins with a brief reflection of the historical foundations of contemporary Paraguay, charting the dynamics of repression and co-option during the dictatorship of Alfredo Stroessner (1954–89), as well as the more recent shift in the country's agrarian economy towards agro-extractivism. Section 2 turns to the question of agency and examines the most important social classes in the country: landed oligarchy, the peasantry, and forces of imperialism. The following section explores how this class structure has contributed to the changing forms that the class struggle (from above and below) has taken in Paraguay over the course of the country's protracted transition to democracy (1989–2008). Against this backdrop, the chapter then situates the rise of Lugo to office and traces out the salient feature of the class struggle during his short-lived administration (2008–12). The class interests behind the June 2012 'parliamentary coup' are discussed. Finally, it offers a brief analysis of the class struggle under the current administration of Horacio Cartes (2013 to present).

## Historical foundation

### The Stroessner regime (1954–89)

General Alfredo Stroessner presided over the longest dictatorship in twentieth-century Latin America, between 1954 and 1989. During this period, pervasive corruption and clientelism in their diverse forms – from contraband to money laundering to theft from the state – were justified by Stroessner (in a 1965 interview) as representing *el precio de la paz* (the price of peace), turning Paraguay into what Eduardo Galeano (1973: 196) called 'the kingdom of institutionalized corruption'. Stroessner also sought to justify torture and domestic repression by linking his measure against all perceived and real opponents to the anti-communist doctrine of the Cold War, earning his regime a well-deserved reputation for brutality and human rights abuses, as well as the economic and political support from the US. While disloyalty was punished with persecution and repression, loyalty guaranteed economic reward and privileges, which included lucrative positions in state monopolies, access to public assets, and acquisition of land through the government rural welfare institute (Instituto de Bienestar Rural – IBR).

Kleinpenning and Zoomers write that

> [d]espite the fact that rural ownership and tenure relationships were very unfavourable to the majority when President Stroessner came to power, there was little or no peasant rebellion during his regime, and the rural masses were unable to force the government to improve their situation.
>
> *(Kleinpenning and Zoomers, 1991: 279)*

The quiescence of the peasantry is explained by means of a two-pronged strategy and policy of (i) agricultural colonization, wherein the Stroessner regime institutionalized the traditional patron–client ties of the peasantry and rural elite through land (Setrini, 2010: 14), and (ii) repression, the Stroessner regime managing to defeat or 'bring to ground' the social movements engaged in the land struggle.

**184** Paraguay: extractivism and class struggle

In the 1960s, the Stroessner regime, faced with stagnating agricultural growth and a growing concern over the spreading land conflict between *latifundistas* and *minifundistas*, embarked on an ambitious internal colonization programme, distributing state-owned land, much of it in the sparsely populated interior and border areas. The Agrarian Statute of 1963 provided a new legal basis and the Instituto de Bienestar Rural (Rural Welfare Institute – IBR) was created as the government agency to carry out the reform with the stated intent to increase rural welfare (Kleinpenning, 1984: 164). In practice, however, while the reform was nominally committed to proving land title and support to the landless peasantry, the bulk of the public land was allocated at extremely low official prices to politically connected associates of the regime (e.g. armed forces, rural elites, government officials), who in turn resold part of this land at favourable market prices to Brazilian companies and colonists. The IBR also sold land directly to foreign state agencies and companies (Kleinpenning, 1984: 173).

According to a recent report by the Paraguayan Truth and Justice Commission on illegal land ownership, between 1954 and 2003 a total of 7,851,295 hectares of land (64 per cent of the total land distributed and 19 per cent of Paraguay's total surface area) were allocated to both nationals and foreigners in an irregular and clientelistic manner (CVJ, 2008).[1] The study examined 200,705 awards of land and concluded that many beneficiaries were relatives of Stroessner himself, or politicians and army officers directly associated with his government. As a result, 'almost all members of Congress are also members of Paraguay's tiny landowning elite, with titles held either directly or in the names of friends and family' (Nickson, 2015: 18). As will become clear in discussing the two case studies of Ñacunday and Marina Kue later on, links to the state continue to allow the rural oligarchy to maintain their monopoly of access to land secure, even though this access was often acquired illegally in the first place. Such illegally acquired, or politically constituted, land is known in Paraguay as *tierra malhabida* (ill-gotten land) and continues to be at the heart of the country's agrarian question and land conflicts. Indeed, it was on land to which ex-Colorado Senator Blas N. Riquelme claimed ownership that 17 people were massacred on 15 June 2012, triggering the impeachment of Fernando Lugo a week later, as we shall discuss in detail below.

## From agro-exports to agro-extractivism

Throughout much of its history, Paraguay has been one of the most consistent followers of an open-economy strategy for economic growth (Nickson & Lambert, 2002: 163; Birch, 2014: 271). Unlike most Latin American countries in the mid-twentieth century – particularly its Southern Cone neighbours – Paraguay never experienced a period of import-substituting industrialization, relying instead on an agro-export development model (Baer & Birch, 1984; Weisskoff, 1992). Part of the reason for this was the power of large-landowner and agricultural lobbyists. Stroessner also discouraged industrialization because of the likelihood of it encouraging the rise of trade unions that might pose a threat to his rule. As a result, there is no important manufacturing sector and no industrial bourgeoisie or proletariat, which partially explains why the peasant movement remains the most important social actor challenging the state and political elite (see the discussion below).

Agriculture remains the largest sector in the Paraguayan economy, accounting for a fifth of economic activity, a feature that distinguishes it from the rest of South America (see Table 9.1). In fact, as noted by Kregg Hetherington (2009: 656n8), Paraguay is the only Latin American country featured in the World Bank's *2008 World Development Report: Agriculture for Development* to fit within the Bank's 'agriculture-based economy' category (World Bank, 2007: 31). Moreover, while the relative contribution of agriculture declined steadily and significantly during the 1970s and 1980s, somewhat unexpectedly, Paraguay is a more agricultural economy today than it was in 1990, as measured by its share of GDP (Birch, 2014: 277).[2]

Indeed, since the late-1990s, the pace, direction and consequences of Paraguay's agrarian development model have been radically transformed and it is increasingly becoming characteristic of a type of 'agro-extractivism' (Rojas, 2104; see also Petras & Veltmeyer, 2014), manifested in the conversion of arable land for domestic food production into land for the corporate production of agro-commodities (or 'flex

**TABLE 9.1** Socio-economic indictors in Latin America, 2014

| Country | GDP | | Employment | |
|---|---|---|---|---|
| | *Agriculture* | *Manufacturing* | *Agriculture* | *Manufacturing* |
| **Argentina** | 8.3 | 14.5 | 1.5 | 13.0 |
| **Bolivia** | 12.4 | 12.4 | 29.5[d] | 10.4[d] |
| **Brazil** | 5.6 | 10.9 | 14.2 | 12.3 |
| **Chile** | 3.3 | 12.4 | 9.2[d] | 11.3[d] |
| **Colombia** | 6.3 | 12.2 | 15.9 | 12.0 |
| **Costa Rica** | 5.2 | 15.2 | 10.4 | 11.4 |
| **Ecuador** | 9.1 | 14.5 | 24.4 | 11.3 |
| **El Salvador** | 11.0 | 19.8 | 19.1 | 14.9 |
| **Guatemala** | 11.2 | 19.3 | 30.6[a] | 16.4[a] |
| **Honduras** | 13.0 | 17.4 | 36.2[c] | 12.9[c] |
| **Mexico** | 3.3 | 17.7 | 14.3 | 15.8 |
| **Nicaragua** | 20.5 | 15.4 | 33.5[b] | 11.5[b] |
| **Panama** | 3.1[d] | 6.3[d] | 15.7 | 7.4 |
| **Paraguay** | **20.5** | **12** | **22.1** | **11.4** |
| **Peru** | 7.2 | 15.3 | 26.0 | 9.5 |
| **Uruguay** | 7.9 | 13.7 | 8.1 | 11.6 |
| **Venezuela** | 5.7[b] | 13.6[b] | 7.4[d] | 11.3[d] |

*Source:* CEPALSTAT (Statistical Annex).

*Notes*
a  2006.
b  2009.
c  2010.
d  2013.

**186** Paraguay: extractivism and class struggle

crops' in the lexicon of critical agrarian studies; see Borras et al., 2012: 404–5; Turzi, 2012). In the words of Birch (2014), Paraguay has experienced 'a marked shift away from small-scale production of a variety of agricultural crops for both domestic consumption and export and towards large-scale, mechanized mono-cultivation of soybeans for global commodity markets'.

As a result of these developments, alongside high commodity prices during the 2000s, Paraguay has experienced sustained economic growth, averaging 4.9 per cent between 2003 and 2013, punctuated by particularly large economic swings – with an apex of 13.6 per cent in 2013, and a low of 4.0 per cent in 2009 – often connected to climatic conditions. Notably, in only two years, the economy went from a half-century record low GDP contraction of 4 per cent in 2009 (after the severe and widespread drought of that year and the fall in international prices for agricultural products) to a record high GDP growth of 13.1 per cent in the subsequent year, thanks to a bumper crop from the 2009–10 harvest. The economy then plummeted to 4.3 per cent in 2011 and contracted by 1.2 per cent in 2012 (in the wake of the severe drought that hit the country in late 2011 and early 2012) and then surged again to 13.6 per cent in 2013, making it the fastest-growing country in the region (ECLAC, 2010: 123–8, 2011: 137–42, 2014).

The driving force behind such volatile GDP growth is reducible (almost entirely) to the boom in GM soybean production (see Table 9.2), which accounts for roughly 55 per cent of the value of exports (Guereña, 2013), making Paraguay the most soybean-reliant economy in the world. In this regard, the Paraguayan countryside has been affected by broader shifts in the global food regime towards neo-liberal restructuring and the deployment of transgenic corps in Latin America since the mid-1990s (see Otero, 2012; Otero & Lapegna, 2016). In particular, Paraguay's insertion into the so-called 'Soy Republic' (i.e. the Southern Cone's neo-liberal soy regime) has led to a marked transformation in the agricultural mode of production occasioned by the adoption of genetically modified crops, agrochemicals and no-tilling techniques.

I argue that Paraguay has witnessed and experienced all of the contradictory developments and pitfalls of agro-extractivism. These include increased concentration of landholdings; dampened overall employment as rural labourers are rendered 'surplus' to the requirements of agribusiness capital; and a growing dependence on agrochemicals that compromise environmental quality and human health. At the same time, the 'transgenic soyization' of Paraguay's agriculture has accelerated the forced expulsion of the peasantry. I argue here that the insertion of Paraguay into the Southern Cone's neo-liberal soy regime has engendered a new regime of dispossession driven by the new agro-industrial practices associated with this model. Here, the weak or absent or conniving nature of the Paraguayan state is central to an understanding of how the application of highly globalized capital and chemical intensive agro-industrial practices has recast the dynamics of the historical process of accumulation by dispossession. Specifically, I suggest the process might be termed 'displacement by fumigation and dispossession' (Ezquerro-Cañete, 2016) – the forced displacement from land by the intensive use of agro-toxins, when crops are

**TABLE 9.2** Soybean production and cultivation in Paraguay, 1997–2015

| Year | Area sowed (ha) | Production (tonnes) |
| --- | --- | --- |
| 1997 | 1,050,000 | 2,771,000 |
| 1998 | 1,150,000 | 2,988,201 |
| 1999 | 1,200,000 | 2,980,058 |
| 2000 | 1,200,000 | 2,911,423 |
| 2001 | 1,350,568 | 3,502,179 |
| 2002 | 1,445,365 | 3,546,674 |
| 2003 | 1,550,000 | 4,518,015 |
| 2004 | 1,936,623 | 3,911,415 |
| 2005 | 2,009,474 | 4,040,828 |
| 2006 | 2,227,487 | 3,641,186 |
| 2007 | 2,429,796 | 5,581,117 |
| 2008 | 2,644,856 | 5,968,085 |
| 2009 | 2,524,649 | 3,647,205 |
| 2010 | 2,680,182 | 6,462,429 |
| 2011 | 2,870,539 | 7,128,364 |
| 2012 | 2,957,408 | 4,043,039 |
| 2013 | 3,157,600 | 8,202,190 |
| 2014 | 3,254,982 | 8,189,542 |
| 2015* | 3,264,480 | 8,004,858 |

*Source:* CAPECO (www.tera.com.py/capeco/) (accessed 5 August 2015).

planted next to population centres (i.e. agrochemical drift as a new mechanism of accumulation by environmental dispossession).

The economic, political and distributive shifts associated with the transition to democracy and to the insertion into the neo-liberal food regime have realigned Paraguay's rural class structure. The country's rural class structure includes the elite (cattle ranchers, soybean farmers, army generals and political acolytes that had been awarded large landholdings illegally during the Stroessner regime under the guise of 'land reform') and the broad peasantry (small-scale landowners, the landless and the informal proletariat).[3] As a rough approximation, the 2008 agrarian census suggests the smallest landholdings of 20 hectares or less comprised 83.5 per cent of all agricultural units but accounted for only 4 per cent of the nation's agricultural land (MAG 2009). At the other extreme, 4,691 holdings, barely 1.6 per cent of the total, controlled 79 per cent of all agricultural land. Of these, the 600 largest holdings (0.2 per cent of the total) controlled 40.7 per cent of the nation's agriculture. As a result, a number of studies testify to the fact that the distribution of agricultural landholdings in Paraguay is one of the most – if not the most – unequal in the world. For example, Paraguay's 1991 Gini coefficient of 0.93 ranked highest out of 133 countries surveyed in the World Bank's 2008 *World Development Report* (2007: Table A3), while a more recent Oxfam report revealed an even higher Gini coefficient of 0.94 (Guereña 2013). Such concentration is not a new problem in Paraguay,[4] but, as the following section will make clear, the lack of any sustained, coordinated or

## 188  Paraguay: extractivism and class struggle

significant programmes of land reform or rural poverty alleviation, combined with the promotion of agro-exports, has further exacerbated the situation over the past 20 years (Lambert, 2000).

## Agrarian class structure in Paraguay

Regarding the Paraguay class structure, it is useful to frame our discussion in terms of Argentine Marxist Claudio Katz's (2007; see also Webber, 2015) categorization of the three major social forces with distinct interest and capacities in Latin America: (i) the rural and urban poor classes and oppressed groups, (ii) domestic ruling classes, and (iii) imperialism. Adopting this analytical framework within the Paraguayan context means focusing on the balance and movement in power relations between: (i) the peasantry, which is by and large the most important social movement actor in the country, (ii) the political and economic elite, not least in reference to the long history of Colorado Party hegemony, and landowners' groups and agribusiness organizations, (iii) the dynamics of (agro-)extractive capital and extractive imperialism, particularly in relation to Brazilian sub-imperialism – that is, the agency and role of the Brazilian state in its active support for the operations of agro-extractive capital in Paraguay.

### *The landed oligarchy*

Landowners' groups comprise some of the wealthiest and most influential elites in the country and exert a strong lobbying presence inside Congress, with representation in all major political parties. Broadly speaking, the landed oligarchy can be divided into two main groups: cattle ranchers and soybean farmers. Cattle ranchers have long been a powerful stakeholder group, as major beneficiaries of Paraguay's unequal land tenure system. They are organized through the Rural Association of Paraguay (Asociación Rural del Paraguay – ARP), founded in 1938 in response to the threat of expropriation that had been raised by the short-lived reformist Febrerista government (1936–37). The vast majority of high-income families resident in Asunción own an *estancia* (cattle ranch) so there is considerable overlap between cattle ranchers and other stakeholders, including the Colorado Party (Nickson, 2010: 290). In response to the escalation of land invasions following the overthrow of Alfredo Stroessner, the ARP carried out a vociferous media campaign in favour of private property, arguing that land invasions and expropriations would frighten away foreign direct investment, and this led to the disbandment of rural development commission, Consejo Nacional de Coordinación del Desarrollo Rural (CONCODER) (Nickson, 2015: 57–8).

Soybean farmers emerged as a powerful stakeholder group during the 1990s. There has been a dramatic increase in the area under soybean cultivation, with Brazilian immigrant farmers consolidating their holdings by buying up land from smaller, often impoverished Paraguayan farmers. Soybean farmers are represented by the powerful Paraguayan Association of Producers of Soybeans, Cereals, and

Oilseeds (Asociación de Productores de Soja, Oleaginosas y Cereales del Paraguay – APS), which represents 50,000 *brasiguayo* commercial farmers who control most of Paraguay's huge soybean production, and the Paraguayan Chamber of Exporters of Cereals and Oilseeds (Cámara Paraguaya de Exportadores de Cereales y Oleaginosas – CAPECO). Most of its members are medium-scale family farmers, often second-generation immigrants from Brazil, of European extraction. It is understood that the large transnational soybean companies that operate in Paraguay are not CAPECO members (Nickson, 2010: 290).

ARP, APS and CAPECO are all members of the Unión de Gremios de la Producción (Union of Producer Association – UGP), a powerful umbrella association established in 2005 in order to defend the interests of producers and exporters of agricultural goods.[5] Traditionally these groups have been able to block tax and land reform, not only through lobbying but also through the threat of direct action in the form of *tractorazos* (large disruptive demonstrations that mobilize thousands of farmers to block roads with tractors and farm equipment). In late 2003, for example, a threatened *tractorazo* by the Coordinadora Agrícola de Paraguay (CAP) successfully blocked government plans to impose VAT on unprocessed agricultural products.

## *The* Campesino *movement*

In the absence of a significant industrial proletariat, the *campesino* movement has long been – by far – the most important and strongest social movement challenging the state and political elite (Fogel, 2009: 54–5). This movement, however, has traditionally remained atomized into different social movement organizations that mushroomed since the 1990s, after suffering severe repression throughout the Stroessner regime.[6] An exceptional moment of unity and cohesion was visible during the period 1994–97, when the five major national peasant organizations at the time – the Federación Nacional Campesina (National Peasant Federation – FNC), the Organización de Lucha por la Tierra (Struggle for Land Organization – OLT), the Movimiento Campesino Paraguayo (Paraguyan Peasant Movement – MCP), the Organización Nacional Campesina (National Peasant Organization – ONAC) and the Unión Nacional de Campesinos (National Peasant Union – UNC), as well as 22 different organizations at the regional, departmental and district levels, were agglutinated through the creation of the umbrella organization Mesa Coordinadora Nacional de Organizaciones Campesinas (National Coordinating Committee of Peasant Organizations – MCNOC). On 15 March 1994, the founding event of the MCNOC was a massive protest march of unprecedented scale through Asunción to demand a reform of the government's agrarian policy. Congregating close to 20,000 people, the march represented the first national mobilization by peasant organizations that had previously articulated their demands only at the local or regional level. Each year thereafter, peasant organizations have held a massive protest march in the capital to present their demands in a public show of their strength in numbers (Levy, 2013: 36–7).

**190** Paraguay: extractivism and class struggle

Although the central demand of these various peasant organizations is largely the same (redistributive land reform), the movement is plagued by infighting and divisions. As a result, the movement has been traditionally atomized into different social movements organizations that, at times, have proposed different projects and strategies, but at certain moments have come together to constitute the government (see the discussion below). In 1998, leadership rivalries between FNC and OLT resulted in a split within MCNOC (Piñeiro, 2004: 130). The lack of a single body representing the peasantry, therefore,

> has more to do with personal rivalries and competition for mass support and resources among its leaders than ideological and programmatic differences. However, it is also true that more substantive divisions coincide with and reinforce personal rivalries. Regional differences in political conditions and land tenure structure encourage the use of different tactics by campesino leaders. These differences are compounded by the different base structures possessed by campesino organizations.
>
> *(Setrini, 2010: 30)*

A nationalist orientation has long been visible within the campesino movements. As Beverly Nagel explains, this is partly a consequence of the repression suffered by peasant organizations during the Stroessner regime: 'Since class-based criticism could not be voiced, nationalist appeal provided the only real space for objections' (Nagel, 1999: 157). This nationalist rhetoric is only emphasized by the country's linguistic distinctiveness: Paraguay is the only country in Latin America in which a majority of the population speaks a single indigenous language (Guaraní) even though they do not politically identify as indigenous.[7] According to the 2002 census, Guaraní is preferred by 59 per cent of the households compared with 35.8 per cent that preferred Spanish (DGEEC, 2004). In rural areas, Guaraní remained by far the predominant language, preferred by 82.5 per cent of the population. As a result, there has been a tendency – not unbroken or free of contradictions – for the Guaraní ethno-linguistic composition of the Paraguayan peasant movements to stand in as an analogue for class (Petras, 1997: 21).

This nationalist discourse is particularly evident near the border with Brazil, where native Paraguayans feel aggrieved of their dispossession amid land takeover by Brazilians and *Brasiguayos* (a pejorative label amalgamated from the Spanish words for 'Brazilian' and 'Paraguayan').[8] The arguments and the rhetoric used are decidedly nationalist, with obvious parallels to the past Brazilian invasions. In one poignant example of the growing animosity towards Brasiguayos cited in national newspapers in 2008, peasants burned the Brazilian flag at an independence day celebration at Curupayty in the department of San Pedro (*ABC Color*, 2008).

## Brazilian sub-imperialism

As Veltmeyer and Petras helpfully distinguish, extractive capital is largely seen as 'the multinational corporations, bearers of capital in the form of foreign direct investment' (Veltmeyer & Petras, 2014: 28). Extractive imperialism, on the other hand, refers to 'the state in the exercise and projection of its various powers in support of this capital' (Veltmeyer & Petras, 2014: 28).[9] In the Paraguayan case, however, we also have to make a further distinction related to a healthy renewal of interest in Marini's (1972) concept of sub-imperialism, redirecting our attention to the geopolitical alliance between Brazilian state and private agribusiness interests (for example, see Vuyk, 2014; Zibechi, 2014; Oliveira, 2016). Indeed, the country's soy complex has a distinctly 'trans-Latin' character, owing to the high influx of foreign (particularly Brazilian) capital, which controls 64 per cent of the land cultivated by soy in the country's four most important *sojero* departments – Alto Paraná, Canindeyú, Caaguazú and Itapúa (Galeano, 2012: 461). The correlation between land concentration and foreign ownership is illustrated in Figure 9.1.

This process of foreignization (*extranjerización*) began in the 1970s with the release of state lands for private purchase (Nickson, 1981) but has accelerated in the last two decades as Paraguayan lands are increasingly being integrated into the expanding agricultural frontiers of Brazil and, to a far lesser extent, Argentina (Galeano, 2012). While not yet a direct investor in land, the Brazilian government provides significant support to Brazilian investors, first by monitoring investment deals acquiring or leasing land (via the Brazilian embassy), and second by providing technical assistance (via Brazilian state agencies) in agricultural and cattle ranching ventures (Galeano, 2012: 466). Furthermore, in the face of increasingly militant agitation by landless peasants in Paraguay for the redistribution of Brazilian-owned soybean farms, the Brazilian government issued strong warnings and threatened sanctions against such actions. In early October 2008, for example, Brazilian president Lula signed Decree 6,592, which regulates the National Mobilization System, dedicated to confronting 'foreign aggression'. The first

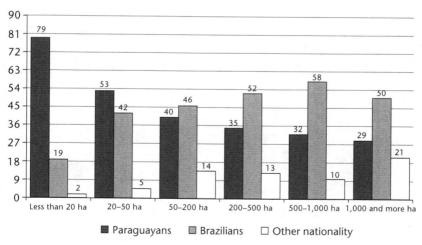

**FIGURE 9.1** Percentage of hectares cultivated with soy, by nationality of producers and farm size, 2008.

*Source:* Galeano (2012).

## 192 Paraguay: extractivism and class struggle

article of the decree defines foreign aggression as 'threats or injurious acts that harm national sovereignty, territorial integrity, the Brazilian people, or national institutions, *even when they do not constitute an invasion of national territory*' (quoted in *Ultima Hora*, 2008; emphasis added). In other words, any expropriation of Brazilian-owned land in Paraguay could be used as a pretext for Brazilian military action against Paraguay. In this regard, Brazilian (sub-imperialist) interests (i.e. the intervention of the Brazilian state in support of its nationals in land conflict) have proved a perennial obstacle to land redistribution, as can be clearly seen in the case of Ñacunday (Fogel, 2013).

## Class struggle in an era of protracted transition to democracy (1989–2008)

The transition from the Stroessner regime to a conservative electoral regime was accompanied by a growing mobilization of peasants. The ebbs and flows of the class struggle for land throughout the protracted transition to democracy are shown in Table 9.3. At a glance, three years stand out in terms of conflicts and arrests: the fall of the Stroessner regime in 1989 opened space for the expression of rural discontent, which was manifested primarily in a wave of land occupations throughout 1990; 1999, which signalled the so-called Marzo Paraguayo; and 2004, which represents the apex in the number of land occupations, evictions and arrest of peasants. The following section provides a brief chronological account of the peaks and troughs of collective action and the associated state repression and criminalization of peasant protests.

**TABLE 9.3** Land conflicts, 1990–2007

| Year | Conflicts | Occupations | Evictions | Arrests | Marches |
|------|-----------|-------------|-----------|---------|---------|
| 1990 | 99 | 49 | 51 | 820 | 34 |
| 1991 | 66 | 17 | 23 | 566 | 19 |
| 1992 | 50 | 16 | 16 | 120 | 15 |
| 1993 | 46 | 14 | 17 | 128 | 18 |
| 1994 | 57 | 26 | 24 | 411 | 60 |
| 1995 | 49 | 23 | 25 | 359 | 37 |
| 1996 | 54 | 20 | 27 | 553 | 39 |
| 1997 | 43 | 15 | 13 | 137 | 15 |
| 1998 | 28 | 14 | 11 | 429 | 17 |
| 1999 | 52 | 31 | 20 | 1,048 | 54 |
| 2000 | 47 | 19 | 12 | 531 | 34 |
| 2001 | 42 | 17 | 24 | 260 | 73 |
| 2002 | 28 | 16 | 14 | 161 | 49 |
| 2003 | 51 | 30 | 19 | 339 | 41 |
| 2004 | 149 | 75 | 74 | 1,400 | 30 |
| 2005 | 34 | 7 | 7 | 34 | 36 |
| 2006 | 45 | 24 | — | 50 | 69 |
| 2007 | 40 | 20 | 9 | 2 | 45 |

*Source:* CDE (2007).

## 1989–90: wave of occupations

The overthrow of Stroessner stimulated a wave of land occupations and a flourishing of campesino organization. By the mid-1990s, roughly 19,000 families had claimed lands, totalling over 360,000 hectares (Nagel, 1999: 148). The wave of land occupations was followed by a counter-attack from the landlord class; paramilitary forces and then the army intervened to dislodge many families. The government's stance was summarized by the following quote, when President Rodríguez (1989–93) declared, 'We have resolved to declare total war on invaders of private property.... Those who make claims honestly and with justice, will receive positive response from government, but to the invaders, total war, total war' (*ABC*, 28 March 1990, quoted in Nagel, 1999: 166). In 1990, there were 51 land evictions and 820 peasants were arrested. The pattern of invasion and dislodgment has continued under successive Colorado governments. In the mid-1990s, the new government deployed the armed forces to quell the occupations and undertook a campaign to evict occupants forcibly and destroy their shacks and crops (Nagel, 1999: 148–9). The Coordinating Committee for Human Rights in Paraguay (Coordinadora de Derechos Humanos del Paraguay – CODEHUPY) reported the murder of 77 rural leaders in the context of the struggle for land between 1989 and 2005 (CODEHUPY, 2007).

## 1999: Marzo Paraguayo

The first of these junctures occurred in 1999, in what is called the Paraguayan March Massacre. Regular peasant protests were scheduled for March of that year, when the assassination of Vice President Luis Argaña triggered a political crisis. In exchange for the forgiveness of public-sector loans made to their members, national campesino organizations joined student-led opposition to a coup attempt by General Lino Oviedo. Campesino leaders (along with student groups) were able to mobilize large enough numbers to defend constitutional government. As Setrini points out, however,

> [t]he nature of this exchange was plainly clientelistic: political support for the incumbent government in exchange for debt forgiveness. Furthermore, leader's [*sic*] secured material benefits for their followers by betraying the political preferences of their bases, among which were many Oviedo supporters.
>
> *(Setrini, 2010: 29; also see Hetherington, 2011: 47–56)*

## The 2000s: from anti-neo-liberal mobilization to ongoing class struggle

In the new millennium, the class struggle once again assumed a different role under conditions of several epoch-defining changes in the global economy. Alongside the unresolved land question, the class struggle in this period took the form of uprisings and widespread resistance against the neo-liberal agenda of structural reform in

**194** Paraguay: extractivism and class struggle

macroeconomic public policy and, later, against the predatory activities associated with the operations of agro-extractive capital.

The former centred on an unprecedented wave of anti-neo-liberal resistance in 2002 against government policies to privatize state-owned enterprises and an IMF-backed economic austerity package of policies of the Colorado administration of President González Macchi (1999–2003). The FNC and MCNOC, both vociferous in their opposition to private-sector involvement in public services and in defence of the existing institutional arrangement for provision of water supply, electricity and telecom, unified again in 2002 and provided the backbone of the Democratic Congress of Paraguay (Congress Democratico del Pueblo – CDP), a broad coalition with leftist political parties and over 60 peasant, union and community groups in opposition to the government's IMF-imposed privatization programme. Between June and September 2002, the CDP organized large-scale marches on Asunción that forced the government to make a volte-face on the privatization of three state-owned companies (water and electricity utilities and the railways).[10] Following widespread protest and conflict, the government was forced to accept all of the CDP's demands, including an indefinite suspension of all privatization plans included in the IMF package.[11] Further demonstrations also led to the repeal of government legislation that sought to introduce more belt-tightening measures, including a price hike in public services. Faced with such a resurrection of civil society organization, it was clear that any incoming government would have to take on this deep-seated opposition to neo-liberal reforms (Lambert, 2000: 108–9; Nickson, 2010: Setrini, 2010; see also Palau, 2002).

### *Ongoing land struggle*

Following repeated promises of reform alongside government inaction over the growing crisis, numbers started climbing again in the mid-2000s.[12] As can be observed in Table 9.3, the number of land occupations reached an apex in the year 2004, when there were 75 land occupations and 74 evictions and 1,400 arrests. Following repeated promises of land reform alongside continued government inaction, the patience of the two major peasant unions finally ran out. In September 2004, the MCNOC and FNC organized a series of nationwide mass land occupations and protests, demanding immediate land reform (Lambert, 2005). In much the same fashion as the Rodríguez quote above, President Nicanor Duarte Frutos (2003–08) declared in a meeting he had with big landowners, referring to the peasants occupying estates, 'We are going to bring them in by the ear, and those who have small ears we will bring in by the hair' (quoted in González Bozzolasco, 2005). In early December, the FNC resumed land invasions (Lambert, 2005).

### *Class struggle on the extractive frontier*

The second major form of the class struggle at the time had to do with resistance against the dynamics of agro-extractivism. I argue that Paraguay has witnessed and

Paraguay: extractivism and class struggle **195**

experienced all of the contradictory developments and pitfalls of agro-extractivism. These include increased concentration of landholdings; dampened overall employment, which accelerated the forced expulsion of the peasantry, as rural labourers are rendered 'surplus' to the requirements of agribusiness capital; and a growing dependence on agrochemicals that compromise environmental quality and human health.[13] Regarding the latter issue of agrochemicals, the transgenic soyization of land in Paraguay has engendered a new regime of dispossession driven by new agro-industrial practices associated with this model. Specifically, I suggest the process might be termed 'accumulation by fumigation and dispossession' (Ezquerro-Cañete, 2016) – i.e. the forced displacement from land by the intensive use of agro-toxins, when crops are planted next to population centres (i.e. agrochemical drift as a new mechanism/instrument in displacement). Here, the weak or absent or conniving nature of the Paraguayan state is central to an understanding of how the application of highly globalized capital and chemical intensive agro-industrial practices has recast the dynamics of the historical process of primitive accumulation, unleashing powerful forces of resistance. Perhaps the case to garner the most public outrage against the soy sector was the 2003 poisoning death of Silvino Talavera, an 11-year-old boy who was sprayed by a crop duster on his way home from school (Hetherington, 2013).[14] As the son of a CONAMUR member, Talavera's death led to widespread mobilization against the indiscriminate use of agrochemicals (see Palau & Kretschmer, 2004; Fogel, 2005).

These forces of development and change provide the context and set the stage for the issues addressed in the follow section of this chapter – namely, the dynamics of the class struggle during the 'rise and fall' of Fernando Lugo. By examining the prior distribution of power in society and within the state, the constellations of state and societal actors and their alliances, actions and strategies, we can begin to identify the nature of the political problem facing any attempt of major redistributive land reform in this country: the legacy of a predatory state, the changing character of contemporary agro-extractive capitalism (particularly in relation to the sub-imperial interests of Brazilian capital) and growing violence, corruption and contestation over land. It is against this backdrop that we need to situate our analysis of the political economy and dynamics of social change during the almost four years (August 2008–June 2012) of the Lugo government in office.

## The Lugo interregnum (2008–12)[15]

Fernando Lugo, a political outsider and former Catholic bishop, assumed the presidential office in August 2008 the leader of a fragmented and ideologically divided electoral coalition, the Patriotic Alliance for Change (Alianza Patriótica para el Cambio – APC). As Andrew Nickson (2009) pointed out, Lugo's victory entailed three 'firsts'. This was the first time in over 60 years that a non-Partido Colorado candidate in Paraguay would rule the country. Amazingly, it foreshadowed the first peaceful handover of power from one political party to another in Paraguay's history. Curiously enough, it was also the first time anywhere in the world that a man had gone directly from the priesthood to the presidency.[16]

## 196 Paraguay: extractivism and class struggle

At the same time, Lugo's rise to office took place close to decade into a significant, if uneven, social and political shift to the left across large parts of Latin America (Petras & Veltmeyer, 2009; Webber & Carr, 2013). That being said, however, Lugo was constrained by his dependence on the centre-right coalition partners, making the status of his election more ambiguous and 'something of a red herring' (Hetherington, 2011: 227). Indeed, setting aside some initial attempts to portray Lugo's election as yet 'another feather in the cap' for '21st century socialism' (for example, O'Shaughnessy, 2009), a number of more balanced observers were quick to shed light on the significant structural-institutional constraints and limitations that Lugo's administration would face from its onset. Nickson (2008), for instance, discarded celebratory comparison to the 'twenty-first-century socialism' as misguided, pointing out that, while Lugo was 'influenced by liberation theology', he 'has been at great pains to present himself as a 'centre-left' candidate and to downplay the image as a radical with any natural affinity to the broad populist movement sweeping the rest of Latin America'. In much the same vein, Kregg Hetherington (2011: 227) suggested that, 'A more instructive parallel in recent history is not Chávez's victory in Venezuela, but Vicente Fox's victory, in 2000, over Mexico's Partido Revolucionario Institucional (PRI), which held power, under different names, since 1928'. Yates and Bakker (2014: Table I), in their survey of 'post neo-liberalism' in Latin America, go further, locating the Lugo administration within the political ideology of 'inclusive neo-liberalism' and 'nationalism', although they provide no analysis to substantiate their claim. Perhaps the most compelling interpretation, however, can be found in the expanding literature that illustrates that Lugo's administration broadly fitted into the Gramscian regime known as regressive Caesarism (González Bozzolasco, 2009; Bourscheid, 2016; Ezquerro-Cañete & Fogel, forthcoming). This consists of 'the particular solution in which a great personality is entrusted with the task of 'arbitration' over a historico-political situation characterized by equilibrium of forces leading towards catastrophe' (Gramsci, 1971: 219).

Lugo had been ordained in 1994 by Pope John Paul II as the bishop of San Pedro, Paraguay's poorest department and a diocese rife with social conflict (Abente-Brun, 2009: 143). In San Pedro, Lugo began his gradual ascent, working alongside peasants and campaigning alongside them in their struggles for land (Nickson, 2009: 146). He was catapulted onto the political arena in March 2006 when he led a march and rally of 40,000 people in Asunción to protest against the unconstitutional plan of the incumbent president, Nicanor Duarte, to seek re-election (Nickson, 2009: 146). The country's social movements assembled 40,000 people in March 2006, and Duarte's plan was defeated. Such was the disillusionment with politicians that Lugo was immediately catapulted to the national political arena; more than 100,000 people signed a petition requesting him to give up the priesthood and to put his name forwards as presidential candidate.[17] Later that year, Lugo helped to create a new political movement, Tekojojá (meaning 'life and equality' in Guaraní), and on 25 December 2006 Lugo announced that he would stand in the 2008 presidential election as a consensus candidate for the fractured opposition (Nickson, 2009: 146). This led to the creation of the APC, an electoral organization formed from a wide spectrum of social movements, trade unions and a myriad of small left-wing parties, strong in militancy but electorally weak in Paraguay's patronage-based political culture – including the Christian Democrats, socialists of various hues, and radical splinters from the Colorado Party. Crucial to its eventual success (but also to its eventual demise) was a strategic alliance with the old Liberal Party, the PLRA, which agreed to support Lugo's candidacy in exchange for the vice presidency nomination (Nickson, 2009: 147). In the presidential campaign of 2008, Lugo faced off against Colorado Party challenger Blanca Ovelar. Lugo offered vague promises on far-reaching socio-economic reforms to address Paraguay's long-standing issues of poverty, inequality and corruption. Critically, land reform was placed squarely back on the political agenda, an issue of particular importance in a country with the highest inequality of land in all of Latin America and where over 40 per cent of the population live in the countryside.

Once in presidency, Lugo made some modest moves towards progressive social and economic reform. He expanded a series of social policies in favour of families in extreme poverty (Tekoporã), child labour (Abrazo), students (Complemento Nutricional, Kits Escolares), and indigenous groups (Desarrollo Comunitario). He successfully renegotiated a partial improvement of the 1973 Itaipú Treaty with Brazil, which had long been a source of contention in Paraguay.[18] However, Lugo's central electoral promise – agrarian reform – faced deadlock. According to Peter Lambert (2011: 185–6),

> The inability of the government to implement its agrarian reform programme was the consequence not so much of a lack of will or even resources, but rather of the existence of a coordinated, well resourced and powerful opposition. Landowners' groups ... comprise some of the wealthiest and most influential elites in the country, and enjoy a strong lobbying presence, with representation in all major political parties.

Opposition from the Colorado Party and the Unión Nacional de Ciudadanos Éticos (National Union of Ethical Citizens – UNACE), as well as from dissident factions within the APC, sought to block key legislation pertaining to Lugo's reform agenda. On 4 June 2009, Congress voted to further postpone a personal income tax bill, thus cutting a key revenue stream (around $160 million), while on the same day it refused to approve an agreement between the hydroelectric plant Itaipú Binacional and CEPRA to finance new settlements for landless families; in the same session, and against the wishes of finance minister Dinonisio Borda, it also voted to increase state pensions and double the salaries of departmental governors and members of the National Electoral Commission, at a combined cost of $118 million (EIU, 2009). In other words, Congress voted to block vital funding streams, while simultaneously voting to increase spending, generating the possibility of an unsustainable deficit. As a result, INDERT's ability to settle landless peasants continued to be severely restrained by its limited budget and its requirement to compensate owners of expropriated land at market price (Nickson, 2015: 35)

**198** Paraguay: extractivism and class struggle

In the domain of agro-exports, the 'left turn' in Paraguay did not coincide with the regional shift towards neo-developmentalism (or 'progressive neo-extractivism'), as exemplified by a number of the contributions to this special issue. In stark contrast to the neo-developmentalist policies implemented in, for example, Argentina under the Kirchner regimes, wherein part of the rents produced by a 35 per cent tax on soy was redistributed. Lugo's attempts to pass a bill to introduce a 6 per cent tax on unprocessed cereal exports (soybean, maize and rapeseed) were repeatedly opposed by Congress. As a result, Lugo's administration was unable to move Paraguay beyond fundamentalist free-market policies, wherein taxes on commercial agriculture are kept at derisory levels (the amount netted in 2011 was only $13m, equivalent to 0.5 per cent of total tax revenue).

Despite growing demands from civil society organizations, no moves were made by the government of Fernando Lugo to recoup land illegally awarded by IBR and INDERT, which could have provided the basis for redistribution to landless farmers (Nickson, 2015: 575). Worse still is the fact that Lugo was incapable of halting the illegal transfer of land, which continued throughout his presidency. In September 2011, Alberto Antebi Duarte, son of Paraguay's second richest landowner, Roberto Antebi, was awarded 4,000 hectares by this means thanks to high-level corruption in INDERT (Nickson, 2012).

> The slow pace of reform under Lugo led to a rise in land occupations, an increasingly militant discourse among peasant organizations and clashes with armed, often Brazilian, security guards.... As Lugo's land reform project stagnated, social conflict became increasingly likely.
>
> *(Lambert, 2011: 186)*

On 15 June 2012, 11 squatters and six police officers were killed in a shootout during a botched security operation by 324 police to evict 60 members of the peasant organization Movimiento por la Recuperación Campesina de Canindeyú (MRCC), who had occupied land near Curuguaty. The tragedy was the worst incident of political violence for decades, igniting criticism from peasant movements and opposition leaders, albeit for very different reasons. It took place on a 2,000-hectare section of property in Marina Kue (Department of Canindeyú) that had been spuriously obtained during the Stroessner era by a corrupt businessman and former Colorado senator, Blas Riquelme, under the guise of agrarian reform (Fogel, 2012).

On 11 July 2016 the Paraguayan court sentenced 11 peasants (eight men and three women) for the killings of the six police officers during the Curuguaty massacre. Rubén Villaba, who was identified as the squatters' ringleader, was given a 30-year prison sentence. Luis Olmedo was sentenced to 20 years as the main co-author of the crime, and two other men, Arnaldo Quintana and Néstor Castro, were given 18 years each for the same charge. Seven other peasants received sentences of between four and six years for criminal association and invasion of private property (LAWR, 2016a). Concerns over the lack of impartiality and independence in the investigations into the events in Curuguaty are captured in a press release from the United Nations Commissioner for Human Rights, Zeid Ra'ad Al Hussein:

> The conviction of 11 peasants in the Curuguaty case following a trial that allegedly did not respect judicial guarantees is deeply troubling ... [also concerning is] the fact that, up to now, the deaths of 11 peasants, killed in the same incident, have not been investigated by Paraguayan authorities, nor have the allegations that some were summarily executed after being subjected to torture and other human rights violations.[19]

The official version of what happened stated that squatters had fired at police first but this view was strongly contested by human rights and activist organizations (CODEHUPY, 2012; PEICC, 2012). Investigations have been cast in a shadow of doubt owing to 'allegations of serious irregularities in the actions of the Public Prosecution Service, the judiciary and the security forces in relation to the police raid in Curuguaty in June 2012' (2013 Human Rights Committee findings on Paraguay). Accusations have also been made regarding the involvement of hidden marksmen, planted to spark a political crisis in order to oust Lugo from office. In such a climate of suspicion, conspiracy theories abound.[20]

In the immediate aftermath of the Curuguaty massacre, a medley of conservative social forces saw their opportunity and converged around the impeachment and removal of Lugo. Accusations of negligence, ineptitude and incapacity to act decisively, spearheaded by highly placed spokespeople for the soy producers (such as Hector Cristaldo, head of the UGP, as well as spokespeople for Cargill and Monsanto), blamed Lugo for the deaths and called for his immediate impeachment (*Ultima Hora*, 2012). Given that Lugo's position vis-à-vis the legislature was never strong, it is no surprise that the opposition struck when the opportunity arose and that Lugo was not able to withstand the attack.

## Democratic rollback: re-establishing the status quo (2012–15)

In the aftermath of the impeachment and removal of Fernando Lugo in June 2012, there was a fast approval of various other varieties of GM crops – indeed, eight new approvals during the interim presidency of Franco alone (see Table 9.4).

The administration of Cartes (2013–present) has returned Paraguay to the orthodox neo-liberal camp of Latin American politics, alongside Mexico, Chile, Peru, Colombia and the majority of the countries of Central America (López & Vértiz, 2015: 156).[21] Since assuming the presidency in August 2013, the Horacio Cartes government has reinforced the repressive role of the state, such as the criminalization of the campesino movement (Areco & Palau, 2016). Criminalization in this context is characterized not so much by the overt use of force by police or armed militias to repress social protest (Palau, 2007), as it is by judicialization (*judicialización*), subjecting various acts to the penal code using a widening repertoire

**200** Paraguay: extractivism and class struggle

**TABLE 9.4** Transgenic crops approved in Paraguay

| Crop | Name | Corporation | Date | Government |
|---|---|---|---|---|
| Soy | RR | Monsanto | 20 October 2004 | Nicanor Duarte |
| Cotton | Bt | Monsanto | 7 July 2012 | Federico Franco |
| Cotton | BtRR | Monsanto | 20 August 2012 | Federico Franco |
| Cotton | Mon 1445 | Monsanto | 20 August 2012 | Federico Franco |
| Corn | Vt Triple Pro | Monsanto | 24 October 2012 | Federico Franco |
| Corn | Bt 11 | Syngenta | 24 October 2012 | Federico Franco |
| Corn | Mon 810 | Monsanto | 24 October 2012 | Federico Franco |
| Corn | TC 1507 | Dow | 24 October 2012 | Federico Franco |
| Soy | BtRR2Y Intacta | Monsanto | 11 February 2013 | Federico Franco |
| Corn | NK603 | Monsanto | 8 January 2014 | Horacio Cartes |
| Corn | MIR 162 | Syngenta | 20 February 2014 | Horacio Cartes |
| Soy | CV 127 | BASF | 20 February 2014 | Horacio Cartes |
| Corn | Powercore | Dow | 4 March 2014 | Horacio Cartes |

*Source:* BASE-IS (2015).

of accusations (Areco & Palau, 2016). According to Areco and Palau (2016), there were four charges between 2004 and 2012; this process escalated to 39 in the first two years of Cartes' administration (2013–15).

The post-coup political and economic environment has ensured that the political ground is fertile for ongoing peasant agitation for land reform as well as the increasing presence of insurgent armed groups. This form of class struggle is on the rise in Paraguay. The self-proclaimed Paraguayan People's Army (Ejército del Pueblo Paraguayo – EPP), an insurgency movement operating in northern Paraguay since the mid-2000s, has been at the centre of various dark episodes in recent history, including the kidnapping and murder of Cecilia Cubas, daughter of former president Raul Cubas (1998–99). The most recent incident at the time of writing occurred on 27 August 2016, involving a deadly attack on a military–police task force (FTC) patrol. The patrol vehicle was hit by a roadside bomb as it travelled on a back road in the Arroyito area of the municipality of Horqueta (Concepción department), in the so-called EPP 'area of influence'. Eight soldiers were killed in the attack, with those surviving the blast being shot dead by hidden gunmen, making it the deadliest attack perpetrated by the group against the security forces to date (LAWR, 2016b). The attack is a clear reflection of the growing explosiveness in the countryside and may be followed by further explosions with a similar character in the months and years to come.

## Conclusion

This chapter has sought to shed light on the ongoing struggle for land and democracy in Paraguay. After some 25 years of democratic transition, Paraguay has stalled at a stage broadly known as 'defective democracy', characterized by clientelism, authoritarian enclaves and inequity (Merkel, 2004; Lambert, 2011). The ousting of Fernando Lugo from office reveals the inordinate level of influence exerted by the landowning elite on Paraguayan politics, as well as the very feeble nature of the country's democracy. The vehemence of the opposition to a centre-left president, whose policies were more social democratic than revolutionary and who actually achieved very little, serves as a potent reminder that 'it is hardly necessary for the Latin American governments to adopt social-revolutionary measures before the traditional elite … feel threatened and act violently in protection of their interests' (Gordon & Webber, 2013: 36).

All in all, the Paraguayan experience is a powerful reminder of how fragile the prospects for redistributive land reform continue to be in the post-authoritarian and post-neo-liberal period of Latin American politics. Without addressing the legacy of the predatory state in Paraguay, and understanding how the power structure left by this legacy is intertwined with new accumulation regimes (extractive capitalism) in the wider political economy, the current agro-extractive export model will continue to reproduce the conditions of a class struggle rooted in relations of class exploitation and rural injustice. In these conditions, not even the redistributive policies of a progressive neo-developmentalist and post-neo-liberal regime can work to keep the peace. With a mobilized working class and peasantry the ruling class will likely have to resort to violence and repression – class struggle from above.

## Notes

1 The accuracy of such figures is often open to debate (e.g. see Hetherington 2011: Ch. 2).
2 'Agriculture as a share of GDP for the period 1968 to 1988 averaged 14.2 per cent, while it stood at 18.4 per cent for the period 2003–2010' (Borda, 2012, cited in Birch, 2014: 288n2).
3 For similar analyses, see Nickson (2010), Palau (2010), Setrini (2010), Levy (2013) and Fogel (2015).
4 The historical context of Paraguay's scandalously unequal distribution of land has a long and tortuous antecedence that can be traced back almost a century and a half. Unlike much of Latin America (e.g. see Kay, 1974), the development of Paraguay's *hacienda* system (i.e. a dualistic agrarian structure composed of *latifundias*, or large hacienda-type estates or landholdings, and *minifundias*, which are small subsistence-oriented farms) is not primarily rooted in sixteenth-century European colonization (Kleinpenning 1984: 164). Instead, the concentration of landholdings and marginalization of the peasantry are largely grounded in the aftermath of the defeat of Paraguay in the War of the Triple Alliance (1864–70), whereby large tracts of the country's unique state-dominated land system were sold to foreign investors and Paraguayan elite as a means to pay off war debt (Pastore, 1972; Riquelme, 2003). This established a highly unequal system of land tenure that remains virtually unchanged to the present day.
5 Its membership includes the Coordinadora Agrícola del Paraguay and the Federación de Cooperativas de Producción.
6 In 1976, for example, the Stroessner government violently repressed and disarticulated an attempted student–peasant opposition alliance based on a Church-backed peasant movement called the Ligas Agrarias (peasant leagues).
7 Paraguay has a largely homogenous *mestizo* population. The 2012 census numbered the indigenous population at 117,150 (DGEEC, 2013), equivalent to roughly 2 per cent of the national population.

**202** Paraguay: extractivism and class struggle

8 The use of the term *brasiguayos* has been subject to particular critique for its implied dichotomy between wealthy Brazilian agriculturalists devoted to soybean production on the one hand, and impoverished and marginalized Paraguayan small-scale farmers on the other (Blanc, 2015). In reality, 'the majority of Brazilian immigrants in Paraguay are small-scale farmers who, like many of their impoverished Paraguayan neighbours, have faced constant marginalization' (Blanc, 2015: 145).

9 For a fuller discussion on the intimate relationship between (extractive) imperialism and capitalism, see Veltmeyer and Petras (2015).

10 Ironically, by preventing privatization, *campesino* organizations also lent their support to the rent-seeking elements of the state whose interests lie in the permanent derailing of public-sector reform in Paraguay (Setrini, 2010).

11 With an opposition-led congress initiating impeachment proceedings against the President, the general elections a year away, and General Oviedo mounting support for another potential coup attempt from abroad, Colorado legislators negotiated the repeal of the privatization programme with union and peasant leaders in exchange for the dismantling of the protest movement.

*(Setrini, 2010)*

12 Following a series of peasant protests, the González Macchi government (1999–2003) allocated agricultural project monies to the FNC and MCNOC. The funds, however, were granted without any administrative controls, prompting immediate charges that the government was trying to 'buy off' the peasant leadership (Lambert, 2005).

13 The exclusionary and socially problematic nature of what we might call the 'transgenic soyization' of Paraguay's agriculture is analysed in far greater detail in Fogel and Riquelme (2005), Palau et al. (2007), Rulli (2007), Guereña (2013), Hetherington (2013), Riquelme and Vera (2013), Elgert (2016) and Ezquerro-Cañete (2016).

14 While cases like this one were widely rumoured to have occurred throughout the countryside, this was the first one in which a team of activists and lawyers managed to get medical proof, in the form of tests on the boy's blood – performed in Buenos Aires – that pesticides killed him (Hetherington, 2014).

15 Much of the following section derives from Ezquerro-Cañete and Fogel (forthcoming).

16 'In a major climb down, on 30 July 2008, the Vatican granted Lugo the first ever papal wavier for a Catholic bishop to return to lay status' (Nickson, 2009: 148n10).

17 Under the Paraguayan constitution, a priest cannot be elected president.

18 Although each country owns an equal (50 per cent) share of the energy produced, the treaty obliges Paraguay to sell any unused electricity at an established cost price to Brazil, rather than at market value or to third parties. In practice, Paraguay uses barely 7 per cent of the energy output and so sells the remainder of its half share to Brazil. Although Paraguay receives a 'compensation' fee of $120 million per year, it has long argued that this is a 'scandalously unfair' treaty, by which Paraguay provides a subsidy on approximately 20 per cent of Brazilian domestic energy use – put at $3 billion per year. After repeated refusals by Brazil to renegotiate conditions until 2023, constant pressure from Lugo, including veiled threats to take the matter to the International Court of Justice, led to an unprecedented agreement in July 2009. Brazil promised to triple 'compensation' royalties to Paraguay to $360 million per year, to complete the substation and transmission line to Asunción, to agree to auditing and transparency, to allow Paraguay to gradually begin to sell electricity to Brazil (but not other countries) at market price, and to share management. This was seen in Paraguay as a major victory, since the extra annual revenue could potentially double public investment from central government and finance major poverty reduction and social expenditure programmes. However, it took until May 2011 for both houses of the Brazilian legislature to approve the agreement.

*(Lambert, 2011)*

19 See www.ohchr.org/EN/NewsEvents/Pages/DisplayNews.aspx?NewsID=20289&Lang ID=E.
20 An independent examination of audio footage by Spanish ballistics experts stated that the police were killed by automatic fire, incompatible with the rudimentary old hunting rifles captured from the squatters. The presence of women and children suggested that they were not expecting violence. Many believed that the shootout was orchestrated by hidden marksmen, a view detailed by the Plataforma de Estudio e Investigación de Conflictos Campesinos (PEICC, 2012), which argued that the police, who were wearing bulletproof vests, were all killed by shots to the head and neck.
21 Similar analysis from Petras and Veltmeyer (2015: 140) places Paraguay within the 'colonial-extractive regimes'.

## References

*ABC Color*. (2008, 16 May). 'Declaran 'guerra' a sojeros y queman bandera brasileña'.

Abente-Brun, D. (2009). 'Paraguay: The unravelling of one-party rule'. *Journal of Democracy*, 20(1), pp. 143–56.

Areco, A. & Palau, M. (2016). *Judicialización y violencia contra la lucha campesina (2013–2015).* BASE Investigaciones Sociales.

Baer, W. & Birch, M. (1984). 'Expansion of the economic frontier: Paraguayan growth in the 1970s'. *World Development*, 12(8), pp. 783–98.

Birch, M. (2014). 'Paraguay and Mercosur: The lesser of two evils?' *Latin American Business Review*, 15(3–4), pp. 269–90.

Blanc, J. (2015). 'Enclaves of inequality: Brasiguaios and the transformation of the Brazil-Paraguay borderlands'. *The Journal of Peasant Studies*, 42(1), pp. 145–58.

Borras, S. M., Kay, C., Gómez, S. & Wilkinson, J. (2012). 'Land grabbing and global capitalist accumulation: Key features in Latin America'. *Canadian Journal of Development Studies*, 33(4), pp. 402–16.

Bourscheid, J. I. (2016). 'Entre la hegemonía y el Cesarismo: Un análisis Gramsciano del gobierno de Fernando Lugo (2008–2012)'. *Pensamiento Plural*, 17, pp. 51–76.

Cannon, B. (2016). *The Right in Latin America: Elite power, hegemony and the struggle for the state.* New York, NY: Routledge.

CDE. (2007). *Informativo campesino*, 231, December. Asunción: Centro de Documentación y Estudios.

CODEHUPY. (2007). *Informe chokokue.* Asunción: Coordinadora Derechos Humanos Paraguay.

CODEHUPY. (2012). *Informe de derechos humanos sobre el caso Marina Kue.* Asunción: Coordinadora Derechos Humanos Paraguay.

CVJ. (2008). *Informe final: Tierras mal habidas, tomo IV.* Asunción: Comisión de Verdad y Justicia.

DGEEC. (2004). *Principales resultados del censo 2002: Vivienda y población.* Fernando de la Mora: Dirección General de Estadística, Encuestas y Censos.

DGEEC. (2013). Fernando de la Mora: Dirección General de Estadística, Encuestas y Censos.

ECLAC. (various years). *Economic survey of Latin America and the Caribbean.* Santiago: United Nations, Economic Commission for Latin America and the Caribbean.

ECLAC. (2005). *Statistical yearbook for Latin America and the Caribbean 2004.* Santiago: United Nations, Economic Commission for Latin America and the Caribbean.

EIU – Economist Intelligence Unit. (2009). *Paraguay politics: President's weakness shows*, 22 July.

Elgert, L. (2016). '"More soy on fewer farms" in Paraguay: Challenging neoliberal agriculture's claims to sustainability'. *Journal of Peasant Studies*, 43(2), pp. 537–61.

Ezquerro-Cañete, A. (2016). 'Poisoned, dispossessed and excluded: A critique of the neoliberal soy regime in Paraguay'. *Journal of Agrarian Change*, 16(4), pp. 702–10.

Ezquerro-Cañete, A. & Fogel, R. (forthcoming, 2017). 'A coup foretold: Fernando Lugo and the lost promise of agrarian reform in Paraguay'. *Journal of Agrarian Change*, 17(2).

Fogel, R. (2005). 'Efectos ambientales del Enclave Sojero', in R. Fogel & M. Riquelme (eds) *Enclave Sojero: Merma de soberanía y pobreza*. Asunción: Centro de Estudios Rurales Interdisciplinarios, pp. 35–112.

Fogel, R. (2009). 'El gobierno de Lugo, el Parlamento y los movimientos sociales'. *OSAL*, 25. Buenos Aires: Consejo Latinoamericano de Ciencias Sociales.

Fogel, R. (2012). 'El Movimiento de los Carperos'. *Novapolis*, 5, pp. 11–30.

Fogel, R. (2013). *Las Tierras de Ñacunday, Marina Kue y otras calamidades*. Asunción: Centro de Estudios Rurales Interdisciplinarios/Servi Libro.

Fogel, R. (2015). 'Clases sociales y poder político en Paraguay'. *Novapolis*, 8, pp. 103–16.

Fogel, R. & Riquelme, M. (eds) (2005). *Enclave Sojero: Merma de soberanía y pobreza*. Asunción: Centro de Estudios Rurales Interdisciplinarios.

Galeano, E. (1973). *The open veins of Latin America*. New York, NY: Monthly Review.

Galeano, L. A. (2012). 'Paraguay and the expansion of Brazilian and Argentinian agribusinesses frontiers'. *Canadian Journal of Development Studies*, 33(4), pp. 458–70.

González Bozzolasco, I. (2005). 'Peasant in Paraguay fight for land, end of repression'. *The Militant*, 69(5).

González Bozzolasco, I. (2009). '{IQM}Bonapartismo a la Paraguaya?' *Novapolis*, 4, pp. 37–50.

Gordon T. & Webber, J. (2013). 'Post-coup Honduras: Latin America's corridor of reaction'. *Historical Materialism*, 21(3), pp. 16–56.

Gramsci, A. (1971). *Selections from the prison notebooks*. New York, NY: International.

Guereña, A. (2013). *The soy mirage: The limits of corporate social responsibility: The case of the company Desarrollo Agrícola del Paraguay*. Oxford: Oxfam.

Hetherington, K. (2009). 'The strategic incoherence of development: Marketing expertise in the World Development Report'. *Journal of Peasant Studies*, 36(3), pp. 653–61.

Hetherington, K. (2011). *Guerrilla auditors: The politics of transparency in neoliberal Paraguay*. Durham, NC, and London: Duke University Press.

Hetherington, K. (2013). 'Beans before the law: Knowledge practices, responsibility, and the Paraguayan soy boom'. *Cultural Anthropology*, 28(1), pp. 65–85.

Hetherington, K. (2014). 'Regular soybeans: Translating and framing in the ontological politics of a coup'. *Indiana Journal of Global Legal Studies*, 21(1), pp. 55–78.

Katz, C. (2007). 'Socialist strategies in Latin America'. *Monthly Review*, 59(4).

Kay, C. (1974). 'Comparative development of the European manorial system and the Latin American hacienda system'. *The Journal of Peasant Studies*, 2(1), pp. 69–98.

Kleinpenning, J. M. G. (1984). 'Rural development policy in Paraguay since 1960'. *Tijdschrift voor Eonomische en Sociale Geografie*, 75(3), pp. 164–76.

Kleinpenning, J. M. G. & Zoomers, E. B. (1991). 'Elites, the rural masses, and land in Paraguay: The subordination of the rural masses to the ruling class'. *Development and Change*, 22(2), pp. 279–95.

Lambert, P. (2000). 'A decade of electoral democracy continuity, change and crisis in Paraguay'. *Bulletin of Latin American Research*, 19(3), pp. 379–96.

Lambert, P. (2005). 'Paraguay's enigmatic president'. *NACLA Report on the Americas*, 38, pp. 10–12.

Lambert, P. (2011). 'Undermining the new dawn: Opposition to Lugo in Paraguay', in F. Dominguez, G. Lievesley & S. Ludlam (eds) *Right-wing politics in the new Latin America: Reaction and revolt*. London and New York, NY: Zed, pp. 177–93.

LAWR – Latin American Weekly Review. (2016a). 'Court rules on "Curuguaty massacre"'. *Latin American Weekly Review*, 14 July.

LAWR – Latin American Weekly Review. (2016b). 'Deadly EPP attack puts Cartes on the back foot'. *Latin American Weekly Review*, 1 September.

Levy, C. (2013). 'Working towards *tekojojá*: The political struggles of the Paraguayan Left'. *Studies in Political Economy*, 92, pp. 29–56.

López, E. & Vértiz, F. (2015). 'Extractivism, transnational capital, and subaltern struggles in Latin America'. *Latin American Perspectives*, 42(5), pp. 152–68.

MAG. (2009). *Censo Agropecuario Nacional de 2008*. San Lorenzo: Ministerio de Agricultura y Ganadería.

Marini, R. (1972). 'Brazilian subimperialism'. *Monthly Review*, 23(9), pp. 14–24.

Merkel, W. (2004). 'Embedded and defective democracies'. *Democratization*, 11(5), December, pp. 33–58.

Nagel, B. Y. (1999). '"Unleashing the fury": The cultural discourse of rural violence and land rights in Paraguay'. *Comparative Studies in Society and History*, 41(1), pp. 148–81.

Nickson, A. (1981). 'Brazilian colonization of the eastern border region of Paraguay'. *Journal of Latin American Studies*, 13(10), pp. 111–31.

Nickson, A. (2008). 'An opportunity for Paraguay: The challenges for Fernando Lugo'. *Nueva Sociedad*, 216.

Nickson, A. (2009). 'The general election in Paraguay, April 2008'. *Electoral Studies*, 28(1), pp. 145–9.

Nickson, A. (2010). 'Political economy of policymaking in Paraguay', in R. A. Berry (ed.) *Losing ground in the employment challenge: The case of Paraguay*. New Brunswick, NJ, and London: Transaction, pp. 265–94.

Nickson, A. (2012). 'Paraguay's presidential coup: The inside story'. *Open Democracy*, 10 July.

Nickson, A. (2015). *Historical dictionary of Paraguay*, 3rd edn. Lanham, MD, and Boulder, CO: Rowman & Littlefield.

Nickson, A. & Lambert, P. (2002). 'State reform and the "privatized state in Paraguay"'. *Public Administration and Development*, 22, pp. 163–74.

O'Shaughnessy, H. (2009). *The Priest of Paraguay: Fernando Lugo and the making of a nation*. London: Zed.

Oliveira, G. L. T. (2016). 'The geopolitics of Brazilian soybeans'. *The Journal of Peasant Studies*, 43(2). pp. 348–72.

Otero, G. (2012). 'The neoliberal food regime in Latin America: State, agribusiness transnational corporations and biotechnology'. *Canadian Journal of Development Studies*, 33(3), pp. 282–94.

Otero, G. & Lapegna, P. (2016). 'Transgenic crops in Latin America: Expropriation, negative value and the state'. *Journal of Agrarian Change*, 16(4), pp. 665–74.

Palau, M. (2002). 'Luchas sociales obligan a retroceder al gobierno y detienen el proceso de privatización'. *OSAL*, 8, pp. 20–5. Buenos Aries: Consejo Latinoamericana de Ciencias Sociales.

Palau, M. (2007). *Criminalización a la lucha campesina*. Asunción: BASE Investigaciones Sociales.

Palau, M. (2010). 'La política y su Trasfondo: El poder real en Paraguay'. *Nueva Sociedad*, 229, pp. 134–50.

Palau, M. & Kretschmer, R. (2004). 'La "guerra del a soja" y el avance del neoliberalismo en el campo Paraguayo'. *OSAL*, 13, pp. 105–15. Buenos Aries: Consejo Latinoamericana de Ciencias Sociales.

Palau, T., Cabello, D., Maeyens, A., Rulli, J. & Segovia, D. (2007). *Los refugiados del modelo agroexportador: Impactos del monocultivo de soja en las comunidades campesinas Paraguayas*. Asunción: BASE Investigaciones Sociales.

Pastore, C. (1972). *La lucha por la tierra en el Paraguay*. Montevideo: Editorial Antequera.

PEICC. (2012). *Informe masacre de curuguaty*. Asunción: Plataforma de Estudio e Investigación de Conflictos Campesinos.

Petras, J. (1997). 'Latin America: The resurgence of the Left'. *New Left Review*, 233, pp. 17–47.

Petras, J. &Veltmeyer, H. (2009). *What's left in Latin America*. Farnham: Ashgate.

Petras, J. & Veltmeyer, H. (2014). 'Agro-extractivism: The agrarian question of the 21st century', in J. Petras & H. Veltmeyer (eds), *Extractive imperialism in the Americas: Capitalism's new frontier*. Leiden: Brill, pp. 62–100.

Petras, J. & Veltmeyer, H. (2015). *Power and resistance: US imperialism in Latin America*. Leiden: Brill.

Piñeiro, D. E. (2004). *En busca de la identidad. La acción colectiva en los conflictos agrarios de América Latina*. Buenos Aires: Consejo Latinoamericano de Ciencias Sociales.

Riquelme, Q. (2003). *Los sin tierra en Paraguay: Conflictos agrarios y movimientos campesino*. Buenos Aires: Consejo Latinoamericano de Ciencias Sociales.

Riquelme, Q. & Vera, E. (2013). *La otra cara de la soja: El impacto del agronegocio en la agricultura familiar y la producción de alimentos*. Asunción: Proyecto Acción Ciudadana contra el Hambre y por el Derecho a la Alimentación.

Rojas, L. (2014). *La tierra en disputa: Extractivismo, exclusión y resistencia*. Asunción, Paraguay: BASE Investigaciones Sociales.

Rulli, J. (2007). 'The refugees of the agroexport model', in J. Rulli (ed.) *United soya republics: The truth about soya production in South America*. Buenos Aires: Grupo de Reflexión Rural, pp. 194–216.

Setrini, G. (2010). 'Twenty years of Paraguayan electoral democracy: From monopolistic to pluralistic clientelism'. *Working Paper No. 3*. Asunción: Centro de Análisis y Difusión de la Economía Paraguaya.

Turzi, M. (2012). 'Grown in the cone: South America's soybean boom'. *Current History*, 111(742), pp. 50–5.

Ultima Hora. (2008). 'Decreto Lude da Silva: Brasil amenaza a Paraguay y vecinos'. *Ultima Hora*, 14 October.

Ultima Hora. (2012). 'Los agroempresarios apoyan proceso de destitución del presidente Lugo'. *Ultima Hora*, 22 June.

Veltmeyer, H. & Petras, J. (2014). 'A new model or extractivist imperialism?' in H. Veltmeyer & J. Petras (eds) *The new extractivism: A post-neoliberal development model or imperialism of the twenty-first century?* London: Zed, pp. 21–46.

Veltmeyer, H. & Petras, J. (2015). 'Imperialism and capitalism: Rethinking an intimate relationship'. *International Critical Thought*, 5(2), pp. 164–82.

Vuyk, C. (2014). *Subimperialismo brasileño y dependencia del Paraguay: Los intereses económicos detrás del golpe de estado de 2012*. Asunción: Cultura y Participación.

Webber, J. (2015). 'Crisis and class, advance and retreat: The political economy of the new Latin American Left', in L. Pradella & T. Marois (eds) *Polarising development: Alternatives to neoliberalism and the crisis*. London: Pluto, pp. 157–68.

Webber, J. R. & Carr, B. (2013). 'Introduction: The Latin American Left in theory and practice', in J. R. Webber & B. Carr (eds) *The new Latin American Left: Cracks in the empire*. Plymouth: Rowan & Littlefield, pp. 1–27.

Weisskoff, R. (1992). 'The Paraguayan agro-export model of development'. *World Development*, 20(10), pp. 1531–40.

World Bank. (2007). *2008 World Development Report: Agriculture for development*. Washington, DC: World Bank.

Yates, J. S. & Bakker, K. (2014). 'Debating the "post-neoliberal turn" in Latin America'. *Progress in Human Geography*, 38(1), pp. 62–90.

Zibechi, R. (2014). *The new Brazil: Regional imperialism and the new democracy*. Edinburgh: AK Press.

# 10

## PERU

## Return of the class struggle from below

*Jan Lust*

Since the beginning of the third millennium, the class struggle in Peru has shown an upward trend. Even so, the class struggle over the last 15 years cannot be compared with the heights of the class struggle from below in the 1980s and the ferocity of the class struggle from above in the 1990s.

In the decade of the 1980s, the strength of the working-class organizations and their political representatives made it possible to successfully defend the interests of the working population. The heights of the class struggle were expressed in the electoral power of the Left, the development of the guerrilla struggle and the ability of the trade unions and the popular movement to organize massive strikes and demonstrations against the state and capital.[1] In the 1990s, when a radical form of neo-liberalism was introduced by President Fujimori, the state and capital initiated a savage class struggle from above. The attack on labour stability and the organizations of the working class, coupled with the repression of whatever movement that questioned the development model in place, helped to change the correlation of class forces in favour of capital.[2]

The class struggle in the third millennium is partly characterized by the struggle of the Peruvian working-class organizations to recuperate lost terrain and partly by the return of the class struggle to the countryside. Currently, the vanguard of the class struggle is formed by peasant and indigenous-based social movements that fight against the invasion of extractive capital in their territories.

The 'return' of the class struggle from below may not be overestimated. In the 1980s, the presence of strong legally functioning socialist-oriented political organizations and the widespread activities of the guerrillas made it possible for the class struggle to easily pass from economistic to political demands. The current political and organizational weakness of the socialist Left owing in part to political repression in the 1990s and the ideological hegemony of the bourgeoisie makes the organization of an anti-capitalist battle extremely difficult. In fact, over the last 25 years the

## 208 Peru: the class struggle from below

predominance of neo-liberalism as an ideology has eradicated the notion that society is made up of socially antagonistic classes, and that development is not possible without the free and unregulated functioning of the markets. When actors of social change start to fundamentally question this model, the state uses the spectre of terrorism and the trauma of inflation (and the crisis of the 1980s) to publicly delegitimize these oppositional forces. If this does not work, the police and the military are instructed to repress protests, a state of emergency is declared, new laws to criminalize protests are implemented and paramilitary organizations are used to eliminate whatever opposition against the development model in place.

This chapter analyses the dynamics of the class struggle in Peru in the period 2000–2015. The objective of this analysis is to determine the vanguard and the rearguard of the class struggle and the possibilities for the class struggle to pass from an economistic level to a political level, i.e. from a battle for reforms to a struggle for power. It analyses the class struggle in urban as well as in rural areas, especially the class struggle of the communities against mining capital.

The chapter is organized into six parts. Part 1 defines the political character of the Peruvian governments since the beginning of the third millennium and describes the economic developments in the period 1980–2015. Part 2 is dedicated to the social and economic situation of the working population. This part demonstrates that the continuation of the development model based on the extraction of natural resources has not improved the social situation of the working population. In Part 3 we analyse the class struggle in the urban areas, mainly the strikes in the years between 2000 and 2015. In Part 4 we turn to the class struggle in the countryside. As an example of this class struggle, we concentrate on the vanguard of the resistance against mining capital, i.e. the indigenous and peasant-based social movements in the department of Cajamarca. It demonstrates how an economistic struggle has turned into a political struggle for changing the extractivist development model. In Part 5 we analyse the weaknesses of the locally and/or regionally organized struggle against mining capital before presenting our conclusions.

## The character of Peruvian governments and their economic context

In November 2000 President Fujimori fled the country, a few months after having won the presidential elections. In general terms, the regimes that came after Fujimori continued the development model implemented by Fujimori in the 1990s. This development model is based on the export of the country's abundant mineral resources and is accompanied by free and (relatively) unregulated markets. Private national and foreign investments are considered to be the motors for economic development. Business activities of the state are reduced to those areas in which the market has not yet entered (Parodi Trece, 2010: 298; Ruiz Caro, 2002: 22, 24).

The government of Toledo (2001–06) declared its intention to combine market-oriented policies with projects that pointed to social inclusion. Unfortunately, projects of social inclusion were never implemented. In order to comply with the rules of the International Monetary Fund (IMF), the reduction of public-sector deficits was considered more important.

In 2006 Alan García became president of Peru for the second time. García's second term cannot be compared with his first government. While in the years 1985–90 the first APRA regime in Peruvian history intended to follow an independent capitalist development path, in the period 2006–11 the APRA government continued the policies of the former Toledo regime and fully 'accepted' the political and economic 'consequences' of what might be called globalization.

The APRA government benefitted from the commodities boom that started to unfold in the first decade of the new millennium. As mining is the principal export sector of Peru, it has a dominant influence on the GDP growth rate and has a positive effect on the country's terms of trade. According to data presented by the government, the contribution of the mining sector to FDI inflows increased from 2000 to 2015 – from 13.9 to 23.3 per cent (Proinversión, 2016). Other data provided by Proinversión point towards negative and diminishing growth rates of the export value of non-traditional products over the same period.

The increase in the export value of Peru's traditional products and the cycle of economic growth since 2002 (until 2011, according to official data) is the consequence of the primary commodities boom on the world market as well as a credit boom in Europe and the US (Parodi Trece, 2014: 221, 255–6). In 2011 the presidential elections were won by Ollanta Humala, who was supported by a variety of progressive and left-wing organizations and intellectuals. He was also able to count on a large popular base in the countryside. His election gave rise to many expectations, although in order to win what might be called the centre of the Peruvian electorate his election programme of the first round, The Great Transformation (*La Gran Transformación*) was put aside in favour of the Route Sheet (*Hoja de la Ruta*).

In December 2011 the first Humala government almost fell over the issue of how to manage the protests in the department of Cajamarca against the Conga Project. The substitution of progressive individuals by neoliberals was, in fact, a 'natural' consequence of the logic of the *Hoja de la Ruta*. The *Hoja de la Ruta* implied that the interests of (transnational) capital, especially mining capital, were not going to be attacked. It was argued that mining was fundamental for economic growth.

Since 2011–12, commodity prices have declined and the export volumes of the country's minerals have diminished. This is expressed in the worsening of the country's terms of trade, the negative growth rates of the export value of the mining products and economic slowdown. Slow economic growth in the advanced capitalist countries and India was the main cause for Peruvian exports to diminish (Parodi Trece, 2014: 337–8). As a consequence, in 2013 Peru had its first trade deficit since 2001. A year later the situation became worse: the country faced the highest trade deficit since 1998. In the same year, Peru had its first fiscal deficit since 2010.

The trap of the current development model is that it urges the government to deepen the model in the context of diminishing export values for the country's

**210** Peru: the class struggle from below

minerals. In March 2014, the government began to discuss the possibility of eliminating the request to submit an environmental impact report for oil companies in the case of exploration through seismic testing. In June the government announced measures that were expected to increase investment in the mining sector. For example, new tax stability pacts to protect mining companies for changes in the tax regime were approved. These pacts were signed for periods of 10 to 15 years. Measures that were intended to accelerate the process of approval of mining concessions were introduced and the Ministry of Environment was stripped of its jurisdiction over air, soil and water quality standards, as well as its ability to set limits for harmful substances. Also its power to establish nature reserves exempt from mining and oil drilling was eliminated. In January 2015, and precisely in the style of the policies introduced by Alan García just before the massacre in Bagua in 2010,[3] the government enacted a Supreme Decree Law with the intention of dividing the communities and exposing the administration of the communities to manipulation and bribes. In April, measures were proclaimed to make it easier for companies in the extractive sector to obtain an environmental certificate and to acquire land that was not in use by the state (but could be the property of the communities, although these communities do not have the 'adequate' property titles). In May, the army was mobilized and a state of emergency was declared in the province of Islay (department of Arequipa) to put down protests against the opencast project of the Mexican Southern Copper Corporation. In September, the army was authorized to 'help' the police forces to 'tame' the protests against the Bambas mine project in the department of Apurimac.

## The social and economic situation of the working population

The development model implemented by the Fujimori regime did not favour the working population. As the governments of Toledo, García and Humala did not modify the 'basics' of the economic policies implemented by Fujimori, the economic situation of the working population did not structurally improve since the 'fall' of Fujimori. Although unemployment diminished in the period 2000–2015 when compared to the 1990s, the underemployment rates did not decrease. In the period 1995–2000 the rates of underemployment fluctuated around 43 per cent.[4]

During the Toledo government there had been much talk about *chorreo* ('trickle-down'). Toledo had promised that economic progress would 'trickle down' to the population, i.e. their disposable income would increase. As *chorreo* did not occur and the economy started to grow, protests were nothing but a 'natural' consequence. The economic boom that started to unfold in 2005, mainly caused by the international demand for the country's mineral resources and their subsequent price increases, was also not translated in considerable wage and income increases for the working population.

In contrast to the Toledo regime, the García government never declared its intention to improve the social and economic situation of the working population. It seems that García wanted to erase the disastrous image of his first government

(1985–90).[5] In fact García's second term cannot be compared with his first government. While in the years 1985–90 the first APRA regime in Peruvian history intended to follow an independent capitalist development path, in the period 2006–11 the APRA government continued the policies of the former Toledo regime. The main objective of the García regime was to expand and deepen the development model based on the extraction of natural resources. Processes were speeded up to parcel out indigenous and peasant land and to provide individual ownership titles of this land. During García's second government, wages were allowed to fall below the nominal minimum wage level.

The Humala government did not comply with the social and economic expectations of the population, although social expenditures increased. Increased taxation of mining capital did not go hand in hand with increased income for the working population. In Tables 10.1 and 10.2 we present data on the evolution of labour remuneration and the exploitation surplus in the years 2001–14. The exploitation surplus includes not only the profits of the corporations but also other company income such as leasing and renting, and the wages of what are called the independent

**TABLE 10.1** Remuneration and exploitation surplus: 2000–06 (as a % of GDP)

| Year | Remuneration | Exploitation surplus |
| --- | --- | --- |
| 2000 | 24.4 | 59.1 |
| 2001 | 25.1 | 58.3 |
| 2002 | 25.0 | 58.7 |
| 2003 | 25.0 | 58.7 |
| 2004 | 23.9 | 59.6 |
| 2005 | 23.1 | 60.4 |
| 2006 | 21.9 | 61.9 |

*Source:* INEI. http://series.inei.gob.pe:8080/sirtod-series.

**TABLE 10.2** Remuneration and exploitation surplus: 2007–14 (as a % of GDP)

| Year | Remuneration | Exploitation surplus |
| --- | --- | --- |
| 2007 | 30.7 | 40.1 |
| 2008 | 30.8 | 39.5 |
| 2009 | 31.4 | 37.5 |
| 2010 | 30.2 | 39.6 |
| 2011 | 30.0 | 41.1 |
| 2012 | 29.8 | 40.6 |
| 2013 | 29.9 | 41.0 |
| 2014 | 29.9 | 41.0 |

*Source:* http://series.inei.gob.pe:8080/sirtod-series/.

workers (INEI, n.d.: 6; Alarco, 2011: 135). Although the exploitation surplus is not the same as profit, it can be considered an indicator of the expropriation of value by non-labour.[6] We have elected to present the data for the periods 2000–06 and 2007–14 separately. Notwithstanding differences in remuneration and profits, both tables show the same trend, i.e. no structural change in the capital and labour relation.

The Peruvian working population is in large part concentrated in small businesses. As a matter of fact, the Peruvian economy can be divided into an economy at the service of the major private corporations – especially the transnational corporations in the extractive sector – and an economy of small businesses and micro-enterprises characterized by low levels of productivity and expressed in remuneration rates and wages at or near the minimum wage level. We term this a capitalist subsistence economy.

During the governments of Toledo, García and Humala no policies were implemented that might have helped to change the country's economic structure according to company size in terms of employment. Data of household surveys show that in 2000 79.7 per cent of the economically active population (EAP) worked in companies that employed from two to nine workers; in 2014 this percentage was slightly reduced to 77.2 per cent. When the minimum wage is compared with the average nominal remuneration of individuals who worked in companies that employed between one and 10 individuals, it becomes clear that the absolute majority of the working population has not at all been favoured by increasing GDP growth rates caused by the commodities boom in the period 2005–11. The absolute majority, employed in very small companies with no union representation, earned a wage or salary just above the minimum wage level. This situation, coupled with policies that favour capital, was in the last 15 years the main trigger for social protests in the urban areas.

## The trade unions and the popular movement

The replacement of Fujimori by Toledo had an important effect on the political space for oppositional forces. It seems that Fujimori's 'fall' released latent social unrest and anger. Social protests rose spectacularly (Garay & Tanaka, 2009: 60).

The rise of social protests during the Toledo regime was met, just as before, with police repression, deaths, detentions and declaration of a state of emergency in different parts of the country. The government was afraid of the possible negative effects of increasing social struggle on economic development (Pajuelo, 2004: 58–9). However, while during the Fujimori regime repression was a frequent and effective method to suffocate the battles of the people, the Toledo government did not succeed in obtaining the same results. In June 2002 the people of Arequipa rose against the intentions of the regime to privatize the state-owned electricity companies. Notwithstanding the repressive measures against the people of Arequipa, in the months and years after the *Arequipazo* social struggle continued.

Together with the 'return' of social protests, the trade unions reappeared at the negotiation table with the government. The unions demanded, among other things, the reconsideration of anti-labour laws and decrees that had been passed under Fujimori's regime. It asked, among others, for the restoration of collective bargaining at economic sector level, the participation of labour in the profits of the companies, the extension of the right of unionization to the public sector, the improvement of the labour conditions and the reinstatement of those workers who had been fired during the Fujimori regime (Solfrini, 2001: 71; Garay & Tanaka, 2009: 67).

The 'return' of the trade unions in the political and economic arena is obvious when we look at the evolution of the strike movement. However, their power must not be overestimated. Union membership has reduced significantly in comparison with the 1980s. According to Juan José Gorriti (interview, 2015), currently the vice president of the main workers' organization, the General Confederation of the Workers of Peru (Confederación General de Trabajadores del Perú – CGTP), around 10 per cent of the formal EAP of the private sector (25 per cent of total EAP of the private sector) is affiliated to a union. In 1980 it was estimated that 40 per cent of the economic active population was a union member (Barba Caballero, 1981: 235). Yepez del Castillo and Bernedo Alvarado (1985: 52) calculate that in the period 1981–82 17.5 per cent of the occupied EAP was affiliated to a union. And while in the period 2000–14, in the case of the private sector, 1,128 strikes took place that involved 413,297 workers and caused a loss of 18,845,939 labour hours, in the years 1980–90 and 1991–99 these figures were respectively 7,612 strikes, 5,346,638 workers and 201,755,074 labour hours, and 1,227 strikes, 552,831 workers and 19,120,157 labour hours.[7]

A detailed analysis of the strikes according to economic activities reveals that the vanguard of the urban class struggle is formed by workers and/or employees in mining, manufacturing and construction. Workers and employees in transport and, in 2014, those who were employed in public administration and defence can be found in the front ranks of the class struggle in the urban areas.

The evolution of the strike movement in the last 15 years is directly related to the expectations that were fostered by the governments of Toledo, García and Humala. Wage-workers assumed that the Toledo and Humala regimes would increase the income of the working population. However, economic progress did not 'trickle down', the rates of remuneration as a percentage of GDP kept falling in favour of the exploitation surplus, and the remuneration of the absolute majority of the working population was still near the minimum wage level. The commodities boom during the García regime was not translated in income increases of the working population. Average remuneration was even allowed to decrease below the official minimum wage level. Hence, the urban class struggle in the years 2000 to 2014 has been mainly fought for social and economic issues such as wage and salary demands and the improvement of the labour conditions and against the renewed attacks on what is left of labour rights.

The fact that individuals working in mining, manufacturing and construction are leading the urban class struggle, i.e. their organizations form the vanguard of the

**214**   Peru: the class struggle from below

class struggle in the urban areas, does not tell us anything about its real power in society. In order to assess this power we should analyse the importance of the mining, manufacturing and construction sectors for employment and economic development.

In the years 2001 to 2014, data of the Peruvian National Institute of Statistics and Informatics (Instituto Nacional de Estadística e Informática – INEI) showed that the mining, manufacturing and construction sectors employed between 14 and 17 per cent of the occupied EAP.[8] According to data of the Peruvian Central Bank, in the period 2000–14 the contribution of these sectors to GDP (in 2007 prices) fluctuated between 32.7 and 36.5 per cent.[9] The particular importance of the mining sector for investment and exports is demonstrated in Part 1 of this chapter.

The power of the vanguard of the class struggle is based on the economic importance of the mining, manufacturing and construction sectors. In terms of the vanguard's impact on workers and employees in other economic sectors, the picture is not at all clear. The effect of the vanguard on individuals working in other economic sectors might be considered limited because of the small proportion of Peruvians who work in mining, manufacturing and construction. However, more than just its reduced size in terms of employment, the fundamental reasons for the weak impact of the vanguard on the rearguard have to be sought in the political and social weakness of the trade unions in general.

The current political and social weakness of the trade unions can be explained by the changes in the Peruvian class structure. Individuals who in the 1980s and 1990s were wage-workers have become own-account workers or 'independents' (interview, Checa, 2015). The classic working class, considered as all those individuals who principally perform (relatively simple) manual activities, has diminished in quantity and has been replaced by highly skilled workers. 'Many of these colleagues,' as Gorriti (interview, 2015) points out, 'no longer feel themselves to be part of the working class.'

A second cause of the weakness of the trade unions is the fact that a considerable portion of the EAP is still not adequately employed. While in 1979 51.4 per cent of the EAP was underemployed, in 1984 this had grown to 54.2 per cent. In 1990, for metropolitan Lima, this reached 73.1 per cent (INEi, 1983: 99; INEi 1987: 150). Although in Peru a 48-hour working week is mandated by law, these long hours do not seem to be enough to generate sufficient income to 'survive', forcing workers to look for a second job. The struggle for survival reduces time available for union activities.

A third element that has a negative impact on the power of the trade unions is the generalized use of temporary contracts by the state and capital. While in 1990 39 per cent of the working population was hired on a temporary basis, in 2003 this had increased to 77 per cent. In 2012 the majority of the contracts in whatever type of company and of whatever size were temporary contracts (Instituto de Estudios Sindicales, 2012: 3). As Gorriti explains, '[t]emporary contracts eliminate whole unions'. Ibis Fernández (interview, 2015), a leader of the CGTP who works in the municipality of Lima, says, 'Every time there are lesser and lesser unions. Individuals on a contract-base do not affiliate with a union. The only ones who dare to join are those who are affiliated years ago.'

A fourth negative influence on the possibilities of the organized working population to make a fist against the state and capital is the problem of informality.[10] Gorriti (interview, 2015) explains: 'The working class of manual workers, including highly skilled workers, was in the 1980s mostly replaced by informal workers and even by self-employed formal or informal workers'. According to different studies (Gamero Requena & Carrasco, n.d.; Díaz, 2014: 228), in the period 2002–11 informal employment as a percentage of total employment fluctuated between 76 and 85 per cent. In 2015, the Peruvian minister of labour and the promotion of employment announced that the rate of informality amounted to 72.8 per cent.[11]

Informality is used as a threat against wage and salary demands of the working population in the formal sector and as an argument to *lower* its remuneration. Informality is also a perfect tool to divide the working population in their struggle against capital. Formal workers and employees might consider the lower remuneration of their informal colleagues to be the cause of their wage and salary reductions.

The fifth reason for the weakness of the trade unions can be traced back to the neo-liberal 'reforms' of the 1990s. According to Fernández (interview, 2015), the privatization of the economic activities of the municipalities fragmented the union power of the municipality workers. Instead of two big unions (of workers and employees), nowadays, in Lima there is a whole range of small unions that organize individuals employed in the municipality of Lima. In addition, individuals that are employed in the privatized municipality services are working on a contract basis instead of being employed.

## Class struggle in the countryside

Since the 'fall' of the Fujimori government in November 2000, social struggles in Peru show an upward trend. The monthly bulletins of the governmental agency Defensoria del Pueblo on social conflicts demonstrate the predominance of conflicts related to the operations of extractive capital. In recent years the fight of the indigenous and peasant communities has literally got bloody. During the Humala government up to mid-2016, more than 20 people died as a consequence of the repression of the protests against the operations of extractive capital.

The communities fight principally to defend their land and water resources. Extractive capital, especially mining capital, has set its eye on the land, beneath which gold, copper and other lucrative mineral resources can be found. The operations of mining capital negatively affect the quality of the water of the communities and even cause the disappearance of complete water basins. The battle of the communities is also against the policies of the Peruvian state to further a development model based on the extraction of natural resources.

The peasants and indigenous-based social movements might be considered the vanguard of the class struggle in Peru. The struggle of these movements to protect

**216** Peru: the class struggle from below

their habitats and livelihoods has not only expanded to all parts where extractive capital has set foot. These battles are putting the current development model in check. That is, the struggle of these movements is primarily a political battle against the Peruvian state and extractive capital, especially transnational mining capital.

The struggle of the Peruvian communities against mining capital can be divided into two phases. While in the first phase indigenous and peasant communities accepted the presence of the mining corporations but fought for economic and social issues related to mining, in the second phase the communities struggled against the presence of the mining companies in their territories.

The struggle in the first phase was, among others, about compensation for the land the communities were willing to sell to the companies, job opportunities in the mine, compensation for environmental damage, and the recognition of the communities' economic, social and cultural rights that were affected by the mine, and against the pressure exercised by the corporations on peasant families to sell their lands (Bebbington, 2009: 135–6; De Echave, 2009: 3; Padilla, 2009: 157; Aliaga Díaz, 2014: 2).

The first phase of the battle of the Peruvian communities started to come to an end in the first years of the third millennium after a truck of Yanacocha[12] spilled 152 kilos of mercury, affecting at least 1,700 individuals in Choropampa, a district in the province of Chota of the department of Cajamarca. The adverse effects of mining became widely known. The receptiveness of the communities ended when they became aware of the negative effects of mining on the environment (interview, Vásquez Huamán & Vásquez Becerra, 2015; interview, Sánchez, 2015).

The second phase of the struggle of the communities is characterized by the fight against the presence of mining capital in their territories. The battle for Hill Quillish in 2004 in the department of Cajamarca might be considered a turning point. At Hill Quillish originates the rivers Grande and Porcón that provide 72 per cent of the water of the city of Cajamarca. The Hill is also an important gold reservoir. It is estimated that it 'covers' 4.2 million ounces of gold (Rodríguez Carmona, Castro & Sánchez, 2013: 128). When it became known that Yanacocha was intending to start explorations at the Hill, tens of thousands of persons demonstrated in the city of Cajamarca. They succeeded in stopping the mining explorations (interview, Sánchez, 2015).

The protests in the department of Cajamarca against mining capital might be considered the vanguard of the class struggle that is returning to the countryside since the start of the third millennium. In November 2015 the struggle entered its fifth year and there are no indications that it is coming to an end soon.

Over the last four years, the struggle of the municipalities, communities and the people of Cajamarca affected by Yanacocha has become an example of how the battle against mining capital can be organized and sustained. The struggle in Cajamarca also perfectly exemplifies how the mining corporations try to gain the population for their business undertakings. It is furthermore a good illustration of the 'natural' repressive reaction of governments that are confronted with massive and sustained popular protests against the economical foundation of their political programmes.

The fight against the Conga Project began at the outset of the third millennium. The initial problems to organize the population have definitively been influenced by the 10 years of class struggle from above that characterized the period 1990–2000. The depoliticization of society and the elite's ideological dominance ensured that private initiative instead of collective decision making would be the point of departure for the allocation of returns to different factors of production (i.e. income distribution).

Since 2004 the fight against the Conga Project has been organized by the people of the provinces of Cajamarca, Bambamarca, San Marcos, Celendín and San Pablo. These provinces are directly affected by the project.

In the province of Cajamarca the struggle is organized by the Environmental Defence Front of Cajamarca (Frente de Defensa Ambiental de Cajamarca – FDAC).[13] The FDAC is composed of a variety of social organizations such as representatives of the neighbourhoods of the city of Cajamarca, the trade union of the professors of the National University of Cajamarca (UNC), the student federation of the UNC, the mothers of the social Glass of Milk (*Vaso de Leche*) programme,[14] and some peasant self-defence committees (*rondas campesinas*). Political parties are not allowed in the FDAC (interview, Saavedra, 2015; interview, Silva, 2015).

The battle in the province of Celendín, one of the provinces directly affected by the Conga Project, is led by the Inter-institutional Platform of Celendín (PIC). This platform is made up of different social organizations, such as the *rondas campesinas* of Celendín, the trade union of schoolteachers of Celendín, and associations of producers and irrigators. At the end of 2009, 37 organizations formed part of the PIC. The main objective of the PIC is to defend and protect the headwater basins of Celendín. Currently, the PIC also struggles against hydroelectric power stations that the Brazilian company Odebrecht is planning to build in Celendín (Interview, Sánchez, 2015).

In 2009, Yanacocha started its campaign to present its environmental impact study (interview, Sánchez, 2015). This campaign meant the beginning of a prolonged battle of the communities that were going to be affected by the Conga Project. As the authorities of the provinces to which these communities pertain had been 'bought' by the corporation, the only force restraining Conga was the resistance mounted by the population. However, as the population was not informed about the devastating environmental impact of the project, a counter-information campaign was started.

In Celendín, several individuals independently in small groups took the initiative to launch this counter-campaign. Although different activities against Yanacocha were developed, these had not a lasting effect (interview, Livaque, 2015). Later, under the flag of the PIC, this work got a more structural and organizational character when members of the PIC began to visit the communities that were going to be affected by the Conga Project and to inform these communities about the consequences of the project. According to Sánchez (interview, 2015), the information caused a change of opinion. Instead of favouring the project, the population started to turn against it.

**218** Peru: the class struggle from below

The counter-campaign was not limited to the province of Celendín. As it was not only Celendín that would be affected by the Conga Project, it was important to educate the population of other provinces as well. With the help of the FDAC, defence fronts were erected in the provinces of San Pablo, Bambamarca, Chota, Cajabamba and San Marcos (interview, Saavedra, 2015).

Yanacocha did not sit aside when the protests against the Conga Project began. On the one hand, it used the Peruvian judicial system to denounce the leaders of the resistance against the Conga Project and monitored these leaders by using paramilitary forces (for instance, in the case of the battle for Hill Quillish). On the other hand, it tried to 'buy' the political consciousness of the population (interview, Sánchez, 2015; interview, Vásquez Huamán & Vásquez Becerra, 2015; interview, Livaque, 2015; interview, Silva, 2015; interview, Hernández, 2015) and to misinform the population, speaking 'bad of us, demonize us, sow discord, fear, mistrust' (interview, Hernández, 2015).

On 9 November 2011, the first regional strike against the Conga Project was organized. A few days earlier, three ministers had visited the area of the mining operations. The regional president, Gregorio Santos, a member of the left wing-oriented organization MAS rallied behind the protest. Fifteen days later a second regional strike was organized. This strike lasted 11 days. Seventeen people were hurt, six of them showed bullet wounds. The city of Cajamarca was the central focus of the struggle. Thousands of persons coming from surrounding provinces were received and nourished by FDAC. According to the president of the FDAC, at a certain moment the central square of Cajamarca was filled with around 75,000 demonstrators (interview, Saavedra, 2015).

The organizational committee in the city Cajamarca, the FDAC, succeeded in controlling all economic activities. Also the highways around and in the city were under the control of the FDAC. On the request of the FDAC, transport in the city came to a complete standstill (interview, Saavedra, 2015). The FDAC received the support of a variety of social actors such as the associations of motor taxis, market vendors and street vendors (interview, Saavedra, 2015; interview, Silva, 2015). Saavedra (interview, 2015) explains:

> We have been in control of the city. All authorities and private institutions were subordinated to the Environmental Defence Front, including Goyo....[15] We, the Environmental Defence Front, issued decrees.... During our struggle there was no police in the streets ... because the *rondas urbanas* controlled the whole city.... The city was ours.

On 29 November 2011, the Conga Project was suspended. On 4 December the government declared a state of emergency in the provinces of Cajamarca, Celendín, Hualgayoc and Contumazá. According to Sánchez (interview, 2015), the police and the army were everywhere in Celendín, 'doing their military aerobatics, scaring people, with a naked torso and well-armed. It seemed like a war scenario.' Livaque (interview, 2015) tells us that around 1,500 soldiers were 'doing war practices in the streets, frightening the children.... In the streets they were doing their exercises with their weapons ready to fire.'

Before the state of emergency was declared, conversations were held in the city of Cajamarca between the resistance front and premier Salomón Lerner. While the government considered it impermissible to affect the interests of transnational capital, the anti-Conga coalition would only end the strike 'provided that the mining company would withdraw all its machinery' (interview, Saavedra, 2015). Naturally, the government could not fulfil this demand and, as a consequence, the conversations ended in an impasse.

Between 31 May and 3 July 2012, a new regional strike was organized. In the city of Celendín the strike occasioned the death of four persons. In the city of Bambamarca one person died.

The killings intensified the struggle. However, when in October 2012 Yanacocha tried to install some of its equipment, again the population of Celendín mobilized itself.

The struggle against the Conga Project entered a new phase. Sánchez (interview, 2015) explains: 'The fight has cycles and I think that you have to weigh the struggle. Knowing that this is a long battle, you are not going to have 365 days to mobilize the people'. According to Saavedra (interview, 2015), the defence fronts have reduced their activities because Yanacocha has stopped its work near the lakes.

## Weaknesses of the struggle against mining capital

The protests against the mining corporations are generally being organized and led by local and/or regional organizations around environmental issues and life-threatening situations caused by mining operations. The struggle for these concrete local issues assures a popular local base.

At the same time that it assures a popular local base, the struggle lacks a national political and organizational projection that enables it to pass the local and/or regional frontiers and to convert the local and/or regional battles into a nationwide struggle for another development model. According to De Echave (2009: 16), the locally organized indigenous and peasant-based social movements against mining capital might be effective in responding to local conflicts, issues and cases, but it is not able to articulate a national agenda related to mining. The fact that the objectives of these different battles are very diverse also hampers the national unity of these dispersed struggles (Comisiones de Investigacion Politai, 2013: 106).

The first weakness of the struggle is not only that it is local but also that it has a local projection. However, since September 2014 the indigenous and peasant communities in the highlands of Cajamarca and communities in the Amazon region seem to have united in their struggle against extractive capital.[16] Processes of articulation of the struggles against the mining and oil companies as well as against projects that point to the installation of hydroelectric power plants in different parts of Peru are confirmed by Sánchez (interview, 2015) and Livaque (interview, 2015).[17]

Even coordination at the international level is starting to take place. Members of the resistance in Celendín have participated in the Political School of the Landless Workers Movement of Brazil (Movimento dos Trabalhadores Rurais Sem Terra – MST). Members of the MST have visited Celendín to learn from the battle against the Conga Project. Also, individuals from the United States and Bolivia and representatives of the Zapatistas from Mexico and the Mapuches from Chile have visited Celendín (interview, Livaque, 2015).

It might be thought that it would not be so difficult to unite the struggles in the different localities in Peru as in general terms the communities face the same problems. Unfortunately this is not case. First of all, the National Confederation of Communities Affected by Mining in Peru (Confederación Nacional de Comunidades del Perú Afectadas por la Minería – CONACAMI) has been deactivated. Its foundation in 1999 was a big step forwards in the centralization of the local struggles, in the coordinated support of these local battles and in the elevation of the debates on the negative impacts of mining to a national level (Padilla, 2009: 158–9). Second, the Peasants Confederation of Peru (Confederación Campesina del Perú – CCP) and the National Agrarian Confederation (Confederación Nacional Agraria – CNA) are not involved in the struggle.[18] Third, there are almost no political parties with a national presence that defend the interests of the communities affected by mining or struggle against extractivist capital in general. Although the MAS in Cajamarca occupies the regional presidency and is directly affiliated to the PCP–PR, a national organization, it has not been able to become central for the national articulation of the struggles of the communities against extractive capital.[19]

To unite the local and regional struggles is crucial for winning the battle against extractive capital as capital not only forms a big united front against the interests of the exploited and oppressed majorities, but also because it has the support of the Peruvian state and the multilateral institutions of imperialism. The unity of the struggle in the rural areas is important to 'get' the battles in small and 'forgotten' communities on the agenda of the population in the urban areas. This brings us to the relation between rural and urban areas.

Another weakness has to do with the lack of ties between the movements against extractive capital in the rural areas and working class and popular organizations in the urban areas. Although these relations might exist, there is no evidence of a strategic alliance between the movements and organizations of the two areas.[20] It is interesting to note, for example, that the current mayor of the capital of the department of Cajamarca is a member of the right-wing Fujimori political party. The regional presidency, as mentioned above, is in the hands of MAS.

The difficulties of developing strategic ties between the urban and rural areas are caused mainly by class differences. In the case of the struggle in the province of San Marcos in the department of Cajamarca against the intentions of Miski Mayo, a Peruvian subsidiary of the Brazilian corporation Vale, to exploit gold and copper deposits located at the Cerro Mogol (2005–09), for instance, Taylor (2011: 431) describes these problems as follows:

A second thorny issue that emerged when Miski Mayo first appeared in the zone concerned divisions between town and country. A sector of the petit-bourgeoisie settled in the town of San Marcos looked favourably on the project, anticipating that an upsurge in mining activity would increase sales in shops, restaurants and bars, as well as boost the market for rented accommodation. One activist from San Marcos noted: 'Until now, we have been growing strongly in the countryside. With the townspeople it is more complicated. Many are undecided, as they hope to take advantage and make money. They expect more business, but don't realize how they could be affected'.

In the case of the city of Cajamarca the same applies. Yanacocha converted the city of Cajamarca into a 'mining camp' and managed to 'generate an enclave' in which everybody is connected and dependent on each other (interview, Saavedra, 2015) This brings us to the third weakness.

The organizations that are leading the struggle are not necessarily class-based. Everybody who is negatively impacted in a certain way by mining operations forms part of the organization/group/network. Hence, within the local or regional move-ment there exist different points of view on the principal demands of the move-ment (Comisiones de Investigaciones Politai, 2013: 106). This is definitely an important condition for the struggle to weaken during a prolonged battle.

This non-class-based struggle is a strength as well as a weakness. As the struggle might be able to count on a range of different social actors that are united on one specific issue, the access to water for instance, it is very difficult to connect this battle to other social struggles. The contradictory class interests between the dif-ferent social actors that are united on one specific issue do not permit broadening the fight to other social issues. In other words, one-item non-class-based alliances do not allow for a broad programmatic alliance.

The fourth and last weakness of the struggle of the social movements against mining capital is the fact that they do not seem to have a strategy that might enable these movements to determine the course of the battle. The movements only react on what happens in their direct environment instead of trying to determine the course of future events. The activities of the mining corporations and the measures taken by the gov-ernment that favour mining capital determine the actions of the social movements.

## Conclusion

The Peruvian economy depends for its growth on the investments in the mining sector and the export of its abundant mineral resources. A radical change of the Peru-vian development model is demanded by the communities that struggle against the invasion of mining capital in their territories which have a major impact on the economy. The deep crisis of the extractive development model has forced the current Peruvian government, in the context of diminishing export values and stagnating FDI, to deepen the same development model. This shows the crisis of the development model based on the extraction of the country's natural resources.

The current development model is basically a continuation of the development model that was implemented in the 1990s. The working population has not benefitted from the introduction of neo-liberalism by former President Fujimori. The regimes after Fujimori did not structurally change the social and economic situation of the majority of the Peruvian population. Even during the commodities boom of the years between 2005 and 2011 the wages and salaries of the majority of the population did not increase significantly. Underemployment rates have not decreased and the absolute majority of the EAP earns a living below or near the minimum wage level.

Since the 1990s the correlation of class forces has been in favour of capital. The 'fall' of Fujimori in 2000 'liberated' latent social anger and 'permitted' the trade unions to return to the political and economic arena. Although strikes show an upward trend, the strength of the organized working class is incomparable with previous decades. The power of the vanguard of the trade unions formed by workers and/or employees in mining, manufacturing and construction is based on the economic importance of these sectors. Its struggle seems to have had a lesser impact on workers and employees in other economic sectors or on the working population in general.

The vanguard of the class struggle in Peru is located in the rural areas. In the urban areas the class struggle is fought mainly around social and economic issues. The struggle of the indigenous and peasant-based social movements to protect their habitats and livelihoods has expanded to all regions where extractive capital is heavily involved. The battles are holding the current development model in check. An example of the battle in the department of Cajamarca shows that it is impossible to conciliate the interests of mining capital and the population affected by mining. The organizations that lead the struggle are firmly based in the communities and the population has a high level of political consciousness. The Peruvian state has taken the side of mining capital, expressed in the indiscriminate use of political violence against the communities that defend their land and water resources against the invasion of mining capital.

In the context of slow economic growth and declining commodity prices, it is expected that key class battles are on the horizon. The development model will be deepened and its scope broadened. This might push the class struggle to new heights. Slow growth will negatively affect the income of the working population and increase the rate of underemployment. As the correlation of class forces is still in favour of capital, the attacks on labour rights will be intensified. This difficult panorama should stimulate the workers' organizations and the social movements that fight against mining capital to unite forces and to work towards a nationwide battle against capital and the Peruvian state.

## Notes

1  On the class struggle in the 1980s, see Parodi (1986), Balbi (1988, 1989) and Balbi and Gamero (1990).
2  On the class struggle in the 1990s, see Bernedo Alverado (1999), Verdera (2000) and Chacaltana and García (2001).
3  In 2010, the struggle of communities in the Amazon region against the privatization of their land was choked in blood. The repression of the protests in the city of Bagua caused the death of 23 policemen and 10 civilians.

# Peru: the class struggle from below **223**

4 On the rates of unemployment and underemployment during the Fujimori regime, see INEI (2001: 235) and Murakami (2007: 374, 430).

5 On this regime see Crabtree (2005) and Reyna (2000).

6 According to Cuadros Luque (2015: 2tft32), 90 per cent of the exploitation surplus is comprised of the profits of the companies.

7 Source: www.inei.gob.pe/estadisticas/indice-tematico/ocupacion-y-vivienda/ (accessed 27 August 2015).

8 See on these data INEI (2010: 97) and www.inei.gob.pe/estadisticas/indice-tematico/ocupacion-y-vivienda (accessed 26 December 2015).

9 Source: www.bcrp.gob.pe/estadisticas/cuadros-anuales-historicos.html (consulted 26 December 2015).

10 Informality may have a *positive* effect on profits as (i) the wages in the informal sector are lower than the gross wages in the formal sector; (ii) owing to the absence of labour rights and union representatives, the rates of exploitation and/or economic oppression in the informal sector might be higher than in the formal sector; and, (iii) economic insecurity of the workers in the informal sector makes it much easier to increase the work intensity.

11 'Informalidad laboral en el país llega hasta el 72,8%', in http://larepublica.pe/impresa/politica/708987-informalidad-laboural-en-el-pais-llega-hasta-el-728 (consulted 8 October 2015).

12 Yanacocha is one of the major mining projects in Peru and, according to the mining company Newmont, South America's largest gold mine. The Conga Project is a new joint venture of the same companies that exploit Yanacocha. These companies are Newmont Mining Corporation, Minas Buenaventura and the International Finance Corporation, i.e. the World Bank. The project is three times the size of Yanacocha (Sullivan, 2013) and implies an investment of US$4.800 million. The Conga Project will 'empty' four lakes. The water of two lakes covers enormous reserves of copper and gold. Two other lakes are planned to be used as waste bins for the 80,000 tons of toxic waste tailings per day that the project will generate for the next 17 years. The four lakes will be replaced by four artificial water reservoirs. The project will affect five rivers, six lakes, 682 natural water springs, 18 irrigation canals and 102 catchments of water for human consumption (Sánchez, 2015). When we refer to the companies that intend to exploit the Conga Project we use the name Yanacocha.

13 The FDAC initiated its activities in 1993. As the name suggests, the FDAC is only dedicated to environmental issues. The FDAC was first called the Defence Front of the Interests of the Cajamarca Region, but in 2007 it changed its name to FDAC as the activities were only concentrated in the province of Cajamarca. It was also thought that the Cajamarca Defence Front could not represent the other provinces of the department of Cajamarca as it did not know these provinces (interview, Saavedra, 2015). The Defence Front of the Interests of the Cajamarca Region (Frente de Defense de los Intereses de la Región Cajamarca) still exists and is led by Ydelso Hernández, a cadre of the political party Movement of Social Affirmation (Movimiento de Afirmación Social – MAS), the Communist Party of Peru Red Fatherland (Partido Comunista del Perú Patria Roja – PCP–PR) and the *rondas campesinas* (regionally and nationally). This Defence Front consists of different social organizations and political parties and is focused on social issues in general such as labour rights, environmental problems related to mining, the defence of the authority of the *rondas campesinas* etc. (interview, Hernández, 2015).

14 *Vaso de Leche* is an organization that provides breakfasts to poor children.

15 Goyo is the nickname of the regional president of Cajamarca, Gregorio Santos.

16 'Perú: Ronderos y comunidades nativas del norte exigen anular permisos a minera Águila Dorada'. http://servindi.org/actualidad/113609.

17 According to Minguillo (interview, 2015), a former cadre of the Revolutionary Socialist Party and currently working with communities in the Amazon region, the main weakness of the struggle against extractive capital is the 'lack of articulation' of all the battles in the country. Olmedo Auris (interview, 2015), a cadre of the PCP–PR and the MAS,

224 Peru: the class struggle from below

says that the weakness of the struggle is the fact that the battles of the different communities are not articulated, i.e. 'there is no organization that unites all these struggles'.

18 According to Eguren (2014: 184), the fact that the large majority of the peasantry is composed of small and very small landowners and do not depend on an employer, might be considered the principal cause for the absence of a rural trade union movement.

19 It should be mentioned, however, that according to Hernández (interview, 2015) and Mendoza (interview, 2015), another cadre of the MAS, the MAS is not against the mining corporations but against mining at headwater basins. According to both, what is needed is a 'territorial zoning' that establishes, for instance, which areas are destined for agriculture and which for mining.

20 The exception is the struggle at Hill Quillish in 2004 in the Department of Cajamarca.

## List of interviews

Checa, Pablo, a leader of the General Confederation of the Workers of Peru and former vice minister of labour and employment promotion (2011–12), Lima, 10 April 2015.

Fernández, Ibis, a leader of the General Confederation of the Workers of Peru, Lima, 29 May 2015.

Gorriti, Juan José, vice president of the General Confederation of the Workers of Peru, Lima, 10 April 2015.

Hernández, Ydelso, cadre of the political parties Communist Party of Peru Red Fatherland and the Movement of Social Affirmation, and the peasant self-defence committees (regionally and nationally), Cajamarca, 19 April 2015.

Livaque, Marle, member of the Inter-institutional Platform of Celendín and secretary of the political party Land and Freedom in the city of Celendín, Celendín, 16 April 2015.

Mendoza, Segundo, cadre of the political parties Communist Party of Peru Red Fatherland and the Movement of Social Affirmation, Cajamarca, 19 April 2015.

Minguillo, Héctor, former cadre of the Revolutionary Socialist Party and currently working with the communities in the Amazon region, interview by telephone, 6 April 2015.

President of the Movement of Social Affirmation, Lima, 31 March 2015.

Saavedra, Wilfredo, president of the Environmental Defence Front of Cajamarca, Cajamarca, 18 April 2015.

Sánchez, Milton, secretary general of the Inter-institutional Platform of Celendín, Celendín, 16 April 2015.

Silva, Narda, militant of the Environmental Defence Front of Cajamarca, Cajamarca, 19 April 2015.

Vásquez Becerra, Alamiro, president of the Defence Front of the Basin of the River Jadibamba, Celendín, 17 April 2015.

Vásquez Huamán, Elvira, secretary of the Defence Front of the Basin of the River Jadibamba, Celendín, 17 April 2015.

## References

Alarco, G. (2011). 'Márgenes de ganancia, financiamiento e inversión del sector empresarial peruano (1998–2008)'. *Revista Cepal 105*, Santiago de Chile. Available at: www.cepal.org/publicaciones/xml/1/45201/RVE105Alarco.pdf [accessed 23 February 2016].

Aliaga Díaz, C. A. (2014). 'Una experiencia de construcción de poder popular. El caso de Cajamarca'. Provided by Aliaga Diaz. In archive of author.

Balbi, C. R. (1988). 'Las relaciones estado-sindicalismo en el Perú 1985–1987'. *Diagnóstica y debate*, 34. Lima: Fundación Friedrich Ebert, pp. 9–60.

Balbi, C. R. (1989). *Identidad clasista en el sindicalismo. Su impacto en las fábricas*. Lima: Desco.

Balbi, C. R. & Gamero, J. (1990). 'Los trabajadores en los 80s: entre la formalidad y la informalidad', in C. R. Balbi, *Movimientos sociales: elementos para una relectura*. Lima: Centro de Estudios y Promoción de Desarrollo, pp. 55–109.

Barba Caballero, J. (1981). *Historia del movimiento obrero peruano*. Lima: Ediciones Signo.

Bebbington, A. (2009). 'Industrias extractivas, actores sociales y conflictos', Chapter 5 in CAAP/CLAES (eds) *Extractivismo, política y sociedad*. Quito: CAAP/CLAES, pp. 131–56. Available at: http://ambiental.net/wp-content/uploads/2009/11/BebbingtonExtract ivismoSociedadDesarrollo09.pdf [accessed 3 June 2016].

Bernedo Alvarado, J. (1999). 'Reforma laboural, empleo y salarios en el Perú', in V. E. Tokman & D. Martínez (eds) *Flexibilización en el margen: la reforma del contrato de trabajo*. Geneva: Organización Internacional de Trabajo, pp. 171–99.

Chacaltana, J. and García, N. (2001). *Reforma laboural, capacitación y productividad*. Working Paper no. 139. Lima: Organización Internacional del Trabajo.

Crabtree, J. (2005). *Alan García en el poder. Perú: 1985–1990*. Lima: Ediciones Peisa S.A.C.

Cuadros Luque, F. (2015). 'Situación del mercado de trabajo y costos labourales en el Perú'. Provided by Guillermo Rochabrun. In archive of author.

De Echave, J. (2009). 'Los retos actuales del movimiento social vinculado a la lucha por los derechos de las comunidades frente a las industrias extractivas: el caso peruano'. Available at: www.yorku.ca/cerlac/EI/papers/De%20Echave.pdf [accessed 8 November 2010].

Díaz, J. J. (2014). 'Formalización empresarial y laboural', in R. Infante and J. Chacaltana (eds) *Hacia un Desarrollo inclusivo. El caso del Perú*. Santiago: Cepal, pp. 173–259.

Eguren, F. (2014). 'De la reforma agraria neolatifundio: el crecimiento capitalista del campo peruano', in G. Almeyra, L. Concheiro Bórquez, J. M. Mendes Pereira & C. W. Porto-Gonçalves (eds) *Capitalismo: tierra y poder en América Latina (1982–2012). Bolivia, Colombia, Ecuador, Perú, Venezuela*, Vol. II. Mexico: Universidad Autónoma Metropolitana/CLACSO, pp. 159–92.

Gamero Requena, J. and Carrasco, G. (n.d.). Trabajo informal y políticas de protección social, *Comunidad Andina*. Available at: www.comunidadandina.org/camtandinos/OLA/Documentos/Pdf/trabajo-informal-y-politicas.pdf [accessed 13 July 2016].

Garay, C. & Tanaka, M. (2009). 'Las protestas en el Perú entre 1995 y el 2006', in R. Grompone & M. Tanaka (eds) *Entre el crecimiento económico y la insatisfacción social*. Lima: Instituto de Estudios Peruanos, pp. 59–123.

INEI. (1983, 1987, 1995, 2001, 2006, 2008). *Perú: Compendio Estadístico*. Lima: INEI.

INEI. (2010). *Perú: Evolución de los indicadores de empleo e ingresos por departamentos, 2001–2009*. Lima: INEI.

INEI. (n.d.). Metodología de Cálculo del Producto Bruto Interno Anual. Available at: www.inei.gob.pe/media/MenuRecursivo/metodologias/pbi02.pdf [accessed 22 May 2016].

Instituto de Estudios Sindicales. (2012). 'La situación laboural y sindical en el Perú'. Working Paper No. 1. Available at: www.iesiperu.org.pe/documentos/LASITUACION LABOURALYSINDICALENEL PERU.pdf [accessed 8 October 2015].

Murakami, Y. (2007). *Perú en la era del Chino. La política no institucionalizada y el pueblo en busca de un Salvador*. Kyoto: Instituto de Estudios Peruanos & Center for Integrated Area Studies, Kyoto University.

Padilla, C. (2009). 'El caso CONACAMI en el contexto latinoamericano', in C. José de Echave, R. Hoetmer & M. Palacios Panéz (eds) *Minería y territorio en el Perú. Conflictos, resistencias y propuestas en tiempos de globalización*. Lima: Confederación Nacional de Comunidades del Perú Afectadas por la Minería/CooperAcción/Fondo Editorial de la Facultad de Ciencias Sociales Unidad de Posgrado UNMSM, pp. 155–82.

Pajuelo Teves, R. (2004). 'Perú: crisis política permanente y nuevas protestas sociales'. *OSAL*, 5(14) pp. 51–68.

Parodi, J. (1986). 'La desmovilización del sindicalismo industrial peruano en el segundo Belaundismo', in Comisión de Movimientos Labourales de CLACSO (ed.) *El sindicalismo latinoamericano en los ochenta*. Santiago de Chile: CLACSO, pp. 325–36.

Parodi Trece, C. (2010). *Perú 1960–2000. Políticas económicas y sociales en entornos cambiantes*. Lima: Centro de la Investigación de la Universidad del Pacífico.

Parodi Trece, C. (2014). *Perú 1995–2012. Cambios y continuidades*. Lima: Universidad del Pacífico.

Proinversión. (2016). *Inversión extranjera*. Available at: www.investinperu.pe/default.aspx [accessed 18 April 2016].

Rodríguez-Carmona, A., Castro, M. & Sánchez, P. (2013). *Imaginarios a cielo abierto. Una mirada alternativa a los conflictos mineros en Perú y Bolivia*. Madrid: ACSUR Las Segovias.

Ruiz Caro, A. (2002). *El proceso de privatizaciones en el Perú durante el periodo 1991–2002*. Santiago: Instituto Latinoamericano y del Caribe de Planificación Económica y Social (ILPES), Serie de Gestión Pública, no. 22. Available at: http://repositorio.cepal.org/bitstream/handle/11362/7273/S027489_es.pdf [accessed 12 January 2016].

Sánchez, M. (2015). Perú: Minería y energía. Proyecto conga. *Plataforma Interinstitucional Celendína*. Available at: http://es.slideshare.net/RossanaMendoza/minera-48498149 [accessed 30 June 2016].

Solfrini, G. (2001). 'The Peruvian labour movement under authoritarian neoliberalism: From decline to demise'. *International Journal of Political Economy*, 1(2), pp. 44–77.

Sullivan, L. (2013). 'Peru: Andean self-determination struggles against extractive capitalism'. *Upside-Down World*. Available at: http://upsidedownworld.org/main/peru-archives-76/4438-peru-andean-self-determination-struggles-against-extractive-capitalism- [accessed 2 August 2016].

Taylor, L. (2011). 'Environmentalism and social protest: The contemporary anti-mining mobilization in the province of San Marcos and the Condebamba Valley, Peru'. *Journal of Agrarian Change*, 11(2), pp. 420–39.

Verdera, F. (2000). 'Cambio en el modelo de relaciones laborales en el Perú, 1970–1996'. *JCAS Occasional Paper*, no. 5, JCAS-IEP Series iii. Available at: http://repositorio.iep.org.pe/handle/IEP/122 [accessed 11 May 2016].

Yepez del Castillo, I. and Bernedo Alvarado, J. (1985). *La sindicalización en el Perú*. Lima: Fundación Friedrich Ebert, Pontificia Universidad Católica.

# 11

# VENEZUELA

## In the eye of the storm

For almost three decades the Latin American Right has been immersed in a rebuilding process that, as Alejandro Fierro (2016) notes, 'never reaches an end'. For one thing, the neo-liberal experiment of the 1980s and 1990s failed miserably, leading to what has been widely described and we have discussed in this book as a 'progressive cycle' in Latin American politics. For another, under the post-neo-liberal regimes formed in this cycle the elites and their subordinate classes were forced to give up some political and social privileges, even though in the case of Venezuela they managed to maintain their enormous economic power in a regime that, notwithstanding the rhetoric of a 'Bolivarian Revolution' and a series of progressive and anti-imperialist measures,[1] was non-revolutionary in that rather than expropriating their property and ill-gotten wealth the government allowed the elite and the economically dominant class their prerogatives of private property. Even so, the elites feared that as the Chavista regime advanced towards their plan for a socialist society they would eventually be forced to surrender their well-deserved if not hard-earned wealth to the masses of the urban poor that had thus far been confined to their ghettos in the favelas or slums.

The response of the various forces that made up the political right to this existential threat to their class privileges was to launch a class war against the regime, with the enthusiastic support of the US, which rightly saw the regime as the greatest regional threat to US hegemony. But to understand why the forces of opposition to the Chavista regime have thus far, after a decade and a half of concerted efforts and US aid, failed to bring the regime down, we need to understand an important feature of the Venezuelan – and Latin American – Right, namely that it is fundamentally divided within itself. You cannot unite politically what is structurally divided. Fierro (2016) makes this point in distinguishing three sectors of the Venezuelan Right.

**228** Venezuela: in the eye of the storm

First, we have a *sociological Right* consisting mostly of the middle class, which is bigger in Venezuela than in other Latin American countries thanks to the avails of the oil industry, but it is much smaller than the popular classes, which represent 70 per cent of the population. It has always been a class at the service of the oligarchy and the elites, since members of this middle class make their living by providing the oligarchy and the elites with all manner of professional and personal services. Fearing (or made to fear) that the dispossessed were coming to rob them and dispossess them of their property and power, they maintain a racist, classist and meritocratic world view, and a negative outlook on the country as well as the Chavista regime.

Second, we have a *political hard Right* composed predominantly of the traditional oligarchy and the economic and political elites linked to oil, imports and land ownership. The rise of Chavism and the resounding failures in attempting to bring it down (the 2002 coup, 2002–03 oil sabotage) forced some members of these elites to come out of the shadows and the rearguard and enter the political arena. Like the sociological base it stands on, as Fierro sees it, the political Right is a prisoner of yesterday's habits. Its proposals and political project lack a clear objective, although they cannot hide their desire to return to the previous state of affairs. It feeds off the voters' disenchantment with the complex economic situation of the country, but it is unable to seduce the electorate with arguments and proposals for democratic change because its image has been tarnished by a history of attempted coups and destabilization.

And then we have what Fierro describes as *the neo-liberal Right*. They are mostly liberal professionals such as Luis Vicente León, president of the Datanálisis polling company; the economist and deputy José Guerra; economist Asdrúbal Oliveros; or electoral adviser Juan José Rendón. They have understood the political moment better than anybody else. Upon seeing the paralysis of the Right, which is tangled in its own internal disputes, the neo-liberal Right is designing the most efficient plan to retake power (but their opinions do not always reach the social right or other sectors, because those who should act as mediators – that is, the political Right – are impervious to their discourse). They firmly believe that the way to reach power is through elections and that the best tactic is an economic offensive. Therefore, they do not participate in accusing the government of authoritarianism or of alleged human rights violations. They have learned, through years of experience, that accusing the other side of being anti-democratic only appeals to the most radicalized portion of the masses. But most do not see Chavism as anti-democratic. This is because democratic participation has grown notoriously under Chavism. This group's hidden agenda is neo-liberalism, which is disguised under a cascade of criticism of the 'intrinsic inefficiency of socialism' and advanced with arguments that appear to be rational or that appeal to common sense, combined with a direct appeal to the working class. They know that they cannot win without the working class. It is the main lesson they have extracted from the past. But, given that notions of neo-liberal capitalism are fundamentally antagonistic, it is still unclear how they will redirect this novel interest in the poor should their campaign succeed.

## Capitalism, socialism and the social economy: the Venezuelan model

Although the Bolivarian Constitution of 1999 focused upon the development of human capacity, it also retained the support for capitalism – and support for continued capitalist development was precisely the direction of the initial plan developed for 2001–07. While rejecting neo-liberalism and stressing the importance of the state presence in strategic industries, the focus of that plan was to encourage investment by private capital – both domestic and foreign – by creating an 'atmosphere of trust'. To this was to be added the development of a 'social economy' – conceived as an 'alternative and complementary road' to the private sector and the public sector. But it is significant how little a role was conceived for self-managing and cooperative activities. Essentially, this was a programme to incorporate the informal sector into the social economy; it is necessary, the plan argued, 'to transform the informal workers into small managers'. Accordingly, family, cooperative and self-managed micro-enterprises were to be encouraged through training and micro-financing (from institutions such as the Women's Development Bank) and by reducing regulations and tax burdens. The goal of the state was explicitly described as one of 'creating an emergent managerial class' (Lebowitz, 2015).

Thus, as Lebowitz noted, the social economy was to play the role it plays in Brazil and elsewhere – as islands of cooperation nurtured by states, NGOs, Grameen-type banks and church charities, that serve as shock absorbers for the economic and political effects of capitalist globalization. Of course, if seriously pursued, this could make things easier for the unemployed and excluded (the half of the Venezuelan working class in the informal sector), by providing them with a better opportunity for survival and improving their social condition. But the point is that the social economy in Venezuela's 2001–07 plan was not envisioned as an alternative to capitalism (except insofar as survival within the nooks and crannies of global capitalism constitutes an alternative). The goal, in short, was not socialism as we tend to understand it but a different capitalism; i.e. socialism was conceived of as a different more human form of capitalism – based on popular or social participation – to ensure the complete development of people, both individual and collective (which is, of course, a socialist ideal and nothing to do with capitalism, the logic of which runs in an entirely different direction).

In any case – 'bracketing' the question of socialism vs. capitalism – there is a fundamental difference between the 'development of the social economy' in the context of the Bolivarian Revolution, such as it is as an idea and project, and the social economy/solidarity economics as understood and promoted by ECLAC, FAO, ILO and the development agencies of international cooperation (including the World Bank), and as conceived by Chávez and the ideologues/theorists of the Bolivarian Revolution. For the former, the social economy is a mechanism of adjustment to the forces of capitalist development, a way of creating spaces within the system for poverty reduction based on local sustainable self-development, the social capital of the poor and the empowerment and agency of the poor (and a

**230** Venezuela: in the eye of the storm

means of converting the informal sector into a more productive sphere of economic development).

However, for the theorists and architects of the Bolivarian Revolution – see Articles 62 and 70 of the 1999 Constitution – the social economy or solidarity economics is viewed through the lens of socialist human development, i.e. 'self-management, co-management, cooperatives in all forms' as examples of 'forms of association guided by the values of mutual cooperation and solidarity'. With its emphasis upon a 'democratic, participatory and protagonistic' society, the Bolivarian Constitution contains the seeds of the 'social economy', conceived of not as a supplement to the dominant private and public sectors but as nuclei of socialism for the twenty-first century, i.e. as a national not just local development model, brought about from below as well as above.

## A new development path

Cooperatives and cooperativism play an important role in this model. Any form of development requires an institutional framework. The framework of endogenous socialist human development brought about by the Bolivarian Revolution is based on the institution of the *misiones* and the *comuna* (or commune), which are oriented towards and designed to bring about the building of new human capacities both by teaching specific skills and preparing people to enter into new productive relations through courses in cooperation and self-management. The effect of this development programme was dramatic: the number of cooperatives increased from under 800 when Chávez was first elected in 1998 to almost 84,000 by August 2005.

All this occurred in the context of Chávez's attack upon the 'perverse logic' of capital and his stress upon the alternative – a social economy whose purpose is 'the construction of the new man, of the new woman, of the new society'. The deepening of this ideological offensive was marked by the renaming of the social economy as 'socialism'. In January 2005 at the World Social Forum, Chávez explicitly called for the reinventing of socialism – different from what existed in the Soviet Union – 'We must reclaim socialism as a thesis, a project and a path, but a new type of socialism, a humanist one, which puts humans and not machines or the state ahead of everything'.

Six months later, influenced – according to Michael Lebowitz, an advisor to the minister of the economy at the time – by István Mészáros's *Beyond Capital*, Chávez stressed the importance of building a new communal system of production and consumption, in which there is an exchange of activities determined by communal needs and communal purposes, not just what Marx described as the 'cash nexus' or the profit motive, the incentive to make money, accumulate capital. 'We have to help to create it, from the popular bases, with the participation of the communities, through the community organizations, the cooperatives, self-management and different ways to create this system.' The occasion was the creation of a new institution – the Empresas de Producción Social (EPS). Drawn from a number of sources – existing cooperatives (pledged to commit themselves to the community rather than only collective self-interest), smaller state enterprises, and private firms anxious to obtain access to state business and favourable credit terms – these new enterprises of social production were to be committed to both serving community needs and incorporating worker participation.

Upon Chávez's re-election in December 2006 a new building block was added: the communal councils (based upon 200–400 families in existing urban neighbourhoods and 20–50 in the rural areas). These were established to democratically diagnose community needs and priorities. With the shift of substantial resources from municipal levels to the community level, the support of new communal banks for local projects, and a size which permits the general assembly rather than elected representatives to be the supreme decision-making body, the councils have been envisioned as a basis not only for the transformation of people in the course of changing circumstances but also for productive activity which really is based upon communal needs and communal purposes.

These new councils were identified as the fundamental cell of Bolivarian socialism and the basis for a new state. 'All power to the communal councils!' Chávez declared. An 'explosion in communal power', designated as the fifth of the 'five motors' driving the path towards socialism. The logic is one of a profound decentralization of decision-making and power; and, as with the third motor, 'moral y luces' (morality and enlightenment), a major educational and ideological campaign, the consistent theme was the stress upon revolutionary practice in order to build socialism. Citing Marx and Che Guevara, Chávez (*Aló Presidente*, No. 279, 27 March 2007, cited in Lebowitz (2007); see also Veltmeyer, 2014, on this point in the Cuban context) insisted that it is only through practice that new socialist human beings produce themselves.

## Communes or nothing? Three years after a change of direction

It was on 20 October 2012, 13 days after the new electoral victory of Hugo Chávez as president of Venezuela. The meeting, a cabinet broadcast on national television, was deemed a 'change of direction' (*golpe de timón*) and had a central slogan: *communes or nothing*. Duiliam Virigay, spokesman of the Revolutionary Bolivar and Zamora Organization (CRBZ), which currently accompanies, 'directly, with leadership, and with organizational structures', 450 of the existing communes and that are 300 under construction, said the following:

> For us, the change of direction is a claim collected by *the Commander* directly from people, which is felt in all territories where the people want to empower themselves, and there is resistance within the government itself, which he himself instils; where are the communes? How do we build socialism if we don't empower the people? How will we build a process if each leader is not committed, and if they don't give space to the people?
>
> The change of direction is a public demand in view that only the people can save the people, in order to deepen the construction of socialism, in concrete, the direct and participative democracy.

**232** Venezuela: in the eye of the storm

The bet on the communes from the CRBZ is prior to the change of direction of 20 October. It comes from the attempt of the constitutional change in 2007:

> There, the Commander raised the new geometry of power, the structural re-foundation of the Republic, from a political, organizational point of view, to change a State that was mainly a rentier, oil-dealing, and bourgeois State to set the foundations of a socialist State, a native socialism, built by our people.

That is when, from below, began the construction of communal councils, socialist communes, and − first tested and now a reality − socialist cities.

With the development of the lines of work, tensions began: 'All processes of empowerment of the people in the framework of the Bolivarian revolution have met much resistance from colleagues who have institutional spaces, sometimes due to lack of awareness, or by not understanding the Commander's vision'. That is why, says Virigay, he wanted to transmit the meeting by national television, to accelerate the transition process:

> Three years after 'the change of direction' it is more alive than ever, it seems like we are still making the same claim. There are still many obstacles, the same happens to the President of the Republic: things are oriented, the presidential council is organized nationally, but in the States, the empowerment of the people is not achieved without a fight. It would be much easier if every person who is in the head of the process in the different structures would facilitate the process of empowering the people, the construction of that instrument, of the people of the territory, where all social actors coincide.

When the presidential term of Nicolas Maduro started, the number of registered communities was less than 100. Today, there are more than 1,300 throughout the national territory. How can we measure the depth of this process of communalization of life, the 'spirit of the commune?' One thing is the written record: 'that's a quantitative way to measure, but it is not enough. Another thing is the process within the commune, their empowerment,' Chávez said in a speech at the National Assembly. The people's power, he added, should be institutionalized progressively in its territory,

> and in that matter we have much to do, because you can register the commune but the process of transferring powers to the commune is still slow, as is the management of some political and economic issues, and also the recognition of the old institutional framework to the new one, these new socialist institutions. The commune could be legally recognized but not recognized as a political player in the process, as an economic actor.

The scenario of the difficulties should not overshadow the strengths that the revolutionary process has, emphasizes the leader of the CRBZ. One of them is the existing will: 'The people want to empower themselves, take the leading role, fight for their spaces, have courage to continue building this political and economical subject, which is the commune'.

The stage we are currently emerged on, which it is always necessary to remember, has a structural difficulty from its start:

> We must review the history of the continent, the world and revolutions. Which processes were maintained after the loss of their historic leader? Our historical leadership was and remains to be Commander Chávez, and even though he is not with us today, even after this loss, this process continues.

At this stage, Virigay notes, there are many strengths: 'That level of consciousness that the Commander Chávez created is alive today, as if he were here today, all he did to raise awareness to the people is still present today'. Therefore,

> [i]t is important to highlight President Maduro's will, expressed in the conclusions of the last Congress of the national leadership of the United Socialist Party of Venezuela (PSUV), that the legacy of Commander is maintained, but above all, to support, encourage and try to consolidate the people's power and ensure that slogan from October 20th: communes or nothing. Calling popular government to the presidential council is a strategic investment.

There are more advantages, such as the unity that exists today within Chavism, through its two main policy tools: the PSUV and the Great Patriotic Pole, and also that, according to the polls,

> Over 60 per cent of the population it remains *Chavistas*, and over 50 per cent believe in building socialism. Not one country in the world, at any point in history, has had such a high level of acceptance for the construction of a socialist project, an alternative to capitalism and neoliberalism.

These are the foundations on which Virigay considers that is possible and necessary to deepen the line of work proposed on 20 October, addressing weaknesses such as continuing to disarm the oil rentier model:

> We can only leave behind that model by building a new one, and in Venezuela there are possibilities of that happening through the communes, so, we, as actors of this process, have to dedicate ourselves to that, so that any grassroots leader, even the ones that write articles for newspaper, opinion pieces, are able to start building socialism through the commune.

The alternative to the legacy in the communes is articulated in a powerful movement:

> It is important that the whole communal movement bets on unity for it to become a major player in the process, that when we talk we build the agenda,

that despite the differences, strategic unity is not lost. We need the empowerment of the commune along the territory, to have a growing importance in the national dynamic, politically, economically, and even in the dynamic of the Party.

For this to continue, the parliamentary elections on 6 December 2015 were viewed as key:

We must close ranks in the elections of December 6th, in order for President Nicolas Maduro, and the entire military-political process, continue to be at the head of this government because a right-wing government would completely eliminate the possibilities of building the dreams that Commander left open for us, such as the construction of the communal State, the social State of law and justice.

Maduro totally underestimated the severity of the economic crises and popular disenchantment, and the government's incapacity to confront capitalist-induced shortages.

The legislative defeat on 6 December revealed that Chavista unity and the growing role of communes on a strategic perspective were inoperative. The right-wing legislative majority emptied the slogan of Chavista party ideologues who claimed that:

*Commune or nothing* is what we can say in these times to make the revolution irreversible, to continue to transform our economic model, and keep Venezuela in the forefront of the process of building socialism in the continent and in the world.

Clearly the Chavistas were in retreat, their leaders on the defensive, and their dependence on the oil-extractive development model in shambles.

## The US and Venezuela: decades of defeats and destabilization

Although Venezuela was regarded by the US under President Obama as the region's main 'threat' to US security interests – replacing Cuba in this regard (the challenge presented by its alternative socialist development model) – current US policy towards Venezuela is a microcosm of its broader strategy vis-à-vis Latin America. The aim of this strategy is to reverse the regional trend towards the construction of an independent foreign policy and to restore US dominance; replace regional integration pacts with US-centred economic integration schemes; realign the international relations and foreign policies of governments in the region with US interests; and reverse the nationalization and socialization processes that the red wave of post-neo-liberal regimes in the new millennium have given rise to.

The resort to several 'hard' military coups in Venezuela was a strategy designed to impose a client regime. This was a replay of US strategy during the 1964–83 period. In those two decades US strategists successfully collaborated with business-military elites to overthrow nationalist and socialist governments, privatize public enterprises and reverse social, labour and welfare policies. These client regimes implemented the neo-liberal policies of the Washington Consensus and supported US-aligned 'integration'. The entire spectrum of representative institutions, political parties, trade unions and civil society organizations were banned and replaced by the empire-funded NGOs, state-controlled parties and trade unions. With this perspective in mind, the US has returned to all-out 'regime change' in Venezuela as the first step to a continent-wide transformation to reassert political, economic and social dominance.

Washington's resort to political violence, all-out media warfare, economic sabotage and military coups in Venezuela is an attempt to discover the effectiveness of these tactics under favourable conditions, including a deepening economic recession, double-digit inflation, declining living standards and weakening political support, as a dress rehearsal for other countries in the region.

Washington's earlier resort to a 'regime change' strategy in Venezuela, Bolivia, Argentina and Ecuador failed because objective circumstances were unfavourable. Between 2003 and 2012 the national-populist or centre-left regimes were increasing political support, their economies were growing, incomes and consumption were improving and pro-US regimes and clients had previously collapsed under the weight of systemic crises. Moreover, the negative consequences of military coups were fresh in people's minds. Today Washington's strategists believe that Venezuela is the easiest and most important target because of its structural vulnerabilities and because Caracas is the linchpin of Latin American integration and welfare populism.

The concentrated and prolonged US war against Venezuela and the resort to extremist tactics and groups can only be accounted for by what US strategists perceive as the large-scale (continent-wide) long-term interests at stake. The war waged by the US against Venezuela started shortly after President Chávez's election in 1999. His convoking of a constitutional assembly and referendum and the subsequent inclusion of a strong component of popular participatory and nationalist clauses 'rang bells' in Washington. The presence of a large contingent of former guerrillas, Marxists and leftists in the Chávez electoral campaign and regime was the signal for Washington to develop a strategy of regrouping traditional business and political clients to pressure and limit changes.

Subsequent to 9/11 Washington launched its global military offensive, projecting power via the so-called 'war on terror'. Washington's quest to reassert dominance in the Americas included demands that Venezuela fall into line and back Washington's global military offensive. President Chávez refused and set an example of independent politics for the nationalist-populist movements and emerging centre-left regimes in Latin America. Chávez told President Bush 'you don't fight terror with terror'. In response, by November 2001 Washington strategists shifted

**236** Venezuela: in the eye of the storm

from a policy of pressure to contain change to a strategy of all-out warfare to overthrow the Chávez regime via a business-military coup in April 2002.

The US-backed coup was defeated in less than 72 hours and Chávez was restored to power by an alliance of loyalist military forces backed by a spontaneous million-person march led by thousands of supporters from the popular or working-class neighbourhoods and barrios, the social base of the grass-roots revolutionary collectives that would come to make up the most organized element of *Chavismo*. Washington lost important 'assets' among the military and business elite, who fled into exile or were jailed.

From December 2002 to February 2003, the White House backed a lockout by executives in the strategic oil industry, supported by corrupt trade union officials aligned with Washington and the AFL-CIO. After three months the lockout was defeated through an alliance of loyalist trade unionists, mass organizations and overseas petrol-producing countries. The US lost strategic assets in the oil industry as over 15,000 executives, managers and workers were fired and replaced by nationalist loyalists. The oil industry was renationalized and its earnings were put at the service of social welfare.

Having lost assets essential to violent warfare, Washington promoted a strategy of electoral politics – organizing a referendum in 2004, which was won by Chávez and a boycott of the 2005 congressional elections, which failed and led to an overwhelming majority for the pro-Chávez forces.

Having failed to secure regime change via internal violent and electoral warfare, and having suffered a serious loss of internal assets, Washington turned outside by organizing paramilitary death squads and the Colombian military to engage in cross border conflicts in alliance with the far-right regime of Álvaro Uribe. Colombia's military incursions led Venezuela to break economic ties, costing influential Colombian agro-business exporters and manufacturers' losses exceeding US$8 billion. Uribe backed off and signed a non-aggression accord with President Chávez, undermining the US 'proxy war' strategy. At this point Washington revised its tactics, returning to electoral politics and street fighting. Between 2008 and 2012, Washington channelled millions of dollars to finance electoral party politicians, NGOs, mass media outlets (newspapers, television and radio) and direct action saboteurs of public energy, electricity and power stations.

The US's 'internal' political offensive had limited success – a coalition of warring right-wing political groups elected a minority of officials, thus regaining an institutional presence. A Chávez-backed overtly socialist referendum was defeated (but by less than 1 per cent). NGOs gained influence in the universities and in some popular neighbourhoods, exploiting the corruption and ineptness of local Chavista elected officials. But the US strategy failed to dislodge or weaken the Chávez-led regime for several reasons. Venezuela's economy was riding the prolonged commodity boom. Oil prices were soaring above $100 a barrel, financing free health, education, housing, fuel and food subsidy programmes, undercutting the so-called 'grass-roots' agitation of US-funded NGOs.

The entire electoral strategy of the US depended on fomenting an economic crisis – and given the favourable world prices for oil on the world market it failed. As a result, Washington depended on non-market strategies to disrupt the socio-economic links between mass consumers and the Chávez government. Washington encouraged sabotage of the power and electrical grid. It encouraged hoarding and price gouging by commercial capitalists (supermarket owners). It encouraged smugglers to purchase thousands of tons of subsidized consumer goods and sell them across the border in Colombia. In other words, the US combined its electoral strategy with violent sabotage and illegal economic disruption.

This strategy was intensified with the onset of the economic crisis following the financial crash of 2009, the decline of commodity prices and the death of President Hugo Chávez. The US and its mass media megaphones went all-out to defend the protagonists and practitioners of illegal violent actions – branding arrested saboteurs, assassins, street fighters and assailants of public institutions as 'political prisoners'. Washington and its media branded the government 'authoritarian' for protecting the constitution. It accused the independent judiciary as biased. The police and military were labelled 'repressive' for arresting fire bombers of schools, transport and clinics. No violent crime or criminal behaviour by opposition politicos was exempt from Washington's scrofulous screeds about defending 'human rights'.

The crisis and collapse of oil prices greatly enhanced the opportunities for the US and its Venezuelan collaborator's campaign to weaken the government. Under these conditions the US relaunched a multi-pronged offensive to undermine and overthrow the newly elected Nicolas Maduro regime. Washington at first promoted the *via electoral* as the route to regime change, funding opposition leader Henrique Capriles.

After Capriles's electoral defeat, Washington resorted to an intense post-electoral propaganda campaign to delegitimize the voting outcome. It promoted street violence and sabotage of the electrical grid. For over a year the Obama regime refused to recognize the electoral outcome, accepted and recognized throughout Latin America and the world. In the subsequent congressional, gubernatorial and municipal elections the US-backed candidates suffered resounding defeats. Maduro's United Socialist Party of Venezuela (PSUV) won three-quarters of the governorships and retained a solid two-thirds majority in Congress.

Beginning in 2013, the US escalated its 'extra-parliamentary' offensive – a massive hoarding of consumer goods by wholesale distributors and retail supermarkets led to acute shortages, long lines, long waits and empty shelves. Hoarding, black-market speculation of the currency and wholesale smuggling of shipments of consumer goods across the border to Colombia (facilitated by opposition officials governing in border states and corrupt National Guard commanders) exacerbated shortages.

US strategists sought to drive a political wedge between the consumer-driven middle class and the popular classes and the Maduro government. Over time they succeeded in fomenting discontent within the lower middle class and directing it against the government rather than the big business elite and US-financed opposition politicians, NGOs and parties.

**238** Venezuela: in the eye of the storm

In February 2014, emboldened by growing discontent, the US moved rapidly towards a decisive confrontation. Washington backed the most violent extra-parliamentary opposition. Led by Leopoldo López, an ultra-rightist who openly called for a coup and launched a nationwide assault on public buildings, authorities and pro-democracy activists. As a result 43 people were killed and 870 injured – mostly government supporters and military and police officials – and hundreds of millions of dollars of damage was inflicted on schools, hospitals and state supermarkets.

After two months, the uprising was finally put down and the street barricades were dismantled – as even right-wing business operators suffered losses as their revenues diminished and there was no chance for victory.

Washington accelerated the pace of planning, organizing and executing the next coup throughout 2014. Taking advantage of the Maduro regime's lax or non-existent enforcement of laws forbidding 'foreign funding of political organizations', the US via the agency of the National Endowment for Democracy (NED) and its 'front groups' poured tens of millions of dollars into NGOs, political parties, leaders and active and retired military officials willing and able to bring about 'regime change' by means of a coup d'état.

Exactly one year following the violent uprising of 2014, on 14 February 2015, the US backed a civilian-military coup. The coup was thwarted by military intelligence and denunciations by lower level loyalist soldiers.

Two power grabs in a year is a clear indication that Washington is accelerating its move to establish a client regime. But what makes these policies especially dangerous, is not simply their proximity but the context in which they occur and the recruits who Washington is targeting. Unlike the coup of 2002, which occurred at a time of an improving economy, the most recent failed coup took place in the context of declining economic indicators – declining incomes, a devaluation that further reduced purchasing power, rising inflation (62 per cent), and plummeting oil prices.

In 2015 Washington embraced the 2002 strategy of combining multiple forms of attack including economic destabilization, electoral politics, sabotage and military penetration – all directed towards a military-civilian coalition seizing power.

## Obama's imperialist offensive against Venezuela

Venezuela today leads the anti-imperialist struggle in Latin America. This struggle, in the current form of the Bolivarian Revolution, according to President Maduro, can be traced back 26 years (27–28 February 1989) to the popular rebellion against the neo-liberal policies of the Carlos Andrés Pérez government that produced the *Caracazo* – the massacre by government security forces of at least 3,000 protesters. 'This was,' he noted (in a telephone conversation with the governor of the state Aragua), 'the beginning of the Bolivarian Revolution to escape the mistreatment [of the people], the pillaging and neo-colonialism, [and] the false democracy' of the republic (Petras, 2015). Venezuela under the leadership of Hugo Chávez, he noted – in a televised broadcast at the time – was the

Venezuela: in the eye of the storm **239**

first country in the region to say 'no' to the concerted effort of imperialist forces to convert the countries in the region into 'colonies of the IMF' and to reject capitalism in its current neo-liberalism form.

Maduro in this televised broadcast also alluded to the form that the anti-imperialist struggle would take under Chávez's leadership, that of the Bolivarian Revolution, or, as he put it: 'the miracle of the socialist revolution and *las misiones*'.

Obama, as it turned out, led the opposition to this 'miracle', labelling it the greatest threat to the security of the region and thus to the US. In confronting this threat and to bring about the required regime change, the US under President Obama escalated its efforts to overthrow the government, using its full arsenal of weapons short of the 'military option'. One of these weapons included mobilizing the large retailers to provoke artificial shortages and thus rebellion. Also, with the aid of the local and international mass media and corporate- and state-funded NGOs they accuse the Maduro government of being 'authoritarian'. Mobilizing the massive resources of the NED and other US-funded NGOs and self-styled human rights groups concerned with 'democratic development', the US launched and orchestrated a virulent propaganda campaign against the government for jailing oppositionists that have been exposed in their plotting of terrorist activity and a military coup – oppositionists like the mayor of Caracas, Antonio Ledesma, who, it was later revealed, signed a document endorsing a coup programmed for February 2015.

The staged propaganda campaign was designed to take advantage of the economic crisis to discredit the government by exaggerating the deterioration and labelling the government as incompetent.

The US government's second serious attempt to provoke a coup – the first being in April 2002 – was in February 2015 in the context of Operation Jericó, a US operation supported by Germany, Canada, Israel and the UK (Meyssan, 2015). The plan for this military operation kicked in on 12 February 2015. A aeroplane owned by Academi (formerly Blackwater), disguised with the insignia of the armed forces of Venezuela, would bomb the presidential palace in Caracas and kill President Nicolas Maduro. The conspirators planned to put into power former congressional deputy Maria Corina Machado and seek the support of several former Latin American presidents who would acclaim the necessity and legitimacy of the coup as an act of restoring democracy.

President Obama issued a clear warning and put it in writing in his new defence doctrine (National Security Strategy): 'We are on the side of citizens whose full exercise of democracy is in danger, as in the case of Venezuelans'. In reality, Venezuela, since the adoption of the 1999 constitution, has been one of the most democratic states in the world. Obama's bellicose rhetoric presaged a worst-case scenario in terms of the US government's attempts to impede Venezuela's march on the road of national independence and the redistribution of national wealth – towards the socialism of the twenty-first century. By 6 February 2015. Washington was in the process of finishing planning the overthrow of Venezuela's democratic institutions. The coup was planned for 12 February.

**240** Venezuela: in the eye of the storm

Operation Jericó had the oversight of the National Security Council, under the responsibility of Ricardo Zuniga. This 'diplomat' is the grandson of another Ricardo Zuniga, president of the National Party of Honduras, who organized the military coups of 1963 and 1972 on behalf of General López Arellano. The Ricardo Zuniga who worked in the Obama White House directed the CIA station in Havana from 2009–11, where he recruited agents and funded a feeble opposition against Fidel Castro.

As always in such operations Washington strove not to seem to be involved in the events that it led. The CIA organized and directed the coup through 'non-governmental organizations' or 'civil society': the National Endowment for Democracy (NED) and its two tentacles on the right and the left – the International Republican Institute (IRI) and the National Democratic Institute (NDI); Freedom House; and the International Centre for Non-Profit Law. Moreover, the US always uses its domestic clients as contractors in organizing or conducting certain aspects of the coup. This time at least Germany was an active participant, charged with the responsibility of ensuring the protection of citizens of NATO countries during the coup. As for Canada, an avid supporter of Obama's campaign against Venezuela, it was assigned control over Caracas's international airport. And Israel was put in charge of ensuring the murder of several Chavista personalities, while the UK was put in charge of propaganda for the coup, putting a 'democratic' spin on it. Finally, the US government planned to mobilize its political networks in securing recognition of the coup: in Washington, Senator Marco Rubio; in Chile, former president Sebastián Piñera; in Colombia, former presidents Álvaro Uribe Vélez; in Mexico, former presidents Felipe Calderón and Vicente Fox; and, in Spain, the former prime minister José María Aznar.

To justify the coup, the White House encouraged large Venezuelan companies to hoard their store of staples and sabotage the economy. The non-distribution of these products was aimed at causing large queues at the shops and the outbreak of riots provoked by the action of provocateurs infiltrated among disgruntled consumers. But the manoeuvre failed because, despite the artificially induced scarcity during January and February and the queues at the shops, Venezuelans did not riot or attack the shops as was hoped.

To strengthen the planned economic sabotage, on 18 December 2014 President Obama signed a decree imposing sanctions against Venezuela and several of its leaders. Officially Washington said it wanted to punish the persons responsible for the 'repression' of student demonstrations. But, in actual fact, since the beginning of the year Washington had been paying a salary – at four times the average income of Venezuelans – to gang members to engage them in assaulting the police. The pseudo-student riot led to the killing of 43 people, mostly police and regime supporters, and spread terror in the streets of Caracas.

The military action was put under the supervision of General Thomas W. Geary, from SOUTHCOM headquarters in Miami, and Rebecca Chavez, from the Pentagon. The actual military operation was subcontracted to Academi (formerly Blackwater), currently administered by Admiral Bobby R. Inman (former head of the NSA) and John Ashcroft (former Attorney General of the Bush administration). According to this part of the plan, a Super-Tucano military aircraft, with the registration N314TG, purchased by Academi in Virginia in 2008, was to be used. The plane, to be falsely identified with the insignia of the armed forces of Venezuela, would bomb the Miraflores presidential palace and other targets such as the headquarters of the Ministry of Defence, the intelligence directorate and the headquarters of Telesur, a multinational television channel created by the ALBA. The plane was parked in Colombia, the headquarters of the coup-makers, who were installed in the US Embassy in Bogota with the participation of US Ambassador Kevin Whitaker and his deputy, Benjamin Ziff.

Several senior officers, active and retired, had prepared a pre-recorded message to the nation announcing that they had seized power to restore order in the country. They were also expected to underwrite the transition plan, drafted by the Department of State and published on the morning of 12 February 2015 in *El Nacional*. The plan included the formation of a new government, led by former deputy Maria Corina Machado, president of Súmate, the association that organized and lost the recall referendum against President Hugo Chávez in 2004. Machado's funds came from the NED. Maria Corina Machado had been received with honours by President George W. Bush in the Oval Office of the White House on 21 March 2005. But, after being elected in 2011 as a representative from the state of Miranda, on 21 March 2014 Machado appeared before the OAS as head of the delegation of Panama to the continental forum and was immediately dismissed from her post as deputy for having violated Articles 149 and 191 of the Constitution of Venezuela.

Unfortunately for the coup-makers, Venezuelan military intelligence had under surveillance individuals suspected of having fomented a previous plot to assassinate President Maduro. On the night of 11 February the main leaders of the conspiracy, and an agent of the Israeli Mossad, were arrested and aerial protection of the Venezuelan capital was reinforced. Others involved were arrested on 12 February. On 20 February, the confessions of those arrested led to the arrest of another accomplice: the mayor of Caracas, Antonio Ledezma, a liaison officer with Israel. The coup had totally unravelled (but not without the attempt of the White House to accuse the Maduro regime of actions to subvert democracy).

When the plan of the parliamentary and extra-parliamentary opposition to overthrow the democratically elected Maduro government, by diverse measures including destabilizing the economy in an effort to provoke street violence and repression by the government, was discovered and made public, editorials in the *Washington Post* on 23 February and the *New York Times* on 14 February 2015 denounced the 'conspiracy' as a 'distraction' engineered by the government to divert attention away from the growing economic crisis, and denounced the government's response (arresting the plotters) as the actions of a 'repressive government'. They called on the government to resign and supported the opposition's call for Maduro to step down in favour of a regime that would implement the 'transition programme' elaborated and presented by the undemocratic and authoritarian opposition forces.

**242** Venezuela: in the eye of the storm

On 9 March 2015, Obama signed an executive order declaring Venezuela to be a threat to national security and US foreign policy. Why at this time did Obama declare a 'national emergency', claim that Venezuela represented a threat to US national security and foreign policy, assume executive prerogatives and decree sanctions against top Venezuelan officials in charge of national security? To answer this question it is essential to begin by addressing Obama's specious and unsubstantiated charges of Venezuela constituting an 'extraordinary threat to national security and foreign policy'.

First, the White House presented no evidence whatsoever. There were no Venezuelan missiles, fighter planes, warships, special forces, secret agents or military bases poised to attack US domestic facilities or its overseas installations. By contrast, the US had warships in the Caribbean, seven military bases just across the border in Colombia manned by over 2,000 US special forces, and air force bases in Central America. Washington has financed proxy political and military operations intervening in Venezuela with the intent of overthrowing the legally constituted and elected government.

Obama's claims resemble a ploy that totalitarian and imperialist rulers frequently use: accusing their imminent victims of the crimes they are preparing to perpetrate against them. No country or leader, friend or foe, supported Obama's accusations against Venezuela. His charge that Venezuela represented a 'threat' to US foreign policy requires clarification. First, which elements of US foreign policy are threatened? Venezuela has successfully proposed and supported several regional integration organizations, which are voluntarily supported by their fellow Latin American and Caribbean members. These regional organizations, in large part, replaced US-dominated organizations that served Washington's imperial interests. In other words, Venezuela supports alternative diplomatic and economic organizations, which its members believe would better serve their national interests. For example, Petrocaribe, a Central American and Caribbean association of countries supported by Venezuela, addresses the development needs of its members better than US-dominated organizations like the OAS or the so-called 'Caribbean Initiative'. And the same is true of Venezuela's support of CELAC (the Community of Latin American and Caribbean States) and UNASUR (the Union of South American Nations). These are Latin American organizations that exclude the dominating presence of the US and Canada and are designed to promote greater regional independence. Both ELAC and UNASUR, together with the G77 within the UN, and China, have denounced the Obama government's decree regarding Venezuela as a threat to regional and national security.

Obama's charge that Venezuela represents a threat to US foreign policy is an accusation directed at all governments that have freely chosen to abandon US-centred organizations and who reject US hegemony. In other words, what aroused Obama's ire and motivates his aggressive stance towards Venezuela is Caracas's political leadership in challenging US imperialist foreign policy.

## The 6 December 2015 election. What was at stake and what were the odds?

Hugo Chávez's first attempt to gain control of the state was by leading an armed rebellion of military officers against an oppressive government. But, having failed in this tactic, Chávez turned towards the institutional mechanism of democratic elections to achieve state power as a means of advancing his political project. Once Chávez gained state power by winning the December 1998 presidential elections he made maximum use of the state's legislative and executive powers to advance the project of a Bolivarian revolution that would work to bring about what he described as the 'socialism of the 21st century' (Chávez, 2007).[2] The project was to bring about socialism from above, by means of a policy of missions and support of a community-based strategy of socialist development, organizing communes and from below by empowering the poor in their communities to act for themselves.

Subsequently, the government made maximum advantage of its broad popular support by contesting a series of local and national elections, winning each one by an increasing plurality. The level of electoral support for the government and the Chavista project of the Bolivarian Revolution over the years was impressive, even after Chávez's death, when Maduro took over as head of state and government leader and went back to the people several times for an extension of the government's popular mandate.

The right-wing parliamentary and extra-parliamentary opposition to the Chavismo fervently supported the 2002 coup. It seems that when they orchestrated the assault on the Miraflores presidential palace they thought that Chavista supporters and the population would be indifferent to the usurpation of presidential power. They also actively supported – as did the US government – the antipatriotic strike by the executives of the state oil company on December 2002–February 2003, and more recently they supported the actions of ultra-rightists led by Leopoldo López, who openly called for a coup and launched a nationwide assault on public buildings, authorities and pro-democracy activists, leading to 43 deaths that were cynically blamed on the government.

Having failed in several coup attempts, and subsequently having lost one election after another, in the wake of the 2013 presidential elections the right-wing opposition turned up the heat on the government by opening up various new fronts in its class struggle and by changing some of its tactics. Among the new tactics was to orchestrate a shortage of basic consumer goods in order to provoke popular discontent and ire – to 'heat up the streets' (*calentar la calle*) by means of an orchestrated media campaign of disinformation (media terrorism); destabilization measures, articulating actions across the country with paramilitary actions orchestrated by Álvaro Uribe Vélez from Colombia; and contributing to an international disinformation and propaganda campaign designed to 'Satanize' Venezuela's socialist government and the Bolivarian Revolution, a campaign orchestrated by José Maria Aznar, former prime minister of Spain, in his capacity as a lieutenant of a legion of self-styled guardians of the Washington-based global campaign and fight for imperial controlled electoral regimes.

**244** Venezuela: in the eye of the storm

You only need to search the internet for 'Venezuelan Opposition Primaries+2015' to find a number of imperial-slanted propaganda articles in English from *Fox News*, *Yahoo*, *International Business Times* and *Reuters*, among others. All of these articles forecast that 'this is the best chance that the Venezuelan opposition has had in a decade to recoup control of the national parliament'. In other words, they continue to parrot politicians such as the secretary general of the Democratic Unity Round-table (MUD), Jesus 'Chuo' Torrealba. In a carbon copy of the last national elections for mayoralties, the argument was that, according to twice-defeated presidential candidate Henrique Capriles Radonski, the vote would be a plebiscite and Maduro would have to resign when the opposition won that vote. But, in fact, the opposition lost by 11 points to Chavismo and only won control of 24 per cent of the 335 mayoralties in the country. This was opposition defeat number 18 of 19 since Chávez won the presidency in December 1998. Evidently, after two years of an 'economic war' orchestrated by the far Right, many Venezuelans had come to realize that shortages, inflation, devaluation of the currency and other ills were manipulated if not created by the opposition and their gringo handlers, as had been the case in Bolivia and Argentina (Rosales, 2015).

In response to a spate of electoral defeats, the right-wing opposition to the government redoubled its tactical manoeuvres and began to experiment with a range of other tactics in its efforts to overthrow the government and return to power. In addition to contesting whatever elections with whatever forces they could muster, these tactics included economic warfare measures such as hoarding goods and sabotage, and reliance on massive support from the US, which poured millions of dollars into the coffers of the right-wing opposition in support of their electoral campaigns to oust the dictatorial regime and restore 'democracy', i.e. restore themselves to power. But none of these tactics worked because conditions did not favour them. However, the results of the mid-term referendum on the government's point towards a possible change in the correlation of forces in conditions of a deepening economic crisis and a deteriorating situation that the government had been unable to manage except by some ineffective attempts to regulate the market for welfare goods and counter-hoarding – preferring to rely on charges of economic warfare and sabotage and US imperialist intervention.

Ironically, it was a change made by the government to the constitution to mandate a mid-term referendum on any government's policies that created the political opening for the right-wing opposition forces. The stakes in the referendum, held in the context of the mid-term parliamentary elections on 6 December 2015 were high. It would either strengthen Maduro's mandate to deepen the Bolivarian Revolution, even under conditions of economic crisis, or it would strengthen the position of groups positioned on the far Right.

Both the government and the opposition came to the mid-term parliamentary elections in the hope and expectation that they would win. On the government's side were the evident gains made in the social condition of the popular classes after 15 years of efforts from both below and above to push the country in a socialist direction. The government has done much over the years to dramatically improve the social condition of the masses, including dramatically improved access to education and health services, and to housing, meeting the basic needs of the rural and urban poor, and lifting many thousands out of poverty. According to ECLAC data, the rate of poverty over the years was reduced by about two-thirds.

It was expected that the government could count on the support of around a third of the electorate whose condition improved immeasurably or were ideologically – and politically – committed to the government's vision of a socialist future, or the belief that things would improve or that the gains would be reversed if the government were to lose state power. On the other hand, the opposition counted on the widespread social discontent generated by the conditions of a protracted economic crisis, including runaway inflation and the shortage of consumer goods, exacerbated by the economic sabotage engineered by groups and enterprises in the private sector and the collapse of oil prices in recent years. According to several polls conducted just before the elections, the opposition would also be able to count on around 35 per cent of the electorate, leaving about a third of the electorate undecided or vacillating between the two electoral options.

Before the referendum both the government and the right-wing opposition made efforts to increase their electoral support. On the government's side, this meant more spending and infrastructure and social investment, as well as heated rhetoric about the non-democratic right-wing opposition and US intervention. The problem for the government, however, was its inability to confront the crisis and to control inflation, which had reached 200 per cent and was decimating the living standards of the working and popular classes, pushing many of them back into poverty. After losing the previous elections it now confronted a right wing-dominated Congress, which made it impossible to advance any progressive legislation and to rely on governing by decree. As for the right-wing opposition, they had an easier path towards increased electoral support, paved by themselves and US government support in the form of economic sabotage and endless propaganda, as well as a deteriorating economic situation of the middle and lower classes that were particularly susceptible to ideological appeal and propaganda about the current problems and impending disaster of socialist policies.

The US was particularly aggressive in its support of the forces of opposition and reaction. It intervened in the political process in diverse ways, including declaring Venezuela a threat to the security of the US. It poured millions of dollars into the opposition referendum campaign, channelling this money to the opposition via the National Endowment for Democracy and other NGOs. Washington's plan was for the opposition to gain control of the Congress and to generate the conditions that would lead to the removal of the president – a strategy of a soft coup that had worked in Honduras and Paraguay, and that was also in the works in Brazil.

As it turned out the opposition won the congressional mid-term elections, gaining the support of 52.1 per cent of the electorate. This was evidently a setback to the government's political project, although the government put a positive spin on the electoral outcome, viewing it as a challenge. The 'fight for socialism', Maduro declared, would continue. Even so, a poll of voters showed that up to 90.9

per cent considered the economic and political situation to be 'bad', and this included 75 per cent of Chavista supporters. As for the image held by the electorate of political leaders Henry Ramos Allup, current speaker of the National Assembly and former leader of the social democratic Democratic Action Party, was viewed in positive terms by 51.1 per cent of the electorate, while Leopoldo López, the currently imprisoned opposition leader, and Henrique Capriles (of the Justice First party), seen as the parliamentary opposition's 'best democratic hope' – i.e. for a 'democratic' alternative to right-wing violence – had positive images of 47.8 and 47 per cent, respectively. Maduro meanwhile received a positive rating from only 33.1 per cent of the voters who were polled.

## Venezuela in the crosshairs

In just the years 2014–15 the National Endowment for Democracy (NED) channelled to the Venezuelan opposition almost US$3 million in support of their electoral campaign for the mid-term parliamentary elections. For example, US$125,000 was turned over to the opposition group Súmate, created by the NED in 2003 to lead the recall referendum against President Hugo Chávez. Another US$400,000 was channelled towards a programme to 'assist members of the National Assembly in the development of policies'. And over US$40,000 was dedicated to 'monitoring the National Assembly'. This raises the question as to what right an organization of one country has to 'monitor' the legislative body of another. Worse still when organizations of one country are financed by a foreign government to spy on their own government. But this is par for the course for the United States, which has taken upon itself the responsibility for democratic development across the world as the leader of the free world, and to intervene in the political affairs of any country that is deemed to be a security threat to its national interest – and this includes the deployment of any and all of its state powers to bring about regime change when and where it is called for.

The agency of the NED, one of US imperialism's most effective weapons for 'democratic development' (the spread of US values and the idea of democracy), in promoting the parliamentary and non-parliamentary opposition to the Chavista regime includes the channelling of close to half a million dollars (US$410,155) to improve the strategic and communication capacity of targeted political organizations by creating and promoting alternative communication and media outlets (as if the right-wing of the opposition did not already have at their disposal diverse media outlets that are all too keen to disseminate their ideas and projects). This includes the financing of diverse social networks to project an anti-government vision in the social media and influence public opinion both within Venezuela and abroad. The NED has channelled another US$73,654 to 'strengthen the technical capacity' of targeted opposition groups and promote 'freedom of expression' and human rights via Twitter, and US$63,421 for 'training [of groups] in the effective use of social networks and alternative media'. The social networks embedded in what the NED and USAID term 'civil society' have in effect been converted into a battlefield in the imperialist class war that the US state has launched against Venezuela.

In this context it is not a coincidence or at all surprising that the US and its allies over the last year have strongly criticized the Maduro government for presumed violations of human rights. The NED has channelled close to half a million dollars to the opposition to finance their 'documentation and dissemination' of information regarding the human right situation in Venezuela, and in preparation of denunciations of the government's violation of human rights in the international arena.

In addition to the millions of dollars channelled through the NED, a foundation created by the US Congress in 1983 to 'do the work that the CIA cannot do publically', the State Department and its Agency for International Cooperation (USAID), funnelled more than US$15 million to opposition groups in Venezuela during the period 2014–15. In the State Department's budget for overseas operations for 2016, which began in October 2015, US$5.5 million was set aside to 'defend and strengthen the democratic practices, institutions and values that advance the respect for human rights in Venezuela'. According to the budget already approved by Congress, a large part of this money will be used to 'help civil society promote institutional transparency, the democratic process and the defence of human rights'.

## Conclusion

How is it possible that a mediocre opposition without a political programme beyond a desire for revenge against Chavism achieved such a favourable result in the 2015 parliamentary elections? There are undoubtedly a number of reasons for this result and the current political situation, some of which relate to the agency of US imperialism and the enemy within, and some caused by contradictions and mistakes of the revolutionary process itself.

Maduro was possibly right when he pointed out, early in the morning following the 6 December 2015 parliamentary mid-term elections, where the opposition garnered over 50 per cent of the popular vote, that with this result the economic war launched by the right-wing opposition had triumphed, setting the counter-revolution on the brink of achieving the power so longed for by these groups and their masters in Washington.

The economic war launched by the right-wing opposition forces, and financed by the US, translates into women and men anxious to feed their children having to endure long hours of waiting outside the supermarkets, the lack of milk, flour, toilet paper, soap and other products that are criminally kept under lock and key by the big economic groups and companies, or smuggled to Colombia. One has to live this situation to understand the frustration, anger and despair that this situation causes, which is not necessarily directed at the unscrupulous millionaire entrepreneurs and actual operators of these lethal strategies linked to a most despicable Right, but illogically at the government regime.

The second key negative factor was the Chavista policy of depending on oil for 95 per cent of its exports and the terrible losses resulting from the decline of prices from $100 a barrel to $35. The extractive strategy and the failure to diversify the economy led to shortages, inflation and economic recession.

**248** Venezuela: in the eye of the storm

Given the heightened level of class consciousness acquired over the course of a 15-year revolutionary process, it is understandable that Venezuelans would demand that the government give immediate solution to the economic crisis and not to hesitate if this means further nationalization or filling the jails with commercial criminals and traitors, or the expropriation of their ill-gotten gains. To acknowledge the government's inability to redress these problems and to respond to the concerns of the populace led to despair – or, as it turned out, electoral support for the opposition in the hope that that the class war might be brought to an end.

But there are other reasons for the success of the right-wing opposition in gaining the support of that one-third of vacillating electors who can always be swayed either to the right or the left. One of these is what Golinger (2015) describes as

> the deadly cascade of lies coming from local and foreign media, creators of imaginary scenarios, managers of destabilization manoeuvres and masters of the production of new 'leaders' – like imprisoned coup-maker Leopoldo López – who appeal to the institutionalization of the oppressors as victims.

Another reason for the electoral success of the right-wing opposition to the government and its political project is the anti-Chavist international campaign orchestrated by an imperialist coalition that includes Aznar, Felipe González, Pastrana, Tuto Quiroga and Uribe Vélez. And we should not underestimate the impact of the machinations of the US administration and the offensive launched against Venezuela by President Obama.

Imperialism is undoubtedly the main enemy of the revolutionary process under way in Venezuela and elsewhere, which, in the case of Venezuela, is on the brink of failing. On the other hand, US imperialism is a two-edged sword that could very well be turned against its wielders and be used to bring the Revolution back from the brink by helping to reconstruct an anti-hegemonic bloc of popular forces – to harness the revolutionary forces and protect Venezuela's social conquests, the *misiones* and *comunas*, the advances made in poverty eradication and education, the housing projects and the redistribution of land and wealth.

## Notes

1 These socialist measures included the nationalization of enterprises in strategic sectors of the economy (the oil sector was already a state monopoly) and the creation of a system of community councils and cooperatives. The regime's anti-imperialist measures included the promotion of a series of anti-imperialist regional institutions such as ALBA (which today serves not only as an alternative regional trade regime but as a clearing-house for a regional alliance of social movements). Other anti-imperialist institutions created at the behest or with the instigation of Hugo Chávez are UNASUR, CELAC, Petrocaribe, Telesur and el Banco del Sur. Together these institutions constitute what might be described as an alternative world/regional order, a regional socialist system.
2 According to Lebowitz (2015), Chávez's ideological commitment towards socialism and the revolution was formed while in prison for having staged a military rebellion.

## References

Chávez, H. R. (2007). 'El socialismo del siglo XXI', in N. Kohan (ed.) *Introducción al pensamiento socialista*. Bogotá: Ocean Sur.

Fierro, A. (2016). 'Las tres derechas'. *Rebelión*, 21 September. Available at: www.rebelion.org/noticia.php?id=216988 [accessed 22 September 2016].

Golinger, E. (2015). 'Venezuela: A coup in real time'. *Counterpunch*, 2 February. Available at: www.counterpunch.org/2015/02/02/venezuela-a-coup-in-real-time [accessed 1 April 2016].

Lebowitz, M. (2007). 'Venezuela: A good example of the bad Left of Latin America'. *Monthly Review*, 59(3), July–August. Available at: http://monthlyreview.org/2007/07/01/venezuela-a-good-example-of-the-bad-left-of-latin-america/ [accessed 12 March 2016].

Lebowitz, M. (2015). *The path towards the socialism of the 21st century in Venezuela*. IDS Working Paper, 20 November. Halifax: Saint Mary's University.

Meyssan, T. (2015). 'Falla el putsch de Obama en Venezuela'. *VoltaireNet*, 23 February. Available at: www.voltairenet.org/article186818.html [accessed 24 September 2016].

Petras, J. (2015). 'El análisis de James Petras en CX36–15feb29.docx'. *El Jorope*, 28 February. Transcript available from author: jpetras@binghamton.edu.

Rosales, A. (2015). 'Venezuelan opposition setting new records in a democratic disaster'. *Axis of Logic*, 20 May. Caracas. Available at: http://axisoflogic.com/artman/publish/Article_70438.shtml [accessed 17 September 2016].

Veltmeyer, H. (2014). *Human development: Lessons from the Cuban Revolution*. Halifax: Fernwood.

# 12

# THE RETURN OF THE RIGHT

After the elections in Argentina that brought Mauricio Macri to power, the parliamentary coup against Dilma Roussef in Brazil, a deep economic crisis in Venezuela, the end of the primary commodities boom that served to finance progressive post-neo-liberal reform, and enhanced support from the US centre of imperial power, the Right across Latin America sought to build momentum for a return to power. But, although now on the defensive on the fronts of both economic development and electoral politics, the Left is counter-attacking. The years ahead into the new future augur a renewed and vigorous class struggle, albeit with a very uncertain outcome. This chapter lays out the possible shape and some of the likely conditions of this outcome.

## Argentina: the rise of the hard Right

The resurgence of the Right and the class struggle from above has found its most intense, comprehensive and retrograde expression in Argentina with the election of Mauricio Macri. During the first two months in office, through the arbitrary assumption of emergency powers, Macri reversed by decree a multitude of progressive socio-economic policies passed by the previous regime, and has sought to purge public institutions of independent voices. Facing a hostile majority in Congress, he seized legislative powers and proceeded to name two Supreme Court judges in violation of the constitution. He purged all the ministries and agencies of perceived critics and appointees of the previous government and replaced those officials with loyalist neo-liberal functionaries. Popular movement leaders were jailed and former cabinet members were prosecuted.

Parallel to the reconfiguration of the state, President Macri launched a neo-liberal counter-revolution with a 40 per cent devaluation of the currency, which raised prices of the basic canasta by 30 per cent; the termination of an export tax for all agro-mineral exporters (except soya farmers); a salary and wage cap 20 per cent below the rise in the cost of living; a 400 per cent increase in electrical bills and a 200 per cent increase in transport; large-scale firing of public and private employees; strike-breaking using rubber bullets; preparations for large-scale privatizations of strategic economic sectors; and a 6.5 billion dollar payout to vulture-fund debt holders and speculators – a 1,000 per cent return – while contracting new debts.

Macri's high-intensity class warfare is intended to reverse the social welfare and progressive policies implemented by the Kirchner regimes over the past 12 years. To do so he launched a virulent new version of the class struggle from above, following several twists and turns in a long-term neo-liberal cycle pattern that included:

1   a period of authoritarian military rule (1966–72), which was accompanied by intense class struggle from below, leading to a period of democratic elections (1973–76);
2   a period of military dictatorship and intense class struggle from above (1976–82), which resulted in the 'disappearances' and murders of 30,000 workers and activists;
3   a negotiated transition (in 1983), leading to a period of liberal democratic electoral politics, a hyper-inflationary crisis and the institution of a harsh neo-liberal policy regime (1989–2000);
4   a period of crisis and insurrectionary class struggle from below that led to the collapse of the neo-liberal regime (2001–03), the formation of a centre-left post-neo-liberal 'progressive regime' based on inclusionary state activism, a labour–capital–regime social pact and a neo-developmentalist model as per the post-Washington Consensus (2003–15); and
5   the election and formation of an authoritarian neo-liberal regime, initiating or presaging a period of intense class struggle from above.

Macri's strategic perspective is to deploy all of the powers of the state, including the police–military apparatus, so as to consolidate a new power bloc of local agro-mineral interests and banking oligarchs, foreign bankers and investors, and to reactivate the accumulation process by cheapening the cost of labour and massively increasing profits. Macri's election to the presidency signalled a new phase or cycle in the imperialist class war launched against labour from above in the 1970s in the form of military dictatorship.

Ironically, the roots of the rise of the neo-liberal power bloc can be found in the practices and policies of the previous Kirchner–Fernández regimes. Their policies were designed to overcome the capitalist crises of 2000–02 by channelling mass discontent towards social reforms, stimulating agro-mineral exports and increasing living standards via progressive taxes, electricity and food subsidies, and pension increases. As noted above, the progressive policies of the Kirchners, like those implemented by other 'progressive' regimes in the region, were based on the boom in commodity prices. When these collapsed the capital–labour co-existence pact dissolved and the Macri-led business–middle class–foreign capital alliance was well placed to take advantage of the demise of the model.

The class struggle from below was severely weakened by the labour alliance with the Kirchner regime. This was not because labour benefitted economically but because the pact demobilized the mass organizations of the 2001–03 period. Over the course of the next 12 years, labour entered into sectoral negotiations (*paritarias*), mediated by a 'friendly government'. Class consciousness was replaced by sectoral allegiances and bread-and-butter issues. Labour unions lost their capacity to wage class struggle from below – or even influence sectors of the popular classes. Labour was vulnerable and is in a weak position to confront President Macri's virulent neo-liberal counter-reform offensive.

Nevertheless, the extreme measures adopted by Macri within a few months in power – the deep cuts in purchasing power of wages, spiralling inflation and the mass firings – have already led a renewal of the class struggle from below. Strikes by teachers and public employees over salaries and firings have flared up in response to the barrage of public-sector cuts and arbitrary executive decrees. Sporadic mass demonstrations were called by social and human rights movements in response to Macri's dismantling of the institutions prosecuting military officials responsible for the killing and disappearance of 30,000 victims during the 1976–83 'dirty war'.

As the Macri regime proceeds to deepen and extend his regressive measures, designed to entice capital with higher profits by lowering the cost of labour as well as business taxes and living standards, and as inflation soars and the economy stagnates due to the decline of public investment and consumption, the class struggle from below is very likely to intensify: general strikes and related forms of direct action have emerged by the end of the first half-year of the Macri regime.

Large-scale class-based organizations capable of engaging in intense class struggle from below but weakened by the decade-long 'corporate model' of the Kitchener era will take time to reconstruct. The question is when and what it will take to organize a class-wide (national) political movement which can move beyond an electoral repudiation of Macri-allied candidates in upcoming legislative, provincial and municipal elections.

## Brazil: a new phase in the class struggle?

On 16 January 2016, the national leadership (*coordinación nacional*) of the Rural Landless Workers movement of Brazil (MST), which in the 1990s had mobilized the most powerful anti-capitalist land reform movement in Latin America, announced that the MST, together with the working classes across the world, was entering a new period of class struggle – a new phase in the global class war (Stedile, 2016). In the analysis made by the leadership, conditions of the current conjuncture included a capitalist system in crisis – a profound and protracted crisis whose social outcomes are impossible to predict – a dramatic expansion of uneven development and social inequalities, the concentration of wealth and income across the world and intensified use of the state's repressive apparatus and the projection of imperial

The return of the Right **253**

power. The crisis is multidimensional. Two important dimensions of this crisis insofar as Latin America – and Brazil – is concerned are (i) the exhaustion of the neo-developmentalist model used by the progressive regimes in the region to make public policy; and (ii) the downward turn in the commodities boom, which has pushed both Brazil and Argentina into a deepening recession – with negative economic growth rates since 2012, down to 3.8 per cent in 2015 and no sign of a recovery in 2016 (indeed a contraction of 3.6 per cent is predicted).

The MST, however, is not alone in this assessment of the economic situation and the balance of forces in the class struggle. Another assessment, typical of many groups on the political Left, was provided by Valter Pomar, a sociologist connected to the left wing of the PT and now a representative of an emerging 'popular front' (Pomar, 2015). The gist of Pomar's assessment, which is more or less representative of the 'mainstream' political left which has positioned itself in support of the construction of a popular front within the working class, can be summarized as follows.

The year 2015 is nearly over. What was the role of Brazil Popular Front in 2015? What is the current situation in the class struggle? And what challenges await us in 2016? As Pomar sees it:

1 The main feature of 2015 was the offensive of the elite against the popular sectors. This offensive had different protagonists (the reactionary middle class, big business, the right-wing parties, the media oligopoly, segments of the state apparatus – with emphasis on the judiciary, public prosecutors, the federal police and the armed forces) and had multiple targets (labour rights, social rights, democratic freedoms, women, blacks, youth especially the periphery, social movements, leftist parties, government policy, the presidential term).

2 The offensive of the elite did not have a single command, or adopt just one tactic. On the contrary, since the beginning of 2015, the elites were divided around two tactics: those who considered most important the recessionary fiscal adjustment, which would have the side effect of wearing the Dilma government and the left, helping to create the environment for the elites' candidates to win in 2016 and 2018; and those who considered it a priority to create the conditions to immediately stop the tenure of President Dilma, Lula and the PT ban, in order to take full control of the federal government.

3 Despite tactical differences, the offensive of the elite was and continues to be animated by common strategic objectives: to realign Brazil to the United States (away from BRIC and Latin American and Caribbean integration); reduce the wages and incomes of ordinary people (decreasing budgets of social policies, changing labour laws, reducing rights without adjusting salaries and pensions, causing unemployment and crunch); and reduce people's access to democratic freedoms (criminalizing politics, social movements and leftist parties, *partidarizar* justice, expand military–police terrorism, especially against the poor outskirts of residents and blacks, subordinating the secular state to religious fundamentalism and assaulting the rights of women, ordinary people and indigenous populations).

4   Throughout 2015, the elites within the dominant and ruling class adopted various tactics but maintained their strategy unity. The popular camp, in turn, was divided both in strategy and in tactics, with different readings of international, continental and national political situations, different positions across the offensive tactics of the elites and different strategic alternatives.

5   Despite this, the year 2015 began with 'drumsticks' dominating the streets and ended with the popular sectors dominating the streets. And while the year began with the ultra-rightist Joaquim Levy in charge of the treasury it ended with his dismissal as minister of finance. In other words, although the elites continued to have the political initiative, and although the conflicts and dangers remain intense, in 2015 Christmas Eve was better than Epiphany.

6   Nothing has only one explanation. The year ended better than it started for several reasons, two in particular: in December 2015 the elites experienced a moment of strong division, while the popular camp unified its actions.

7   The division within the elite occurred when the speaker of the house, Deputy Eduardo Cunha, who is still in post, in order to protect the personal interests of the elite triggered the impeachment process, used the well-known 'manoeuvres' regime when composing both the commission that would review the impeachment request and the Congressional Board of Ethics. While the elites supported the initiative, the impeachment process was born under the stigma of a coup motivated by criminal objectives. As I said of the elites in an editorial in a major newspaper, Cunha became 'dysfunctional'. As a result, the demonstrations of 13 December 2015 represented a dismal failure for the elite in their tactical manoeuvre against the sitting president.

8   The beginning of the impeachment proceedings, marked by criminal characteristics, confronted forces in the popular sectors with a dilemma: to seek unity in action or defeat without penalty. True, some minority groups (not just the left-wing opposition, but also those within the party system and the government) 'turned up their noses' against the idea of unity. But the vast majority of progressive, democratic and leftist sectors initiated and engaged in a spontaneous process that produced a great measure of unity, which was visible in the heterogeneous character and massive scale of the demonstrations of 16 December 2015.

9   Expressions of the 16 December demonstrations were dominated by a call for unity around the following slogans: 'against the coup for democracy!' (what analysts have conceptualized as a 'soft' coup, along the lines experimented with by the hard Right in Venezuela, Paraguay and Honduras), 'Away with Cunha!' and 'For a new economic policy'. Mobilized by three rather than a single slogan, every sector in this popular front was left the freedom to establish their own hierarchies and links between the different issues.

10  Soon after the demonstrations, President Dilma received the support of the Frente Brasil Popular (the FBP), the Supreme Court defeated the most aberrant aspects of the procedures adopted by Eduardo Cunha, and the minister of finance, Joaquim Levy, was forced out of office. These were measures that did

not result from the success of the 16 December mobilization but that resulted in a positive balance for the popular sectors at the end of a year marked by an elite offensive.

11 What was the role of the FBP in the process? Without prejudice to a more detailed balance sheet, while taking care not to incite a divisive debate that might affect a unity of purpose and action, we consider that the Brazil Popular Front, as well as each of the organizations and activists belonging to it, contributed greatly to the process described above. Especially because from the beginning we believe in unity, bet on social mobilization, and bet on the combination of slogans. This was the path that led us to the current result.

12 However, the FBP did not want to have a great past ahead of them. Our greatest challenges in the future are: the defence of rights, the defence of democracy, the defence of national sovereignty, the struggle for structural reforms and the defence of Latin American integration. And, as in 2015, the years 2016 and 2017 will see major clashes between elites and popular sectors.

13 For one thing, the struggle against the coup-making activities of the hard Right continues and will continue even with the ousting of Rousseff and the PT regime. The issue is not to just remove Eduardo Cunha from the presidency of the Chamber. The elites will try to place someone more 'functional' in the position, and certainly some groups will seek to continue the impeachment process. Moreover, the importance assumed by the Supreme Court and the role that the court has assigned to the Senate constituted a 'mixed blessing'. This is because you cannot take away from the people the right to elect the President, although the impeachment and ousting of Dilma Rousseff in April 2016 showed the power of the Right in its control of the legislative apparatus to subvert the 'will of the people' expressed in the electoral process.

14 The struggle for an alternative economic policy continues. Again, the issue is not to just replace the minister of finance. We must take action against policy measures that interrupt the recessionary fiscal adjustment, and restore policies that secure and advance social and labour rights and encourage employment and development. We must destroy the dictatorship of finance capital. If the government insist on economic policy that causes, directly or indirectly, unemployment, recession and lack of assistance, it will become much harder to defeat the elite offensive.

15 The struggle for structural reforms continues. Without structural reforms, the elites will still have the means to sabotage, stop and try to reverse the processes of change in our country. Without structural reforms, most of the Brazilian people remain without enjoying the riches it produces. Without structural reforms, our development will remain conservative, dependent and short of potential for the needs of the country.

16 The struggle for regional integration continues. The advance of the elites and the hard Right in countries such as Argentina and Venezuela magnifies the importance of Brazil remaining firm in defending the process of South American and Latin Caribbean integration, especially Mercosur, UNASUR and CELAC.

17  The struggle for the construction of the Brazil Popular Front continues. You have to launch the FBP in all states, in all Brazilian cities. Encourage instances of FBP to have a regular operation, able to offer a welcoming policy discussion space, especially for the hundreds of thousands of militants who are not yet part of, nor intend to take part in any partisan organization or popular, trade union or youth movement. Investing energies in the creation of unitary communication space, built from the cooperation between existing instruments. And keep betting on a unity of action with other sectors and fronts and discuss how to deal with the 2016 elections.

18  We should not rule out that in the 2015 holiday season the Right will promote some spectacular action, for example, the so-called *Lava-Jato*. However, without lowering our guard and not to rest on our laurels, we can say we fought the good fight and we were successful because we are on the right side and adopted the correct policy. We will seek to do the same in 2016.

This is the analysis and conclusions drawn by Pomar and the left wing of the PT in the current conjuncture. What can be said about it? One thing is that they were wrong on most counts of fact and outcome. To wit:

1  The PT was deeply involved in corruption and discredited among many popular sectors, as evidenced in the mass protests.

2  President Dilma Rousseff was ousted by what many observers have described as a coup – a soft coup in which Roussef's PT parliamentary allies abandoned ship and joined the opposition.

3  The model and disastrous economic policies that tied the PT to agro-mineral exporters were not sustainable and led to a precipitous fall in jobs and income in 2016–17.

4  The Brazilian Left and the mass popular movements that protested against the coup, corruption and the government's disastrous economic policies in 2016 are independent and generally critical of the PT.

In effect, Pomar speaks for few activists outside of his rather reduced ideological circle. The demise of the coup, if it comes about, would largely be the result of a judiciary inquiry and mass protests, and not the action of a corruption-infested PT.

## Bolivia: radical populism, post-development or political coitus interruptus

The election of Maurice Macro in December 2015 was a clear signal of the beginning of the end of the latest progressive cycle in Latin American class politics. And, as outlined above, the downturn of Brazil's economy since 2012 has also activated a turn to the right in Brazilian class politics, as well as a new phase in the class struggle. Another sign that the progressive cycle has come to a temporary end was the failure of Evo Morales to get popular support for the proposal to modify the constitution so as to allow him to contest the next presidential elections and possibly extend his term in office.

The failure to win the constitutional referendum does not necessarily mean the ascension of the Right to power, or even the end of the progressive cycle in Bolivia. As Morales himself noted in a news conference held a few days after the referendum results were published (24 February 2016), it meant that they – i.e. the forces for progressive change – had admittedly lost an important battle, but by no means the war. Indeed, Morales continued, 'We will continue to fight harder, with more unity and experience'. But losing this battle also meant that in order for the progressive forces to overcome this setback in the struggle for change, and to retain power for the battles ahead of them in this struggle, there was a pressing need for the regime to engage in a process of critical self-reflection – something patently absent to date.

Some issues to reflect upon were immediately evident. One was the role of the US state – 'imperialism', in the discourse of class politics – in engineering, as well as financing the opposition and the 'no' campaign in the referendum. As the Argentine analyst Atilio Borón noted in the lead-up to the referendum (and he was by no means alone in this denunciation): 'A conspiracy against the process of change that Evo Morales leads is underway. It has its epicentre in Washington DC and is implemented by Bolivian and foreign political operators' (Borón, 2016). However, it was as evident that losing the referendum also reflected a swing to the right and a change in the correlation of class forces that pointed towards a fundamental failure of the regime to bring about any substantive change in the economic model used to guide macroeconomic policy over 10 years in power.

Despite rhetorical reference to an entirely new agenda based on an indigenous cosmovision of 'living well' in social solidarity and harmony with nature, and rhetorical reference to an ongoing 'socialist revolution' and a 'patriotic agenda' for the industrialization of the country, the country had not managed to escape the trap of an extractivist strategy of national development and its relation of dependence on foreign direct investment. Indeed, the Morales–García Linera regime embraced this strategy, and even today continues to rely on foreign investors and the multinational corporations in the extractive sector for an important source of fiscal revenues.

The problem that the Morales–García Linera regime needs to confront in the process of self-reflection and continuing class struggle is itself – a problem that is rooted in the beginnings of the regime.

Evo Morales came to power by leading a popular uprising and then channelling the forces of progressive or revolutionary change in the popular sector – political forces that had been mobilized by the indigenous social movement – into an electoral contest. Having won this electoral contest, backed by the popular masses, the regime initiated a process of partial nationalization in the strategic sector of fossil fuels (gas and oil), declaring these resources to be the property of the 'people'. This nationalization policy was not designed to lead to the socialization of production.

Rather, it served to increase the capacity of the state to strike a better deals with foreign capital – to exact a greater share of the value of the social product on the global market, providing the government with enhanced fiscal resources that it could use to finance a process of inclusive development, i.e. reduce the rate of poverty. As it turned out, the regime was able to lift a substantial number of poor people out of poverty, reducing the rate of poverty by 50 per cent from 2007 to 2012, but the process did not lead to any substantive or structural change or decreased dependence on foreign capital and multinational corporations to extract the country's strategic resources and bring them to market.

What has kept Morales in power for close to 10 years with an extraordinarily high level of popular support is inclusionary state activism based on the use of resource rents to finance a programme of welfare benefits and conditional cash transfers to the poor. However, he did not change the fundamental social structure of wealth and income distribution or touch the power structure: 100 large families still control most of the productive land in Santa Cruz and the export market. Over two dozen large foreign companies still control production and occupy very lucrative positions in the strategic sector of oil and gas extraction and mining. Manufacturers still earn a lot of money because wages continue to rise incrementally.

The government's social programmes were financed by the high prices of oil and gas, metals and other commodities, but when prices began to fall in 2013 the regime lost its ability to maintain this balance between popular support and the incentives provided to capital. And in this context other factors came into play – problems that affected many supporters of the regime, hoping against hope that the revolutionary process would succeed. One was the contradiction between a post-neo-liberal and post-development radical discourse on living well and a development model predicated on foreign direct investment, which provided privileged access of extractive capital to the country's productive resources but was destructive of both 'mother nature' and indigenous livelihoods. Other problems included a failure to institutionalize a process of revolutionary change based on the ideology of living well in social solidarity and harmony with nature. Increasing the weight of technocrats and bureaucrats in the state apparatus, indigenous elements in the MAS's social base were marginalized, with policies designed to reassure foreign investors and international financial institutions rather than deal with the country's social problems.

These policies led to Bolivia maintaining the largest international currency reserves of any country in the region. Meanwhile, 40 per cent of the population continued to live in poverty – immiserated by policies that favoured capital over the population. Even though many peasant and union leaders stayed on side, consumed by the rot that had begun to infect the MAS party apparatus, discontent spread within the social base of the movement as well as the middle class. This was undoubtedly reflected in the failure of Evo Morales to win the referendum. The government had counted on Morales's popularity – as well as populist and anti-imperialist demagoguery – to win the referendum, so much so that Morales had declared that he would not stand for re-election if he did not garner at least 70 per cent of the vote. But the evidence provided by the government regarding the role of the US in the financing of the 'no' campaign was not enough to overcome the widespread disenchantment with the regime, the contradictions between the government's populist and indigenist *pachamama* discourse and its actual policies, the evident corruption of MAS officials and the failure of the government to deliver on its promises.

Government officials like to believe that the failure to win the referendum reflected the machinations of foreign intervention and the right-wing opposition within the oligarchy. However, even a cursory review of the voting dynamics shows that the problem is not simply the oligarchy or US imperialism but rather the failure of the regime to deliver on its key promises as well as the corruption of MAS officials and the lack of popular consultation on key policy measures. For example, El Alto, a proletarian city on the highlands of La Paz that was a former bastion of support for the regime, turned against Morales in the referendum, with almost 50 per cent voting 'no'. Was this the product of foreign intervention or the machinations of the oligarchy and the US-funded right-wing opposition? Or was it the result of problems internal to the regime? Did it reflect a pendulum swing of support away from progressive policies towards the reactionary policies advocated by the right-wing opposition? What allowed a divided right, confronted with an unexpected victory in its 'no' campaign, to attempt and pretend to lead and represent the broad masses of workers and peasants who in actual fact voted not for them but for democracy – voting against the corruption of the MAS and even the vice president, but not against the government's policies as such, and even less against Evo Morales?

Without a doubt, Morales's prestige as a winner and mediator was diminished as a result of the referendum. On the other hand, the government has another few years of life (the next elections are not until 2019). And Evo Morales certainly retains the mass support to complete his current term of office – and the time to bring about a revolutionary process of transformative change. But this would require a radical change of direction and politics – abandonment of the government's pact with global extractive capital, mobilization of the forces of popular resistance in support of an anti-capitalist policy regime, and engagement with the class struggle.

## The social foundations of the new Latin American Right

A new Right with distinctive characteristics and electoral support is emerging in the world and has emerged in Latin America. To grasp the nature of this new Right – so as to avoid simplistic judgements and combat it effectively – it is useful to differentiate Carlos Menem, who embodied the old Right (espousal of neo-liberalism but respectful of Peronism and the legislature) from Mauricio Macri, a disciple of neo-liberalism but wedded to the extractive model of capitalist development, even more than the Kirchners (i.e. plunder, rather than labour exploitation, as the modus operandi of capitalism), and willing to discard any vestige of democracy.

Something similar can be said of the Venezuelan Right. It tried to seize executive power without regard to the constitution. As for the new Brazilian Right today in opposition to the PT regime, it can also be distinguished from the political Right in the 1990s behind the neo-liberal/privatizing regimes of Fernando Henrique Cardoso, who was constrained by providing a social democratic veil over his neo-liberal policies. As Mendes Pereira and Alentejano argue in Chapter 6, the right-wing opposition to the PT regime has no such qualms or need for subterfuge. It is outright undemocratic and, while prepared to play the democratic political game, views the trappings of liberal democracy as a hindrance rather than an institutional means of achieving its agenda. Like the Venezuelan Right it is fundamentally authoritarian and quite prepared to resort to violence and force in achieving executive power. The new Latin American Right has its reference points in Washington and the neo-liberal model of free-market capitalism. It is not above strict conformity with the full application of radical structural adjustment policies even as it claims autonomy in defending its own agro-mining interests, as well as the full use of the state apparatus to do so.

Perhaps what is most distinctive about the new Right, notwithstanding its instrumental view of the state and disdain for democracy, is its appeal to and roots in 'civil society', an amalgam of associations and interest groups formed in the broad expanse between the state and the family. In the 1980s and 1990s, 'civil society' took form as a complex of non-governmental organizations (NGOs). They were enlisted by the development associations and organizations of international cooperation, and increasingly by governments in the region, as a strategic partner in its development agenda – to provide an alternative to the confrontational politics of the social movements and to mediate between the donors and recipients of development assistance.

In other words, the social base of the new Right is found not only in the elites of the dominant class, and in the political opposition that represents the economic interests of this class, as well as the mass media that are generally owned by scions of this class, but in the conservative sector increasingly taking organizational form as 'civil society' – organized not in support of but in opposition to the left-of-centre governments with a progressive policy regime.

However, once state power is achieved – usually, as in Macri's case, by the institutional means of electoral politics – the latent authoritarianism of the new Right comes to the fore. In the case of Macri this is expressed in the immediate resort to the powers of the state – to both legislate and issue executive decrees – to reverse the progressive policies of the previous Kirchner regime and repress any protests. Because the ultimate political costs of these policies thus far are not apparent or bearably low – protests that can easily be ignored or repressed – the new right-wing regime can indulge its belief that state workers are privileged and their wages and benefits on the public payroll undeserved.

How long these reactionary views can be indulged and the policies associated with them sustained is hard to say. But there are also clear indications that in the pursuit of its political agenda – to advance the interests of capital and the dominant class – the new Right will galvanize powerful forces of resistance, which in the years to come will be its undoing. On this see our discussion below.

## Capital, labour and the class struggle: whither the working class?

Gonzalez Casanova, a distinguished Mexican academic famous for his analysis of the indigenous question in Latin American politics, noted at a rally of labour organizations in Mexico City at the end of August 2014 that 'the long night of neo-liberalism' was by no means over and that in order to defeat the forces of capitalist development and reaction the working class should unite with other forces of resistance in the popular sector. The problem to which Casanova made reference – the class war launched decades ago by capital against labour – is truly global in scope, although his concern (and ours) is with Latin America, on the periphery of the world capitalist system.

Throughout the first three decades of capitalist development after World War II the working class led the struggle against capitalism. And it bore the brunt of the class war launched by capital against labour in a context of a system-wide production crisis. On the periphery of the system, the struggle of workers against wage exploitation combined with the struggle of landless rural workers ('peasants') and the broader anti-imperialist struggle in a war of national liberation. There were numerous battlefronts to this war, with significant regional variations in the form of struggle. In Africa and Asia the class struggle was more or less subordinated to the war for national independence that brought the workers and peasants into a common front with the petit bourgeoisie and nationalist elements of the bourgeoisie. In Latin America, where, with the exception of Cuba, the war for national independence had been settled a century earlier, the class struggle predominantly took the form of a worker–peasant alliance against the machinations of US imperialism on the political dynamics of this struggle. However, in the heat of different battles in this war, the workers and peasants were in many cases divided by the forces ranged against them, allowing them to be isolated, picked off and defeated. The agency of this defeat was the state, aided and abetted by imperial power and international cooperation. By the turn into the 1980s and a new world order, the land struggle and associated social movement were brought to ground and had subsided, and the labour movement had been weakened where it had not been destroyed, its organizational and political capacity seriously diminished.

Over the subsequent three decades of capitalist development in the era of neo-liberal globalization, the working class was never able to regain the offensive. The labour movement was in decline and in some cases free fall, the result of structural forces generated in the capitalist development process (for example, the disappearance in the 1990s of up to 250,000 industrial jobs and with them the industrial proletariat, in just Brazil). And the leadership of the popular movement was taken over by a semi-proletariat of landless rural workers, peasants and, in some contexts (Chiapas, Bolivia, Ecuador ...), the indigenous communities. Peasant-based and -led social movements in this context mobilized the forces of resistance against neo-liberalism in the 1990s, holding the entire neo-liberal policy agenda at bay and arresting its advance. As for the industrial and public-sector working class, it was but a shadow of its former self. With the destruction of the forces of production in industry, a process that accelerated in conditions of neo-liberal globalization, and the privatization of the key firms in the strategic sectors of the regional economy, the working class was gradually transformed from an industrial state-sector proletariat into an urban proletariat of informal street workers – the 'urban poor', in the development discourse of the agencies of international cooperation. Under these conditions, most of the unions in the labour movement were seriously weakened or brought into line via an alliance with the state, the leadership either accommodated or corrupted.

Fast-forward to 2010, and an entirely new context defined by the ascension of the centre-left to political power, the demise of neo-liberalism, the declining influence and power of US imperialism, and a system in crisis. At the centre of the system, in Europe and North America, the most surprising political development was the relative absence of any resistance to the machinations of capital and the class war launched by capital against labour in the 1970s. With a few exceptions the political landscape in Europe was marked by a relative absence of organized protests in response to the latest attacks on what remains of the welfare state in Europe (in France, Greece and Spain). The weakened condition and virtual demise of the labour movement were reflected in a steady decline in trade union density (the proportion of paid workers who are union members, which had declined compared to the early 1970s, when the class war was launched) in many countries, especially in the Anglo-American countries (US, Canada, Australia) but also a number of European countries – from an all-time high in 1964 to an all-time low in 2016. On the Latin American periphery, however – for example, in Chile (see Gaudichaud's chapter in this volume) and Argentina (see the discussion above) – there are signs of positive change that point to the possibility of rebuilding a socialist movement on the basis of organized labour – organizing and bringing together the diverse sectors of a divided and fragmented working class and mobilizing the forces of resistance against capitalism in its neo-liberal and post-neo-liberal forms, and against imperialism.

In Bolivia, in May 2011 the workers organized and represented by the COB finally revolted against the policies of a government that was formed with the promise to abandon neo-liberalism and the expectation of a socialist programme, but that in four years of state power utterly failed to institute any fundamental change in the social structure of national production and development. With a working class brought to its knees by over two decades of neo-liberalism, and the arteries of the treasury literally clogged with money held in hard currency reserve so as to assuage the fears and whet the appetites of potential foreign investors, the government adamantly refused to accede to the modest demands of the workers for a living wage. The government finally settled the labour strike and subdued a spreading labour movement by offering the workers a miserly 11 per cent wage increase. The leadership of the emerging movement, in the form of the COB, was constrained to settle with the government. But it is evident that in Bolivia we have the makings of a more powerful labour movement. Already, as also in neighbouring Argentina, the revolutionary as well as the parliamentary Left have begun the process of rebuilding the forces of popular resistance – and rebuilding the movement.[1]

Similar and potentially more powerful forces of resistance are also being built in the indigenous sector of the popular movement. If or when these forces are combined with the forces marshalled by the organizations of an incipient labour movement, conditions could rapidly change. One manifestation of this is the Unity Pact (Pacto de Unidad), established by indigenous groups and working-class organizations in Bolivia, Colombia, Ecuador and Peru on 26 February 2009. This pact follows a series of meetings, forums and congresses held to the same purpose – to unify the indigenous social movement Left – over the past four years.

This is one change that can be attributed to the rise of Evo Morales to state power and to the so-called red tide in national politics in the first decade of the new millennium. Another apparent trigger for a re-emergence of the social movements is the so-called global financial crisis, which in the Latin American context turns out to be a crisis of the neo-liberal model of capitalist development. This model has attracted and appears to be the unifying factor in the emerging forces of resistance. A major conglomeration of these forces of popular resistance was generated in response to the US proposal, in 2001, to establish the Latin American Free Trade Agreement (LAFTA, or ALCA in its Spanish acronym).

In opposition to ALCA, ALBA proposed an alternative model of regional integration based on the socialist principles of social justice, fair trade and the equitable development of the forces of production. ALBA turned out to be a key point and centre of reference, and an organizing space, for the formation of a region-wide articulation of diverse social movements able to incorporate and unite in support of a common programme the diverse forces of resistance in the popular sector against the neo-liberal model and the underlying capitalist system.[2]

Lines of proposed action based on shared principles, agreed upon and ratified in several subsequent ALBA summits, include:

1   defence of the sovereignty of the people and their right of self-determination, supported with policies of autonomous development, equity, internationalism, and solidarity with the people in struggle;
2   constitute a united front against neo-liberal policies, including in particular privatization and denationalization;
3   support forms of agricultural production that guarantee food sovereignty and that respect life and mother earth;
4   promote solidarity among people and nations;
5   unite in support of the feminist struggle against patriarchy and sexism in all of its forms;
6   support an emancipatory [anti-capitalist] culture; and
7   recognize the need for the political participation of the people in the construction of a new state committed to the consolidation of ALBA and its objectives.

It would appear that the eclipse of the social movements in the wake of the red tide and the economic crisis has passed. And with each passing day the movement appears to be rebuilding, auguring well for the battle ahead – for the world to win.

**264** The return of the Right

## Conclusion

While on the surface there is an evident decline of revolutionary political class struggle from below, there is the potential for economic struggles to become political in so far as inflation erodes gains and political leaders fix rigid guidelines on wage advances. Also, as the case of Venezuela illustrates, political leaders can provide conditions that favour the advance from economic to political class struggle. But at the moment (in the current swing in the correlation of class power) the most dynamic advance in the class struggle, at least on the fronts of electoral politics and state power, comes from above – and this appears to be a worldwide phenomenon. Witness the systematic assault on wages, social legislation, employment and working conditions launched in the US, Spain, Greece, Ireland, Portugal, England and the Baltic/Balkan states. In these countries the economic crisis has yet to precipitate mass revolt; instead, we see defensive actions, even large-scale strikes, in an attempt to defend the historic gains of labour eroded over the past three decades of neo-liberalism. This has been an unbalanced struggle where the capitalist class holds political and economic institutional levers backed by the international power of imperial banks and states. The working class has little in the way of comparable international solidarity.[3] What it had has been steadily eroded in a series of losing battles fought by organized labour against an ascendant and powerful capitalist class in firm control of the state apparatus and all of its powers.

The most helpful signs in the global class struggle are found in the dynamic direct action of the Latin American and Asian working class. Here steady economic gains have led to the strengthening of class power and organization. Moreover, the workers can draw on revolutionary traditions to create the bases for a relaunching of the socialist project. What could detonate a new round of political and economic class warfare from below? Possibly the resurgence of inflation, recession and a further deterioration in the condition of the working class, repression of the class struggle and an ever-deepening cutback of the welfare state that will expose workers to the barbarism of capitalism in the twenty-first century.

## Notes

1  In this connection, see, for example, the calls for unity and the formation of a Popular Front in Brazil and a United Front in Argentina and Bolivia. In Bolivia, the COB is taking the lead, together with a social movement Left; in Argentina, the so-called Leftist Front (the Frente de Izquierda) encompasses only a fraction of the revolutionary Left, and envisages a electoral process rather than a broader class struggle for power, but even so the seeds of an broader labour movement have been sown.

2  Among the more than 160 movements that constitute the Council of the Movements for ALBA (Consejo de Movimientos Sociales del ALBA), formed on 20 May 2007 at an ALBA summit meeting in Venezuela, can be found the Movimiento de Pobladoras y Pobladores, the Asociación Nacional de Medios Comunitarios Libres y Alternativos (ANMCLA), the Frente Nacional Campesino Ezequiel Zamora, the Frente Nacional de Campesinos y Pescadores 'Simón Bolívar', CONIVE, el Frente Bicentenario de Mujeres 200, La Red de Colectivos La Araña Feminista, la Red Nacional de Sistemas de Truke, el Frente Nacional Comunal 'Simón Bolívar', Red Nacional de Comuneros, the Red de

Organizaciones Afrovenezolanas, Movimiento Nacional de Televisoras Comunitarias-ALBA TV, Movimiento de Mujeres Ana Soto, Movimiento Gayones, OPR Bravo Sur, Compañía Nacional de Circo, Colectivo Nuevo Circo, Jóvenes por el ALBA, and la Alianza Sexo – Genero Diversa Revolucionaria.

3 The World Social Forum and other such 'Left forums' are mainly speech-making opportunities for the chattering classes made up of academics and NGOs. In most cases the foundations and sponsors explicitly prohibit them from taking a political position, let alone organize material support for ongoing class struggles. None of the major working-class general strikes in Europe, Latin America or Asia has ever received material support from the perpetual Left forum attendees. The decline of workers' internationalism has not been in any way replaced by the international gatherings of these disparate forces.

## References

Borón, A. (2016). 'The Bolivian vote for "No" is born in Washington, DC'. *Resumen Latinoamericano/Dawn News*. Available at: www.thedawn-news.org/2016/02/12/the-bolivian-vote-for-no-is-born-in-washington-dc/ [accessed 18 September 2016]. Cited in E. Sarría, 'Bolivia: the process of change does not stop'. *The Dawn News*, 24 February. Available at: www.thedawn-news.org/2016/02/25/bolivia-the-process-of-change-does-not-stop [accessed 18 September 2016].

Pomar, V. (2015). 'Roteiro para análise de conjuntura', 14 October. Available at: http://valterpomar.blogspot.com.br/2015/10/roteiro-para-analise-de-conjuntura.html [accessed 16 June 2016].

Stedile, J. P. (2016). 'Welcome to the Class Struggle'. *The Dawn*, 27 April. Available at: www.thedawn-news.org/2016/04/25/welcome-to-the-class-struggle/

# CONCLUSION

The class struggle from below has taken different forms and directions, with greater or lesser intensity between countries and within countries in different time periods. In general terms, the countries with relative higher levels of urbanization and industrialization experience the greatest urban-centred struggles – as is the case with Argentina, Venezuela and Chile, though not with Brazil and Mexico.

Among the urban-based class struggles, there is a further distinction between factory-based class struggles based on workers' strikes (Argentina) and mass street action in the form of marches (Venezuela and Chile). Urban-based class struggles generally rely on coalitions formed with distinct segments of the popular classes. For example, in Argentina, pensioners, human rights groups and lately owners of small and medium-sized businesses have joined the class struggle around diverse issues ranging from soaring unemployment, reductions of pensions and wages and astronomical increases of the tariff on utilities. Chile, in contrast, experiences mass struggles including indigenous people, university, technical and high school students and popular community-based movements with unionized teachers and medical personnel.

In Venezuela, urban class struggles have taken and are largely taking the form of community-based mobilizations in support of the government and its social welfare programme in opposition to US-backed coups. Brazil is highly urbanized but yet in recent decades the class struggle has revolved around the land occupation movements led by the rural landless movement (the MST). To the extent that urban struggles play a role they revolve around the 'homeless peoples' movements' and popular protests against public services. As for the industrial proletariat, which played a leading role in the class struggle in the 1980s and 1990s, its leadership in the labour movement formed an alliance and 'corporate relations' with the urban political elites and the centre-left Workers' Party. Together with the blows received in the 1980s' transition to a neo-liberal model of capitalist development, and the

Conclusion **267**

associated transformation of a solid industrial proletariat into a precariat, an informal working class disconnected from the capital–labour relationship of the capitalist system, the dynamics of this corporatist alliance essentially took the urban industrial working class out of the class struggle. Despite the existence of several federations of labour unions with millions of members – Central Única dos Trabalhadores (CUT), Brazil's main national trade union centre, by itself has over seven million affiliated workers – the urban working class, while not quiescent, has not demonstrated any capacity to mobilize the forces of resistance let alone lead the popular movement for social change.

The class struggles in Paraguay, Peru and Mexico form a distinct cluster. Paraguay's class struggles are predominantly led by rural peasant movements that are linked to the demand for land reform and that rely on mobilizations and direct action – land occupations and marches in the provincial and state capitals. The sharing of ethno-class identity (Guaraní-speaking peasants in Paraguay) fortifies class solidarity, as is also the case in Peru among the Quechua and Aymara peasants.

The class struggle in Peru has centred in the provincial and regional areas. The centrepiece has been peasant and provincial communities struggling against dispossession by foreign-owned mining conglomerates. In their struggle, mining workers' trade unions, at best, play an auxiliary or secondary role. The community-based struggles are local and multi-sectoral, as mining exploitation pollutes water, air, land and food and undermines local commerce, thus unifying a broad spectrum of otherwise 'intermediary classes'. The urban working classes have offered symbolic support but have yet to become the protagonists that they were in the 1970s and 1980s.

Mexico is the country with the greatest variety and volume of class struggles in Latin America, but at the same time the country with the least popular impact of these struggles on the political elite and national politics. A key problem with the class struggle in Mexico is the dispersal of class forces – it is regional, sectoral and politically fragmented. Mexican authorities and their narco-death squads are notorious for assassinating emergent class-based opposition: the most flagrant case is the murder of 43 rural students attending a teachers' college. The range of militant groups includes mining workers, teachers in Oaxaca, peasants in Guerrero, indigenous communities in Chiapas, and the national electrical workers' union, which was severely repressed.

In terms of social welfare, the class struggle has advanced the furthest in Venezuela, largely under the political direction of Hugo Chávez. However, the precarious dependent state of the oil economy and the top-down leadership have precluded a sustainable social transformation. The most advanced land reform struggles occur in Brazil, where the MST was able to 'occupy, transform and produce', settling over 300,000 families in expropriated farming estates over two decades. Sustainable advances by the MST reflected its cohesive organization and broad social alliances in civil society.

The advance of the class struggle in Paraguay and Peru has linked land, environmental and indigenous movements in concerted and combative struggles that apply

**268** Conclusion

massive pressure to secure incremental gains, from the formidable ruling class bloc of local oligarchs, foreign multinationals and US military advisers.

Argentina's formidable trade unions in industry, services and transport have repeatedly demonstrated their capacity to successfully convoke general strikes over wages and employment. Yet their hierarchical structure and bureaucratic leaderships preclude structural changes. Only in times of systemic crises – as in 2001–03 – when a massive movement of unemployed workers took to the streets and ousted a series of presidents, was there a serious struggle that demanded structural changes.

A comparable analysis of case studies of seven countries reveals a veritable mosaic of differences and similarities of class struggle in Latin America. The tempo and intensity of class struggle has shifted: in times of crises formidable popular advances occur; in other times when economic reversals occur under centre-left electoral regimes the ruling classes have led counter-reform regimes. Given the structural failures of the ruling classes and the legacy of class struggle from below, the reality is that any 'rightist return' is tenuous, unsustainable and reversible.

## The foundation of the new Latin American Right

A new Right with distinctive characteristics and electoral support is emerging in Latin America. To grasp the nature of this new Right – so as to avoid simplistic judgements and combat it effectively – it is useful to differentiate Carlos Menem, who embodied the old Right (espousal of neo-liberalism but respectful of Peronism and the legislature), from Mauricio Macri, a disciple of neo-liberalism but wedded to the extractive model of capitalist development, even more than the Kirchners (i.e. plunder rather than labour exploitation as the modus operandi of capitalism), and willing to discard any vestige of democracy.

Something similar can be said of the Venezuelan Right. It tries to seize executive power without regard to the constitution. As for the new Brazilian Right, today in opposition to the PT regime, it can also be distinguished from the political Right in the 1990s behind the neo-liberal/privatizing regimes of Fernando Henrique Cardoso, who was constrained by providing a social democratic veil over his neo-liberal policies. As Mendes Pereira and Alentejano argue in Chapter 6, the right-wing opposition to the PT regime has no such qualms or need for subterfuge. It is outright undemocratic and, while prepared to play the democratic political game, views the trappings of liberal democracy as a hindrance rather than an institutional means of achieving its agenda. Like the Venezuelan Right, it is fundamentally authoritarian and quite prepared to resort to violence and force to achieve executive power. The new Latin American Right has its reference points in Washington and the neo-liberal model of free-market capitalism. It is not above strict conformity with the full application of radical structural adjustment policies even as it claims autonomy in defending its own agro-mining interests, as well as the full use of the state apparatus to do so.

Perhaps what is most distinctive about the new Right, despite its instrumental view and disdain for democracy, is its appeal to and roots in 'civil society', an amalgam of associations and interest groups formed in the space between the state and the family. In the 1980s and 1990s, 'civil society' took form as a complex of non-governmental organizations (NGOs). They were enlisted by the development associations, organizations of international cooperation, and increasingly by governments in the region, as a strategic partner in its development agenda – to provide an alternative to the confrontational politics of the social movements and mediate between the donors and recipients of development assistance.

In other words, the social base of the new Right is found not only in the elites of the dominant class, in the political opposition that represent the economic interests of this class, and in the mass media that are generally owned by scions of this class, but also in the conservative sector of the middle class, which increasingly takes organizational form as 'civil society', organized not in support of but in opposition to left-of-centre governments.

However, once state power is achieved – usually, as in the case of Macri, by the institutional means of electoral politics – the latent authoritarianism of the new Right comes to the fore. In the case of Macri this is expressed in the immediate resort to the powers of the state to legislate and to issue executive decrees – and to reverse the progressive policies of the previous Kirchner regime and repress any protests. Because the ultimate political costs of these policies thus far are not apparent or bearably low – protests that can easily be ignored or repressed – the new right-wing regime can indulge its belief that state workers are privileged and their wages and benefits on the public payroll undeserved.

How long these reactionary views can be indulged and the policies associated with them sustained is hard to say. But there are also clear indications that in the pursuit of its political agenda – to advance the interests of capital and the dominant class – the new Right will galvanize powerful forces of resistance, which in the years to come will be its undoing.

## Argentina: the end of the progressive cycle and the rise of the hard Right

The class struggle from above in Latin America has found its most intense, comprehensive and retrograde expression in Argentina, with the election of Mauricio Macri (December 2015). During his first two months in office, through the arbitrary assumption of emergency powers, he reversed by decree a multitude of progressive socio-economic policies passed over the previous decade and has sought to purge public institutions of independent voices.

Facing a hostile majority in Congress, he seized legislative powers and proceeded to name two Supreme Court judges in violation of the constitution. And he purged all the ministries and agencies of perceived critics and appointees of the previous government and replaced those officials with loyalist neo-liberal functionaries. Popular movement leaders were jailed, and former cabinet members were prosecuted.

Parallel to the reconfiguration of the state, Macri launched a neo-liberal counter-revolution: a 40 per cent devaluation that raised prices of the *canasta básica* by more

**270** Conclusion

than 30 per cent; the termination of an export tax for all agro-mineral exporters (except soya farmers); a salary and wage cap 20 per cent below the rise in the cost of living; a 400 per cent increase in electrical bills and a 200 per cent increase in transport; large-scale firing of public and private employees; strike-breaking using rubber bullets; preparations for large-scale privatizations of strategic economic sectors; a US$6.5 billion payout to vulture-fund debt holders and speculators – a 1,000 per cent return – while contracting new debts.

Clearly President Macri's high-intensity class warfare is intended not only to halt but to reverse the social welfare and progressive policies implemented by the Kirchner regimes over the previous 12 years (2003–15). One reason for moving so quickly in dismantling the progressive reforms and policies of the Kirchner regime is that Macri and his government faces another round of elections in 2017, and he is evidently laying the groundwork for another mandate, which will allow him to reinstate a neo-liberal programme of privatization, trade liberalization and labour flexibility.

As part of this agenda President Macri has launched a virulent new version of the class struggle from above, following a long-term neo-liberal cycle that has witnessed (i) a period of authoritarian military rule (1966–72), accompanied by intense class struggle from below followed by democratic elections (1973–76); (ii) a period of military dictatorship and intense class struggle from above (1976–82), resulting in the murder of 30,000 workers; (iii) a period of negotiated transition to electoral politics (1983) and a hyper-inflationary crisis that ended in a decade-long programme of radical 'structural reforms' under the Washington Consensus and the deepening of neo-liberalism (1989–2000); (iv) a period of crises and the collapse of neo-liberalism, and insurrectionary class struggle from below (2001–03); (v) the installation of a centre-left policy regime based on a post-Washington Consensus on the need to bring the state back into the development process and secure a more inclusive form of development as well as a labour–capital–regime social pact (2003–15); and (vi) installation of an authoritarian neo-liberal regime led by Macri and an intense class struggle from above (2015–16). Macri's strategic perspective in this latest political development is to consolidate a new power bloc of local agromineral and banking oligarchs, foreign bankers and investors, and the police–military apparatus to massively increase profits by cheapening labour.

The roots of the rise of this neo-liberal power bloc can be found in the practices and policies of the previous Kirchner–Fernandez regimes. Their policies were designed to overcome the capitalist crises of 2000–02 by channelling mass discontent towards social reforms, stimulating agro-mineral exports and increasing living standards via progressive taxes, electricity and food subsidies and pension increases. Kirchner's progressive policies were based on the boom in commodity prices. When they collapsed, the capital–labour 'co-existence' dissolved and the Macri-led business–middle class–foreign capital alliance was well placed to take advantage of the demise of the model.

The class struggle from below was severely weakened by the labour alliance with the centre-left Kirchner regime, not because labour benefitted economically but because the pact demobilized the mass organizations of the 2001–03 period. Over the course of the following decade labour entered into sectoral negotiations (*paritarias*), mediated by a 'friendly government'. Class consciousness was replaced by 'sectoral' allegiances and bread-and-butter issues. Labour unions lost their capacity to wage class struggle from below – or even to influence sectors of the popular classes. In these circumstances and conditions labour was vulnerable and is in a weak position to confront President Macri's virulent neo-liberal counter-reform offensive.

Nevertheless, the extreme measures adopted by Macri – the deep cuts in purchasing power, spiralling inflation and mass firings – have led to the first phases of a renewal of the class struggle from below. Strikes by teachers and public employees over wages, salaries and firings have flared up in response to the barrage of public-sector cuts and arbitrary executive decrees. Sporadic mass demonstrations have been called by social and human rights movements in response to Macri's dismantling of the institutions prosecuting military officials responsible for the killing and disappearance of 30,000 victims during the 'dirty war' (1976–83).

As the Macri regime proceeds to deepen and extend his regressive measures designed to lower labour costs, business taxes and living standards to entice capital with higher profits, as inflation soars and the economy stagnates owing to the decline of public investment and consumption, the class struggle from below is likely to intensify – general strikes and related forms of direct action are likely before the end of the first year of the Macri regime. However, large-scale class-based organizations capable of engaging in intense class struggle from below, weakened by the decade-long 'corporate model' of the Kirchner era, will take time to reconstruct. The question is when and what it will take to organize a class-wide (national) political movement which can move beyond an electoral repudiation of Macri-allied candidates in upcoming legislative, provincial and municipal elections.

## Regional and international alignments

The large-scale class struggles from above and below that we have reviewed and analysed have had a profound impact on regional and international alignments. Venezuela, Brazil and Argentina have favoured regional integration and political associations that exclude the US. On the other hand, Colombia, Peru and Paraguay, where the ruling class's struggles from above have been successful, have supported free trade agreements and political alliances aligned with the United States. One victim of the return to the right in Argentina, Brazil and Paraguay is ALBA. Towards the end of the year 2016 the right-wing regimes in these countries formed a 'triple alliance' to suspend Venezuela from participating as a member of Mercosur, and prevent Venezuelan Chancellor Delcy Rodríguez from assuming her right on behalf of Venezuela to assume the presidency of the organization.

The most immediate period is one of great uncertainty. The previous alliances between the centre-left and the popular movements have either weakened or

**272** Conclusion

disintegrated, while the ruling class advances under the umbrella of an aggressive class struggle from below. However, the demise of the commodity boom – the sharp decline of soya and oil prices – erodes the capacity of the ruling class to sustain their economic advance. The peace negotiations in Colombia and the Framework Agreement may favour the ruling class, but the end of the commodities boom and the consequent decline in export revenues limit the possibility of consolidating the extractive economic model. The emerging ascendancy of the Right will probably not be of long duration. As demonstrated by the rapid and widespread growth of class struggle from below in Argentina in response to the ascendancy of the hard Right (Macri) to state power, the pendulum swing to the right in the class struggle across Latin America might be short-lived. President Macri himself may not serve out his tenure, beset as he is by a mobilizing working class and the expectations of private investors, who will face considerable uncertainty in the near future.

While the class struggle plays a decisive role in shaping development regimes and processes of capital accumulation, there is no certainty that each turn in the struggle cycle reproduces or repeats the previous configuration of power. While the previous turn in the class struggle from below led to the emergence of progressive extractive regimes and changes in budget allocations, the next turn may lead to structural transformations in which sustainable development and the socialization of the financial, productive and commercial systems will be undertaken.

## A final note

It is our hope that our modest text will help academics and scholars shed their blinders, take account of the centrality of the class struggle in the development process, and recognize how it influences the formation and decline of regimes, development models, productive systems and variations in the way countries intersect with the world capitalist system. We draw attention to the failure of almost all development and political writing to take account of this pervasive social reality.

# INDEX

Page numbers in *italics* denote tables, those in **bold** denote figures.

accumulation: by dispossession 40, 42, 50, 51, 53, 54–5, 55n1; by fumigation and dispossession 195; primitive 41, 42; *see also* displacement by fumigation and dispossession
Acosta, Alberto 47, 49
Africa, land-grabbing in 41
agrarian conflict: in Argentina 87, 89
agrarian reform *see* land reform
agribusiness 5, 22, 51, 52, 88, 191; in Brazil 130; in Paraguay 10
Agricultural Modernization Act (Mexico) 153
agriculture: agricultural credit per harvest in Brazil *121*; internationalization of 121–2; in Paraguay 185–8; soybean production and cultivation in Paraguay *187*; transgenic crops approved in Paraguay *200*; *see also* soybean/soya cultivation
agrochemicals 195
agro-development, and class struggle 128–9
agro-extractivism 9–10, 48, 51, 130, 194–5; in Paraguay 185–6
agro-toxins 125, 186–7
Águila, R. 144
Al Hussein, Zeid Ra'ad 199
Alarcón, Roberto 139
ALBA (Alianza Bolivariana para los Pueblos de Nuestra América) 36, 263, 255n26, 271
Albuja, V. 47–8, 49
ALCA 73; *see also* Latin American Free Trade Agreement (LAFTA)

Alentejano, Paulo 260, 268
Alianza Bolivariana para los Pueblos de Nuestra América *see* ALBA (Alianza Bolivariana para los Pueblos de Nuestra América)
Alianza Civica 172
Alianza PAIS 70
Alianza Patriótica para el Cambio (APC) 182, 195
Alianza Sexo – Genero Diversa Revolucionaria 265n2
Alliance for Democracy 59
Allup, Henry Ramos 246
Antebi, Roberto 198
Antebi Duarte, Alberto 198
anti-capitalism 35–6; *see also* capitalism
anti-imperialism 29, 36, 227, 238, 261; *see also* imperialism
Areco, A. 200
Arellano, López 240
Argaña, Luis 193
Argentina: agrarian conflict in 87, 89; bank failures in 65; class struggle in 6, 20, 21, 25, 64–6, 266; and the commodity boom 165; convertibility of the currency 81–2; foreign direct investment in 29, 46; Heads of Household Plan 85; land-grabbing in 51–2; and the Latin American Right 250–2; and the Macri regime 7, 93–7, 269–71; and Mercosur 60; military coup in 24; neo-liberalism in 21; new financial policies in 90–1;

**274** Index

Argentina *continued*
political developments in 7, 9, 17, 60, 61, 62, 64–5, 72–80; popular uprisings in 22; post-neo-liberalism in 6; public investment in 83; recovered factory movement in 20; relationship with the U.S. 271; resistance to Macri 97–103; state-labour relations 100; and the structural reform agenda 61; trade unions in 4, 268; Universal Child Allowance (AUH) 90; worker lay-offs in 100–3; *see also* Kirchner regime(s)
Arizpe, Lourdes 162
Armstrong, A. 144
Ashcroft, John 241
Asia, land-grabbing in 41
Asian Crisis 135, 139, 140
Asociación Nacional de Medios Comunitarios Libres y Alternativos (ANMCLA) 264n2
Association of Producers of Soybeans, Cereals, and Oilseeds (Asociación de Productores de Soja, Oleaginosas y Cereales del Paraguay – APS) 188–9
Association of State Workers (ATE) 97–8, 103
ATES 127
austerity measures 13, 14–15, 93, 194
Authentic Labour Front (FAT) 171
Aylwin, Patricio 136, 137–8
Aznar, José María 240, 243, 248

Bachelet government 144
Barrientos, Rene 66
Bebbington, A. 54
Bernedo Alvarado, J. 213
biofuels 10, 27, 41, 46, 48, 51, 52
biotechnology 48
bituminous shale industrialization 48
Bolivarian Revolution (Venezuela) 29, 60, 72, 74–5, 227, 229–30, 238, 239, 243, 244
Bolivia: accumulation by dispossession in 40; agrarian reform in 66; anti-capitalist coalition in 36; class struggle in 20, 25, 66–9; and the commodity boom 165; 'democratic and cultural revolution' 29; extractivist economy in 33; indigenous movement in 47–8; land-grabbing in 51–2; and the Latin American Right 256–9; mineral exports in 30; neo-liberalism in 21; political developments in 8, 46, 47, 60, 61, 62, 66, 72, 73, 74, 76; popular uprisings in 22; post-neo-liberalism in 6; progressive policy regime

in 32; rebellion in 80; TIPNIS controversy 48, 75
Bolivian Labour Confederation (COB) 66, 68, 69, 262, 264n1
*Bolsa Família* programme 127
Borda, Dinonisio 197
Borón, Atilio 257
Borras, S. M. 51
Brazil: 1989 presidential election 108–9; agrarian reform in 105–8; agrarian reform settlements 117–19; agro-development and class struggle in the countryside 128–9; Cardoso and the agrarian question 109–14; class struggle in 6, 16, 20, 24, 62–4; Collor and Itamar regimes 109; food insecurity 122–4; foreign direct investment in 29, 45–6; internationalization of agriculture 121–2; land occupation tactic 126–7; land-grabbing in 51; landholding structure and agricultural production 119–21; and the landless workers movement 9; and the Latin American Right 252–6; Lula da Silva and Rousseff PT regime 114–16; and Mercosur 60; military coup in 24; murders of rural workers and judgments *124*; neo-liberalism in 21; political developments in 7–8, 22, 61, 62, 72, 75–9, 105; post-neo-liberalism in 6; primarization in 45–6; relationship with the U.S. 271; settled families and area occupied *117*; and the structural reform agenda 61; union membership in 3–4; urban mass movements in 4; worker exploitation and environmental issues 124–5
Brazil Popular Front 253
Brazilian Right 260, 268
Bresser-Pereira, L. C. 44
Bretton Wood system 61
BRIC countries 16, 253
Bridge, G. 52
Bury, J. 54
Buryaile, Ricardo 97
Bush, George W. 235, 241

Cabanas, Lucio 163
Calderón, Felipe 159, 160, 161, 169, 240
Caló, Antonio 100
*Campesino* movement 189–90
Canada 16, 21, 240; Latin/South American investment by 28, 31; and NAFTA 156
Cananea Consolidated Copper Company (CCCC) 152
capital: geoeconomics and geopolitics of 8, 45–6; *see also* extractive capital

Index **275**

capitalism 1, 2, 5, 8–9, 26, 27, 239, 264; and class struggle 12; crisis of 14–15, 17; free-market 14, 27, 41, 43–4, 50, 59, 61, 71, 97, 198, 260, 268; industrial 33; in Latin America 164; in Mexico 151–4; neo-liberal 42, 44; *see also* anti-capitalism; extractive capitalism; neo-liberalism

Capriles Radonski, Henrique 237, 244, 246

*Caracazo* 238

Cárdenas, Lazaro 152, 174n3; redistributive policies 174n1

Cardoso, Fernando Henrique 63, 75, 110; agrarian reform settlements under 117; initiatives of 112–13

Cardoso government, and the agrarian question 109–14

Caribbean nations 28, 60, 89, 242, 253n3, 255n26

Cartes, Horacio 182, 199–200

Casanova, Gonzalez 261

Castro, Néstor 198

CELAC *see* Community of Latin American and Caribbean States (CELAC)

Central Única dos Trabalhadores *see* CUT (Central Única dos Trabalhadores)

Central Independiente de Obreros Agricolas y Campesinos/Partido Comunista Mexicana (COAC/PCM) 163

Chávez, Hugo 21, 23, 36, 60, 72, 76, 229, 267; U.S. opposition to 234–7

Chavez, Rebecca 240

Chavista regime 227–8, 246–7

Chediack, Juan 100–1

Chile: class struggle in 25; and the commodity boom 165; CUT election results by party **147**; evolution of the minimum wage **148**; foreign direct investment in 29, 46; Labour Plan 135; military coup 24; mineral exports 30; number of legal strikes **147**; number of workers on legal strike **147**; percentage distribution of the labour force by sector **148**; political developments in 9, 59, 139–40; rate or unionization and population with union affiliation **148**; socio-political syndicalism and workers' strikes 140–4; trade unionism in 4, 145–9; union affiliation by economic activity **148**; union movement and neo-liberal democracy 136–40; urban class struggle in 266; workers' movement in 134–5

Chilean Path to Socialism 134

China: class struggle in 14, 16; foreign direct investment from 70, 78, 91, 95, 96, 116; as world economic power 3, 45, 55, 59, 72, 88

Christian Democratic Party (DC) 135, 137, 139, 140, 141, 145, 146, 197

Citizens' Revolution (Ecuador) 29, 70

civil society 36, 37, 44, 53, 66, 139, 160, 164, 172, 194, 198, 235, 240, 246, 247, 260, 267–9

class struggle: and agro-extractivism 194–5; in Argentina 6, 20, 21, 25, 64–6, 266; in Bolivia 20, 25, 66–9; in Brazil 6, 16, 20, 24, 62–4; changing anatomy of 4–5; in Chile 25, 266; in Colombia 6, 25, 34; dynamics of 18; in Ecuador 25, 69–73; and the eviction of the peasant class 52; and extractive capital/capitalism 33–4, 166–7; history of 5, 19–21; involving land and labour 3; key dimensions of 18–19; in Latin America 17, 19; and the Latin American Right 261–3; in Mexico 152, 153, 160, 173; and neo-liberal politics 3, 8–9; in Paraguay 192–5, 200; in Peru 6, 20, 23, 25, 34, 215–19, 222, 267; as in Southern Europe 17; theoretical framework 8; transition from intense to limited 73–5; urban 213–14, 266; *see also* class struggle from above; class struggle from below

class struggle from above 5, 12, 13–14, 19, 20, 24, 76, 264; in Argentina 251, 269–70; in Mexico 153; in Peru 207

class struggle from below 5, 12, 14, 19, 63, 75, 266; 2010–2014 22–3; in Argentina 270–1; in Mexico 172; in Peru 207; in times of crisis 15–17

COB *see* Bolivian Labour Confederation

CODELCO copper company 143

Colectivo Nuevo Circo 265n2

collective bargaining 15–16, 68, 84–5, 135, 142, 213

Collier, Paul 31

Collor de Mello, Fernando 63, 108, 109

Colombia: class struggle in 6, 21, 25, 34; economic development in 6; foreign direct investment in 29, 45–6; mineral exports in 30; neo-liberalism in 29, 33; political developments in 59; primarization in 45–6; relationship with the U.S. 271

Colorado Party 182, 188, 193, 194, 195, 197

commodification of resources 26, 48, 50

commodity boom 45, 46, 59, 60, 69, 71, 74, 165, 209

**276** Index

commodity traders 52
commons, enclosure of 49–53
communes, in Venezuela 230–4
communism 2
Communist Party (PC) 135, 140
Community of Latin American and Caribbean States (CELAC) 225, 242
Compañía Nacional de Ciro 265n2
CONAIE *see* Confederation of Indigenous Nationalities of Ecuador
Concertación 138–40, 142, 145
CONFECH 139
Confederación General de Trabajadores (CGT) 97
Confederation of Copper Workers (CTC) 143
Confederation of Indigenous Nationalities of Ecuador (CONAIE) 47, 70, 71, 73, 75
Confederation of Mexican Workers (Confederación de Trabajadores Mexicanos – CTM) 179n36
CONFUSAM 146
Conga Project 209, 223n12; opposition to 217–19
Congress of Labour (CT) 171, 179n36
CONIVE 264n2
Consejo Nacional de Coordinación del Desarrollo Rural (CONCODER) 188
CONTAG trade union 106, 110, 112, 114, 126
cooperatives (communes), in Venezuela 230–4
Coordinadora Agrícola de Paraguay (CAP) 189
Coordinating Committee for Human Rights in Paraguay (Coordinadora de Derechos Humanos del Paraguay – CODE-HUPY) 193
corporate social responsibility (CSR) 31
Correa, Rafael 23, 47, 48–9, 70, 71, 73
Council of the Movements for ALBA (Consejo de Movimientos Sociales del ALBA) 264n2
counter-revolution 5; in Mexico 172; neoliberal 250, 252, 269, 271
Cristaldo, Hector 198–9
Cuba 24, 60, 261
Cubas, Cecilia 200
Cubas, Raul 200
Cuevas, Christian 143
cultural diversity 44
Cunha, Eduardo 254, 255
Curuguaty massacre 198–9
CUT (Central Única dos Trabalhadores)

62–3, 135–8, 139, 140, 141, 142, 144, 146, 267; election results by political party 147

Dávalos, P. 47–8, 49
Davos Consensus 62
DC *see* Christian Democratic Party (DC)
De Echave, J. 219
de la Madrid, Miguel 155
De la Rúa, Fernando 75
decentralization 45
decolonization 2
deforestation 125
*democracia tutelada* 6
democratic and cultural revolution (Bolivia) 29
Democratic Congress of Paraguay (Congress Democratico del Pueblo – CDP) 194
Democratic Ruralist Union (União Democrática Ruralista – UDR) 107
Democratic Unity Movement/Roundtable (MUD) 77, 244
dependency theory 110
deregulation 45, 52, 55n2
development 1–2; capitalist 2, 19–20, 26–7, 40, 46, 263, 266; economic 1
development assistance 61
direct foreign investment *see* foreign direct investment (FDI)
displacement by fumigation and dispossession 186; *see also* accumulation
DNTR-CUT 113–14
drug trafficking, in Mexico 159–60
Duarte Frutos, Nicanor 194, 196
Duhalde, Eduardo 81, 85
Dutch disease 86, 175n7

ECLAC (UN Economic Commission for Latin America and the Caribbean) 28, 43, 45, 61, 89, 154, 175n8, 229, 245
ecology, political 34
economic growth, inclusive 32, 62
Ecuador: 'Citizens' revolution' 29; class struggle in 20, 25, 69–73; and the commodity boom 165; environmental issues in 48–9; extractivist economy in 33; neo-liberalism in 21; political developments in 46–9, 60, 62, 72, 75–7; popular uprisings in 22; populism in 30; post-neo-liberalism in 6; poverty in 49; progressive policy regime in 32
ELAC 242
Empresas de Producción Social (EPS) 231
England 16

Environmental Defence Front of Cajamarca (Frente de Defensa Ambiental de Cajamarca – FDAC) 217–18, 223n13
environmental issues 44; agro-toxins 125, 186–7, 195; in Argentina 75; in Bolivia 68; in Brazil 124–5; deforestation 125; in Ecuador 48–9, 75; and the enclosure of the commons 49–53; hydroelectricity 50, 197, 217, 219; and the mining industry 51, 55, 166, 179n34, 215–17; in Peru 210
environmental movements 34, 36
Esparza, Martín 161
European Central Bank 15
European Commission 15
European Union 15, 21
Evans, G. 52
exploitation 1, 26; in Ecuador 69–70; of labour 2, 164; in Mexico 151–2; of workers 124–5
export of primary commodities 27–8, 29
extractive capital 3, 4, 9–10, 26, 190, 220, 261; contradictions of 31–3; in Latin America 29–30, 45; as new phase of development 27–9; regulation of 31; *see also* foreign direct investment (FDI)
extractive capitalism 33, 54, 164–70; resistance to 34–5, 37, 53–4
extractive imperialism 191
extractivism 43, 59–60; and agro-development 128–9; contradictions of 32; as a form of capitalism 32; and new developmentalism 46–9; opposition to 47, 167; progressive 29; *see also* extractive capital; extractive capitalism; extractive imperialism
Extraordinary Ministry of Land Policy (Ministério Extraordinário de Política Fundiária – MEPF) 110–11
EZLN *see* Zapatista Army of National Liberation (EZLN)

FARC 21
farming communities 34, 35, 36
FDAC *see* Frente de Defensa Ambiental de Cajamarca
Federación Nacional Campesina (National Peasant Federation – FNC) 189–90, 194
Federation of Metal Workers of Peru 168
Federation of Workers in Family Farming (Federação dos Trabalhadores na Agricultura Familiar – Fetraf) 114
Felipe González 248
Fernández, Ibis 214–15
Fernandez de Kirchner, Cristina 65, 73, 74,

75, 81, 87–8, 91, 251, 259; *see also* Kirchner regime
Fernando Lugo 182, 195–9; impeachment of 199, 201
Fierro, Alejandro 227–8
Figueroa, Barbara 145
flexibilization 169
FNC *see* Federación Nacional Campesina (National Peasant Federation – FNC)
food insecurity 122–4
foreign direct investment (FDI) 27–9, 36, 55n2, 61, 165, 190–1; in Argentina 29, 46; in Brazil 29, 45–6; in Chile 29, 46; in Colombia 29, 45–6; dependence on 33; in Ecuador 71; pattern of 45–6; percentage distribution by sector in Latin America 28; 'resource-seeking' 30; *see also* extractive capital
Fox, Vicente 159, 168, 170, 196, 240
fracking 75
Framework Agreement *see* Tripartite Framework Agreements (Acuerdos Marco Tripartitos)
France, class struggle in 16
Franco, Federic 182, 199
Free Trade Area of the Americas (ALCA) 73; *see also* Latin American Free Trade Agreement (LAFTA)
Frei, Eduardo 138
Frente Bicentenario de Mujeres 200 264n2
Frente Brasil Popular (FBP) 254–6
Frente de Defensa Ambiental de Cajamarca (FDAC) 217–28, 223n13
Frente de Izquierda (Leftist Front) 264n1
Frente Nacional Campesino Ezequiel Zamora 264n2
Frente Nacional Comunal 'Simón Bolívar' 264n2
Frente Nacional de Campesinos y Pescadores 'Simón Bolívar' 264n2
Frente Popular Darío Santillán 91
Front for Victory (FPV) 81, 100
Fuerzas de Liberación Nacional (FLN) 163
Fujimori, Alberto 77, 95, 96, 207, 208, 212

G77 242
Galeano, Eduardo 183
García, Alan 209, 210–11, 212
Garcia Rivas, M. A. 50
García Linera, Álvaro 257
Geary, Thomas W. 240
General Confederation of the Workers of Peru (Confederación General de Trabajadores del Perú – CGTP) 213

**278** Index

General Workers Union (UNT) 141
geotechnics 48
Germany 16
Giarracca, Norma 52
Glass of Milk (*Vaso de Leche*) 217, 223n14
global capitalist financial crisis 90, 263
globalization 45, 165, 209, 261, 262
Godoy, Hugo 'Puppy' 97
Golinger, E. 248
Gómez Urrutia, Napoleón 168
Goodman, J. 52
Gorriti, Juan José 213, 214, 215
Greece, class struggle in 16
Greene, William C. 152
Grupo México 167–8, 169, 170, 179n35
Guaraní language 190
Guerra, José 228
Guevara, Che 231
Gutiérrez, Lucio 70, 75

Hamm, Bernd 54
Harper, Stephen 31
Harvey, David 40, 41, 42, 49–50, 53, 154
Hetherington, Kregg 185, 196
Hill Quillish 216, 218
Holloway, J. 53
Honduras 21
Humala, Ollanta 209, 210, 211–12, 213
human rights movements 271
hydroelectric dams and plants 50, 197, 217, 219

IDB (Inter-American Development Bank) 21, 176n17
imperialism 1, 2, 8, 182; extractive 191; in Paraguay 188; US 72, 77, 153, 156, 242, 246, 248, 250, 257, 261; *see also* anti-imperialism
import substitution industrialization (ISI), 32, 84
inclusionary state activism 31, 43, 46, 59–60, 62, 73; *see also* new developmentalism
INCRA *see* National Institute of Colonization and Agrarian Reform (Instituto Nacional de Colonização e Reforma Agraria – INCRA)
India 16, 88
Indian nations, autonomy of 67
indigenous communities 34, 35, 261; in Bolivia 67–8; in Ecuador 69, 72–3; in Mexico 151–2, 162, 174, 178n28, 178n31; territorial rights of 48–9; *see also* Indian nations

indigenous movements 56n6, 67; in Bolivia 47–8
industrialization 27; substitution 84, 165
inequality and inequalities: of landholding structure 119–21; in Mexico, 151; social 32, 82, 89
Inman, Bobby R. 240
Institutional Revolutionary Party (PRI) 157
Instituto de Bienestar Rural (Rural Welfare Institute – IBR) 184
Inter-institutional Platform of Celendin (PIC) 217
International Metalworkers Federation 169
International Monetary Fund (IMF) 15, 21, 51, 95, 112, 154, 156, 209, 239
International Republican Institute (IRI) 240
Ireland, class struggle in 16
Itaipú Treaty 197
Italy, class struggle in 16
Itamar administration 109

Jimenez, Clever 70
Jóvenes por el ALBA 265n2
Jozami, Eduardo 92

Katz, Claudio 82, 188
Kiciloff, Axel 91
Kirchner, Cristina *see* Fernandez de Kirchner, Cristina
Kirchner, Nestor 65, 73, 251, 259; election of 80–1
Kirchner regime(s) 198, 251–2, 268, 269, 270; convertibility and wages 81–2; demise of 91–3; departure of Lavagna 85–7; failure of bourgeois nationalism 89–91; growth of employment and collective bargaining 84–5; new expansionary phase 82–4; and progressivism 80–1; re-composition of state power 87–9
Kleinpenning, J. M. G. 183
Kuczynski, Pedro Pablo 8, 77

La Botz 170
Labour Central 141, 144
labour force, distribution by sector **148**
labour movement 2, 262; and flexibilization 169; and the informal sector 154–6; in Mexico 152–4, 170–2; *see also* trade unions
labour unions *see* trade unions
Lagos, Ricardo 139–40, 141–2
Land Bank (Brazil) 112–13

land occupations 110, 118–19, 126–7, 198; in Paraguay 192–3, 194
land reform 189–90; agricultural credit per harvest *121*; in Bolivia 66; in Brazil 105–8; conflicts in Paraguay (1990–2007) *192*; landholding structure according to family farming criteria *120*; market-assisted 111–13; in Paraguay 184, 200; settled families and area occupied in Brazil *117*
land-grabbing 41, 51, 52, 55
landless rural workers: in Brazil 16, 20, 131, 252, 266; and the class struggle 2, 4, 7, 9, 19–20, 34, 35, 37, 62, 72, 153, 261; in Colombia 34; and land reform 106–8, 110–13, 115, 117; in Mexico 158, 172, 173; in Paraguay 184, 187, 191, 197, 198; in Peru 220; urban migration of 23, 42, 155
Landless Workers Movement of Brazil (Movimento dos Trabalhadores Rurais Sem Terra – MST) 62–3, 109, 110–11, 114, 126–7, 129, 130, 220, 252–3, 266, 267
Lansbury, N. 52
Lasso, Guillermo 71
Lastra, Ana Laura 98
Latin America: percentage distribution of FDI by sector *28*; socio-economic indictors *185*; see also *specific Latin American countries by name*
Latin American Free Trade Agreement (LAFTA) 263
Latin American Left 30, 59
Latin American Right 182, 259–60, 268; in Argentina 250–2; in Bolivia 256–9; in Brazil 252–6; class struggle and the working class 261–3; social foundations of 259–60; in Venezuela 227–8
Lavagna, Roberto 85
*Lava-Jato* 256
Lebowitz, Michael 229
Ledesma (Ledezma), Antonio 239, 241
Leftist Workers Front (FIT) 90–1
León, Luis Vicente 228
Lerner, Salomón 219
Levy, Joaquin 77, 254
Ley Corta Portuaria 144
liberalization 45, 52, 55n2
liberation movements 2
liberation theology 196
Ligas Agrarias 201n4
Lillo, Manuel Ahumada 141
Loeb, Daniel 93
López, Leopoldo 238, 243, 246

Lopez Obrador, Andres Manuel 158–9
Lopez Portillo, José 155, 175n7
López Rega, José 64
*los Ninis* 175n6
Low Countries 16
Lozano, Javier 170
Luksoc Group (COSILUK) 142
Lula da Silva, Luiz Inácio 3, 63, 92, 108, 110; agrarian policies of 114–16; agrarian reform settlements under 117; land occupations under 126
Lust, J. 34, 37

Macchi, González 194, 202n12
Machado, Maria Corina 239, 241
Macri, Mauricio (Macro, Maurice) 7, 60, 61, 76, 77, 78, 250, 256–7, 259, 260, 268, 269, 272; and the class war 251–2; election of 93–7; resistance to 97–100
Macrismo 92
Maduro, Nicolas 232–4, 237; failed U.S. coup against 239–41
Maduro regime 8, 74–5, 77, 239
Mahuad, Jamil 70, 75
Malvinas, battle of 64
manufactures of agricultural origin (MOA) 83
manufactures of industrial origin (MIO) 83
Mapuches 220
Maquila Health and Safety Support Network (MHSSN) 169
*maquiladoras* 156
Marini, R.191
market deregulation 42
market-assisted land reform (MALR) 111–13; *see also* land reform
Martínez, Arturo 140
Marx, Karl 5, 12, 13, 18, 19, 26, 41, 42, 54, 151, 182, 231
Marxism 6, 175n9
Marzo Paraguayo (Paraguayan March Massacre, 1999) 192, 193
MAS *see* Movement to Socialism (MAS) party
MCNOC *see* Mesa Coordinadora Nacional de Organizaciones Campesinas (National Coordinating Committee of Peasant Organizations – MCNOC)
Medeiros, L. S. 127
Mendes Pereira, J. M. 260, 268
Menem, Carlos 80, 87, 259, 268
Mercado Común del Sur (Mercosur) 60, 93, 95, 96, 182, 255n16, 271
Mesa, Carlos 66

**280** Index

Mesa Coordinadora Nacional de Organizaciones Campesinas (National Coordinating Committee of Peasant Organizations – MCNOC) 189–90, 194
Mesa regime 22
Mészáros, István 231
Mexican Electrical Workers Union (SME) 171
Mexican Revolution (1910) 152, 172
Mexican Southern Copper Corporation 210
Mexican Union Front (FSM) 171
Mexico: capitalism in 151–4; class struggle in 9, 21, 151, 173–4, 259–61, 267; class struggle on the extractive frontier 164–70; educational reform 160; exploitation of natural resources by MNCs 41; extractive sectors 165; foreign direct investment in 52–3; hydroelectric dams in 50; indigenous communities in 151–2; labour movement in 152–4, 170–2; mineral exports in 30; neo-liberalism in 29, 33, 154–7; peso crisis 157–8, 176nn13–14; political developments in 59; privatization in 50; resistance to extractivism in 37; union membership in 4; and the war on drugs 159–60; Zapatista factor in class politics 161–4; from Zedillo to Peña Nieto 157–9
Micheli, Paul 102
middle class: and the commodity consensus 34–5; impoverishment and mobilization of 81
Millennium Development Goal (UN) 49
mine workers, violence against 167–9
mineral extraction 29, 46; *see also* mining industry; opencast mining
*Minga Informativa de Movimientos Sociales* 36
minimum wage 21, 23, 138–40, 211–13, 222; in Chile **147**
mining industry 55; for industrial minerals and precious metals 51; in Mexico 167, 178nn32–3; in Peru 209–10, 214; Peruvian protests against 216–19; resistance to 53; weakness of Peruvian struggle against 219–21; *see also* mineral extraction; opencast mining
MiningWatch 166
Ministry of Reform and Agrarian Development (Ministério da Reforma e do Desenvolvimento Agrário – MIRAD) 106, 107
Miski Mayo 220–1
Moraga, Etile 140

Morales, Evo 8, 23, 56n7, 66–9, 73, 74, 75, 257–8
Morales-Garcia Linera regime 69
MOSICAM (Trade Union Movement for Change) 141
Movement for Latin American Unity and Social Change (MULCS) 91
movement of unemployed workers (*los piqueteros*) 25, 73, 85
Movement to Socialism (MAS) party 22–3, 67, 68–9, 73–4, 258–9
Movimiento Campesino Paraguayo (Paraguayan Peasant Movement – MCP) 189
Movimiento de Mujeres Ana Soto 265n2
Movimiento de Pobladoras y Pobladores 264n2
Movimiento Gayones 265n2
Movimiento Nacional de Televisoras Comunitarias-ALBA TV 265n2
Movimiento por la Recuperación Campesina de Canindeyú (MRCC) 198
MST *see* Landless Workers Movement of Brazil (Movimento dos Trabalhadores Rurais Sem Terra – MST)
MUD *see* Democratic Unity Movement/ Roundtable
multinational corporations (MNCs) 3, 7, 27, 33, 40–1, 60, 190

Nagel, Beverly 190
National Action Party (PAN) 152, 159, 166, 170
National Agrarian Confederation (Confederación Nacional Agraria – CNA) 220
National Agrarian Reform Plan (PNRA; Brazil) 106–7
National Campaign for Agrarian Reform (Brazil) 107–8
National Confederation of Communities Affected by Mining in Peru (Confederación Nacional de Comunidades del Perú Afectadas por la Minería – CONACAMI) 220
National Coordinator of Education Workers (CNTE) 160–1, 177n19, 177nn22–3
National Democratic Institute (NDI) 240
National Endowment for Democracy (NED) 238, 240, 245, 246
National Forum for Agrarian Reform and Justice in the Countryside 113
National Indigenous Council (Consejo Nacional Indígena) 174
National Institute of Colonization and

Agrarian Reform (Instituto Nacional de Colonização e Reforma Agraria – INCRA) 109, 113, 114, 115, 117
National March for Agrarian Reform, Employment, and Justice 110
National Party of Honduras 240
National Plan of Agrarian Reform (II PNRA) 115, 126
National Program for Strengthening Family Farming (Programa Nacional de Fortalecimento da Agricultura Familiar – PRONAF) 114, 121, 127
National Program of Land Credit (Programa Nacional de Crédito Fundiário – PNCF) 115
National Regeneration Movement (Mexico) 158
National Revolutionary Movement (MNR) 66
National Union of Social Security Workers (SNTSS) 171
National Union of Workers (UNT) 142, 171
National University of Cajamarca (UNC) 217
nationalization, in Mexico 152
nationalized property 90
Nebot, Jaime 71
neo-colonialism 17
neo-developmentalism 198
neo-Keynesian economics 6
neo-liberalism 3, 6, 13, 41, 61, 79, 239, 262, 268; in Brazil 105, 109; in Chile 135; demise of 23, 59–60, 76, 262; in Latin America 20–1; in Mexico 154–5, 157–8, 160, 162; opposition to 5, 110, 193–4; in Paraguay 199; in Peru 208, 222; rejection of 62; and the trade union movement 141; *see also* capitalism, neo-liberal; post-neo-liberalism
new developmentalism 43, 44, 59–60; and extractivism 46–9; *see also* inclusionary state activism
New Majority 146
new social movements 54; *see also* social movements
Nickson, Andrew 195, 196
non-governmental organizations (NGOs) 34, 166, 236, 238, 239, 245, 260, 265n3, 269
North American Free Trade Agreement (NAFTA) 156, 163, 173, 178n27

Obama, Barack 237, 248; opposition to Venezuela 238–42

oil reserves 48
Oliveros, Asdrúbal 228
Olmedo, Luis 198
opencast mining 48, 51, 167, 210; *see also* mining industry
Operation Jericó 239–40
OPR Bravo Sur 265n2
Organización de Lucha por la Tierra (Struggle for Land Organization – OLT) 189–90
Organización Nacional Campesina (National Peasant Organization – ONAC) 189
organized labour *see* labour movement; trade unions
outmigration, forced 51
Ovando Candía, Alfredo 66
Oviedo, Lino 193
Oxford Centre for the Analysis of Resource Rich Economies 31

Pachakutik 70, 71
Padres, Guillermo 170
Palau, M. 200
Paraguay: agrarian class structure (*Campesino* movement) 189–90; agrarian class structure (landed oligarchy) 188–9; agro-exports and agro-extractivism 184–8; anti-neo-liberal mobilization and ongoing class struggle (2000s) 193–4; and Brazilian sub-imperialism 190–2; class struggle and transition to democracy (1989–2008) 192; class struggle in 6, 267; class struggle on the extractive frontier 194–5; and the commodity boom 165; democratic rollback (2012–15) 199–200; economic growth and development 6, 186; land conflicts *192*, 194; land-grabbing 51; the Lugo interregnum (2008–12) 195–9; Marzo Paraguayo (1999) 192, 193; and Mercosur 60; percentage of hectares cultivated with soy **191**; political developments in 9–10, 21; relationship with the U.S. 271; soybean production and cultivation 186–9; Stroessner regime (1954–89) 183–4; transgenic crops approved *200*; wave of occupations (1989–90) 193
Paraguayan Chamber of Exporters of Cereals and Oilseeds (Cámara Paraguaya de Exportadores de Cereales y Oleaginosas – CAPECO) 189
Paraguayan March Massacre *see* Marzo Paraguayo (1999)

**282** Index

Paraguayan People's Army (Ejército del Pueblo Paraguayo – EPP) 200
Paraguayan Truth and Justice Commission 184
Partido del Acción Nacional (PAN) 169
Partido Democrático (Democratic Party) 134
Partido Obrero Socialista (Socialist Workers Party) 134
Partido Revolucionario Mexicano (PRM) 152, 174n3
Party of Order 146
Party of the Democratic Revolution (PRD) 156, 158, 170, 172
Pastrana 248
Patriotic Alliance for Change (Alianza Patriótica para el Cambio – APC) 182, 195
peasant farmers 42; in Mexico 155; violence against 110, 124–5, *124*
Peasants Confederation of Peru (Confederación Campesina del Perú – CCP) 220
Peña Nieto, Enrique 160, 170, 179n38
Pérez, Carlos Andrés 238
Peru: class struggle in 6, 20, 23, 25, 34, 222, 267; class struggle in the countryside 215–19; and the commodity boom 165; economic development in 6; exploitation of natural resources by MNCs 41; extractivist economy in 33; FDI in 52–3; exports in 30; neo-liberalism in 21; political developments in 8, 22, 59, 62, 77; populism in 30; relationship with the U.S. 271; remuneration and exploitation surplus (2000–6) *211*; remuneration and exploitation surplus (2007–14) *211*; resistance to extractive capitalism in 37; social and economic situation of the working population 210–11; and the structural reform agenda 61; struggle against mining capital 219–21; trade unions and the popular movement 212–15; urban labour in 10
Petras 190–2
Petrocaribe 242
Piketty, Thomas 32
Piñera, Sebastián 240
Pinochet, Augusto 134, 145
*piqueteros* 25, 73, 85
Plá, Romina 99–100
Plan Colombia 7
Plan of Ayala 174n1

Partido Revolucionario Clandestino Union del Pueblo (Procup) 163
political ecology 34
Pomar, Valter 253
Popular Front (Brazil) 264n1
Popular Movement Dignity 91
Port Union of Chile 144
Portugal, class struggle in 16
post-colonialism 1
postmodernism 53
post-neo-liberalism 5, 6, 10, 30, 31, 46, 59–60, 196, 234; *see also* neo-liberalism
poverty 44, 175n10; in Bolivia 258; in Ecuador 49; increase in 103; in Mexico 151, 156, 158, 162
poverty reduction 60, 61, 62, 65, 75, 89, 140–1, 245; in Bolivia 68
PREALC 154
primarization 45
privatization 42, 45, 48, 49–51, 52, 54, 55n2, 70, 171, 194; in Bolivia 40; in Mexico 157
Programa Nacional de Fortalecimento da Agricultura Familiar (PRONAF) 114, 121, 127
Proletarian Line 163
PRONERA 127
PS *see* Socialst Party (PS)
PT *see* Workers' Party (PT)
Pueblo en Marcha 90–1
Pueblo Unido 163

Quintana, Arnaldo 198
Quiroga, Jorge Fernando 'Tuto' 248

racism, in Mexico 151
Recabarren, Luis Emilio 134
recovered factory movement (Argentina) 20
Red de Colectivos La Araña Feminista 264n2
Red de Organizaciones Afrovenezolanas 265n2
Red Nacional de Comuneros 264n2
Red Nacional de Sistemas de Truke 264n2
redistributive policies 6, 174n1
Rendón, Juan José 228
resistance 1, 3, 4; anti-neo-liberal 193–4; to capitalist development 40; to extractive capitalism 34–5, 37, 53–4; and to extractivism 33–4, 167; to mining 53; to neo-liberalism 44; in the popular sector 46
resource curse 32
Revolutionary Bolivar and Zamora Organization (CRBZ) 231–2

Riquelme, Blas N. 184, 198
Rocca, Paolo 102
Rodríguez, Andrés 193
Rodríguez, Delcy 271
Roman, R. 170
Rousseff, Dilma 7, 10n1, 63, 77, 92, 116, 117, 130, 250, 254–5, 256; land occupations under 126
Rubio, Marco 240
Rural Association of Paraguay (Asociación Rural del Paraguay – ARP) 188
rural landless workers *see* landless rural workers
Rural Landless Workers movement *see* Landless Workers Movement of Brazil (Movimento dos Trabalhadores Rurais Sem Terra – MST)
Russia 16

Salinas de Gortari, Carlos 153, 156, 157–8, 162, 168, 173, 176n12
Sánchez, Milton 218–19
Sánchez de Losada/Lozado regime 22, 75
Sankey, K. 34, 37
Santos, Gregorio 218
Scandinavia 16
Setrini, G. 193
Simioni, Luana 98
Singer, Paul 93, 94
slave labour 124–5
social economy 229
social justice 113
social movements 46, 53, 271; community-based 266; indigenous 219; Latin American 263; against mining capital 219–21; new 54; peasant-based 219, 261; in Peru 215–16
Social Movements for ALBA 36–7
social organizations 34
socialism 35–6, 73, 233; in Bolivia 262; of the twenty-first century 29, 46, 60, 196, 243; in Venezuela 229–30
Socialist Democracy movement 91
Socialist Party (PS) 135, 139, 146
Soros, George 93
South Africa 14, 16
Southern Common Market *see* Mercado Común del Sur (Mercosur)
soybean/soya cultivation 52; in Paraguay 187; percentage of hectares cultivated in Paraguay 191; *see also* agriculture
Spain, class struggle in 16
Spronk, S. 50
state activism, inclusionary *see* inclusionary state activism

State Council of Indigenous and Peasant Organizations (CEOIC) 164
Stédile, Pedro 130, 159
strikes 4, 77, 95; in Argentina 97–9, 266; in Brazil 109; in Chile 134, 139–4, 147; in Mexico 152, 167–9, 170; in Peru 213
Stroessner, Alfredo 183–4
structural reform 43–4, 55n2, 61, 72, 255; in Mexico 154; opposition to 193–4
student movement, in Mexico 153
sub-imperialism, Brazilian 188, 190–2
substitution industrialization 84, 165

Taylor, L. 220–1
Tekojojá 196
Telephone Workers Union 171
Tenner, Michael 130
Tetreault, D. 34, 37, 167
Teubal, Miguel 52
Third World debt 175n5
TIPNIS controversy 48, 75
Toledo, Alejandro 208, 210, 212, 213
Torrealba, Jesus 'Chuo' 244
Torres, J. J. 66
Trade Union Law 137
trade unions 3–4, 15–16, 35, 77; in Argentina 64, 268; in Chile 134–5, 139–42, 143–4, 148; in Mexico 155, 179n36; in Peru 212–15; union affiliation by economic activity 149; *see also* labour movement
Trans-Pacific Free Trade Alliance 73
Trans-Pacific Partnership (TPP) 59, 61, 95, 96
Tripartite Framework Agreements (Acuerdos Marco Tripartitos) 136, 137, 138, 140, 145, 272

UNASUR *see* Union of South American Nations (Unión de Naciones Suramericanas – UNASUR)
unemployment 21, 65, 82, 86, 87, 141
Unión de Gremios de la Producción (Union of Producer Associations – UGP) 189
union movement *see* labour movement; trade unions
Unión Nacional de Ciudadanos Éticos (National Union of Ethical Citizens – UNACE) 197
Union of South American Nations (Unión de Naciones Suramericanas – UNASUR) 182, 242, 255
Union of Workers of the National Autonimous University of Mexico (STUNAM) 171

Union/Peasant/Social/Indigenous and Popular Front (FSCISP) 170
United Front: in Argentina 264n1; in Bolivia 264n1
United Nations Economic Commission for Latin America and the Caribbean (ECLAC) 28, 43, 45, 61, 89, 154, 175n8, 229, 245
United Socialist Party of Venezuela (PSUV) 237
United States 16–17, 21; as imperialist power 2, 8; influence in Latin America 96; investment in South America 72; involvement in Latin American politics 60, 64, 66, 70, 73, 77, 134, 234–8, 259, 271; Latin American regimes aligned with 59; migration to from Mexico 155; and NAFTA 156; and Plan Colombia 7; relationship with Venezuela 234–8; representatives expelled from Bolivia 67
United Workers Front 71
Unity Pact (Pacto de Unidad) 263
Universal Child Allowance (AUH) 90
urban labour, in Peru 10
Uribe Vélez, Álvaro 236, 240, 243, 248
Uruguay: and the commodity boom 165; and Mercosur 60; political developments in 22
USAID (UN Agency for International Cooperation) 247

Vanoli, Alejandro 94
Vaso de Leche (Glass of Milk) 217, 223n14
Velasco Arregui, E. 170
Veltmeyer, H. 190–2
Venables, Tony 31
Venezuela: 2015 election 243–6; 'Bolivarian revolution' 60, 72, 74–5, 227, 229–30, 238, 239, 243, 244; capitalism, socialism, and the social economy 229–30; change of direction and communes 231–4; class struggle in 6, 23; development in 230–1; economic development in 6; and the Latin American Right 227–8; nationalist-populist policies in 7; neo-liberalism in 21; paramilitary power in 7; political developments in 8, 10, 21, 22, 30, 46, 60, 62, 72, 74–5, 77, 79, 243–6; post-neo-liberalism in 6; rebellion in 80; relationship with the U.S. 234–8, 271; social welfare in 267; urban class struggle in 266; U.S. imperialism against 238–42

Venezuelan Right 260, 268
Venezuelan United Socialist Party (PSUV) 77
Vía Campesina 36, 114
Villa, Pancho 172
Villaba, Rubén 198
violence: against mine workers 167–9; against rural workers 124
Virigay, Duiliam 231–3
vulture funds 95, 96, 270

War of the Triple Alliance 201n4
war on terror 235
Warhurst, A. 52
Washington Consensus 20, 27, 30, 42, 55n2, 61, 62, 70, 72, 79, 126, 156, 172, 235; and neo-developmentalism 43–4
water war (Cochabamba) 66, 73
Webber, J. R. 50
welfare policies 6, 43, 50, 85, 153, 165, 184, 251, 262, 267
Whitaker, Kevin 241
Williamson, John 43
Womack, J. 143
women, in the workforce 156
worker exploitation, in Brazil 124–5
Workers' Left Front (FIT) 90–1
Workers' Party (PT) 24, 63–4, 75, 110, 126, 129, 266; and the Lula da Silva and Rousseff regimes 114–16
Workers Trade Union Federation see CUT (Central Única dos Trabalhadores)
World Bank 21, 31, 43, 51, 52–3, 61–2, 68, 69, 70, 79, 111, 113, 154, 156, 185
World Social Forum 265n3

Yanacocha 216, 217–19, 221, 223n12
Yasky, Hugo 103
Yasuni-ITT project 48
Yepez del Castillo, I. 213

Zapata, Emilio 152, 172, 174n1
Zapatista Army of National Liberation (EZLN) 154, 156, 161–4, 170, 172, 173
Zapatista rebellion 178n25, 178n28
Zapatistas 220
Zedillo, Ernesto 157, 168
Zibechi, Raul 35, 54
Ziff, Benjamin 241
Zoomers, E. B. 183
Zuniga, Ricardo 240